NAVAL WARFARE UNDER OARS

4th to 16th Centuries

A STUDY OF STRATEGY, TACTICS AND SHIP DESIGN

By

WILLIAM LEDYARD RODGERS
Vice Admiral, U. S. Navy (Retired)

NAVAL INSTITUTE PRESS
ANNAPOLIS, MARYLAND

NAVAL WARFARE UNDER OARS
4th to 16th Centuries

A Study of Strategy, Tactics and Ship Design

CONTENTS

CHAPTER		PAGE
	PREFACE	xi
I	THE NAVY OF THE ROMAN EMPIRE	3
	Appendix I	24
	Appendix II The Fleet of Belisarius in 533 A.D.	27
II	THE NAVAL WARS WITH THE SARACENS	30
	Appendix Greek Fire	41
III	THE NAVY OF THE LATER ROMAN EMPIRE	46
IV	THE FIRST CRUSADE	53
V	THE ORGANIZATION OF ANCIENT NAVIES	59
	Appendix	63
VI	THE VIKINGS	69
VII	MEDIEVAL WARS OF FRENCH AND ENGLISH	88
	Appendix	106
VIII	ITALIAN NAVAL WARS	109
IX	WAR OF CYPRUS AND CAMPAIGN OF LEPANTO	143
	Appendix	230
X	THE WAR OF ELIZABETH OF ENGLAND WITH PHILIP II OF SPAIN AND THE CAMPAIGN OF THE GREAT ARMADA	240
	APPENDIX	336
	INDEX	345

ILLUSTRATIONS

FIGURE   PAGE

1 Ships from Trajan's Column .... *opp.* 24
2 Reconstruction, man-of-war, second century 25
3 Ships from walls of Pompeii .... *opp.* 26
4 Reconstruction of Byzantine dromon (Pamphylian type) 64
5 Reconstruction of Byzantine dromon (large type) 66
6 Gokstad ship, present condition .... *opp.* 72
7 Gokstad ship, model of reconstruction .... *opp.* 73
8 Reconstruction of "Great Serpent" 74
9 Norman ships from Bayeux Tapestry .... *opp.* 88
10 English King's ship .... *opp.* 92
11 Crossbow, cranequin, and bolts .... *opp.* 106
12 Merchant galley .... *opp.* 112
13 Ships sculptured on Pisa's Leaning Tower .... *opp.* 113
14 Latin assault from the sea on the walls of Constantinople .. *opp.* 126
15 Pope Pius V .... *opp.* 152
16 Marc Antonio Colonna .... *opp.* 154
17 Sebastiano Veniero .... *opp.* 166
18 Don John of Austria .... *opp.* 168
19 Battle of Lepanto (1st diagram) 190
20 Venetian contemporary Plan of Battle of Lepanto ...... *opp.* 194
21 Battle of Lepanto (2d diagram) 196
22 Battle of Lepanto (3d diagram) 197
23 Sketch of fireball 200
24 Battle of Lepanto (4th diagram) 206
25 Battle of Lepanto (5th diagram) 208
26 Battle of Lepanto by Vasari .... *opp.* 210
27 Venetian map of Modon 224
28 Cross section of galley and varying arrangements of rowers .. 230
29 Side views of galley 231
30 Venetian galley .... *opp.* 232
31 Galleass model in Naval Museum of Venice .... *opp.* 234
32 Venetian galleass under sail .... *opp.* 236
33 Galleass (cross section) 236
34 Rowers at large oar 238
35 Nef (from tomb of Contarini in Padua) .... *opp.* 238
36 Nef (section and half-plan) 239
37 King Philip II of Spain .... *opp.* 242

38 Sir Francis Drake .... *opp.* 246
39 Queen Elizabeth of England .... *opp.* 250
40 Battle and cruising formation of Great Armada 276
41 Lord Howard of Effingham .... *opp.* 280
42 British man-of-war at period of the Armada .... *opp.* 288
43 Action off Plymouth (diagram) 294
44 *Ark Royal* (British flagship) .... *opp.* 296
45 Action off Portland 299
46 Action off Isle of Wight (contemporary drawing) 302
47 Action off Isle of Wight (diagram) 305
48 Bombard on ship's deck mount .... *opp.* 336
49 Bombard (sectional drawing) 337
50 Types of guns and mounts 338
51 Breech-loader on swivel rail mount with sectional drawing *opp.* 338

MAPS

MAP NO.   PAGE

I Wars of Justinian in the West . . . . *opp.*   8

II To illustrate Byzantine and Saracen naval campaigns   32

III Constantinople   34

IV To illustrate Italian and Spanish naval wars . . . . *opp.*   48

V Viking Campaigns   70

VI North Sea and English Channel   90

VII Map of Spain   134

VIII Campaigns of the Holy League 1570-72 . . . . *opp.*   150

IX Neighborhood of Corfu   156

X Fleets on August 7, 1572   219

XI Voyage of Spanish Armada   308

PUBLISHER'S PREFACE

This book, and its companion, GREEK AND ROMAN NAVAL WARFARE, was originally published in the late 1930's, when naval warfare still centered on big guns and the battle line, much as it had for centuries past. The technological era that came with World War II vastly complicated the art of war with sophisticated weapons, complex communications, and electronic search, detection and guidance systems which have taken much of the control of battle away from the admiral on his bridge and turned it over to a computer in the combat information center. Accordingly, the big guns and the battle line have become history.

But though the weapons and tactics have changes, the basic reason for the existence of any naval force is as it was when the Venetians and Spaniards engaged their enemies centuries ago—to control what happens at sea. The principles of strategy which the ancients developed still remain valid, and a thorough understanding of them as they are presented in this text might well tip the balance in favor of the better informed of two otherwise equal opponents.

Admiral Rodgers spent many years in preparing this work, a classic in the history of naval warfare. Long out of print, it has been reissued in keeping with the U.S. Naval Institute's editorial policy of making such material readily available for professional naval officers.

PREFACE

Like my preceding volume, *Greek and Roman Naval Warfare*, this is a study of fleet naval tactics in the days of rowing ships, but during the Christian era. Incidentally, it gives a brief sketch of the political and economic conditions underlying military and naval efforts. Also, as in the earlier work, I have attempted to reconstruct some of the earlier types of men-of-war, for which direct and positive evidence is lacking. Naturally, the worth of such attempts will be better evaluated by, and have more appeal to, seamen and naval architects who know the sea and the traditions and principles of naval architecture, than they will to historical students whose knowledge of past maritime affairs is chiefly confined to casual mention of them by writers who were concerned more with government and sociology. As for the general objectives of naval warfare in all ages, I refer to the first chapter of my previous volume on *Greek and Roman Naval Warfare*.

Yet it seems worth while to repeat here what was said in the earlier volume, that the duties of navies are primarily concerned with traffic on the seas. They protect the commerce of their own nation; they escort their armies over seas and supply them there; and they check or stop hostile commerce. The enemy may be subdued either by bloodshed or by reduction of supplies and the chief task of navies is to strike at the enemy's property in transit on the water. A great fleet battle is only a means to the end of enabling the navy to control maritime commerce in its own favor. A commander in chief who does not expect a victory to aid the movements of his own merchantmen would have little reason to fight a general action.

When the organized fleet, in greater or less degree, has assured maritime control, cruisers take up the detailed work of patrolling the seas under general protection of the fleet. They keep down hostile raiders and pirates and grant comparative security to the thousands of merchant ships whose voyages support the war and whose collective success is a principal factor in victory. Of these cruisers and their deeds history tells us little in detail, although the sum of their achievements is great. In most cases we

know little more of their particular deeds than we do of the individuals
who man them. For it is the fleets who capture publicity and remembrance
on account of their great battles and the aid they give to armies in attacking seaports.

In these early wars we can learn little of the work of cruisers in sup-
plementing the task of the main fleets, for our sources of information are
scanty. Nevertheless the work must have been done with considerable efficiency and, fortunately, we can see something of it in the account which
Procopius so ably gives of the campaigns of Belisarius in Africa and Italy.

Although the title of this work is *Naval Warfare Under Oars—Fourth
to Sixteenth Century,* I have permitted myself in the last chapter to
include an account of the Anglo-Spanish War of 1585-1604, the chief
event of which was the Expedition of the Great Armada. I do this partly
because there was some attempt to utilize rowing craft in the early part
of the war, although the issue was decided by sailing ships; partly also
because the fleet tactics of sailing ships as later developed were totally
unknown to either side. On the Spanish side, leaders hoped to fight after
the fashion of Lepanto and charge the enemy. When the English declined
to give them this opportunity, the Spanish leaders took their individual
ships where there seemed a chance to engage. On the British side there was
little idea of unison of effort or fleet tactics, such as was the rule in rowing
tactics and still governs today in steam tactics. Indeed, in the British
maneuvers there is apparent only the resolve of individual captains not to
let the Spanish take advantage of their superiority in infantry and small
arms by getting to close quarters and boarding as they had done at Lepanto.
But the English admirals did not yet understand that the basis of all fleet
tactics in all ages is to hold reluctant captains in their assigned positions
and produce co-ordinated action. Therefore, an account of the campaign
of the Armada is scarcely out of place at the close of the history of
rowing ships.

Owing to the recent invention of printing, the contemporary records of
Lepanto and the Armada campaigns are much fuller than of any in
previous centuries and of this I have availed myself both in extracts from
contemporary records and the use of contemporary pictures and works on
naval architecture and armaments. For our ideas of ship architecture in
earlier times we must necessarily rely in great degree on continuity of

tradition in the shipbuilding arts and a reference to later well-known practices.

Money values of various countries have their equivalents given in gold dollars of 1932.

Rear Admiral F. H. Schofield and Captain D. W. Knox were good enough to examine certain chapters and make valuable suggestions by which I have profited. The drawings of ships and diagrams of battles were made by Mr. R. N. Jones of the Bureau of Construction and Repair and the maps by Mr. F. G. Perkins of the Hydrographic Office. My sister, Mrs. Robert Giles, has painstakingly read the manuscript and corrected many errors and lapses. To all, I extend my very hearty thanks.

W. L. RODGERS

NAVAL WARFARE UNDER OARS
4th to 16th Centuries

CHAPTER I

THE NAVY OF THE ROMAN EMPIRE

Its Civil Wars

The Political Background and the Navy

FOR over 350 years after the battle of Actium there was no large-scale naval warfare within the Mediterranean, on whose shores Rome was the only state. As time passed and rival claimants for succession to the Imperium made no use of the navy for moving their armies upon Rome, it became apparent that the fleets served only for the maintenance of good order on the sea and the protection of commerce. Piracy was always present, as, indeed, it was until less than 60 years ago, and the imperial fleets found their principal task in keeping it within tolerable limits. For this purpose, the principal naval station was at Misenum on the Bay of Naples, whence Pliny, the admiral commanding, issued to observe the destruction of Pompeii in 79 A.D. and lost his life in his scientific exertions. The seas governed from Misenum included all the western Mediterranean. The other principal naval station was at Ravenna in the Adriatic, whose chief was responsible for the communications of Italy with the East. Other stations were maintained in the Mediterranean and outside on the ocean and there were flotillas on the Rhine and the Danube. Under such circumstances the size of individual ships decreased in the centuries after Actium, as we may see in the reliefs on Trajan's column (see appendix). In a similar case, we see today in this country that the Coast Guard vessels which are armed for the maintenance of the laws are smaller than battleships which are meant to fight.

The period of two centuries following the establishment of the Empire is regarded by some historians as the happiest period of the human race. But during this peaceful time society weakened. At first, the strong economic demand for unity centering in Rome was upheld by the military authority of the Emperor. But as time passed and the government became more centralized it enjoyed less active support from the local communities, which lost political strength. At the same time, the army, which at first was the chief bond of political unity, lost its own cohesion and the local provincial armies gathered political power, making emperors and requiring bonuses in return. Public opinion, such as it was, supported the idea of political unity and looked to the Emperor for protection against the growing danger from the barbarian tribes beyond the Rhine and the Danube, which were beginning their migrations and raiding the Empire.

In the general weakness of government the navy lost efficiency so far that a tribe of Goths which had established itself on the shores of the Euxine about the middle of the third century was able to man 500 ships in 267 and break out into the Mediterranean. Although we are told these ships had only 25-30 men each, their crews seized Athens and went on to the Adriatic. After the raiders had incurred much loss by disease and battle, the remnant was driven back into the Euxine. Such was the impotence to which three centuries of unemployment had reduced the Roman naval power.

The Civil War of Constantine and Licinius

In the early part of the fourth century there was some revival of the naval service owing to the civil wars arising out of increasing governmental weakness. By the time of Diocletian (283-305) the centralization of government had gone so far and the business of administration had so increased, that to render management more possible the Emperor divided the state into four great regions and, retaining one for his personal supervision, assigned the others to three colleagues (or deputies) whom he associated with himself with the titles of Augustus and of Cæsar, and gave to each the troops necessary to preserve order and guard the frontiers. Thus the army was no longer an imperial unit and lost usefulness as a national bond. Nevertheless, as long as Diocletian reigned, respect for him preserved the political unity of the Empire.

After his abdication, however, civil war arose between the Cæsars. After several years of warfare the Empire found itself under the rule of two men, Constantine in the west, governing Italy and the west, including the Balkan peninsula except Thrace, while Licinius held Thrace, Asia Minor, Syria, and Egypt. The Roman state was now once more divided nearly as it had been in the time of Antony and Octavian, yet, although the economic need for unity was still present, the political conditions had greatly changed. Whereas the government had been an oligarchy of the Roman people, it was now an autocracy. Such was the situation when Constantine and Licinius made peace with each other in 314, without any formal renunciation of the unity of the Roman Empire. Peace was preserved for nine years, during which time the wise government of Constantine reduced taxes, improved the currency, and favored the growing strength of the Christians, while Licinius lost ground through persecuting them. In order to maintain his diminishing authority, Licinius found a pretext for declaring war against Constantine.

As Europe and Asia were once more to meet in arms, fleets were again necessary to cross the water and control the sea communications of the armies. Were either army to cross the Hellespont its fate would depend on its own fleet being able to hold the passage in its rear. Unfortunately, the story of the campaign is very briefly given by early writers. In preparation for coming hostilities, Constantine went to Thessalonica, where he built a port, which the city had never had before, and there fitted out 200 ships of war with from 30 to 50 oars each and 10,000 seamen,* besides 2,000 ships of burden. The size of these ships indicates how much the navy had run down through lack of use, and it was evidently to a great extent a new creation. On his part, Licinius drew 350 ships from his maritime provinces of Asia Minor, Syria, and Egypt. Constantine had 120,000 infantry and 10,000 cavalry, and Licinius considerably more, if we can believe in these great numbers, for the military strength of the state was much decayed since the time of the Republic.**

The two armies met at Adrianople in 324 and Licinius suffered a defeat which obliged him to fall back on Byzantium, where Constantine hastened to besiege him. The fleets now came into use for the control of the passage between Europe and Asia. Licinius relied on his ships to keep his line of supply from Asia, and Constantine needed his fleet in the Bosphorus to complete the blockade of Byzantium, and even more to cover the arrival of his own 2,000 ships of burden bringing him supplies and

---

* NOTE: If we accept the ships as having 30 to 50 oars 3,000 seamen would have been ample with 60 to 80 soldiers per ship at 1 man per yard of length (both sides).

** Delbrueck holds that the fourth century armies were much smaller than in Augustus' time and says that the recorded figures for Constantine's battles are worthless.

munitions. Again, sea power was an important factor in the struggle between Europe and Asia.

Licinius placed his fleet under the command of Abantus who took position in the Hellespont, acting on the defensive. Constantine gave command of his fleet to his son Crispus, with orders to attack. Crispus entered the Hellespont and camped at Elæus, on the European side just within the entrance. From thence, Crispus advanced up the strait with only 80 ships, believing that in the narrow waters he could not make good use of a larger force. Abantus met him and after an indecisive day of battle both fleets retired to their camps. The next day Abantus got under way and ran down to attack Crispus but, on sighting the latter's entire fleet, which had not appeared the day before, Abantus hesitated. While he did so, the wind shifted to southward and blew so hard that his ships were driven ashore and 130 lost. Crispus lay safely on a protected beach and afterwards took advantage of his enemy's misfortune to go to Byzantium and blockade the city by sea while his transports supplied his father's army.

In the meantime Licinius renounced hope of saving the city and crossed to Asia with such troops as he had, in the hope of raising a new army there and continuing his resistance. Constantine followed with his army by the help of a great number of small boats which could land on the shallows, and in a final battle near the shore of the Bosphorus he overcame Licinius and re-established the unity of the Empire. With his success, the supremacy of the Christian religion was secured and with the transfer of the imperial capital from Rome to Byzantium in the following years, the latter city (under the name of Constantinople) became the center of resistance to the disintegrating efforts of the German tribes in the West and of the Persians and, later, the Mohammedans in the East. It must be admitted that the story of Constantine's naval campaign lacks present-day interest, due largely to the scanty accounts which have come to us. Nevertheless, I have told of it because it developed anew the strategic necessity of an effective navy to enable an invading army to cross the Hellespont.

The Vandal Piratical Power

The breakdown of the Roman Empire began again soon after the strong hand of Constantine was removed from affairs. In the middle of the fourth century the Empire was again divided into east and west and the cleavage was permanent, although the Empire was nominally one and undivided. No successful effort to control the seas was made for nearly two centuries after Crispus' victory.

In the early part of the fifth century the Vandals, a German tribe, left its lands in the present Hungary and crossed the Rhine, passing through Gaul into Spain in 409, and took possession of Southwest Spain, the present Andalusia. A few years later, the Roman governor of Africa, Count Boniface, having fallen into disgrace with the Italian court at Ravenna, the western capital, invited the support of the Vandals, and the whole nation, about 80,000 souls under their King Gaiseric, passed into Africa in ships furnished by Boniface in the year 428.* Although Boniface promptly made his peace with the Emperor at Ravenna and opposed the advance of the Vandals as they marched eastward into his province, he was unsuccessful and the Roman government evacuated Africa in 435, with the exception of Carthage which held out till 439.

Thus Gaiseric established the Vandal nation in Africa with the capital at Carthage. With this city as his chief port, he formed a pirate fleet with which he yearly raided the western Mediterranean and even the coasts of Illyria and the Peloponnese. He seized Sicily, Sardinia, Corsica, and the Balearic Islands, and for 30 years Gaiseric controlled what was probably the leading maritime power in those seas. In 455 the Vandal King took his fleet up the Tiber and for 14 days he plundered Rome. To such extremity had fallen the might of the Eternal City. There were several encounters of the Roman shipping with the pirate craft of Gaiseric. In 460 the western Emperor, Majorian, provided a fleet of 300 ships which assembled on the coast of Spain, but Gaiseric raided and destroyed it before it sailed, and the Emperor was stripped of the purple and beheaded as having proved himself "unable to preserve the state of the Roman world." In 467 Gaiseric raided the Peloponnese and Leo I, Emperor of the East, resolved to take decisive action in conjunction with the Italian government. Now that Gaiseric was threatening the commerce and the shores of the entire Mediterranean, it was necessary for the Empire to make united efforts to overthrow him. The Italian forces were under the command of Marcellinus, and his fleet surprised and overcame the Vandals

* Delbrueck estimates the whole tribe as having 8,000 to 10,000 combatants. See *Geschichte der Kriegskunst*, vol. 2.

occupying Sardinia. It was planned that from Sardinia Marcellinus should proceed to Carthage, there to join the expedition from Constantinople. The eastern forces were very much larger than those of Marcellinus. It was alleged that over 1,100 ships conveyed 100,000 men.* The Emperor's choice for commander was one Basiliscus, who himself afterward became Emperor. The plan of operations called for three squadrons to attack simultaneously.

These were the Italian squadron under Marcellinus, which was to move from Sardinia while Basiliscus with one eastern squadron was to move directly on Carthage. A second eastern squadron under Heraclius was to take up re-enforcements in Egypt and then land its troops in Tripolitana and have them march overland to Carthage and join the others at the city. It was a complicated operation to carry out with the slow methods of communication of the times, yet all went well till Basiliscus reached the promontory of Mercury (Cape Bon) after having scattered the ships of Gaiseric off Sicily. But instead of pushing on from the promontory, Basiliscus wasted time. Gaiseric was at first overawed by the prestige of the imperial name, and he had heard of his loss of Tripolitana and Sardinia, but he asked for a delay of five days to arrange for surrender, and of the time thus accorded him he made good use. He armed his subjects and manned many ships while others he prepared as fire ships and towed them empty near the point where Basiliscus' fleet had formed its camp. There Gaiseric waited for a favorable wind and then got his ships under way, under sail, towing the fire ships. When he approached the hostile fleet he set fire to the towed fire ships and cast them off under sail. These found their way among the Romans and set many ships on fire and, at the same time, while tumult arose among the Romans, the Vandal ships came up, ramming and sinking and making prizes. Basiliscus fled with the remainder of his fleet to Sicily and joined Marcellinus there, but before the united forces could undertake a new campaign, Marcellinus was assassinated and Basiliscus returned to Constantinople. In the meantime, Heraclius had gone forward from Tripolitana to the neighborhood of Carthage but, when he heard of the defeat of his colleague, he too retired to Constantinople. The Empire had put forth its entire strength against a single barbarian nation and had lost. It was a dreadful blow to Roman prestige

---

* Probably a great overestimate.

MAP I.

WARS OF JUSTINIAN IN THE WEST

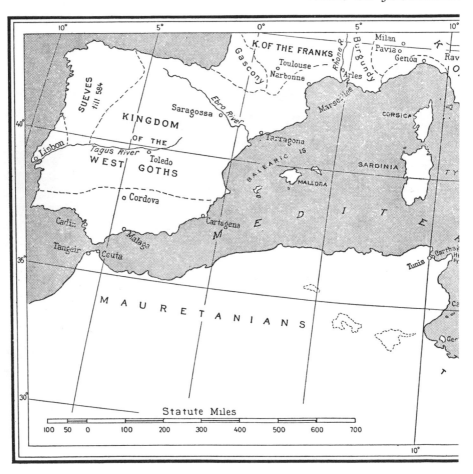

Statute Miles

100 50 0   100   200   300   400   500   600   700

MAP I

at sea, where the Empire had failed as it had failed in Gaul and Britain and even in Italy itself.

The Overthrow of the Vandals

For the next two generations the Roman Empire remained on the defensive against barbarian inroads by sea and land. The chief enemy of the eastern Empire was the Persian Kingdom, with which its military capacities were fully occupied. When Justinian I came to the throne in 527 he was desirous of regaining for the Empire the territories which it had lost in the preceding two centuries. His international policy was one of restoring the Roman prestige and he undoubtedly accomplished much in this direction, although he overstrained the military and financial power of the Empire in his effort. He himself announced his policy early in his reign:

> We have good hopes that God will grant us to restore our authority over the remaining countries which the ancient Romans possessed to the limits of both oceans and lost by subsequent neglect.

Early in the reign of Justinian a pretext arose for a declaration of war against the Vandalic Kingdom of Africa with its seat at Carthage. For over 50 years the Vandal Kings had observed the terms of a treaty which Gaiseric had concluded with the Emperor Zeno, but the Catholic Christians of Africa had always been more or less persecuted by the heretic Vandal conquerors and the Roman Emperors had occasionally protested. In 530 the Vandal Gelimer, a great grandson of Gaiseric, overthrew his cousin on the throne and took his place. Justinian at once remonstrated, demanding the restoration of the rightful King. Gelimer refused compliance, probably realizing that in the end he could not avert war.

In 532 the Empire's current war with Persia was closed and Justinian began preparations for a campaign against Gelimer. It did not seem to the Emperor to be a war of aggression, but rather he was to suppress a tyrant in a province over which the Empire had never renounced its authority. The eastern traders at Carthage saw commercial advantage in political unity and besides the Church was in favor of rescuing Roman African Catholics from their Vandal Arian oppressors. The war was for the re-establishment of just authority, and true religion.

It was long since the Empire had maintained a powerful navy and the imperial ministers pointed out the dangers of the campaign, for the failure of the last African expedition under the Emperor Leo was still well remembered. Although this unfavorable view had much in its justification, its proponents probably did not realize how greatly the military strength of the Vandals had declined in two generations. Justinian relied on the justice of his cause and the expedition took place in the year 533. No important naval action took place. In fact, the Vandal fleet, deemed so strong, made no appearance. So the interest of the expedition to us lies in the minute account which we have of the organization and conduct of an ancient great naval enterprise, which we owe to its historian, Procopius, who was a member of the expedition, acting as Secretary to Belisarius, the Commander in Chief.

The combatant force was made up of 10,000 infantry and 5,000 cavalry besides the private guards to the Commander in Chief. The army was carried by 500 transport ships manned by 20,000 sailors and these ships were all able to carry over 3,000 medimni* (120 tons), but none more than 50,000 medimni (2,000 tons). The transports were escorted by 92 ships-of-war called *dromons*, a new term. These were single-banked ships with high bulwarks above the oars for the protection of the rowers from the missiles of the enemy (see Appendix to this chapter). They were able to attain great speed, Procopius tells us, and they were manned by 2,000 men of Constantinople, all rowers as well as combatants, so that none was superfluous. Calonymus commanded the ships and Archelaus the army. The time was well chosen, for Tripolitana had revolted against Gelimer, and he was planning to recover it. Also the Vandal Governor of Sardinia was in rebellion and asking aid from Justinian, who sent a few soldiers to support him. The Emperor sent an advance squadron ahead of the main fleet. Probably its task was an administrative one, to let the peoples on the route know of the expedition and to make contracts for local supplies to be furnished the expedition.

The departure of the fleet from Constantinople about the summer solstice (June 21) was attended with all the ancient ceremonies modified to suit the Christian faith. The flagship lay off the palace and, after religious services by the principal cleric of Constantinople, Belisarius embarked with his wife Antonina who habitually accompanied him on his campaigns,

* Medimnus, a measure of capacity of about 1½ bushels; 25 medimni of wheat to a ton.

and was sometimes entrusted by him with administrative duties. The flag-ships then got under way, followed by all the fleet and put in at Perinthus on the Propontis (Sea of Marmora) where 5 days were spent in shipping horses. At Abydos 4 days more were spent before putting out into the open sea, and here Belisarius painted red the upper parts of the sails of his own ship and of two others carrying his immediate staff, so that the fleet might know which ships were the guides to be followed. For night guidance the same ships carried lights on staffs at their bows.

A fine breeze carried the fleet out of the Hellespont, but a calm soon fell, which lasted as far as to Malea, but the calm was found advantageous, since the seamen apparently were not yet well trained, and as the ships were numerous and large they were often in collision. But owing to the fine weather they could be kept from damaging each other by the use of boathooks.

And so the fleet came to Tænarum and Methone where it overtook the advance guard. Here Belisarius disembarked the whole army for organization and drill. Unfortunately, a serious pestilence broke out, because, for the sake of graft, a great official in Constantinople had fur-nished badly baked bread (hard tack) which here spoiled and poisoned the army, costing 500 lives. Although Belisarius reported the matter to the Emperor and was praised by the latter for doing so, yet the culprit went unpunished. Politics was much the same then as now.

After some stay at Methone (perhaps as much as 3 weeks), the fleet moved on to Zacynthus (Zante) where much water was taken on board to make the passage across the Adriatic. The winds were light and not until the sixteenth day did the fleet complete a voyage of under 300 miles and arrive at a deserted strand in Sicily near Mount Ætna. Evidently the transport ships did not assist themselves by oars. During the passage the water spoiled, except that of Belisarius and his table companions. For them Antonina provided water in glass jars which she buried in sand in a small compartment of the ship, and this water was unaffected.

After reaching Sicily, Belisarius was somewhat at a loss, for he knew nothing of the situation in Africa and his soldiers announced they would fight well on shore, but would decline to make an effort at sea where, they said, they would have two enemies, the sea and the Vandal fleet. Accordingly, Belisarius sent his Secretary forward in a fast ship to Syracuse to get information and return to meet the fleet at a point 20 miles north of Syracuse. Procopius gave out that he was buying provisions and was fortunate enough to meet an old friend in the market place who pointed out a slave who had left Africa only 3 days before. This man stated that Gelimer knew nothing of the Roman expedition and was 4 days away from Carthage in the interior, and that he had dispatched a force of 5,000 men and 120 ships to recover Sardinia. Thus a large part of the Vandal army was absent from Africa and haste was imperative for Belisarius to seize the opportunity. In spite of protests from the slave's owner, Procopius shanghaied his informant, telling the former that he would pay the man well and send him back. Procopius hurriedly returned to Belisarius, who immediately sailed with the expedition to Malta where it picked up a strong east wind which took it quickly to Caputvada on the gulf of Tunis, about 120 miles SE. of Carthage, or 5 days' march for an unencumbered man, as Procopius puts it.

Before landing, Belisarius assembled a council of war and Archelaus urged that the troops should remain on shipboard and make a quick passage to Carthage and take it by surprise if possible. Belisarius rejected the proposal on the ground that they might meet a hostile fleet, and the soldiers had already said in that case they would not fight. Therefore, Belisarius pointed out it would be wrong to blame the soldiers should a battle at sea be forced on them, and he decided to land where they were, before bad weather should risk both fleet and army. In about 70 days after leaving Constantinople the army was safely on shore in Africa. It had gone about 980 miles as a steamer would now go, but about 1,250 miles on its actual course with probably over 5 weeks in ports by the way and repeatedly at anchor over night.

After landing, the soldiers dug a trench and found good water, so the army bivouacked, leaving a guard of 5 soldiers on each transport and the men-of-war anchored in a circle outside the transports (which were probably drawn close to the shore). The march to Carthage followed. The inhabitants were friendly and gave supplies readily (they were orthodox Christians like the army) and Belisarius took the strictest measures to prevent pillaging by his troops. As far as the road ran near the shore the fleet kept abreast, but when the road left the coast and crossed the neck of the great promontory, the army was obliged to part from the fleet. The latter was ordered not to put in at Carthage, but to remain about 3 miles offshore until summoned by Belisarius. In less than 2 weeks of unmolested march the army was approaching Carthage and about to enter the present Tunis.

But Gelimer had assembled a force and was following, unperceived, intending to fall on the enemy by surprise near Carthage. Here he had prepared an ambush among some hills, whose success would depend on the simultaneous arrival of three detachments to surround the Roman army. One detachment under the King's brother came up several hours too soon, and was defeated with the loss of its leader's life. The second detachment was also defeated a little later, and then the King came up with his main force. He defeated the Romans and drove them back, but the trap had been sprung too soon and so Gelimer had encountered only the advanced cavalry; the infantry had not yet come up. Procopius says that nevertheless, in his opinion, if Gelimer had continued his effort and pushed forward to attack the infantry also, the Romans could not have withstood him. Instead, on entering the little town where his brother had been killed, he found his body and abandoned everything to indulge his grief and bury the body. While the Vandals were thus in confusion, Belisarius rallied the fugitive cavalry and, at its charge, the whole Vandal army fled without offering opposition. The next morning Antonina arrived with the infantry and joined her husband. The whole force then marched to Carthage where it arrived at nightfall on September 14. Belisarius refused to enter in the dark, both to avoid pillaging the city and because he feared an attack. But in fact, the Vandal army had evacuated.

In the meantime the fleet had heard nothing for some days and sent ashore for news. It learned of the battle by Tunis and came towards the city with a good wind and, at the same time, the citizens (opposed to the government), seeing the fleet in the offing, removed the chains from the harbor mouth to afford the fleet free entrance. When still some miles from Carthage, Archelaus and the soldiers on board wished to remain at a distance, according to their orders, but the sailors wished to keep on for they said the weather was threatening and they did not wish to anchor at sea. So the fleet shortened sail to deliberate. The leaders feared to enter the port, for it was not known that the chain had been removed, and besides the harbor seemed small for so many ships, so the fleet ran on 3 miles south and entered the Stagnum, the bay in front of Tunis, about the time Belisarius and the army were camping before the city gates. All the ships anchored except that of the Admiral, Calonymus, who went off with a few sailors and entered the port to pillage. Evidently, he personally had secured accurate information. In the morning Belisarius marched into the city in battle array. The citizens were friendly and Belisarius now learned that the Vandal army had gone. Belisarius had preserved the most remarkable discipline in the army ever since landing and was still maintaining it. The citizens at once informed him of the looting by Calonymus the night before and he compelled restitution of the stolen goods. Calonymus returned to Constantinople, where he soon died insane in a manner which Procopius regarded as the judgment of God.

The Vandal King now recalled his brother Tzazon with his army from Sardinia and together they moved towards Carthage. But of Tzazon's ships which escorted his army to Sardinia, Procopius tells us nothing. About the middle of December, Belisarius marched out of the city and defeated the Vandal army, but after this final victory Belisarius could no longer keep his troops from dispersing to seek booty, and Procopius says that in his opinion, if Gelimer could have rallied only a few of his men, not a Roman would have escaped to enjoy his prize of war. King Gelimer surrendered and Belisarius, with his captive and a vast treasure, returned to Constantinople where he was granted a triumph, which was then an unusual honor for a private man.

So ended a campaign rendered possible only by the Empire's sea power, in which close co-operation by the army and navy was practiced owing to the two services having a common commander in chief, yet, in which, owing to the unexpected absence of the hostile navy, there was no naval battle.

The Gothic War and Naval Battle of Sena Gallica

Having regained the province of Africa, Justinian felt encouraged to attempt the recovery of the orthodox Italians from the rule of the heretical East Goths, who had established themselves in Italy about the middle of the fifth century, and in the long war which ensued Procopius gives a clear account of the naval tactics of the time. The Gothic King Theodoric died in 526 and, after his death, the Goths lost strength and became isolated from the Teutonic tribes elsewhere in Europe. In the civil disturbances which arose among the Goths, Justinian found a pretext for resuming direct authority there, as he had already done in Africa. As the Gothic Kingdom was without a fleet, and as Justinian was in complete control of the waters of the eastern Mediterranean, it was easy to begin his Italian Campaign by a small expedition to Sicily. Belisarius was again made Commander in Chief and was given about half the force which he had taken to Africa 2 years before. He sailed from Constantinople with about 8,000 men at the end of June, 535, and disembarked at Catana. He seems to have met no opposition except at Panormus (Palermo) where the defenses were strong and the Gothic garrison refused to surrender. The harbor was not closed and Belisarius entered with his fleet. As the masts of his ships were higher than the walls of the city, he hoisted boats full of archers to the mastheads so that their fire could overshoot the walls. The garrison yielded at once and by the end of the year Sicily was completely restored to the Empire.

In the war to conquer Italy, which now followed and which lasted until 562, the imperial fleet enabled the army to go where it would and to have necessary supplies, but not until 550 did the Emperor send enough troops to his generals to make a thorough success of their operations.

In the spring of 536 Belisarius crossed the straits to Rhegium and marched to Naples, which he soon captured, and then on Rome, which he entered in December, 536, upon the invitation of the inhabitants. The Gothic King Witigis brought an army against the city and a siege followed which lasted over a year. The Gothic force was too small completely to cut off communications and it was not expert enough to practice formal siege warfare, so it confined itself to assaults which did not bring success. However, the Goths broke all Rome's aqueducts which had supplied the city for centuries, and until their reconstruction about a thousand years afterwards the Romans drew all their water from the Tiber and from wells. During the siege the Romans were somewhat short of supplies, but the Goths also suffered from hunger and disease and Procopius points out that the Gothic scarcity arose from the Roman sea power which prevented Italy from receiving the supplies which were her necessity. The siege was terminated by a truce, after which Belisarius resumed operations and the

Roman arms made progress, largely owing to the security with which supplies came overseas in the absence of any Gothic navy.

By 540 Belisarius controlled Italy south of the Po, he captured the Gothic King, hostilities were suspended, and Belisarius returned to Constantinople. In the fall of 541, a new Gothic King, Totila, reopened hostilities and, leaving the valley of the Po, he marched into South Italy, which he soon regained. In his siege of Naples, which he took in 543, he was much aided by some ships which he had gathered and used to destroy the squadron of provision ships sent to relieve the city. At last the Goths were learning that only on the sea could they destroy the Roman sea power which supported the Roman forces in Italy. Justinian's generals in Italy did little and in 544 he sent Belisarius once more to Italy. The latter at once relieved Otranto which was besieged by a Gothic army, but King Totila began a second blockade of Rome.

Apparently the Emperor expected Belisarius to find the means of supporting the war in Italy itself, but the army he sent was too small to occupy enough territory to find the means of subsistence within the controlled area. In the summer of 545 Belisarius wrote to the Emperor that he could not get revenue from Italy and towards the end of the year the Emperor sent a new army. In the meantime Totila had been successful in Tuscany, and early in 546 he began to press the blockade of Rome in person. He had already shut off the supplies to the city from Sicily and the east by a squadron of light ships stationed at Naples and the Lipari Islands. Besides he had seized one of the two ports at the mouth of the Tiber, so that the imperial garrison held only Portus. Belisarius sent 500 men by sea from the Adriatic to re-enforce the troops at Portus and soon arrived there himself. Rome was greatly suffering and on the point of surrender.

Bessas, commanding the garrison of the city, had been profiting by the distress of the citizens to fill his own purse, and was not greatly inclined to aid his Commander in Chief. Belisarius decided that the forces he had with him (a few thousand only) at Portus were too weak to attack the Gothic camp and thought he could attempt no more than to throw supplies into the city by the river route.

To prevent the passage of supply ships, Totila had anchored a boom across the river, and on each bank at the ends he had erected a tower to contain guards. A little downstream was an iron chain to keep ships from getting at the boom. To overcome this obstacle, Belisarius secured two wide boats to each other and built a tower on them higher than those on shore. Using this tower as a derrick he hoisted high a boat filled with combustibles. To protect this incendiary device Belisarius fitted the decks of 200 dromons, which were to carry the supplies, with high parapets, having embrasures through which archers could shoot, and manned these light craft with soldiers. A sufficient garrison was left in Portus to man the walls and if necessary to issue to counter-attack any onslaught by the Goths. Another division of soldiers was ordered to advance along the shore to accompany the vessels. Belisarius embarked on one of the dromons and the incendiary machine was towed or dragged upstream. The chain was only slightly guarded and was soon hauled away. A little farther the Romans found the boom better protected by some soldiers who rushed from their camp to aid the guards already in the towers. The fire tower was guided to the right bank where the Roman covering party was marching, and the boat load of combustibles was dropped on the tower which was consumed with its guard of 200 Goths. In the meantime the archers in the dromons kept up a heavy rain of arrows on the Goths on shore until these turned and fled. The boom was then destroyed and the way to Rome was open.

At this moment a rider galloped up to say that Isaac, who had been left in command of the garrison of Portus, was in the hands of the enemy. Belisarius lost his presence of mind. He had given orders to Isaac on no account to sally from the walls of Portus and he assumed that the town, and with it his wife Antonina, had been captured by the Goths. He drew back at once with all the relief supply ships to attempt to recover Portus before the enemy could make themselves secure there. On arrival, it turned out that Portus was safe, but that Isaac had gone out with a small detachment to attack a Gothic camp and had been made a prisoner while pillaging the camp from which he had driven the occupants. If Belisarius had promptly returned up the river, the misadventure would probably not have been serious, but the shock and disappointment were so great that he was taken ill, and also the garrison at Rome grew negligent.

The city was taken by the Goths in December, 546. There were only about 500 of the inhabitants left in the city. Bessas and most of the garrison escaped. Totila hoped that this success would end the war, but the Emperor refused his proposals and Totila then moved to South Italy where the division left by Belisarius at Brundisium had been making progress. In the absence of the Gothic army Belisarius undertook to reoccupy Rome and put it in a state of defense. As he was now completely in control of the sea he was readily able to establish a good market in the city through importations from Sicily. The people of the neighborhood were attracted into town by the vacant houses. Totila came back but could not drive Belisarius out. The war ran on for two years more, but Justinian never sent enough troops to enable Belisarius to accomplish his task. In 548 Belisarius sent Antonina to Constantinople to ask her friend, the Empress Theodora, for more troops, but she was dead and, as Belisarius was weary of conducting a war without sufficient forces, it was easy for his wife to procure his recall. He left Italy early in 549; his enemies alleging that he had done nothing but sail about the coasts of Italy, only venturing to land when he had the support of a fortress. During the summer of 549 the Goths besieged Rome a third time and were successful in January, 550.

The Emperor now held only a few posts in South Italy and Totila asked him for peace and recognition, but Justinian arranged to continue operations, so Totila decided to carry the war into Sicily. Totila gathered about 400 men-of-war and some large captured merchantmen to ferry his army into Sicily. He first took Tarentum, the imperial base in South Italy, and besieged Rhegium but without waiting for the latter to fall he crossed to Sicily early in 550 and soon had the whole island in his power except Messina, and after several months the Gothic army returned with much booty.

RENEWAL OF THE WAR IN ITALY

During the past few years the Goths had been steadily gaining in Italy and the only places now held by the Empire were Ravenna, Ancona, Otranto, and Croton. On returning from Sicily (late summer, 550) Totila sent an army to besiege Ancona. Justinian now made a determined effort. By the autumn of 550 a new Roman army of invasion had assembled in Dalmatia and it was thought better to spend the winter there before marching into Venetia. Justinian appointed the Armenian eunuch Narses as Commander in Chief in Italy. He was a very able minister who made no enemies and was believed to have the advice of the Virgin herself in battle. But duties elsewhere delayed his arrival in Dalmatia for nearly a year.

Totila now realized that the Empire was about to make a supreme effort for his destruction. His naval forces had been gradually increasing for several years and he was able to send a fleet of 300 ships (no doubt very small) to ravage the shores of Greece and it intercepted transports conveying supplies to the army of Narses at Salona. At the same time the blockade of Ancona was completed by 47 Gothic ships which closed the sea, in the summer of 551. Valerian, the imperial general at Ravenna, wrote to Salona to tell the relieving army of the gravity of the situation at Ancona. Narses had not yet arrived, but the general in command at Salona, John, by name, took upon himself to disobey the imperial order to make no move before Narses should appear, and with 38 well-manned ships he joined 12 which Valerian brought from Ravenna. The two generals then crossed the Adriatic to Sena Gallica, about 17 miles northwest of Ancona. The Gothic commanders at sea left a force on shore to maintain the blockade of Ancona by land and took the fleet to Sena Gallica where they offered battle. John and Valerian addressed their men, saying that the fight was not for Ancona alone, but that the war depended on supplies and that valor cannot dwell with hunger. On Ancona, they said, depended the possibility of recovering Italy. Ancona was then a base for the Romans, but were the enemy to secure it, the Romans could no longer sail the seas. Anticipating the Emperor Leo's warning in his tactics written 300 years later, they reminded their hearers that they were fighting on a hostile coast where defeat meant destruction. "If we lose," they ended, "God help Italy." The strategy of the war was exposed in this address. A secure port in South Italy was necessary to serve as an over-seas base for the advance of the Roman army which would draw its supplies from beyond the Adriatic.

PROCOPIUS DESCRIBES THE BATTLE OF SENA GALLICA

The two fleets were nearly equal in numbers and lined up facing each other. As the lines approached each other bow to bow the archers opened the engagement, and as the ships moved on and came in contact, the boarders fought from the upper decks (catastroma) with sword and lance. The Goths were without squadron training, so that some of their ships were too distant from each other to give mutual support, and others were so close that they fell foul of each other and became locked together "so that one would say their decks were built into one, like a mat." In such conditions the Goths' archery was inefficient, and as friendly ships collided with each other, the men's attention was diverted from their swords and lances to push the ships apart with boathooks, and all were shouting at each other to their own confusion. They could shoot only slowly at distant enemies, yet could not use side arms well when in contact with the enemy.

On the other hand, the Romans were more practiced in ship handling and kept proper distance from each other, skillfully heading towards the enemy, and when one of the latter separated from his comrades they rammed him, and when ships came near each other the Romans used their arrows and then closed to board. The Goths became discouraged and fought neither in land fashion nor in sea fashion. So in the end the Goths "turned to flight without dignity" with the loss of 36 ships. The 11 ships which reached shore were burned by their own crews which returned to Ancona. When the victorious fleet arrived it found the besiegers had retired. The battle was a great blow to the power and prestige of the Goths and soon after a Roman expedition to Sicily recovered the four fortresses of the island. Nevertheless, the sea power of the Goths was not entirely destroyed. They were still able to control the Tyrrhenian sea and Totila sent to Sardinia and Corsica and overcame the Roman garrisons there. An imperial expedition from Africa late in 551 to recover the islands was defeated after landing and driven back to Africa, returning in greater strength the next year.

Narses' Campaign in Italy

In the spring of 552 Narses set out for Italy. He had the troops assembled at Salona the previous year, besides men from various German tribes and even deserters from Persia. Probably the Empire could not assemble a larger force. It was well supplied with money and munitions and numbered about 25,000 men.* This comparatively small army was able in a little time to conquer Italy south of the Po, a task which Belisarius

---

* Bury, *Later Roman Empire*, vol. 2, p. 262.

had found impossible with 15,000 men and short supplies. But, although the sea as far as Sicily had been Roman throughout the war and Narses' admirals had just won an overwhelming victory, he preferred to march into Italy through Venetia. Probably he did not have enough ships to take all his army across at one time, although he had enough to rule the sea.

In this naval study it is unnecessary to trace the further course of the war. In three great battles Narses overcame the Goths and other Teutonic tribes, and established Roman rule throughout South Italy, but the conquest of the Po Valley was not complete till 562. Following Narses, a Byzantine Exarch (viceroy) at Ravenna held authority over a slowly diminishing territory in Italy for nearly two centuries.

BATTLE OF BUSTA GALLORUM

Pursuant to what was said in my previous volume about naval tactics imitating the military tactics of the day, it is worth while to compare what Procopius tells us of the tactics at Busta Gallorum, the first and principal of Narses' battles in Italy, with the naval tactics at Sena Gallica a few months earlier.

At Salamis and in the Roman wars, the tactical effort of the victors (aside from ramming) was to give opportunity to the spear and sword. But in the days of the Roman Empire, the close-fighting legionary passed out of fashion and, for the principal arm, the military world substituted armored cavalry using the bow, with the sword or lance as secondary weapons.

At Busta Gallorum (33 miles SW. of Sena Gallica), Narses occupied a strong defensive position with perhaps 15,000 men,* and probably had more men than the Goths. He formed his center of dismounted cavalry with a force of mounted men on each side of them, and the wings were made of archers whose outer flanks were advanced, so that the center was somewhat withdrawn. Opposite the center of this line, which was much strengthened by the shape of the ground, Totila drew up his cavalry with his infantry behind the cavalry. He gave the cavalry the unusual order to use their spears only, neglecting their archery. During the forenoon Narses refused opportunities to attack which the enemy offered. In the

---

* Delbrueck, *Geschichte der Kriegskunst,* vol. 2, p. 386.

afternoon the Gothic cavalry charged the Roman center and was met on both sides by the flanking archery discharge. The Goths suffered much loss before they could reach the Romans and the attack was broken up. The Gothic infantry did not move and Narses' whole line then advanced and swept the enemy from the field.

COMPARISON OF THE TWO BATTLES

Although the land battle repeated the tactics of John and Valerian at Sena Gallica, it must be recollected that the tactical method of the navy was imposed upon it by its soldiers' weapons. With their high bulwarks, ships were built to protect the archers' attack instead of to facilitate the old time boarders' battle. At Sena Gallica, as at Busta Gallorum, the Goths charged and through lack of skill they fell into a huddle. Then in both cases the Romans used their archers and after shaking the enemy they charged and destroyed him. The tactical difference between the Roman and the Gothic formation at Sena Gallica was that most of the Goths were so jammed together that those in the rear could not aim at the enemy on account of the intervening ships, but the Romans, who maintained a single line with proper intervals, could bring all their archery and all their rams into action.

While the Goths never equaled the Romans in their fleet, they had seen how much Belisarius multiplied his small forces by his ability to move by sea from the Bosphorus and then from point to point in Italy. In consequence, when they began shipbuilding both belligerents gradually increased the size of ships, for it will always happen that whatever type of ship is in vogue, the bigger the ship, the more effective her fighting, provided her size is not gained at too great an expense to her mobility. It is to be regretted that in the six centuries between Actium and Sena Gallica we are unable to obtain a clear view of the development of naval affairs. This is due to the fact that the rise of Christianity had turned the predilections of historians from politics and war to theology, and only Procopius finds his chief interest in secular matters. Nevertheless, it has been worth while to follow the naval campaigns of Constantine and Belisarius because they needed navies for the same reason that we do today, namely, to guard their commerce and cover the sea communications of their armies which had to be preserved to carry on operations across the water.

AUTHORITIES CHIEFLY CONSULTED FOR THIS CHAPTER

BURY, J. B., *History of Later Roman Empire.*

Cambridge Medieval History, vol. I.

DELBRUECK, H., *Geschichte der Kriegskunst.*

EUSEBIUS, *Life of Constantine.*

FINLAY, G., *History of Greece under the Romans.*

FIRTH, C. H., *Life of Constantine.*

GFRÖRER, A. F., *Byzantinische Seewesen.*

GIBBON, E., *History of the Decline and Fall of the Roman Empire.*

PROCOPIUS, *Histories of the Vandal and Gothic Wars.*

APPENDIX I

CHAPTER I

The Trajan's column at Rome has many representations of ships. It is apparent that they are small and it is what might be expected, for in the absence of great wars the Roman navy for several centuries needed only local coast-guard ships to suppress piracy and preserve order on the seas. With the sculptures on the column and Pompeian wall paintings as our principal sources, we may try to reconstruct the ships which served the Empire probably until the first half of the sixth century A.D., when extended maritime operations required an increase in the size of men-of-war.

The Pompeian paintings show ships with rowers seated on the upper decks and some 15 or 20 oars on a side. On the column the outline of the ships is much conventionalized. The men are out of all proportion to the vessels in which they are seated and the vertical scale is greater than the horizontal. In any reconstruction one must take some particular dimension as a basis and draw the rest of the ship in proportion. Let us take the length of the sternsheets in the column as the standard, and as 7 or 8 feet long. The foresheets is about the same. In medieval ships the remainder of the length, the rowing chamber, was about three times as much. Thus the whole length of the ship would be 60 feet and the rowing chamber would accommodate 12 oars on a side at 3½ feet per oar. Taking the vessel as a bireme, that is, either with 2 men per oar or with 2 oars with 1 man each per bench, we have 48 rowers. Adding 27 men for officers, seamen, and soldiers, we have a crew of 75.* Allowing 350 pounds for each man's weight with clothes and armor and 10 days' rations at 15 pounds per man per day, we have a total weight of 26,250 pounds, which we count as 33 per cent of the displacement. The equipment, ship's stores, and perhaps a small piece of mechanical artillery as 19 per cent and the hull as 48 per cent, making a total displacement of 35.5 tons. At 60 per cent for block coefficient and 12.5 feet beam for stability, we have a draft

---

* Josephus says the Pontic squadron of 40 ships had 3,000 men.

FIG. I.—SHIPS FROM TRAJAN'S COLUMN

Date early second century. See diagram p. 25.

(The middle ship has oars on three levels and by her lantern is probably a flagship.)

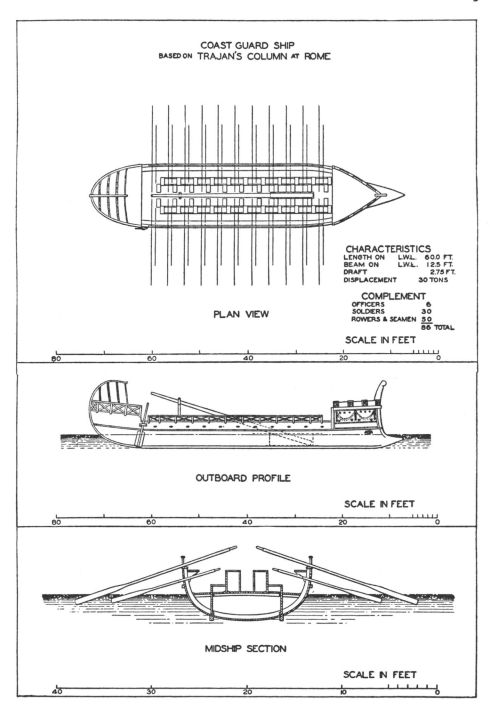

COAST GUARD SHIP
BASED ON TRAJAN'S COLUMN AT ROME

CHARACTERISTICS
LENGTH ON   L.W.L.   60.0 FT.
BEAM ON   L.W.L.   12.5 FT.
DRAFT   2.75 FT.
DISPLACEMENT   30 TONS

COMPLEMENT
OFFICERS   6
SOLDIERS   30
ROWERS & SEAMEN   50
                        86 TOTAL

PLAN VIEW

SCALE IN FEET

80   60   40   20   0

OUTBOARD PROFILE

SCALE IN FEET

80   60   40   20   0

MIDSHIP SECTION

SCALE IN FEET

40   30   20   10   0

FIG. 2.—RECONSTRUCTION, MAN-OF-WAR, SECOND CENTURY

of 2.75 feet. The racing speed would be rather low, about 6.4 knots.*

The Pompeian paintings reproduced herewith show the vessels with a single mast and a sail area which may be guessed as less than the area of the water line. The rowers are protected by their shields hung along the sides. So we may suppose they joined in the fight as Procopius alleges of the dromons in the Vandalic War. The shields are omitted in the drawing.**

I take it that Belisarius' ships differed little from those of the first and second centuries as reconstructed above.

---

* This estimate of size and speed is based on the data given in my previous volume *Greek and Roman Naval Warfare*, pp. 29-53.

** It will be observed that the diagram is of a craft of less displacement, carrying less cargo than that of the text, and a trifle faster.

FIG. 3.—MEN-OF-WAR. FROM FRESCOES POMPEII. DATE ABOUT 60-70 A.D.

The lower fresco, somewhat more defaced, shows a ship under sail of the same size and type. She has a single mast, stepped forward of the middle length of the ship, and raking forward. There is one square sail, spread on a horizontal yard supported by topping lifts.

APPENDIX II

THE FLEET OF BELISARIUS IN 533 A.D.

The account which Procopius gives of the ships of the expedition to Africa shows how much the business of the Empire had fallen off since the comparatively peaceful times of the second century. If 500 ships were needed to carry a total force of 5,000 horses and 36,000 men, including sailors, it is clear that they cannot have been as large as Procopius says. Not only the industries of the Empire had fallen off since its early days, but the machinery of production and distribution was less efficient. Besides, the government had neglected to keep a sufficient fleet on the seas to suppress piracy. This would account for a reduction in sea-borne commerce and further, in such a state of affairs, it is clear that sound principles of insurance demanded that individual ships should be small in order to spread the risks.

We therefore have some difficulty in believing that the transport fleet had many (if any) ships of 50,000 medimni (2,000 tons) burden, for such ships could not find cargoes readily. For the same reason, 80 years ago, the *Great Eastern*, although an admirable ship, was too big to find a cargo at any given time and place. Even the ships of 3,000 medimni (120 tons cargo or 240 tons displacement), which Procopius says were the smallest in the expedition, were not small ships for the times.

It is not difficult to estimate the tonnage of ships necessary to transport the army of Belisarius. The vessels which Napoleon prepared in 1803 and 1804 to carry the French army to England were designed to do much the same type of work that Belisarius required. Both expeditions needed light-draft craft to land their passengers readily, and the day-long voyages of Belisarius were short, like the passage of the Channel for Napoleon. Full accounts of the French craft are to be found in the work of Edouard Desbrières entitled *Projets de Débarquement aux Iles Britanniques* and in Nicolai's *Napoleon at His Camp of Boulogne*. Models of the flotilla may be seen at the Naval Museum at the Louvre and drawings in *Souvenirs de Marine*, by Vice Admiral Paris. From these works it appears that the prams (sailing ships) of about 400 tons' load displacement could each take 80 to 120 soldiers with 50 horses and 38 sailors and 10 days' rations and forage for all, besides some military supplies and guns, amounting to perhaps 60 tons. Commuting the accommodation for horses into that for men at the ratio of 1 for 5, we see that each man had a trifle more than 1 ton of ship displacement and each horse had about 5½ tons. The gunboats (chaloupes-cannonières) of 120 tons' displacement carried 130 men, soldiers and crew, with 10 days' supplies. This is 1 ton per man. Smaller craft of Napoleon's flotilla were even more heavily laden in proportion to their displacement.

Turning now to Belisarius' expedition, besides 2,000 soldiers in the dromons, he had 16,000 soldiers and 5,000 horses in the transports, besides their crews proper. The latter amounted, as is alleged, to 20,000 men. Taking the capacity of the Boulogne prams as a basis and substituting food and water and general supplies for the guns and military supplies on the prams, Belisarius' troop and horse transports could carry 30 days' rations and 16 days' water with 4,000 tons of general supplies on 45,000 tons' displacement. They would have needed crews of about 6,000 men according to the medieval rule for men in proportion to tonnage.

Let us assume that the general supply ships took 60 days' rations at 4 pounds per man and 15 days' horse rations at 20 pounds and a weight twice as much more for siege engines and military equipments of all kinds. The crews of these ships would come to about 5,000 men, to which we may add 2,000 more for camp followers of all kinds. This would give us only 13,000 men in addition to the strictly military force.

So we must choose between accepting a smaller number of sailors or a larger military force in order to preserve a reasonable ratio between the two. Of course, the smaller total is preferable. Taking 31,000 men as the whole number in the expedition we have it that the general supply ships would take about 12,000 tons of cargo on a displacement of about 36,000 tons. The whole fleet would come to about 81,000 tons (besides the dromons) and the average of 500 ships would be 162 tons' displacement.* This average is much less than the size given by Procopius as the minimum, i.e., 3,000 medimni or 120 tons burden.

Procopius introduces us to a new type of man-of-war which he calls "dromon," saying there were 92 of them in Belisarius' fleet manned by 2,000 men, who were all rowers and combatants by turns. A mention of

---

* Dimensions of such a ship would be roughly 60' x 18' x 8'.

dromons by Cassiodorus referring to a period a few years earlier says that Theodoric, King of the Ostrogoths, ordered the construction and manning of 1,000 dromons. As these navigated in the branches of the Po, it is clear that they must have been small. It is therefore plain that the long maritime peace of the early Empire, followed by great weakness in the government, had reduced the size of men-of-war. The officers and the non-combatant men of Procopius' dromons could not have brought the whole crew of each to more than 30 to 35 men. These could readily be placed on a craft 50 feet long and 17 tons' displacement. Such a craft with 22 oars might reach a maximum speed of 6.3 knots.

In his *Vandalic War*, Book II, chap. 11 (consult also Book III, chap. 11), Procopius says the rowers were protected by high bulwarks in which were oarports. The statements about dromons in the Vandalic War may be compared with what the same author says as to the Gothic War, when he tells of the second siege of Rome. During that siege Belisarius used a part of his small relieving army to bring 200 dromons up the Tiber, carrying provisions. As the countryside was deserted and no crews could be found there, the soldiers must have rowed, as well as fought, and Belisarius could have provided no more than 30 to 35 men for each craft. So the dromons were originally small.

As for the ships which fought at Sena Gallica, Procopius tells us little directly, but we may assume that they were larger than the dromons of which he spoke in 533. This is to be inferred from the relatively small numbers at Sena Gallica compared to the figures mentioned earlier and also to the fact that the rowers were protected by a "catastroma" or covered deck, whereas in Belisarius' fleet they were protected only by the bulwarks which also shielded the archers. It is therefore probable that the ships at Sena Gallica had crews of perhaps as many as 150 or 160 men, including mariners, rowers, and soldiers, and may have been of some 80 tons' displacement.

CHAPTER II

THE NAVAL WARS WITH THE SARACENS

Economic Situation

AFTER Narses' conquest of Italy, the Empire was in full control of the Mediterranean and its commerce and, as no one disputed it, the naval forces were again neglected since no demands were made on them. Then, in the early part of the seventh century, Mahomet unified Arabia and the Arabs set out on a career of conquest whose prize would be the tribute and commerce of the Eastern Roman Empire. Consequently the two warring powers developed their navies to secure their maritime positions. Before taking up the naval warfare, it is therefore desirable to survey the commercial field at stake early in the seventh century, which in some respects resembles that at issue in the wars of Alexander's Successors.

The maritime business of the Empire was great and prosperous and trade centered at Constantinople which, besides being the seat of government and commercial distributing point, was a great industrial center. Its chief manufactures were silk goods, domestic pottery utensils, mosaics for churches and palaces, works of religious symbolism, such as crucifixes, jewelry, and munitions of war. The trade of the Mediterranean was mainly in the hands of Greeks and Syrians, even as far as Gaul. The West sent metals and agricultural products. Silk and wrought linen came from Tyre and Berytus, purple from Cæsarea, strong wines from Gaza, furs from Cappadocia. Through the Euxine and the Caspian, Byzantine commerce reached Central Asia and northward to Scandinavia. Russia sent honey, wax, and slaves. The Empire trade with the East was mainly one of imports and there was a drain of money eastwards, as there is now, to pay for silk and spices and only a little glass and enamel work and some embroideries went east from Syria.

By the third century Roman merchants had ceased to control the Red Sea route to India and it fell into the hands of intermediaries, Persians, Abyssinians, and Yemenites (south Arabs). The two latter peoples controlled the Red Sea. Ceylon became the great halfway point for trade between Europe and China, and there the Persians took entire control of the silk which supplied the Syrian factories, and Justinian could neither break their hold nor regulate the price by edict. However, in 551, he succeeded in obtaining silk-worm eggs for Syria through two monks who visited China, and so started a great industry which spread over the Empire.

The great commerce passing through Constantinople enabled the government to obtain a great part of its revenues from the city itself.

Thus at the opening of the seventh century the Byzantine Empire was the most civilized and best organized state of its time, but before the century closed the spread of Mohammedanism threatened its existence. For eight centuries longer its resistance to the Saracens* enabled western Europe to accomplish its development, and during the greater part of this long period, the organized navy of Constantinople, with its new inventions, played a great part.

THE RISE OF MOHAMMEDANISM

The general economic situation which promoted the Arabic development under the impulse of Mahomet had its origin in the conquests of Alexander in the fourth century, B.C., whereby Hellenic culture controlled the development of Semitic peoples and was itself modified by them. In Mahomet's time the economic conditions in South Arabia had long been growing worse. As political authority diminished, the irrigation works suffered and caused population pressure and tribal animosities. Both the Byzantine Empire and its age-long opponent, Persia, suffered from the unrest along their Arabian borders, and the sudden expansion of the Saracens was the culmination of a turbulence of centuries.

With this new religion the prophet Mahomet held in check the political rivalries within the city of Medina and established its supremacy in Arabia. Immediately after his death in 632 the new religion developed a nationalistic policy of Arabianism dictated more by hunger and avarice than by religion. When the Mohammedans pushed outside of Arabia they found their Christian fellow Semites of the Byzantine Empire persecuted as

---

* NOTE: Saracens were the indigenous people of the Syro-Arabian desert. Later than the period now discussed the name was applied to the Mohammedan enemies of Europe.

TO ILLUSTRATE BYZANTINE AND SARACEN NAVAL CAMAPAIGNS

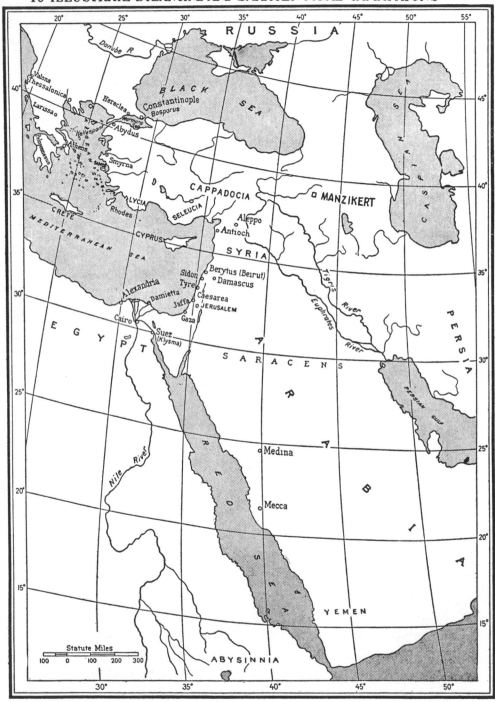

MAP II

heretics and oppressed by excessive taxes. Consequently, the invaders were welcomed by the inhabitants and opposed only by the Byzantine armies. Within two years after the death of Mahomet, the first Caliph had completed the unification of Arabia and entered on the conquest of Syria. In three great battles the armies of the Empire were defeated and Syria was occupied after five vigorous campaigns. The cities of Jerusalem and Cæsarea, which were Greek in culture, held out until 638 and 640, respectively, and the long resistance of the latter sea-coast city doubtless showed the Arab leaders that a navy was indispensable for further advance. In 637 the Arabs attacked the Kingdom of Persia with 5,000 to 6,000 men and were welcomed by the Aramaic part of the population. They routed the Persian army (Aryans) and rapidly advanced to the ethnic boundary at the mountains beyond the Tigris. An extensive tribal migration of Arabs now began into the new-won lands whereby they were garrisoned and made to pay tribute to the conquerors.

The rich province of Egypt furnished a potential base to the Emperor from which he might attempt to recover Syria; so the Arabs now turned their attention in that direction. Amru entered Egypt in January, 640, and advanced with an army of 8,000 to 9,000 men. The governor had been persecuting the heretics and grinding all with taxes, so that here, as in Syria and Persia, the Arabs found little opposition, owing to local dissensions. By 643 Amru was master of all Egypt. The illness of the reigning Emperor at the time of the Arab invasion of Egypt and his death in 641, followed by some years of disorder at Constantinople, prevented the central government from sending timely aid to the patriarch of Egypt in his resistance to the Arabs. But in 645 a naval expedition was sent from Constantinople and the city of Alexandria rose in revolt at its appearance. It was too late and Amru soon had the upper hand again.

The Saracens Start a Navy

The Empire had maintained dock yards at Alexandria and at Klysma (now Suez). They were in communication by a canal from the Nile to the Red Sea and, although the Empire was supreme in the eastern Mediterranean, a local squadron had been needed to maintain maritime good order. Now the situation was altered. The Arab seizure of Alexandria prevented any Byzantine flank attack on Syria, and the possession of the rich Nile

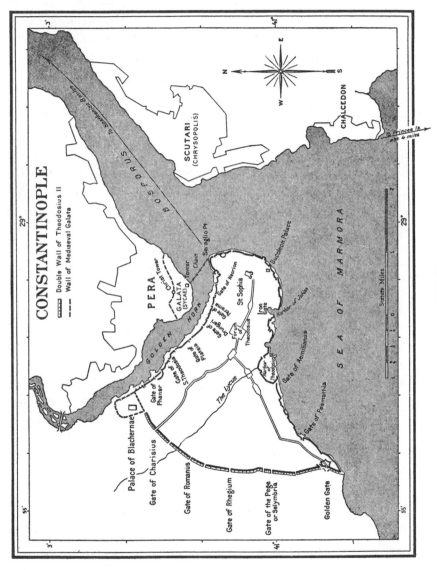

MAP III

This map shows the city at the time of the Fourth Crusade (1205 A.D.)
The wall around Blachernae did not exist in 700 A.D.

valley enabled the exportable surplus of grain to be readily diverted by the canal to the needs of Arabia. Further, the Arabs perceived that maritime strength was essential to hold and pursue their conquests. As long as Constantinople had a navy, Syria could readily be attacked. In consequence, the Arabs utilized the Alexandrian dock yard and began to build their own fleet which they maintained with the maritime population of Egypt. Moaviah, governor of Syria, also built a navy in his Phœnician ports, and the Syrian and Egyptian squadrons worked in tht greatest harmony. The central Arab administration soon began to regard its navy as one of its chief preoccupations. Tribute and the control of maritime trade would be the prize of successful war.

As ruler of the province immediately in contact with the Empire, Moaviah wanted to attack its heart at Constantinople. In 649 Moaviah temporarily seized Cyprus where there had always been a sea-faring population, and also took Rhodes.

The Empire now perceived the necessity of greatly developing its own navy to oppose the growing maritime strength of the Caliphate. In 655 Moaviah contemplated an attack by sea on Constantinople in which the Egyptian squadron was to take part with his own; but the Byzantine fleet, alleged to be 500 strong and led by Emperor Constans II in person, anchored off the coast of Lycia. Here the Saracen fleet encountered him and inflicted a severe defeat. The Emperor himself assumed a disguise and left his flagship to escape on another vessel. Before Moaviah could utilize his victory, the death of the Caliph Othman diverted his attention to the securement of his own succession to the Caliphate. He made an ignominious peace with the Empire and for several years he had many things to do. The Empire thus had time to recover and prepare to repel a great maritime attack which, if it had succeeded, might have overthrown even western Europe.

In spite of his defeat on the Lycian coast, Constans II improved his military forces and did much to re-establish the Roman fleet, but died in 668 before the Arab attack came. In spite of the delay in their great advance, owing to the civil war among the Arabs, raids into Asia Minor occurred every year and in 668 and 669 great overland expeditions against Constantinople reached the Bosphorus, but failed in their purpose, as they could not cross the water owing to the city's maritime defense.

First Great Siege of Constantinople

In 672 Moaviah, who was now Caliph, conceived the plan of attacking Constantinople by water, thinking perhaps that the new Emperor Constantine would be a weaker prince than his father. The fleet intended for the expedition mobilized and spent the winter at Smyrna and in the Cilician ports, and in the spring of 673 it went forward in great strength intending to blockade the city by sea and land. The Emperor had made every preparation to oppose the Arabs and among other arrangements he had adopted the recent invention of Callinicus, a Syrian architect, the celebrated "Greek fire," the forerunner of gunpowder. He had a large number of fire ships and of fast sailing boats equipped with tubes for casting the "fire."

The hostile fleet occupied a base on the shore a little west of the city where it controlled the sea route from Syria, by which it drew supplies. Behind the city, the army extended across the peninsula to the Black Sea and blockaded it, but the Saracens were not an engineering people and no siege attack was made upon the great walls. The hostile ships engaged each other every day, but the blockaders accomplished nothing, for they did not venture to push beyond the city into the Bosphorus, and so the Black Sea protected by the Imperial fleet remained open to supply the city. The blockade lasted from April to September and then the Arabs withdrew to Cyzicus on the Asiatic side of the Sea of Marmora where they had collected supplies and there they passed the winter and in the spring renewed the blockade of Constantinople. So it happened each year till 677 when the invaders "were put to great shame by the help of God and the Mother of God * * * and returned in great shame" to Syria, as the old record puts it. The retiring fleet suffered much from a heavy gale on leaving the Hellespont and a pursuing Byzantine squadron destroyed the ships that escaped the gale. At the same time the army had its own disaster in retiring across Asia Minor. The Caliph was now embarrassed by internal difficulties and he was glad to make peace for a period of 30 years and pay the Emperor a heavy annual tribute for its continuance.

A time of anarchy and bad government of the Empire followed soon after the death of Constantine and the peace of 677 was negligently observed. Nevertheless, the navy was so regenerated that in 697 the Empire sent a fleet to retake Africa from the Arabs. It was able to seize

Carthage, but held it only for the following winter, when the Arabs drove out the Romans and destroyed the city walls as they had done at Alexandria, for their engineering skill was unequal to that of the Romans in the attack or defense of fortifications.

SECOND SIEGE OF CONSTANTINOPLE

Early in the eighth century the Caliph Suleiman had restored strength to the Arab state and prepared another attack on Constantinople for the overthrow of the Roman Empire. As was said a few pages previously, the objective of the Saracen was not so much religious proselytism as the control of trade and the imposition of tribute. In spite of the loss of Syria, Constantinople was still a great manufacturing point and the distributor of an important maritime trade. Suleiman sent two armies into Asia Minor, one under his brother Moslemah and another under a general named Suleiman.

The latter advanced into the province of Leo the Isaurian, one of the most prominent men of the Empire, and, after Leo had some successes against the Moslems, his soldiers proclaimed him Emperor, and he marched on Constantinople, which he entered in March, 717, and was crowned. Moslemah's slow march across Asia Minor gave Leo five months' respite during which he organized the defense of the city and the walls were fully equipped with siege engines, so that the Saracens would have to depend wholly on blockade as they were inexpert in siege work. All inhabitants who could not provide supplies for themselves were warned to leave the city.

Moslemah crossed the Hellespont at Abydos and arrived before Constantinople on August 15, 717, with an army said to be 80,000 strong.* So much had the Saracen power increased since its first eruption from Arabia. He threw a ditch and wall of stones around the city and sent out foragers to collect supplies and destroy what could not be used. Two weeks later Suleiman arrived with the fleet of 1,800 warships and fast sailers (evidently small ships) to complete the blockade and attend to the supply of the army by sea, for without a naval force the wealth of the Caliphate would scarcely avail the army at Constantinople.

Having remained quiet for two days after arrival while he learned of

---

* The army and fleet were probably much exaggerated in strength.

the situation, Suleiman's first effort was to cut off the city both from the Euxine and the Propontis. He took advantage of a south wind to stem the current of the Bosphorus and with a part of the fleet he sailed to the Asiatic shore of the exit of the stream. With another detachment he sailed past the city to secure the channel entrance and cut off the city's communications with the Euxine. Heavy merchantmen, each with 100 soldiers on board, followed the fighting ships. The Emperor led out a squadron from the Golden Horn which attacked the transports and burned 20 of them with "Roman fire," and filled the enemy with terror of the "moist fire." That night, with pretended secrecy, the Emperor removed the chain closing the Golden Horn, hoping the enemy would attempt to enter, but the Arabs feared a snare and moored in the good haven of "Sosthenion," (now Stenia) 8 miles north of the city.

The Saracens had little advantage by their position. Inactivity followed through a long and unusually severe winter. The blockaders, natives of the south, suffered more than the citizens and their losses in horses and camels were disastrous. The Saracen Admiral Suleiman died and the Caliph also. In the spring, two great re-enforcing squadrons with troops and supplies came from Egypt and Syria, respectively, and entering the Bosphorus they also were able to pass above the city and took positions along the Asiatic shore where the current gave them some protection from the Roman fire ships moving up stream. Both these squadrons had many Egyptian Christians among their crews and, by a preconcerted agreement, many of these men deserted one night in their ships' small boats, shouting "long live the Emperor." They gave good information to the Emperor who sent out a squadron with the fire-squirting siphons to consume the hostile shipping. The expedition came back "with much booty"; from which we must conclude that before the fire ships did much damage, the enemy was panic-stricken and deserted their vessels which were then made prize. After this engagement, the Arab fleet did not venture to pass above the Roman naval station in the Bosphorus to complete the blockade by sea. The siege now promised to be a failure. But soon the besiegers were joined by a new army which came up from Syria and occupied the Asiatic shore of the Bosphorus and Propontis.

It is apparent that the Arab fleet was able to cover only the expedition's communications with the Mediterranean, but could not entirely cut off the city's communications with the Black Sea. The new army south of the Bosphorus played a useful part on the Asiatic side by preventing the city from sending there for provisions.

But the Emperor sent a detachment of troops to the Asiatic shore which surprised the enemy, killing many and routing the rest, so that the coast was free for the Roman ferry boats with supplies and for fishing, and the city was once more sufficiently supplied. Famine and plague broke out among the Arabs and in the summer a Bulgar army summoned by the Emperor came down and killed many of the Saracens. The new Caliph was not friendly to the Commander in Chief, his cousin Moslemah, and did not support him cordially.

So in the summer of 718 the siege became untenable and on August 15 Moslemah retired. The army got back with little difficulty to Syria across Asia Minor, but the fleet was less fortunate. It met two tempests, one in the Hellespont and the other after issuing into the Ægean, which left only 10 survivors, and of these, 5 ships were captured by the Romans, so that only 5 got back to tell their tale.

The failure of the Moslem attack was due to the combined defense offered by the great wall on the land side and the strong, although not superior, Greek fleet. The land wall, erected in the fifth century, was a double one, and perhaps the strongest known to antiquity. Each wall had a system of towers about 60 yards apart, reaching above the general line. The inner wall was only a few yards in the rear of the outer one and was higher, so that there was missile fire from mechanical artillery on four different levels against the attacking force. As the Saracens were not good at siege work, assault was impracticable. The sea walls were less formidable, for they were single only, but they were covered by the imperial fleet which lay securely in the Golden Horn, protected by the great chain across the entrance. In consequence, the Saracens could not think of attacking the sea face of the city while subject to a counter-attack from the fleet issuing from the Golden Horn. Thus the outcome turned on sea power and the Saracens did not have sufficient naval superiority to close the Black Sea communications of the city and subdue it by starvation.

THE EMPIRE AFTER SARACENS' DEFEAT

The reaction of this great victory was such that only a few years after-

ward the Roman frontier once more reached the Euphrates. It seems to
be the opinion of modern historians that the failure of these two great
sieges of Constantinople in the height of the Moslem expansion was a
victory for the European type of civilization no less important than that
of Alexander a thousand years before, and far greater than the defeat of
the Saracens before Tours only 14 years after the success of Leo III.
Owing to the great check received by the Moslems before Constantinople
the Empire of New Rome was able to act as Europe's bulwark against the
Moslems for over seven centuries, thus giving time for the Greco-Roman
civilization to impress itself on the invading Teutonic tribes from the
regions of the Baltic and so lay securely the foundations of present life in
Europe and America. Although the naval records of the early Empire are
very brief, except in the history of Procopius, it is worth while to follow
the naval actions of Constantine, Belisarius, and Moslemah, because navies
were needed then for the same reasons that they now are; namely, to carry
on military operations across the water. In the two great attacks on Constantinople the Saracen navy was a necessity not only to complete the
blockade, but also to cover the transport of supplies from the center of the
wealth of the Caliphate in Egypt and Syria. The movement of large
armies and the simultaneous passage of their munitions across the thinly
populated interior of Syria would have been far more difficult than by sea.

Although the Empire lost Syria and Egypt in the first outbreak from
Arabia, and with these provinces the mastery of the southern routes to the
Far East, yet the Empire still governed the Eastern trade by its hold on
the northern route. The commerce of the East with western Europe, both
by the Red Sea and by northern caravans and the Black Sea, still was
directed through Constantinople where it was redistributed and reshipped
in mixed cargoes, to which were added the products and manufactures of
the Imperial City. The importance of this trade to the West enabled the
Byzantine Empire to retain its hold on Italy longer than it otherwise
could have done and it lasted until the great cities of Venice, Genoa, and
Pisa began to develop their own maritime strength and substitute their own
shipping for that of Constantinople.

APPENDIX TO CHAPTER II

GREEK FIRE

In its long contest with the Arabic power the Empire was greatly aided by its superior military organization. In succeeding to Rome as the capital of the Roman Empire, Constantinople had inherited all the former's learning and all its military traditions. Although the practice of the art of war had changed in the course of centuries, yet the army of New Rome was unequaled both in organization and administration and, particularly, it was strong in its array of military engines of every description for use ashore and afloat.

What seems to have turned the scale against the superior forces of the Caliphs in 677 and 718 was the superior equipment of the Romans and the invention at a most opportune time of "Greek fire."

It is not easy to say precisely what it was at any particular time for, like other basic inventions, it grew and changed with time. What we know of its nature is derived from the work of Marcus Græcus, entitled *Liber Ignium*. This book written about the twelfth or thirteenth century, was apparently compiled from earlier sources and reworked. A number of recipes for incendiary compositions which it names are doubtless due to different periods. Before discussing what it was, we should see how it acted and what it did.

As for the method of use, the incendiary material was either thrown in earthen closed pots from ballistæ, or else hurled by hand. In both cases a wick or slow match was attached as igniter to the main incendiary charge. (The match was lighted before discharge without danger to the soldier or the ship.) About 900 A.D. the Emperor Leo VI, the Wise, wrote in his *Military Institutions* of the "fire prepared in tubes whence it issues with a noise of thunder and a fiery smoke which burns the ship at which it is directed." The tubes for discharging the fire were used from the time of its invention two centuries earlier. Although the Empire made great efforts to keep its composition secret, 26 tubes with the material to serve them were captured by the Bulgarians in 812, and in 904 the Saracens used Greek fire at the siege of Thessalonica.

Two hundred years after Leo VI, Anna Comnena, when writing in the *Alexiad* of her father, the Emperor Alexius Comnenus, says,

> On the prow of each ship he had fixed a head of a lion or other land animal made of brass or iron with the mouth open and then gilded over, so that their mere aspect was terrifying. And the fire which was to be directed against the enemy he made to pass through the mouths of the beasts so that it seemed as if the lions * * * were vomiting the fire.

Anna also describes a blow gun for the use of Greek fire as follows:

> Readily combustible rosin is collected from the pine and other evergreen trees and mixed with sulphur. Then it is introduced into reed pipes and blown with a strong continuous breath and at the other end fire is applied to it and it bursts into flame and falls like a streak of lightning on the faces of the men opposite.

Possibly the large ship siphon may have been used with some sort of pneumatic impulse from an air pump such as Anna describes for the mouth blow gun.

Still later, in the thirteenth century, John of Joinville describes the tactical use of Greek fire at the siege of Damietta during Louis IX's crusade in Egypt.

> The Saracens brought an engine called a petrary (stone thrower), which they had not hitherto done and put Greek fire into the sling of the engine. * * * So soon as they hurled the first cast we threw ourselves on our hands and knees. * * * It fell on the place in front of us where the host had been working [*on the defenses*]. * * * Our firemen were ready to put out the fire, and because the Saracens could not shoot directly at them [on account of certain defenses] they shot up into the clouds so that the darts fell on the firemen's heads. The fashion of the Greek fire was that it came frontwise as large as a barrel and the tail of fire that issued from it was as large as a large lance. The noise it made in coming was like heaven's thunder. It had the seeming of a dragon flying through the air. It made so great a light because of the abundance of the fire that one saw clearly throughout the camp as if it had been day. Three times did they hurl Greek fire at us that night with the petraries and four times with the swivel cross bow.

Evidently it was a long task to prepare to discharge the Greek fire.

As an example of the tactical combination of mechanical artillery with Greek fire, Joinville says,

> When the tower was made, the wood of it was valued at 10,000 livres

($30,000) and more. * * * As soon as the King of Sicily came on guard he caused the tower to be pushed forward along the causeway. * * * When the Saracens saw this they so arranged that all their sixteen engines should cast their shot upon the causeway to the place where the tower had been brought and when they saw that our people feared to go to the tower, they cast Greek fire at the tower and burned it utterly.

The same tactics were practicable in ship fighting; that is, the fire could be thrown on the ship and a rain of missiles kept upon the fire fighters. As for throwing Greek fire by hand, Joinville says of two men in front of him,

At last they [the Saracens] brought a churl on foot who thrice threw Greek fire at them. Once William of Boon received the pot of Greek fire on his barge, for if the fire had caught any of his garments he must have been burnt alive. [And again] We who were going by water [on the Nile] came a little before dawn to the passage where were the Soldan's galleys. * * * Here there was great confusion and tumult, for they shot at us and at our mounted folk on the bank so great a quantity of darts with Greek fire that it seemed as if the stars of heaven were falling. [Once more I quote], The Solden fled into the tower. * * * Then they threw at him Greek fire and it caught the tower which was made of pine planks and cotton cloth. The tower flared up quickly nor have I ever seen finer or straighter flame.

Returning now to what Greek fire was, the various compositions named in the *Liber Ignium* fall into two classes, incendiary and explosive. The latter recipes include the ingredients of gunpowder—sulphur, charcoal, and saltpeter. The *Liber Ignium* was fully commentated by the celebrated French chemist, M. Berthelot, in *La Chemie au Moyen Age*. Data may also be found in Gfrörer's *Byzantinische Geschichte*, in H. W. L. Hime's *Gunpowder and Ammunition*, and in T. B. Bury's *Later Roman Empire* and his notes to Gibbon.

Among the ingredients of various compounds we find naphtha, bitumen, and pitch from the oil fields of Asia, sulphur from Sicily, and various vegetable gums and resins, turpentine, and oil. Besides these quick lime was sometimes employed to make the "moist fire." While all burned readily, sulphur made poison gas and quick lime heated on the application of water so it could be extinguished only by sand or, as was then alleged, by vinegar or urine.

As it is doubtful whether saltpeter was known in the seventh century when Greek fire is first mentioned, it is possible to believe that the fire was at first only a specially effective incendiary composition which had been developed through the long experience of the Roman armies, and of which the generals of the day began to make more extensive use; and that the invention of Callinicus was the "moist fire" containing quick lime.

The important doubtful point in the history of Greek fire is when saltpeter was first discovered and utilized as an explosive. Hime supposes that the discovery of saltpeter was late, about 1300 A.D., and that a principal ingredient in Greek fire was quick lime, which heats when wet and that the combustible material, including oils firing at low temperature, was placed in the tube and discharged and ignited by applying the hose of a water engine to the breech of the tube.

On the other hand, Berthelot, who gave great attention to the history of chemistry, believed that Callinicus used saltpeter in the seventh century and that he had real gunpowder, that is, a mixture of salt peter, charcoal and sulphur, which we all know is highly explosive.

The distinction between incendiary mixtures which the early Greeks had and explosive gunpowder is that the former drew the oxygen of combustion from the air and burned from the surface only, and therefore slowly, whereas through the saltpeter, gunpowder in its own substance combined combustibles with oxygen so that the burning took place nearly simultaneously in all parts of the mixture and consequently the pressure of the gases of combustion was high before they could dissipate. The proportions of the three ingredients may be considerably varied and still make an explosive mixture. Saltpeter is always the largest component running from 50 per cent to 75 per cent and charcoal varies from half to two-thirds the remainder. The power also largely depends on the nature of the wood from which the charcoal is made and the method of roasting it, and further on the thoroughness with which the ingredients are ground and incorporated. It is natural to suppose that whenever gunpowder was first made it was of little strength and that a long time must have passed before even what we should call a moderate efficiency was developed.

If we believe that the earliest form of Greek fire was merely a projectile of incendiary material, we know that it could be thrown by mechanical artillery. But we are told it was also thrown from a tube. We may therefore conjecture that either it was blown out by a hydraulic pump as Hime suggests, in which case it would have small velocity and range;

or it may have been thrown by some sort of pneumatic device to serve as the mouth blow gun did for small flaming projectiles.

A small pneumatic tank of 2 cubic feet capacity and 3 atmospheres would throw a 4-pound inflammable projectile a range approaching 200 yards, allowing for air resistance. The ancients could make tight-fitting valves and such a device is quite possible, but mechanical artillery could do as well or better. Berthelot alludes to the explosive tendency of finely divided combustibles floating in the air, but the pressure developed by firing such a mixture would be no more than could be easily developed in a hand pump.

If we accept Berthelot's view that the distinguishing feature of Greek fire in the seventh century was already saltpeter, the explanation of the siphon is simple. The siphon was loaded with a combustible projectile which was both ignited and expelled by the explosive effect of an ounce or two of very imperfect gunpowder. Or the fire ball itself may have had some saltpeter in its composition so that it generated its own driving force of a few atmospheres, as does the Roman candle of our own day.

As the manufacture of explosives improved and saltpeter became more common, after some centuries the light combustible projectiles began to be replaced by stone projectiles and, as the strength of gunpowder increased, iron was substituted for stone. It was found that the mechanical impact of a heavy shot was more effective than a flaming projectile. Thus it is probable that modern artillery developed out of the East Roman siphons for projecting Greek fire.

AUTHORITIES CHIEFLY CONSULTED IN THIS CHAPTER

BERTHELOT, M., *Chemie du Moyen Age.*
COMNENA, Anna, *Alexiad.*
Cambridge Medieval History, vols. II and IV.
FINLAY, G., *History of Greece.*
GIBBON, E., *History of the Decline and Fall of the Roman Empire.*
HIME, H. W. L., *Gunpowder and Ammunition.*
JOINVILLE, Jean, *Chronicle of the Crusade of St. Louis.*

CHAPTER III

THE NAVY OF THE LATER ROMAN EMPIRE

THE WARS OF ALEXIUS COMNENUS

AFTER the defeat of the Saracens before Constantinople in 718, the contemporary historians do not give any clear account of naval tactics for over three centuries. The possession of the maritime cities of Syria and Egypt made the Saracens a naval power. As they extended their conquests along the northern shores of Africa, they found there convenient bases from which to overpower Sicily and raid the coasts of Italy, and even make lodgments in the southern parts of that peninsula. Of course, they needed shipping to cross the water, but their expeditions were predatory and the ships served more as transports than as men-of-war. We can get little distinct view of the methods of naval fighting until the end of the eleventh century when Anna Comnena gives us some account of her father's naval campaigns against the Norman rulers of South Italy and against the Pisans.

Constantinople's hold on Italy, which Justinian had established in the sixth century, was a precarious one which varied from century to century. By the beginning of the eleventh century the Saracens had complete possession of Sicily and held many strong points along the coasts of Italy, but the Empire held the south of the Italian peninsula.

Norman adventurers began to be prominent in South Italy early in the eleventh century. Of the twelve sons of Tancred of Hauteville in Normandy ten went out to Italy. The oldest ones arrived in 1030 and serving first as soldiers of fortune they gradually built up their power. Among Tancred's younger sons, Roger conquered Sicily from the Saracens and Robert Guiscard became master of South Italy and drove the Byzantine governors from Apulia. As the Norman adventurers gained territory, including the maritime cities, they began to pay attention to their shipping, of which they had none at first.

46

VENETIAN SEA POWER

While the Empire was struggling with the Saracens in Asia Minor and Sicily during the ninth and tenth centuries, Venice took advantage of her favorable position on the group of islands at the head of the Adriatic to resist the pretensions to sovereignty of the Successors to Charlemagne in the western Empire, and undertook in great measure the distribution of the markets of Constantinople with the west of Europe.

In 992 a treaty with Constantinople, which took the form of declaring ancient rights, gave Venice commercial privileges beyond those of other Italian maritime cities such as Amalfi. In particular the port tax at Constantinople was made the same for all ships and cargoes regardless of size and thus led to larger ships than had theretofore been customary. While Venice was thus increasing her riches through her commercial and military fleet, the Empire was losing her own sea power to her ally. After the middle of the eleventh century the Seljuk Turks conquered the provinces of Asia Minor on which the Empire's naval strength had depended, and the navy dwindled. Thereafter the industries of the Empire needed the shipping of Venice. In 1075 the Normans of Italy under Robert Guiscard raided the Dalmatian commerce of Venice.

The cause of Robert's displeasure with Venice was probably that the city had taken some advantage of the Amalfi colonists at Constantinople in matters of trade. In the tenth and eleventh centuries Amalfi was a rich commercial city, but she did not insure her maritime position by a navy. The Norman raid on Dalmatia accomplished little and the raiders got away before the Doge of Venice could reach them. Thus began hostilities between Venice and South Italy which were often renewed, even after the Spaniards had replaced the Hauteville dynasty in South Italy.

As long as the Empire was established in Apulia the Venetians had found no difficulties there, but the rule of the Normans and the prospect of having Robert control the egress of their ships from the Adriatic was unendurable. The Doge took means to secure his authority in Dalmatia after the Norman attack, and Robert turned against the Empire as a supporter of Venice on the pretense of restoring an exile to its throne. The Emperor, Alexius Comnenus, noting the preparations of Robert for invading his Empire and knowing his own weakness on the sea, sent to Venice for aid shortly before Robert was ready, and tried unsuccessfully to get help from Pope Gregory VII and from the Emperor Henry IV of Germany. Although the Venetians had at least as much interest as the Empire in restricting the Norman power, yet they drove a hard bargain, by which they agreed to turn out their whole fleet to defend the Byzantine territory, while on his part, Alexius promised that, win or lose, he would pay a large annual sum to Venice, and oblige the Amalfitans at Constantinople to pay a large tax to the church of St. Mark at Venice for the use of warehouses at Constantinople. Thus the Venetians had extended their privileges for trade in the Empire, and above all had no taxes of any kind. This most important treaty, whereby far-reaching commercial advantages were granted as rewards for naval services, was a mile stone in the growth of Venice and marks the extension of her sea power beyond the Adriatic.

In the spring of 1081 Robert Guiscard assembled a force at Brindisi which Anna Comnena says was 30,000 strong, with 150 ships, but Delbrueck says was no more than 1,300 Norman riders and 15,000 others. On the larger ships he built wooden turrets and covered them with hides. The expedition sailed in June, 1081, and the advance guard, with 15 galleys under Bohemund, son of Robert, attacked Corfu (Corcyra) unsuccessfully, whereupon it waited for the rest of the fleet and then took the island. The fleet then moved north to Durazzo (Dyrrachium) where it anchored after receiving much damage on the way from a violent gale, in which the turrets collapsed, although the season of the year was the best. Nevertheless, the Normans landed on June 17 and, occupying the neighboring country, they besieged the city which had a garrison under George Palæologus. In accordance with their treaty, the Venetians came with their entire fleet under command of Doge Silvio himself to the number of 14 galleys, 9 uscieri (huissiers or great ships), and 36 other ships and anchored about 2 miles north of Durazzo, where the shore was bold and steep. Robert immediately sent his son Bohemund to induce the Venetians to renounce their support of the Emperor. But as Duke of Apulia and ruler of Amalfi, the trade rival of Venice, Robert could not make any promises which could persuade the Venetians to

MAP IV.
TO ILLUSTRATE ITALIAN AND SPANISH NAVAL WARS

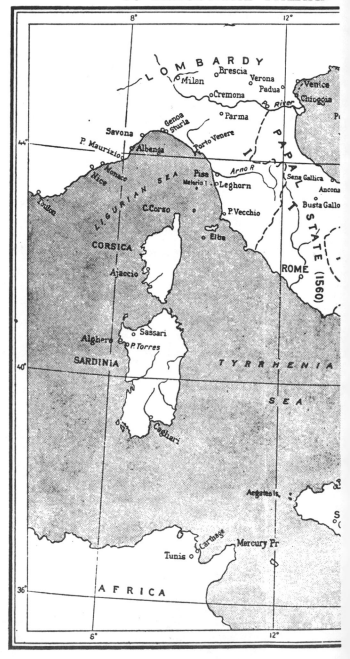

MAP IV.—This map also illustrates the war

of the Roman Empire against Robert Guiscard.

sacrifice their advantageous position which their new agreement with the Emperor gave them with regard to the Amalfitans in the commerce of Constantinople and the East.

The accounts of the early historians are somewhat conflicting, but Anna Comnena says that, when Bohemund came to the Doge to make arrangements, the latter put him off till the morning and during the night made preparations to meet the Norman attack. The shore was occupied by the Normans and therefore the Venetians could not approach it closely to protect their rear, but the sea was calm and might be expected to remain so. So the Venetians built a "sea harbor," of which we have heard in Scipio's time, but this seems to have been particularly elaborate. The larger ships anchored at suitable intervals and were then secured to each other by hawsers, so that the enemy could not pass, but had to fight hand-to-hand. Wooden towers were built at the mastheads and the small boats which usually towed astern were hoisted to the mastheads and filled with armed men. Besides their usual arms, the men aloft were provided with heavy timbers cut to lengths about 18 inches long and studded with iron spikes to be thrown on the enemy's ships. From this we may assume that many of the Norman ships were undecked; otherwise, the plunging timbers would scarcely have been heavy enough to pierce the deck and injure the bottom; and a hole in the deck only would not be serious. Behind the "sea harbor" lay the galleys, the men-of-war.

Anna does not tell us whether there was only one line of Venetian ships with the galleys behind them, or two lines with the galleys between them. In any case, in the morning Bohemund led his fleet in front of the Venetians and again demanded surrender. When this was refused, he charged the ships making the sea harbor and a desperate battle followed in which the greater height of the Venetian ships was advantageous, as always. Soon one of the wooden plungers knocked a hole in the bottom of Bohemund's vessel. While some of the crew continued fighting, others in their panic jumped overboard and were drowned. Bohemund himself escaped to another ship. When at last the attack on the sea harbor had failed and the Norman ships began to withdraw, the Venetian galleys, which had been lying quietly behind the sea harbor, issued out and pursued the enemy to the beach where they landed and continued the battle with the Norman crews and were aided by a sortie of the garrison of Dyrrachium under the command of Palæologus. The allies even entered the Norman camp and withdrew with much booty. However, in spite of the Venetian victory at sea, the siege of Dyrrachium continued. In October, 1081, the Emperor Alexius came with an army to raise the siege, but was defeated and the city surrendered.

Nevertheless, the victory at sea gave the allies control of the communications of the Norman army with Italy during the winter 1081-82, and all the coast towns which had at first paid tribute to the invaders now ceased to do so, and consequent disease and hardship cost the Normans many lives. Although defeated in the field, the Emperor's diplomacy raised enemies against Robert in Italy and he was obliged to return there, leaving his son Bohemund in command of the army in Illyria. The latter had some early success and pushed into the interior as far as Larissa, but there the Emperor's diplomacy again scored by inducing the principal Norman subordinates to insist on receiving their pay and thus Bohemund's position was much weakened. In 1082 the Venetian fleet seems not to have taken the sea, but in 1083 it came out in greater force than before and, after a victory off Durazzo, it was joined by some imperial ships (for Alexius was building a fleet of his own) and regained possession of Corfu for the Empire, with the exception of the citadel, which the Emperor besieged.

In 1084 Robert made every effort to aid Bohemund and assembled 120 vessels of war (galleys and smaller craft) besides cargo ships. Although the force as named appears large considering the unhappy situation at the time in Calabria and Sicily, Manfroni* believes the fleet was greater than that of 1081. Robert was in command himself and his four sons each had a squadron. Two squadrons went to Butrinto and the other two to Valona where they picked up the remains of the army. In November all went to raise the siege of the citadel of Corfu. When the Emperor heard that Robert was about to cross from Italy, he sent to Venice to urge that the city send a great fleet for which he offered to pay, and he himself, as his daughter says, equipped many biremes and triremes, besides piratical craft. (It may be, as Manfroni suggests, that these biremes and triremes were of the new type which replaced the dromons, having rowers sitting in groups of two or three on the same thwart, each with his own oar.) The

---

* *Storia della Marina Italiana.*

Venetians hastened to comply with the Emperor's request, for the Normans in possession of Corfu could put a most serious check on their commerce with the East.

The Venetians joined the Romans and occupied a camp on the mainland opposite the northern end of Corfu, and Robert left the city of Corfu and placed his fleet in the little harbor at the northern end of the island. The allies crossed to Corfu and a desperate but inconclusive sea battle at close quarters took place in which the Normans had rather the worse and the two fleets retired to their previous berths. On the third day after, Robert attempted to clear the enemy from the channel, but was again defeated. The winter season was now approaching (it was November) and the Venetians sent their lighter galleys and smaller ships to their own lagoons for the bad season, retaining only their larger vessels to maintain the blockade.

On learning of this step from a deserter, Robert at once decided to engage for a third time. He took 5 galleys under his own command and gave 5 others to each of his sons and put the rest in the reserve. The Venetians learned of the coming attack in time to prepare a "sea harbor" with their larger ships and placed the others behind it. Robert and his sons made a vigorous attack which caused the imperial ships to make an immediate escape. The Venetians met the onset, but their ships had either consumed or landed their stores and in consequence were so tender that the ships heeled and men lost their footing as they crowded to the engaged side and many fell overboard and were drowned. In the end, after losing 7 galleys and many ships, the others surrendered, for they could not get out of their own "sea harbor." The prisoners were treated with great cruelty by the Normans.

The result of the battle greatly disturbed the Venetians, for they feared to have the mouth of the Adriatic closed. They deposed their Doge, elected another, and in the next spring sent out another force of lighter and more numerous ships. What happened to this fleet is not clear. Anna says it conquered Robert's fleet, while others say it was beaten. At all events, Duke Robert Guiscard died in the summer of this year (1085) and the confusion at home as well as in his army abroad brought relief to the Empire and Venice entered on the enjoyment of her commercial treaties.

The campaigns of this war and the imperial treaties established Venice on firm foundations as a maritime and commercial state, and began the substitution of her own sea power for that of the Empire, which was completed a century later.

It is noteworthy that Anna makes no mention of Greek fire in this war and we may surmise that the Empire did not care to trust its allies with the secret.

AUTHORITIES CHIEFLY CONSULTED IN THIS CHAPTER

Cambridge Medieval History, vol. IV.

COMNENA, Anna, *Alexiad.*

DELBRUECK, H., *Geschichte der Kriegskunst.*

FINLAY, G., *Byzantine Empire.*

GIBBON, E., *Decline and Fall of the Roman Empire.*

MANFRONI, C., *Storia della Marina Italiana.*

CHAPTER IV

THE FIRST CRUSADE (SEE MAP II)

ALTHOUGH Alexius Comnenus did something to revive, or at least check the decline of, the sea power of the East Roman Empire, the crusades, which began in his reign, were a principal reason for the passage of maritime supremacy to the city-states of Italy. At the beginning of his reign Alexius was not only troubled by the rising Norman power in South Italy, as has been told, but he was hard pressed by the Seljuk Turks, who had secured almost the whole of Asia Minor at the battle of Manzikert in 1071, a few years before he came to the throne, and ever since the Emperors had been seeking for help to restrain their conquests. The Turks were less considerate of the pilgrims visiting the Holy Land than the Saracens whom they replaced, and Alexius' appeal for aid from western Europe took a form which he did not expect, for the great migrations of the First Crusade had the religious object of recovering Jerusalem from the infidels, instead of the political one of repelling the advance of the Turks. The greater part of the crusading armies came from Western Europe by land and passed through Constantinople in 1096-97 without serious hostilities or rioting and went on their way across Asia Minor* to the conquest of Palestine where various Christian principalities were established. The movements of these armies do not concern this naval study; but, in crossing the Empire, the leaders had to come to an agreement with the Emperor. Necessarily these vast military expeditions brought great changes in the maritime situation of the Eastern Mediterranean. The Crusaders swore allegiance to the Emperor and promised to deliver to him the cities which the Turks had

---

* *Cambridge Medieval History*, vol. VI, p. 298, puts the number of crusaders marching through Asia Minor to Antioch at 25,000 to 30,000 men. Although there were no open hostilities, yet these semi-disciplined troops did much pillaging and were a burden to the Empire. Alexius tried to make use of them to recover his territory. Besides, there were a large number of peasants, mostly unarmed, of both sexes, and even children, who were inspired to start for the Holy Land from many parts of Europe. Gibbon estimates them at nearly 300,000 souls. Most were lost marching across Europe to Constantinople and, of those who reached there, none got to Jerusalem, being destroyed in Asia Minor.

recently taken from the Empire, while he promised them some military aid and supplies for the armies. The interpretation of this agreement was the occasion for later hostilities.

As has been said, the Venetians had just secured great advantages over other Italian cities in the trade of the Empire, and the Turks, like their predecessors, the Saracens, were always ready to do business with the Christians in spite of warfare. The Italian princes and certain French contingents, who joined the crusade, embarked for the Holy Land in South Italy, and the Italians were anxious to promote the business end of this religious venture and favor the trade of their own Italian cities, Pisa, Genoa, and Amalfi, as against Venice, although Amalfi began to lose its prosperity after Robert Guiscard took it over in 1073. In particular, Bohemund of Taranto, who had been foiled by Alexius and the Venetian fleet in 1081-84, was ill-disposed to both, although he had taken the oath of allegiance to Alexius when he passed through Constantinople on the Crusade.

Thus the support of the crusaders' principalities was not left entirely to the Venetian shipping, but the advance of the armies was followed also by the ships of the western side of Italy, both to supply the Christians and to gather up the spoil. The fleets of four great merchant cities were competing for the new business opened up by the conquests of the crusading princes, although the Venetians were a little later in reaching Syria than the others. While the commercial cities all found profitable business, both with the Moslems and Christian principalities, the latter lacked military strength to occupy the country. They held isolated cities and fortresses, but did not well control communications and the Christian occupation of the Holy Land withered away within two centuries.

Besides attending to their own trade and supplying the Christian armies, the fleets of Italy assured military communications by sea between different parts of the crusaders' forces, supplied good mechanics for the management of siege engines at the besieged seaports, and with their training in piratical warfare in the waters of Spain and Africa they kept the seas clear of the Turkish cruisers. These Italian traders now had the opportunity to tap the commerce of Constantinople with Tyre and Sidon, and even with Egypt, and turn it directly to their home ports. In this great trade movement the Venetians were inclined to stand by the Empire, rather than to seek the favor of the crusaders. Previous to the crusade Genoa and Pisa had had little, if any, business with the East, but had confined themselves to the west and south of the Mediterranean, while Amalfi and Venice had held the eastern trade.

Now commercial greed backed religious enthusiasm to cause Genoa to send a squadron under private management to the East. It arrived at the port of Antioch in time for its crews to take an important part in the siege of that great city which was conquered in June, 1098. Instead of turning the city over to the Emperor, the machinations of Bohemund procured it for himself and most of the crusaders broke with the Emperor.

Bohemund of Taranto, now Prince of Antioch, gave the city of Genoa important trade privileges, as a reward for its aid in the siege. By this wise liberality Bohemund secured his communications by sea in his struggle to hold his own, both against the Empire and the Turks. The advantages of the eastern trade now began to be apparent to the governments in Italy, and in September or October, 1099, about three months after the capture of Jerusalem, a force of 120 Pisan ships under command of the Archbishop of Pisa arrived at Jaffa after aiding Bohemund in further conquests. In the autumn of 1099 the Venetians sent an expedition of 200 ships to Syria, which wintered on the way at Rhodes. Here the ambassadors of the Emperor sought it to urge that it should not help the crusaders, who had become politically minded and were looking for principalities for themselves. In particular, the Emperor was angry with Bohemund. A Pisan squadron of 50 galleys was also in the neighborhood of Rhodes about this time, and the ancient chroniclers disagree as to whether it was attacked by the Venetians or by the Byzantine fleet. Following the Venetian version as summarized by Manfroni,* the Archbishop had allowed the first Pisan squadron to commit many outrages on the imperial cities on the coast of Asia Minor. When the second came to Rhodes the Venetians there, being allies of the Empire and unwilling to see the Pisans replace them in the trade of the East, fell upon the smaller Pisan fleet and inflicted a severe defeat upon it. After the battle it appears that the victors restored ships and prisoners to the Pisans on the condition that they would swear that no Pisan thereafter would set foot in the eastern Empire for trading purposes. Thereupon the Venetian fleet went to Jaffa where Godfrey

* *Storia della Marina Italiana.*

of Bouillon, the new ruler of Jerusalem, asked it to aid in the conquest of the sea coast of Syria. By this time, the Venetian leader, Giovanni Michiel, son of the reigning Doge, saw that the crusaders had firmly established themselves in the Holy Land and was anxious to have a share in the profits of business there. He accordingly agreed to Godfrey's proposal, but in return he secured very advantageous terms for Venice and Venetian commerce. This he was able to do, for the situation of the crusaders was not strong in spite of the capture of Jerusalem, and no other European ships were then in those waters. The Genoese had gone home with great riches, and of the Pisans nothing is known; so they also had probably gone home after their defeat. So much for the economic side of the maritime conduct of the First Crusade; but Anna Comnena gives a different picture of the defeat of the Pisans, putting it at a later date and showing the tactical side of an East Roman naval battle.

According to her, the Pisans under command of their Archbishop pillaged the Ionian Islands, whereupon the Emperor ordered ships to be built in all his countries. As he knew the Pisans were skilled in sea warfare and he dreaded a battle with them, he fixed on the bows of the ships the brazen tubes previously mentioned (p. 42). The ships so armed composed a special squadron and the whole fleet, under the Grand Duke Landulph, left Constantinople in April and sailed to Samos where the ships were hauled ashore for cleaning and retarring the bottoms. The Pisan fleet passed them and the Romans weighed anchor in chase and pursued them from point to point until they overtook the Pisans near Rhodes.

When the Pisans caught sight of them, they speedily set their fleet in battle order and whetted their minds as well as their weapons for the fray. As the Roman fleet was drawing near, a certain Peloponnesian Count, Perichytes by name and a very expert seaman, had his monoreme rowed very quickly against the Pisans directly he saw them and he passed through the midst of them like fire and then returned to the Roman fleet. The Roman fleet, however, did not venture upon a regular sea battle with the Pisans, but made a series of swift irregular attacks upon them. Landulph himself first of all drew near to the Pisan ships and threw fire at them, but aimed badly and accomplished nothing, wasting his fire. Then the man called Count Eleemon very boldly attacked the largest vessel at the stern but got entangled in its rudder; and as he could not free himself readily, he would have been taken, had he not with great presence of mind had recourse to his machine and poured fire upon the enemy very successfully. Then he quickly turned his ship about and on the spot set fire to three more of the largest barbarian ships. At the same time a squall of wind suddenly struck the sea and churned it up and dashed the ships together and almost threatened to sink them, for the waves roared, the yards creaked, and the sails were split. The Barbarians now became thoroughly alarmed, first because of the fire directed upon them because they were not accustomed to that sort of machine nor to fire, which naturally flames upward but in this case was thrown in whatever direction the sender desired, often downwards or laterally, and secondly, they were much upset by the storm, so they fled. The Roman fleet for its part ran to a little island, locally called Seutlus, and when day dawned it sailed away and entered the harbor of Rhodes. There the Romans disembarked and led out all the prisoners they had taken.

In this account of the battle, we again see the surprise and dread of a new weapon bringing disaster. As the Pisans had nothing similar, it was most effective.

A few years later Bohemund of Antioch returned to Italy to lead an attack from thence upon the Empire. During a temporary withdrawal of the imperial fleet in 1107, he crossed the Adriatic to Avlona with an army of 34,000 men including 5,000 cavalry, and 200 transports, and 30 galleys,* but after landing he could do nothing, for the Emperor had profited by his previous campaigns against Bohemund and his father, Robert Guiscard. The superior Byzantine fleet cut off the supplies of the invading army which besieged Dyrrachium. But the place was well supplied and fortified. The Emperor used his army to prevent foraging, but refused to fight and Bohemund broke up his ships to use their material in his siege works. Nearly a year after landing he was compelled to seek terms from the Emperor and renew his oath of allegiance. In this last effort of the Byzantine fleet it brought victory to the imperial arms without a battle merely by ruling the sea in strength. In the course of the next century the Venetian fleet entirely replaced the imperial fleet in the service of the Empire, in return for which Venice enjoyed extensive trade privileges throughout the Empire.

---

* Two hundred transports of the size then usual would probably not carry over 10,000 infantry and 2,000 cavalry. In view of the habitual overstatements of medieval writers as to the size of armies, we might refer to Procopius' precise account of the wars in which he was concerned and believe that 15,000 men made a large army and 25,000 a very great one throughout all this period.

AUTHORITIES CHIEFLY CONSULTED IN THIS CHAPTER

Cambridge Medieval History, vol. IV.
COMNENA, Anna, *Alexiad.*
DELBRUECK, H., *Geschichte der Kriegskunst.*
FINLAY, E., *Byzantine Empire.*
GIBBON, E., *Decline and Fall of the Roman Empire.*
MANFRONI, C., *Storia della Marina Italiana.*

CHAPTER V

THE ORGANIZATION OF ANCIENT NAVIES

VERY little has yet been said as to the organization and administration of the ancient navies, either in my *Greek and Roman Naval Warfare* or in this, and it is summarized here, for the Byzantine navy was a development of the Roman navy.

ATHENIAN FLEET

The Athenian ships were built by the state and when not in use were kept in the vast arsenals built at the Piræus where every ship had her slip and her storeroom. The admiral was appointed by the state. The vice admiral seems to have had the title of fleet pilot. On service, each ship was commanded by a trierarch who was a rich man and required to provide many articles of equipment at his own expense. He drew the pay of the crew from the treasury and paid it over. The trierarch was in military command of the ship but not necessarily a seaman. The second in command, the "kubernetes," or pilot, was an accomplished seaman and responsible for the navigation and handling of the ship. The "Proreus," or boatswain, was stationed at the bow and in command forward, having the lookout and care of soundings and reporting to the kubernetes. He looked out for the sails and gear and also was a seaman by calling. The rowers were commanded by a "keleustes" who had two assistants to watch and control the rowing, one for each side. A flutist played a sharply accented air to mark the stroke for the rowers. There was also a paymaster in charge of the stores and money, who kept the accounts. The majority of the crew were rowers, a triere in the fifth century B.C. had about 170. They were frequently of the poorer class of citizens, but, when permanent rowers were necessary, slaves or hired men were often shipped. For seamen to handle the sails and anchors, steer the ship and keep the lookout, 8 or 10 men were needed. The soldiers on board varied at different periods. At the battle of Ladé in 494 B.C., the Chians had 40 heavy armed soldiers on each ship and 80 years later, at the great siege of Syracuse, the Syracusans had many heavy armed on board as well as slingers and archers.

But at Salamis in 480 B.C., the Athenians had only 14 heavy armed and 4 bowmen. The supplies on board were only enough for a few days, so large expeditions were accompanied by store ships.

ROMAN NAVY

In its early days the Roman navy was less permanent than the Athenian organization. The military command of the fleet, like that of the legions, fell to civil officers who exercised military functions in virtue of their civil office. The admiral might be the consul or a pro-consul or his legate acting as his deputy. Combatants for ships were supplied from the legions, but we have little information as to how the ships and crews were provided in early days. Apparently, the Greek cities in South Italy which were allied with Rome provided some ships in the First Punic War, and Rome built many others, as Polybius tells us. The seamen and rowers must have come from the maritime population and from freedmen and slaves, very much as was the case in Greece. The ship captains seem to have been subordinate to the centurions embarked on each. Apparently there was little attempt to maintain a state navy between wars, for it seems that ships were usually lacking when war was declared. In the early Empire the service took on a more permanent character but became of little importance, as it was only a coast guard. Josephus, writing in the first century, says the Pontic squadron had 40 ships and 3,000 men. Ten times as many ships and men for the whole Empire would be roughly proportional to the coast line.

In the late Empire the organization became very complete. This was brought about by the new sea power on the Mediterranean, the Saracens. By the ninth century there was an imperial squadron at Constantinople and a provincial squadron in each of five maritime provinces (or themes), the·Cibyrrhiot, Ægean, Helladic, Peloponnesian and Cephallenic squadrons.* The imperial squadron was maintained from the imperial treasury and was under the command of an admiral whose title was *drungarios*. At first the imperial squadron seems not to have been maintained in a mobile

---

* These five themes included the greater part of the maritime population of the later Roman Empire. The Cibyrrhiot theme extended along the coast of Asia Minor from and including Rhodes to abreast the eastern end of Cyprus. Ægean—the Ægean Islands, the Dardanelles, and Cyzicus. The Peloponnese—as its name indicates. The Helladic—Northern Greece and Thessaly. The Cephallenic—the Ionian Islands.

state, but to have been manned without much delay by an arrangement with the ship owners of the capital. Later, it was a standing force (Gibbon, *Decline and Fall*, Bury's edition (vol. 9, appendix 10). The navies of the maritime themes were always ready. Each was maintained from the treasury of its own theme and the local governor was admiral of his squadron. The forces which the Empire was able to fit out were very considerable. In 902 an unsuccessful naval expedition for the conquest of Crete included an imperial squadron of 60 dromons with 230 rowers and 70 soldiers each and 40 pamphylians* with crews of 160 men for some and 130 for others. The provincial squadrons added 77 ships and the whole force amounted to 47,127 men, whose pay came to 34 centenaries of gold (about $738,000), probably for the season. It may be mentioned here that the standing army seems to have been about 120,000 men. An allowance table for the imperial dromons, written by Emperor Constantine Porphyrogenitus, has come down to us for each ship. It includes 70 mail coats, 12 light cuirasses for the siphon men and others at the bow, 10 ordinary cuirasses, 10 helmets with visors, 8 pairs of metal brassards, 70 bucklers of sewn leather, 30 lydian bucklers, 80 boat hooks (or poles) with steel-shod ends, 20 scythe lances to cut rigging, 100 spears, 100 javelins, 20 cross bows with spare parts, 10,000 arrows, 200 little arrows called flies to sting horses, 10,000 caltrops, 4 grapnels with chains, 50 surcoats of heavy textiles to wear over armor.

The *Institutions* of Leo included what may be regarded as naval regulations and tactical instructions. Among other directions he tells his commanders in chief to divide their commands into groups of three or five ships and place each under a

> Count, who will take your orders. You will train each soldier individually and also each ship to attack the others. Then you will form all the galleys into two squadrons, which will execute all the battle maneuvers, sometimes in one formation, sometimes in opposition to each other. Long iron-tipped boat hooks will be used to keep the ships from colliding and injuring each other. If you camp on a shore in our own country or where no enemy is to be feared, you will see that the soldiers do no harm to the inhabitants, but when you are on a hostile shore you will have lookouts both at sea and shore and be always ready for battle. Vigilance must be redoubled as dangers increase for if the enemy knows you have landed your crews he will try to burn your ships.

---

* Pamphylian dromons were small ones.

* * * As fortune has her occasions and the events of war are uncertain one should try to win by some stratagem or by surprise and you should not engage in decisive battle without extreme necessity. Therefore you must not go so near the enemy that you can no longer avoid battle unless you have much confidence in the number and strength of your ships and the courage of your soldiers. But above all you must deserve divine protection by an exemplary life, by your integrity, your temperance, your humanity to prisoners, and your care to avoid all disorder.

Your galley being as a head to the rest of the fleet must be distinguished from the others by her size, strength, and soldiers of choice. Similarly, squadron commanders will take the best men in their squadrons for their own flagships. All will watch the flagship and guide themselves by her and look for new orders. Each order must be issued by some particular signal previously agreed upon. Either the flag is held upright or leaning to the right or left or waved or held high or low or made to disappear. The shape of the signal may be altered or only the color, as was formerly the case. The battle signal should be red, raised on a long staff. You should practice the different signals as well as the counts and prefects [captains] so that mistakes will not be made.

* * * You may form your fleet in crescent with the galleys on the one side and the other, like two horns or two hands. You will take care to put the best ships and the best armed at the ends of the line. Your flagship will be at the base of the curve where you will see everything best and give your orders. You can also form in a straight line. In this way you have the bows towards the enemy to burn his ships by the fire from the siphons. You may form into two or three lines according to the number of ships you have. When the first line has engaged the enemy, the other line files to right and left and throws itself on the flanks or rear of the enemy so that he cannot withstand this new attack.

Among the weapons that the Emperor names are the siphons for Greek fire, and pots full of unslaked lime to break on his deck and strangle the enemy.* Above all he prizes pots full of burning combustibles which break on striking. Large caltrops, or wooden balls stuck full of iron points and covered with pitch and sulphured cloth are set on fire and thrown on the enemy's deck where they cannot easily be put out and some will burn their hands and others their feet and the men thus engaged diminish the fighters.

---

* By their dust.

APPENDIX TO CHAPTER V

As time passed, the ships to which the term "dromon" applied became larger, than in the time of Procopius. The Emperor Leo VI, the Wise, who reigned and wrote about 900 A.D., says in his *Tactica*,

Your dromons should be well built and fit for battle. The bulwarks must not be too thick, for they would make the ship heavy; nor yet too thin, for they would be broken by collision with the enemy. All the tackle must be ready and everything necessary to the equipment of the dromons. Some things must have spares provided, such as anchors, oars, tholepins, sails and cordage. It will also be well to have on board some knees, joists, and other timber, and oakum, pitch, nails, and tools for necessary work and repairs.

You will put a tube covered with bronze at the bow to throw flame at the enemy. Above the tube there will be a wooden platform with a solid parapet and soldiers will go there to fight and shoot arrows. On large dromons there will also be a wooden castle amidships, and upon it the soldiers will be stationed to hurl heavy stones against the enemy, or heavy pointed pieces of iron to break or smash, or else [to throw] fire.

Every dromon should be long and of proportional breadth, with two ranks of oars, one above the other. Each rank should have 25 thwarts with two rowers on each, one to port and one to starboard—in all 100 men, rowers or soldiers. Dromons may be built larger with as many as 200 rowers or more with 50 at the lower oars and the rest above. Smaller ships with one rank of oars are called galleys and serve for patrol and reconnaissance and other duties needing speed.

Every dromon will have its captain, a lieutenant, two ensigns, and two pilots as its staff of officers. The two forward rowers will also tend, one the pump and the other the anchor. The pilot stationed forward will sit as high as possible and be well armored. The captain will be aft and in a position where he is alone and well covered from attack and where he can also see well and direct the maneuvers. The rowers of the upper rank and all on the upper deck will be fully armored with helmets, breast plates, and arm and thigh pieces. They will fight with pikes, javelins and swords. Those who have no metal armor will make something of plaited sinews over a double thickness of leather, and keeping behind the others, they will use their arrows and hurl stones, but they must not tire themselves too much with throwing for then the Barbarians, and specially the Saracens, will shelter themselves by locking shields and then will board and easily overcome exhausted men. You will choose the stoutest and bravest men to fight on deck.

63

IMPERIAL DROMON ABOUT 900, A.D.

PLAN VIEW   SCALE IN FEET

120   100   80   60   40   20   0

OUTBOARD PROFILE   SCALE IN FEET

120   100   80   60   40   20   0

MIDSHIP SECTION   SCALE IN FEET

50   40   30   20   10   0

FIG. 4.—RECONSTRUCTION OF BYZANTINE DROMON (PAMPHYLIAN TYPE)
(Explanation on opposite page)

About fifty years later, Leo's son and successor wrote of dromons with 230 rowers and 70 soldiers. Still later, Geoffrey de Vinsauf, who took part in the Third Crusade and wrote its history, mentioned a naval battle off Tyre in 1189 in which a Crusaders' galley (but by its description of the type of a Byzantine dromon) was boarded by the Turks who drove the rowers on the upper deck from their oars and took their places. But the Christians at the lower oars worked them against the efforts of the Turks above and the ship was driven first one way and then the other. At last the Christians rallied and resumed possession of the upper deck and the ship was safe. The account is here quoted merely because it gives an idea of the latest general arrangement of a dromon.

From the above descriptions we may make a series of sketches attempting a reconstruction of the dromon at different periods. First is the small one described by Procopius in the first half of the sixth century. It would be some 50 feet long, 11 feet wide, and 2 feet draft, and displace about 17 tons, a small type of Trajan's vessels shown in Fig. 1 but, instead of shields along the sides, the bulwarks were high. The hull would weigh 8 or 9 tons and the crew and equipment as much more.

The later and larger craft of the ninth century, with 100 rowers in two ranks on the deck and 130 men in all, has been considered by Admiral Serre on whose drawing Fig. 4 has been based. Serre assumes provisions and water for 20 days at 7½ kilograms per day. This seems to me a very high allowance. The Greeks thought 3 days' supply was enough to be remarked and Procopius thought 16 days' water was a great quantity. I believe, therefore, that the same type as Serre assumes, but with less allowance for rations (10 days and 15 pounds per day), could have been built shorter and lighter, say, 109 feet long, 14 feet wide, and 3¼ feet

---

FIG. 4.—PAMPHYLIAN DROMON

Characteristics: Length on L. W. L. ....109 ft.
Beam on L. W. L. ....14 ft.
Draft ....3.25 ft.
Displacement ....78 tons
Complement: Officers and seamen 25
Soldiers 35
Rowers 100

The Emperor's text says that the siphons were mounted under the forecastle instead of on it as here shown.

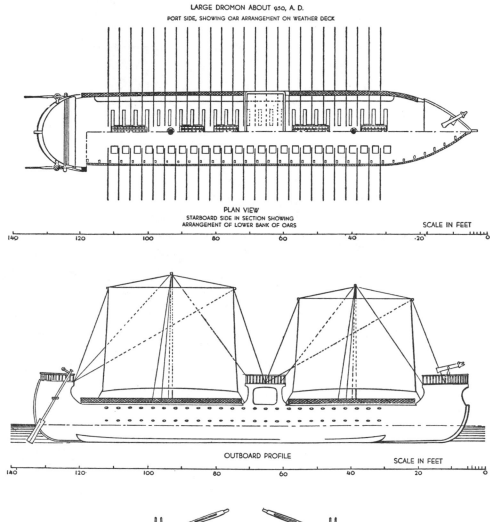

LARGE DROMON ABOUT 950, A. D.
PORT SIDE, SHOWING OAR ARRANGEMENT ON WEATHER DECK

PLAN VIEW
STARBOARD SIDE IN SECTION SHOWING
ARRANGEMENT OF LOWER BANK OF OARS

SCALE IN FEET

OUTBOARD PROFILE

SCALE IN FEET

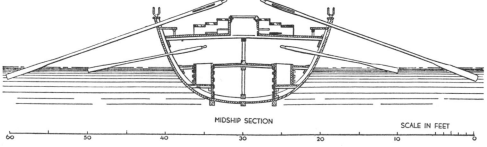

MIDSHIP SECTION

SCALE IN FEET

FIG. 5.—RECONSTRUCTION OF BYZANTINE DROMON (LARGE TYPE)
(*Explanation on opposite page*)

draft, giving a load displacement of 80 tons instead of 100 tons. Such a ship with 100 rowers might reach a speed of 7.3 knots. As for the large ships mentioned by Leo VI and the one of Tyre, where the upper rowers were on deck and the others below, with probably 200 rowers in all, we might assume a ship of 127 feet in length, 18 feet in width, with a draft of 4.7 feet, giving a displacement of 165 tons, and a speed of 7.5 knots for a spurt and 5.0 for a couple of hours. The deck would be 4 feet above the water, the upper tholepins 5¼ feet. The lower rank of rowers would be in the hold with the oar ports 1.5 feet above the water. The castle at the bow carrying the bronze tube and the one amidships are shown on the sheer plan (see Fig. 5). Leo mentions that the dromons with 160 and 130 men were called "pamphylians." There was a still smaller type of dromon called "galley" with a single bank of oars which were used for scouting.

We may therefore conclude that during the golden age of the Empire in the first and second centuries A.D., the traditional type of men-of-war went out of existence as small coast-guard ships were sufficient to keep piracy within limits. Constantine and Licinius probably used small coast-guard ships no larger than are shown on the column of Trajan in a conventionalized style (Fig. 3). During the fifth century the Empire submitted to the Barbarian piratical sea power in Africa, for whose needs small craft were sufficient, and when Belisarius reconquered Africa for Justinian, in the sixth century, his ships were also small. Thereafter the Mohammedans developed a hostile sea power to which the Empire refused to submit, and the combatant ships grew in size to embody greater fighting strength. As the ships grew in size they developed into two classes, the smaller

---

FIG. 5

Characteristics: Length on L. W. L. . . . . .127 ft.
Beam at L. W. L. . . . . .18 ft.
Draft . . . . .5 ft.
Displacement . . . . .175 tons
Complement: Officers and seamen 40
Soldiers 60
Rowers 200

Leo's successor records that in 950 A.D. the dromons had 230 rowers and 70 soldiers. This would make the vessels about 140 feet long with a displacement of about 190 tons.

"galleys" for scouting and reconnaissance, and the larger "dromons" for battle. Apparently, as time passed, the lighter scouts and heavier battle ships were both known as "dromons" which became a generic term serving to distinguish combatant rowing "long" ships from commercial sailing "round" ships. Still later, as the single row of oars in the galley type was found preferable, the double row of oars was disused and the word "dromon" disappeared from the seaman's vocabulary.

AUTHORITIES CHIEFLY CONSULTED FOR THIS APPENDIX

GIBBON, E., *Decline and Fall of the Roman Empire* (Bury's edition).

KROMAYER, J. ⎫
VEITH, G. ⎭ , *Heerwesen und Kriegfuhring der Griechen und Roemer.*

MANFRONI, C., *Storia della Marina Italiana.*

LEO VI (Emperor), *Tactica.*

VEGETIUS, *Military Institutions.*

CHAPTER VI

THE VIKINGS

THE NORTHERN PEOPLES

WE SHALL now turn from the wars of the Mediterranean to consider the naval tactics of the Scandinavian peoples, who spread themselves into England, Ireland, France, Germany, Italy, and Sicily by sea and through Russia by land, so that reaching Constantinople by two routes they left their mark on the development of all Europe. This expansive movement out of Scandinavia began in the last decades of the eighth century and was the final part of the general migrations of the Teutonic peoples which distinguished the first millenium of our era. At first the numbers were very small. The movement reached its greatest activity within the next hundred years, although it did not lose its entire strength until after the eleventh century.

In military and economic relations of nations, one of the most important factors is the relative as well as the actual populations of the countries concerned, and we must not be misled by the vast numbers attributed to the Northmen by contemporary chroniclers. The accounts which have come down to us both in the monkish annals and in the Scandinavian sagas tell of Viking raids by many hundreds of ships manned by many thousands of warriors, but present-day historians agree that the early writers had little sense of numbers and that in reality the Vikings were comparatively few in number. For instance, in their great siege of Paris in 885-86 they are alleged to have gone up the Seine with 700 ships and 40,000 men. At that time the city occupied the present "Ile de Cité," then of about 50 acres, and possibly extended a little on both banks of the Seine with which it was connected by bridges with fortified heads. The Viking army attacked these bridge heads without success and never completely blockaded the city. In the end the French King appeared with an army of relief but, instead of fighting to a finish, he bought off the Viking army at the price of 700 pounds of silver and permission to occupy the province of Burgundy which was then in insurrection. The sum of 700 pounds was not enough to buy a large body of men, for as mentioned in the previous chapter, the great Byzantine expedition of 902, only 16 years later than the siege of Paris, cost only about a pound of silver per man for the whole campaign of 6 months or more (34 centenaries of gold for 47,000 men).

TO ILLUSTRATE VIKING CAMPAIGNS

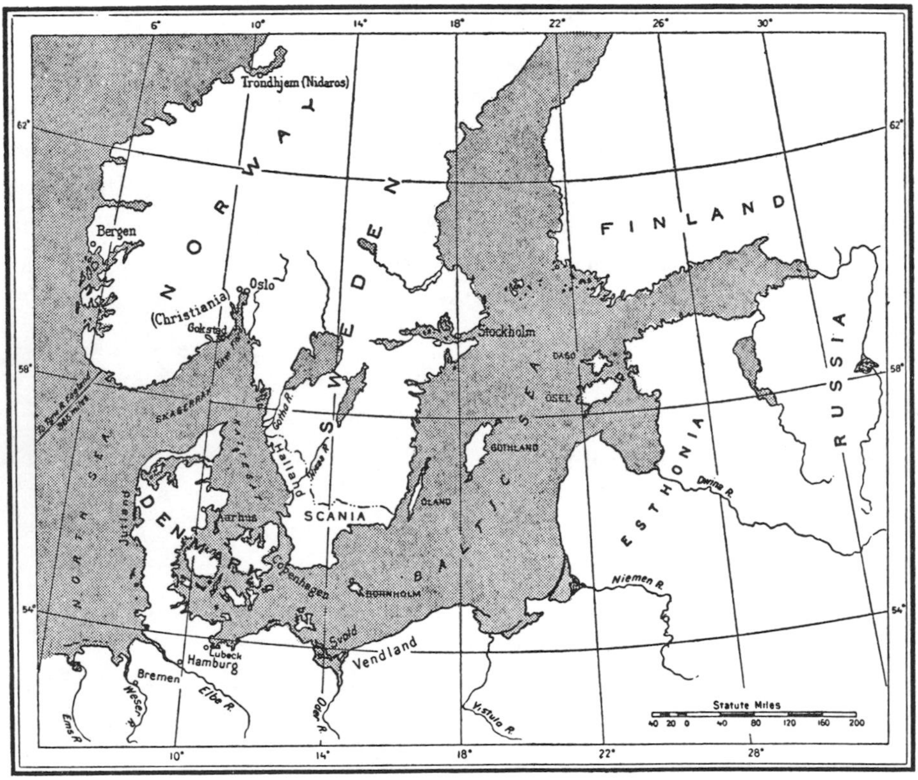

MAP V.—VIKING CAMPAIGNS

This unusually great Viking expedition therefore probably numbered only a very few thousand men.

Although there was then no census, and any estimate of the population of any part of Europe is vague, yet it is asserted by Scandinavian antiquaries that about the year 1000 A.D. all Scandinavia may have had in the neighborhood of 1,000,000 inhabitants, of which Norway and Sweden may each have had a quarter and Denmark, which then included the province of Scania in Southern Sweden, may have had the remaining half.

In their migrations the Swedes went mostly to Russia; the Norsemen to the west, to Ireland, England and France; and the Danes went both east and west into Germany and as far as France and the British islands.

Organization of Scandinavia

Besides, the organization of Scandinavia was not thorough enough to turn out a high percentage of the people for war. Until the ninth century there was no recognized national king in Norway. The country naturally fell into three well-marked geographical regions, the northern one about the present Trondjem, the western one about Bergen, and the eastern one about Oslo. It was always difficult to obtain co-operation among these districts, which were further divided into about 30 "fylker" or sub-districts, each under a petty king, who had in his "fylke" perhaps 6,000 to 10,000 inhabitants, and maintained a body of house guards. The people lived by agriculture and fishing and in the summer popular leaders took their followers across the seas on Viking cruises and these squadrons were ready for commerce as well as for plunder. The warships were often accompanied by merchant ships which carried supplies and were convenient store ships for booty and for commerce. Neither must we think that Viking raids were wholly at the expense of foreigners. An opportunity for plunder among themselves was seldom neglected when occasion occurred. As late as the eleventh century, when the three Kingdoms were marked out much as they now exist, King Harald Hardrada of Norway raided in Denmark precisely as smaller kings raided their neighbors 200 years earlier. The unrest throughout the Northland must have been much like that existing along the border between Scotland and England some centuries later, except that the Norse forays were by sea.

When the Viking movement began, it derived its importance less from the numbers of the raiders than from the fact that they were the best fighters in Europe. Their Frankish and Saxon cousins who had preceded them in occupying the Roman Empire had lost much of their original combatant qualities and made scarcely the opposition that might have been expected. Unlike the soldiers of the eastern Empire, who, although brave, considered it foolish to fight unless the prospects of victory were decidedly in their favor, the gallant Dane or Norwegian thought his life was well spent if he took his enemy with him. When such a man threw off his mail coat and went berserk (bareshirt) in order the more freely to swing his huge two-handed axe, which no armor could resist, there was no one in Europe to match him as a soldier except among his own people.

Early Viking Raids

As was said, the early Viking raids were on a small scale. It seems probable also that the people were poor to such an extent that only the principal leaders were completely armed, while the majority had very little defensive armor, which was sought as plunder nearly as much as gold and silver. Apparently, the raids did not seek to acquire much bulky loot.

As Europe was not then densely populated and communications were poor, it was easy for light-draft ships to land on the beach or go up a river to plunder some rich monastery and get away before the neighborhood could be aroused in its defense, for feudal levies were slow in assembling. As time passed and the Viking raids increased in size, the leaders occupied points of advantage, frequently islands such as Noirmoutier at the mouth of the Loire and Thanet near the Thames River. These they fortified and used as bases for progress inland, and no doubt they served also as trading points. When such a fortunate expedition had established itself firmly, it might be joined later by friends and the raid become a permanent settlement.

Finally, both in England and France, the Vikings seized or were granted territory which they held either in fief or independently, to which they brought their women, and where they became naturalized and ruled the original inhabitants as in Northumberland and Normandy, and elsewhere. Against the Viking attacks the natives could make no effective reply until their rulers also developed shipping, as did King Alfred of England, to pursue them on the sea. But of these naval engagements we have few details and what we know of Viking naval tactics comes from accounts of sea battles between the Scandinavians themselves.

The Gokstad Ship

We are better informed as to Viking ships than we are as to ships of that period in the Mediterranean because of the former's use as tombs.

FIG. 6.—THE GOKSTAD SHIP, TOMB OF OLAF GEIRSTDALF. DATE ABOUT 860-70 A.D.

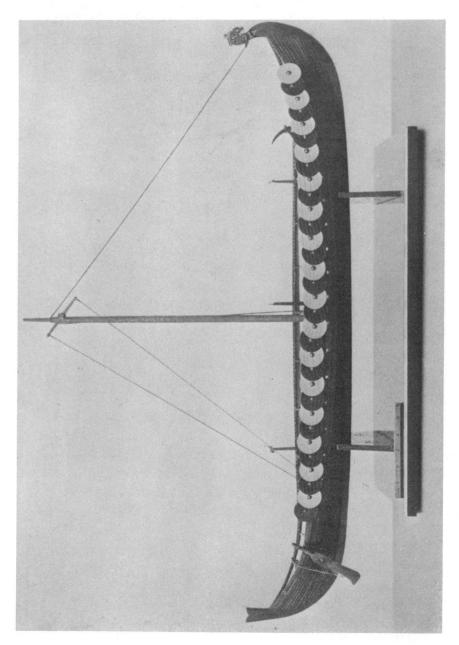

FIG. 7.——MODEL OF THE GOKSTAD SHIP OF THE NINTH CENTURY, RESTORED

Courtesy of the Science Museum, South Kensington.

Several such ships which have been thus preserved under ground have been recently discovered and may now be seen in the National Museum at Oslo. The ship found at Gokstad is a Viking ship (i.e., a warship, not a trader) of the ninth century. She is 78 feet long over all and 16¾ feet extreme beam. Her draft seems to have been about 2.7 feet exclusive of keel and at that draft her water-line length is 72½ feet and her water-line beam 15¾ feet. As her lines are very fine, her load displacement is only about 30 tons. She is clinker built of oak, with 16 oar ports on each side, cut through the planking about 18 inches below the gunwale. The oars found are 17.4 feet long. She is fitted with a single mast amidships probably 42 feet long (not all of it was found) and carried a single square sail. She is undecked, but carried a tent to protect the crew in port and this was secured along its edges to the gunwale. The tent could also be set up on the beach, for the crews liked to spend the night on shore. With two men to each oar she might make 7 knots for a short spurt. A replica of this craft was built for the World's Fair at Chicago in 1893. She crossed the ocean in good time, sometimes doing as much as 11 knots under sail, and proved an excellent sea boat.

THE GREAT SERPENT

From this survival of the old Norse ship and many incidental allusions in the contemporary sagas we are able to derive a fairly clear idea of the much larger ships which were built by the end of the tenth century, and the number of men they carried. The largest ship named in the sagas is one which King Canute of Denmark, England, and Norway built and which had, so it is said, 60 rowers' benches. But this tale may be rejected with little consideration, for until wooden ships were strapped with iron less than a century and a half ago, they lacked sea-going strength if over 200 feet long, and 60 benches would have needed a craft of over 200 feet. The most celebrated ship of the Norsemen was the *Long Serpent* of King Olaf Tryggevesson, built just before the close of the tenth century, and on which he met his death at the battle of Svold in 1000 A.D. She was remembered for several generations as the standard for comparison, and was said to be the most costly ship ever built in Norway.

We are told in the Saga of King Olaf that the *Long Serpent* was 74 ells (122 feet) long on the grass (i.e., the keel) and had 34 benches for

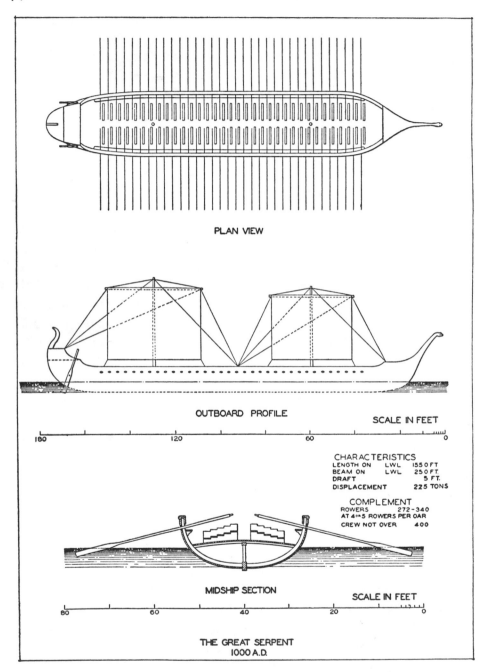

PLAN VIEW

OUTBOARD PROFILE

SCALE IN FEET

180   120   60   0

CHARACTERISTICS

LENGTH ON	LWL	155 0 FT
BEAM ON	LWL	25 0 FT.
DRAFT		5 FT.
DISPLACEMENT		225 TONS

COMPLEMENT

ROWERS	272-340
AT 4 OR 5 ROWERS PER OAR	
CREW NOT OVER	400

MIDSHIP SECTION

SCALE IN FEET

80   60   40   20   0

THE GREAT SERPENT
1000 A.D.

FIG. 8.—RECONSTRUCTION OF "GREAT SERPENT"

oars. She was therefore about 165 feet long over all and perhaps 150 feet
on the water line. Probably she was longer in proportion to her beam
than the Gokstad ship, for we are told in another saga (Flateyarbok) that
to take a certain 30-benched ship to sea through the ice it was necessary
to cut a fairway 24 feet 8 inches (15 ells) wide. At the water line this ship
must have been of less width than the channel, say 23 feet. The *Long
Serpent* was somewhat larger and may have been about 25 feet at the
water line and 27 feet over all at the gunwale. With lines not quite so
fine as the Gokstad ship such a craft at 5 feet draft (excluding keel) would
probably displace 220-230 tons. It is not known if she had one or two
masts.

The remarks in the sagas indicate that the largest ships, unlike the
Gokstad one, which was undecked, had high poops and forecastles and
were low amidships only, and had several men on each oar. The description says that *Long Serpent* carried 8 men to each half-room (between
the thwarts) and 30 men in the foreroom. This makes a crew of 574 men
at the least, and probably is an overstatement even when she was crowded.
The galleys of the Mediterranean in the early sixteenth century carried
225 men on a deck area of a scant 8 feet per man (See *Le Triremi*, by
Luigi Fincati). During the Crimean War French and British three-deckers
took on board as many as 2,000 soldiers in addition to their crews of
about 1,000 and their density of population was then also about 8 square
feet of deck per man. (H.M.S. *Queen* took home 2 regiments and 3
additional companies. See *Military Expeditions*, by Furse.) On this basis
the *Long Serpent* might have carried nearly 400 men.

But it does not seem that the Norsemen crowded their ships as much
as the Mediterranean peoples. The sagas tell us repeatedly of ships with
20 benches and 90 men (2¼ men per oar) and of a ship of 32 benches
which never went to sea with less than 240 men (3¾ men per oar). We
may conclude then that the *Long Serpent*, the largest of all, may have
had 4 to 4½ men per oar, or 272 to 306 men in all as normal crew, with
a possibility of rising to 400 men for battle. The existing Gokstad ship,
with its 16 rowing benches, may be credited with a normal crew of 2 to 2¼
men per oar, a total of 64 to 72 and sometimes 80 to 90. A 10-benched
boat probably had a crew of somewhat less than 2 men per oar, say 35
men in all, yet on occasion they could carry more, for we are told in the

Seventh Saga of the *Heimskringla* that for a short raid within a fiord against a neighbor a certain Harek put 80 of his household in a 10-benched boat and rowed all night to surprise his enemy at dawn and burn him in his house.

AVERAGE SIZE OF SHIPS

Various indications are given in the sagas as to the average size of ships in squadrons. Thus, King Olaf the Saint, in the eleventh century, had 5 ships with 360 men. Einar Tambarskelver had 8 or 9 great ships with nearly 600 men. In the twelfth century Gregorius had 11 ships with nearly 480 men. At the same period King Eystein was deserted by most of his men in a civil war and had left with him 10 ships and 1,440 men. All these squadrons, although of few ships, belonged to great people. It is fair to assume that larger squadrons averaged fewer men per ship and probably no more than 50 to 60 men would be a reasonable average crew for fleets approaching 100 in number, and for over 100 ships the size of the crews would average still less.

SIZE OF FLEETS

As for the size of the fleets which the northern Kingdoms could turn out the Saga of King Canute says that about 850 ships in Denmark alone were subject to his levy (early eleventh century), but it is very unlikely that the entire force ever answered the summons at one time. When King Olaf Tryggevesson met the combined fleets of Denmark and Sweden, supported by the Norwegian squadron of Earl Eric at the battle of Svold, he had only 60 ships and, although 11 of these were of the largest size, he was much inferior in strength. I doubt if he had much over 5,000 men in all. In the naval campaign of the Kings of Norway and Sweden against Denmark in 1026 each assembled 350 ships, but King Olaf of Norway took only 60 across to Denmark. On this occasion King Canute is said to have brought over an English fleet and, with his Danish ships, he had a total force of 1,200.* He had little difficulty in driving the combined fleets before him and, as the chronicle says, he "occupied Norway without stroke of sword."

In 1066, when King Harald Hardrada of Norway went on his last

---

* Probably the number of ships is overestimated and the average size was small. If there were 12,000 men in the fleet, it was a huge force.

campaign against King Harald of England, he made a half-levy and had nearly 240 ships, besides store ships and small craft. As for the men in the levy, we may gain some idea as to their numbers from the effort of King Olaf the Saint to regain his kingdom in the year 1030. With some help from Sweden, Olaf assembled about 3,600 men in Sweden and marched overland on Trondjem, the capital of Norway. He was opposed by the levies of the northern districts and they received some aid from the rest of the Kingdom. According to one account Olaf was opposed by "one hundred times a hundred men" and by another he was outnumbered two to one (*Heimskringla*).* This suggests that for a short and popular campaign all Norway might turn out perhaps over 20,000 men or 8 to 10 per cent of the population. No doubt a single "fylke" could show a higher proportion for strictly local defense or a popular Viking cruise. So the full maritime levy of 480 ships probably did not exceed 20,000 men or an average per ship of about 40 men, or less.

A royal fleet on a foreign cruise usually had 60 to 150 ships, with a few of the largest size, but most of no more than 30 to 60 men per ship. Even Harald Hardrada, on his expedition to England just mentioned, probably had 8,000 to 10,000 at the maximum. The great Viking raids of the ninth century, which were primarily for plunder, were no doubt much smaller. If a popular leader could attract 12 to 30 ships with from 1,000 to 2,000 men, it was a big expedition. The Orvar Odd Saga mentions 15 ships with 120 men each as a very great Viking force.

A TYPICAL VIKING

As an example of the manner of life and of fighting of distinguished Vikings it is worth while to sketch the career of King Olaf Tryggevesson, whose father was grandson of King Harald Haarfager, who first ruled all Norway. Tryggeve was petty king of a district in SE. Norway and, when he was killed by a cousin seeking to replace him, his wife Astrid fled with Olaf to Sweden. When the child was 3 years old his mother attempted to cross into Russia to join her brother, who held there a great position, but was captured at sea by Vikings who sold her and the boy separately as slaves in Russia. When the boy was nine years old he was seen by his

---

* In his *History of Norwegian Peoples*, Gjerson says, vol. II, p. 264, that this estimate is high and that Olaf had only 2,500 and the chiefs only 5,000 men.

uncle in the market place who questioned him and bought him and placed him in a good situation at the Court of King Waldemar of Novgorod, where he grew, as his saga says, "to be the handsomest of men, very strong and stout, and in all bodily exercises he excelled every Northman that was ever heard of." He was very expert at swimming and mountain climbing. He could run along the oars of his ship while the crew was rowing, could play with three daggers in the air at once, and could cut and strike equally well with both hands and could cast two spears at once. He was very merry and frolicsome, gay and social, had great taste in everything, was very generous, careful in his dress, and in battle he exceeded all in bravery. He was distinguished for cruelty when enraged, and thus some obeyed him with friendliest zeal and others out of dread. Withal he was a great ruler, who, in his short reign after seizing the Kingdom of his ancestor, obliged his countrymen to accept Christianity. He was the ideal hero of the Paganism which he made his subjects renounce.

When he had become distinguished in Russia and a favorite of both King and Queen, he was forced by jealousies to ask for release and began his Viking life. He landed, gained booty, and settled for a time in Vendland (now the neighborhood of the Oder mouth). He married the local queen and soon went sailing again. For some years he was successful and got much booty. Under his father-in-law Olaf, he fought in the army of the German Emperor when the latter attacked Denmark and was checked by the ramparts defending its southern frontier. But after three years, Olaf's wife died and he went again on a Viking cruise and plundered in Flanders, Northumberland, Scotland, the Hebrides, and Ireland, became wealthy, and was baptized, thus assuming the faith he was later to enforce on his subjects. A great Irish lady, Gyda, proposed herself in marriage and he won her in a duel in which with his mighty Norwegian axe he struck the sword from the hand of his Irish opponent and then felled and bound him. His twelve seconds in the duel were told to follow his motions and they each did the same to their adversaries. Olaf then lived sometimes in England and sometimes in Ireland.

In 995, when Olaf was about 26 years old, with five ships he returned to Norway, which he had left in his mother's arms, and, owing to dissatisfaction with the current rule of Earl Hakon in the north, he was readily accepted there as King. He soon established his authority and religion over the entire kingdom and in 1000 A.D. he went to Vendland with a fleet to seize his third wife's (Thyra) lands there. He was waylaid on his return by the combined fleets of Sweden and Denmark and that of the sons of Earl Hakon whom he had driven from Norway. When he saw the great odds against him he refused to retreat and in a desperate battle, after his fleet was destroyed and his ship in possession of the enemy, he and Kolbiorn, his marshal, who was dressed and armed like him, leaped overboard on opposite sides of the ship. When the enemy boats tried to pick them up the King threw his shield over his head and sank beneath the waters. It was long before his people gave up hope that he had swum to safety under the water, and he remains the hero of the nation to this day.

The Arms of the Vikings

Returning from this digression. The arms of the Vikings at sea were of course the same as those they used as soldiers. They employed the sword and both the throwing and thrusting spear, and an axe with a 5-foot handle which needed both hands to swing it effectively. Besides they used the bow more than any people they fought with, and kings and leaders were particularly proud of their skill in archery. There was a great deal of stone throwing (from slings and by hand) and ships were well provided with suitable stones. The defensive armor was the helmet and mail shirt to which a hauberk was added for protection of the neck between the shirt and helmet. The shields were at first round, about 3 feet across, such as those found on the side of the Gokstad ship. Afterwards they were long and narrower.

Tactics

The ships were without rams and battles were won, as the Romans won, by hand-to-hand fighting. It was customary for a squadron on the defensive to lash the ships together, so that the side of each was protected by her neighbors. This enabled the ships most heavily engaged to be supported by men from other ships. When thus lashed together, the flank ships were naturally the most favorable point of attack. At the battle of Svold, Earl Eric first attacked the flank ship of King Olaf and when he cleared it of men he cut it away from its neighbor and fell on the latter. It was also practicable and customary for the smaller craft, which were free to move and which lacked the advantage of height, to come up to the great ships heavily engaged and put their own fresh men into the fight and relieve the wounded and those who were exhausted. It was a point of honor for the leaders, who had the largest ships, to lash their own vessels to the others in such a way that the sterns would be on the same line and thus throw the bows of the flagships in advance of the general line so as to take a more prominent part in the action.

BATTLE OF AARHUS

The following is an account (from *Heimskringla,* Saga VIII) of a battle on the east coast of Jutland about Christmas 1044 between Magnus, King of Norway and Denmark, and Earl Swend, a claimant to the throne of Denmark.

Swend's ships were lashed together and were attacked by the King, who naturally had the choice of where to strike.

> They fought at the bows, so that only the men on the bows could strike; the men on the forecastle thrust with spears and all who were farther off shot with light spears or javelins or war arrows. Some fought with stones or short stakes and those who were abaft the mast shot with the bow. The battle was hot with casting weapons. King Magnus stood in the beginning of the battle within a shield rampart [of his followers] but as it appeared to him that matters were going too slowly, he leaped over the shields and rushed forward in the ship, encouraging his men with a loud cheer and springing to the bows where the battle was going on hand-to-hand. When his men saw this they urged each other on with mutual cheering and there was one great hurra through all the ships. And now the battle was exceedingly sharp and in the assault Swend's ship was cleared of all forecastle men on both sides of the forecastle. Then Magnus boarded Swend's ship followed by his men and one after the other came up and made so stout an assault that Swend's men gave way and King Magnus cleared first that ship and then the rest one after the other. Swend fled with a great part of his people, but many fell and many got life and peace. * * * There were seven prizes as the result of the battle (Saga of King Magnus the Good).

BATTLE OF NISAA

In 1062 Harald Hardrada of Norway met Swend, King of Denmark, (above mentioned) in the battle of Nisaa on the coast of Halland a little north of Copenhagen. The previous winter preparations had been made for war. I quote from *Heimskringla,* Saga IX.

King Harald remained all winter at Nidaros and had a ship built on the strand. It was a buss.* The ship was built of the same size as the *Long Serpent* and every part of her was finished with the greatest care. On the stem was a dragon head and on the stern a dragon tail and the sides of the bows were gilt. The vessel was of 35 rowers' benches and was remarkably handsome, for the King had everything belonging to her equipment of the best, both sails and rigging, anchors and cables. King Harald sent a message in winter to Denmark to King Swend that he should come northward in spring, that they should meet at the Gotha River and fight, and that the one who gained the victory should have both Kingdoms. King Harald during this winter called out a general levy of all the people of Norway and assembled a great force towards spring. King Harald had his great ship drawn down and put into the River Nid and set up the dragon's head upon her. Thiodolf, the scald, sang about it thus

> My lovely girl the sight was grand
> When the great war-ship down the strand
> Into the river gently slid
> And all below her sides was hid.
> Come lovely girl and see the show—
> Her sides that on the water glow,
> Her serpent-head with golden mane
> All shining back from Nid again.

Then King Harald rigged his ship, got ready for sea, and when he had all in order went out of the river. His men rowed very skillfully. So says Thiodolf:

> It was upon a Saturday,
> Ship-tilts were struck and stowed away,
> And past the town our dragon glides.
> That girls might see our glancing sides.
> Out from the Nid brave Harald steers
> Westward at first our dragon veers
> Our lads together down their oars
> The splash is echoed round the shores.

> Their oars our king's men handle well,
> One stroke is all the eye can tell:
> All level o'er the water rise,
> The girls look on in sweet surprise,
> Such things they think can ne'er give way.
> They little know the battle-day.
> The Danish girls, who dread our shout,
> Might wish our ship-gear not so stout.

---

* Apparently a ship wider than the usual long ship and with 3 masts.

> 'Tis in the fight, not on the wave
> That oars may break and fail the brave.
> At sea, beneath the ice-cold sky
> Safely our oars o'er ocean ply,
> And when at Trondhjem's holy stream
> Our seventy oars in distance gleam
> We seem when rowing from the sea
> An erne with iron wings to be.

King Harald sailed south along the land and called out the levy everywhere of ships and men. When they came south to Viken [Christiania fiord] they got a strong wind against them and the forces lay dispersed, some in the harbor, some at the isles outside, and some in the fiords. When the weather became favorable King Harald sailed eastward to the Gotha River [boundary of Danish Scania] with his fleet and arrived there in the evening. When the Danes heard that the Northmen's army was come to the Gotha River they all fled who had opportunity to get away [i.e., the local people]. The Northmen heard that the Danish King had also called out his forces and lay in the south, partly at Fyen and partly in Sealand. When King Harald found that King Swend would not hold a meeting with him, nor fight, according to what had been agreed upon between them, he took the same course as before [i.e., in a previous year], letting the bonder [free peasants] troops return home,* but manning 150 ships with which he sailed south along Halland where he harried all round and then brought up with his fleet in Lofo fiord and laid waste the country. A little after King Swend came upon them with all the Danish fleet, consisting of 300 ships.

When the Northmen saw them King Harald ordered a general meeting of the fleet to be called by sound of trumpet and many there said it would be better to fly as it was not advisable to fight. The King replied, "sooner shall all lie dead upon one another than fly." King Harald drew up his ships to attack and brought forward his great dragon in the middle of his fleet. The ship was remarkably well equipped and fully manned. So says Thiodolf:

> The ring of shields seemed to enclose
> The ship's deck from the boarding foes.

> * * *

> The Dragon on the Nisaa flood,
> Beset with men who thickly stood,
> Shield touching shield, was something rare
> That seemed all force of men to dare.

---

* Presumably it was difficult to hold the bonder troops for a prolonged campaign. Those who went on owed personal service.

Ulf, the marshal, laid his ship by the side of the King's and ordered his men to bring her well forward. Hakon Ivarsson lay outside on the other wing and had many ships with him all well equipped. At the extremity of the other side lay the Trondhjem chiefs, who also had a great and strong force.

Swend the Danish King also drew up his fleet and laid his ship forward in the center against King Harald's ship, and Finn Arneson laid his ship next and then the Danes laid their ships according as they were bold or well equipped. Then, on both sides they bound the ships together through all the middle of the fleets, but as they were so large, very many ships remained loose and each laid his ship forward according to his courage and that was very unequal. Although the difference among the men was great, there was a very great force on both sides. As soon as King Harald was ready with his fleet, he ordered the war blast to sound and the men to row forward to the attack.* Soon the battle began and became very sharp, both Kings urging on their men. Stein Herdisarson [who was a scald in the ship next to King Harald] says of the fight

> From fleet to fleet so short the way
> That stones and arrows have full play.

It was late in the day when the battle began and it continued the whole night. King Harald shot for a long time with the bow. So says Thiodolf:

> The upland king was all the night
> Speeding the arrows' deadly flight.
> All in the dark his bowstring's twang
> Was answered, for some white shield rang
> Or yelling shriek gave certain note
> The shaft had pierced some ring-mail coat.

Earl Hakon and the ships that followed him did not make fast their ships in the fleet, but rowed against the Danish ships that were loose and slew the men of all the ships they came up with. When the Danes observed this each drew his ship out of the way of the Earl, but he set upon those who were trying to escape and they were nearly driven to flight. Then a boat came rowing to the Earl's ship and hailed him and said that the other wing of King Harald's fleet was giving way and many of their people had fallen. Then the Earl rowed thither and made so severe an assault that the Danes had to give way before him. The Earl went on in this way all the night, coming forward where he was most wanted and wheresoever he came none could stand against him. Hakon rowed around outside the battle.

Towards the end of the night the greater part of the Danish fleet broke into flight, for then King Harald with his men boarded the vessel of King

---

* Either the unequal length of the ships allowed some to use a few oars forward or aft, or else the smaller boats that were not lashed pushed the ships into battle.

Swend and it was so completely cleared that all the crew fell except those that sprang overboard. When King Swend's banner was cut down and his ship cleared of its crew all his forces took to flight. The ships which were bound together could not be cast loose, so the people who were in them sprang overboard and some got to other ships which were loose and all King Swend's men who could get off rowed away, but many of them were slain. Where the King himself fought the ships were mostly bound together and there were more than 70 of King Swend's left behind.

King Harald rowed after the Danes but that was not easy, for the ships lay so thick together that they could scarcely move. * * * They followed the fugitives only a short way and rowed back to where the deserted ships lay. Then the battle place was ransacked and in King Swend's ship was a heap of dead men but the King's body was not found. * * * Then King Harald had the greatest attention paid to the dead among his men and had the wounds of the living bound up. The dead bodies of Swend's men were brought to the land, and he sent a message to the peasants to come and bury them. * * * In the winter the talk of the countryside was that Earl Hakon had won the battle for the King, and the latter was very jealous and attacked Hakon but did not secure him (*Heimskringla*, Harald Hardrada's Saga).

Battle at the Gotha River

In the middle of the twelfth century Norway was ruled by the three sons of the late King Harald. They divided the kingdom into thirds and were on bad terms with each other. King Inge killed his two brothers, Sigurd and Eystein, but did not thereby gain undivided rule, for the followers of Eystein put forward his nephew Hakon, son of King Sigurd, as heir. Hakon was well received in the northern districts and in 1159 he set out with 37 ships, cruising south. He plundered in the neighborhood of Bergen and, hearing King Inge's fleet was near, he passed outside of it at sea and was pursued by it, being overtaken in the Gotha River. King Inge entered the north arm of the river (it had an island in its mouth) and landed, sending out spies who reported Hakon's fleet above them. They said that Hakon's ships lay at the stakes in the river to which they had moored and had run stern lines to the shore. They had laid two great east-country trading vessels outside the fleet and built high wooden stages on them (or else high fighting tops on the masts). In other words, the flanks of Hakon's fleet were protected in the strongest manner by lofty ships, giving unusual advantage to the spearmen and archers on board and offering difficulties to hostile boarders.

King Inge's fleet rowed up the river but, on coming in sight of the enemy, he turned inshore out of the current and called a council. It seemed too dangerous to row upstream subject to archer fire, under which the rowers would not only be unable to fight, but would need shelter behind the shields of their comrades. It was then decided to send the light craft down stream and up by the other branch around the island to make a charge with the current and cut the enemy away from his moorings at the stakes. When this attack should develop the main body would row up stream and support the others.

When King Hakon's leaders (he was a boy) saw the enemy stop they became confident that the enemy was afraid to attack and when they saw the light craft under way down stream the men could not be restrained. They cast off their lines and made chase. But in a little they came to a turn in the river and saw King Inge's main body lying quietly in the eddy. The latter immediately prepared for battle, but Hakon's fleet turned up-stream again to a stretch of the shore where there was no current owing to a turn in the river. Here they ran inshore and threw out stern lines to the bank, turning their bows outward, and protected their flanks as before with the heavy trading ships, which they managed to move down stream.

> In the middle of the fleet lay the King's ship and next to it Sigurd's and on the other side lay Nicholas. * * * All the smaller ships lay farther off [from the King] and they were nearly all loaded with weapons and stones.

Then Sigurd of Royr made the usual speech of exhortation and the boy King went on board one of the east-country ships where a shield wall was formed around him, but his standard remained on the long ship where it had been.

Seeing that King Hakon and his people were going to fight, King Inge and his men sent to recall the light ships which had got off and in the meantime consulted and arranged for the attack. It was agreed that the enemy was not in such a strong location as when his ships were held in position at the stakes in the river and it was arranged that King Inge himself should hold his ship out of action. When the light ships returned, all advanced against the enemy by rowing up stream and keeping beyond archer fire and then across the current. The attack had to be made by each ship independently, for if lashed together they would be unmanageable. One of King Inge's leaders, Erling Skakke, thrust the bows of his ship between that of King Hakon and the next, but that of Gregorius, the other admiral, grounded and heeled heavily in the current. Hakon's light ships thereupon attacked her, but before she yielded, a friend threw an anchor into her and towed her off. King Inge came up on seeing Gregorius in trouble, for he said he could not let his friends work for him while he kept the best ship idle; so he set up his banner and crossed the river and lay under one of the great east-country ships. This was so high that it hurled stones and spears and iron-shod stakes to great advantage. The King had to withdraw and he entered the fight near the middle of the enemy formation. The battle turned against King Hakon. Slowly his smaller ships were cleared and his men driven into the great merchant ships, but some got on shore and at last with great difficulty the boarders under Erling forced their way into Hakon's high ship and cleared her bows of defenders. Then the whole force gave way and many were killed and many fell overboard, but most, including King Hakon, got to the land. Within two years Hakon overcame and killed King Inge in a battle on the ice.

Summary

The Viking battles are peculiar in galley warfare for the entire renunciation of the ram, and reliance on the infantry weapons. The preference for lashing the main body of ships together so as to make a single battle ground of a large group of ships is also noteworthy. It facilitated the use of reserves of men from the lighter craft at points where the main struggle needed support. The light vessels also found opportunity for service in skirmishing on the flanks and protecting their own flank ships.

Of the three battles described, those at Aarhus and the Gotha were won by breaking through the center, and the other by success on the flanks. As it seems, the peculiarity of the Viking naval tactics arose out of the great personal valor and recklessness of life of the Scandinavian people. Besides, owing to their piratical habits, they probably looked on hostile ships as carriers of booty and did not favor ram tactics which would sacrifice a prize.

AUTHORITIES CHIEFLY CONSULTED IN THIS CHAPTER

Cambridge Medieval History, vol. III.

Du Chaillu, Paul Belloni, *The Viking Age.*

Sturleson, Snorro, *The Heimskringla, or Chronicle of the Kings of Norway.* Translated by S. Laing.

CHAPTER VII

MEDIEVAL WARS OF FRENCH AND ENGLISH

Maritime Conditions in Eleventh and Twelfth Centuries

FOR several centuries after the Viking migrations we know little of maritime affairs in northern waters. Apparently the ships of France, the Low Countries, and England were modeled much after those of the Vikings and were not large. They seem to have depended more on sails than those of the Mediterranean and had yards with square sails instead of antennas with triangular sails. A single mast and sail was the rule until the fourteenth century.

The first great maritime adventure after the Viking conquests was the invasion of England by Norman William late in 1066. Contemporary reports say that William crossed with a huge army of 60,000 men in 700 ships, but modern criticism much reduces these figures. Oman thinks there may have been 12,000 Normans in line at Hastings, Delbrueck says there cannot have been more than 7,000 men with half as many horses. This army, which attracted adventurers from far beyond the limits of Normandy, is shown by the Bayeux tapestry* to have been transported in small ships. Probably few, if any, were decked. If we take Delbrueck's estimates of the size of the Norman army, 35,000 displacement tons of shipping would have been able to carry it with abundant supplies. There may have been 600 to 700 ships, few reaching the size of 100 tons' displacement (dimensions about 55 x 17 x 6.5 feet). The accompanying picture of the ducal flagship from the Bayeux tapestry shows a small craft much like the Gokstad ship at Oslo.

To oppose William's passage, King Harold gathered a fleet on the Kentish shore, but the Normans were delayed by contrary winds and the British squadron ran out of supplies and retired into the Thames to complete and refit. The weather then changed and William crossed and landed without naval opposition, and soon defeated Harold and killed him at

---

* This tapestry was attributed to Matilda, wife of William the Conqueror. It is now said to be a work of the early twelfth century.

FIG. 9.—SHIPS FROM THE BAYEUX TAPESTRY. PROBABLE DATE, EARLY YEARS
OF TWELFTH CENTURY

William the Conqueror's crossing of the Channel, in 1066. Upper vessel Duke William's
ship. The cross at the masthead indicates the Pope's approval of the expedition. The
lower ship is a horse transport with 10 horses, all apparently facing athwartship. Both
ships were presumably from 60 to 70 feet long and of 60 to 80 tons' displacement.
Sixteen oar ports on a side are visible.

Hastings. Thereafter, for a century and a half, there were no naval operations in northern waters on a large scale.

As the English King was Norman Duke and ruler of other vast territories in France, there was little to disturb the peace of the neighboring seas except the usual piracy. During this period ships probably increased somewhat in size and a larger proportion were decked. For the security of shipping the King, the barons with estates on the sea coast, and also some of the seaports maintained a few galleys similar in design to those of the Mediterranean. King John seems to have had about 50 galleys which were used for revenue collection among other purposes. Not only did these public ships protect their own commerce: it seems to have been not uncommon for them to attack strange craft, so that the same ships and crews turned from national defense to piracy with much readiness.

War of 1213-17

The long quiet (except from piracy) in the English Channel was broken in the very last part of the twelfth century when the efforts of the French monarchs to consolidate their Kingdom led to war between Richard of England and Philip Augustus of France. Control of the sea was rendered necessary by military operations and the sovereigns called out their fleets. Sailing ships composed the greater part. The British ship service was on a feudal basis. The King had the right to call out a ship levy. Thus, the Cinque Ports were obliged to grant the King 57 ships for 15 days' service without pay; in return for which duty these towns were granted important commercial privileges. In size these ships were small; a century later the largest could scarcely have exceeded 160 tons.* The organization and administration of these squadrons seems to have been more lax than in the Mediterranean.

War broke out between France and England during King Richard's captivity in Austria, from which he returned in 1194, and lasted until his

---

* Early in the fourteenth century a ship needed a man for every 4 tons' burden and one man for 3 tons in ships under 100 tons. In 1300 a squadron of 30 ships furnished by the Cinque Ports, Hastings, Romney, Hythe, Dover, Sandwich to which were added Winchelsea and Rye, the largest vessel had only 39 men and 3 officers. As the King had the right to double man the ships when he did not levy the full quota, this may mean that the largest vessel was no more than 80 tons. Probably the average size was between 30 and 40 tons' burden or between 60 and 80 tons' deep displacement (see Sir H. Nicolas, *History of the Royal Navy*, vol. I, pp. 285, 295, 363).

MAP VI.—NORTH SEA AND ENGLISH CHANNEL

death in 1199. His successor, John, made peace with France, but hostilities were soon renewed and John lost Normandy and Anjou. Very considerable demands were made on English shipping for the over-seas operations, but no important naval operations occurred in the early part of the war.

Early in 1213 the King of France had been so successful in conquering the King John's French provinces that he prepared to invade England and required his vassal, the Count of Flanders, to aid him. The latter would not sacrifice his people's profitable trade with England and declined obedience. Thereupon King Philip Augustus directed war upon Flanders and all the ships which he had made ready to take his army to England were sent with their supplies to Damme, the port of Bruges, in support of the French army of invasion.

In the meantime King John had been assembling his forces. Men capable of bearing arms were summoned to the fortified port of Dover to oppose the French should they land; and the King's bailiffs at all ports were directed to send to Portsmouth all ships capable of carrying six or more horses (say above 30 tons' burden). The Count of Flanders now called on King John for aid who sent 700 knights and others in 500 ships to the Flemish coast under his half-brother, the Earl of Salisbury.*

BATTLE AT DAMME

Early in June, 1213, Salisbury found the port of Damme full of ships. He sent to reconnoiter and found they were French and that their crews had gone ashore to plunder. He instantly attacked and took 300 ships laden with grain and oil, which were sent to England. About 100 more were burned on the beach.** The English then landed in pursuit of fugitives, but King Philip Augustus sent such a large force against them that the English were driven back to their ships with considerable loss. Nevertheless, the destruction of the French supply ships was the ruin of the campaign against Flanders and King Philip Augustus was obliged to return to France.

A FRENCH ARMY IN ENGLAND

King John's foreign efforts were hampered by his misgovernment at home, where his demands for money provoked the nobles. In 1215 the latter extorted Magna Charta which placed authority in the hands of a committee. A civil war soon resulted in which the rebel barons offered the

---

* We can scarcely believe there were 500 ships. Seven hundred knights implies about 3,000 men in all, with perhaps 1,400 horses. With somewhat less supplies than assumed for the Norman army of William, this force could be shipped in about 200 ships averaging between 60 and 70 tons' displacement. Linear dimensions about 45′ x 14′ x 6′. (See appendix to chapter on "Navy of Roman Empire.")

** Either the ships must have been very small or the number is much exaggerated.

throne to Prince Louis, the heir to the French throne. He sent 7,000 Frenchmen to England in December, 1215, and more the following month. Some landed at London. Under the command of Eustace the Monk, the French fleet seems now to have been in command of the channel in spite of the losses at Damme.

Eustace provided, as is alleged, 600 ships and 80 cogs* to take Prince Louis and 1,200 knights, with many followers, to England, where they arrived in May, 1216, and landed in Kent without opposition. After subduing Kent, with the exception of Dover, which was strongly garrisoned, the French army marched to London, where it was joined by the rebel barons.

The presence of foreigners in the country now began to turn the English people in favor of the King and the traditional sentiment against the French dates from this summer. King John fell back to the west of England when Prince Louis first arrived and the latter committed the serious strategic error of neglecting Dover and marching north, whereby the English royalists were left in possession of a strong naval station and a squadron on the line of French communications. King John recovered much of the country during the summer of 1216, but died that fall, leaving the French and rebels holding the eastern counties and London, but the good wishes of the people returned to his boy successor, Henry III.

Prince Louis saw his error in neglecting Dover and besieged it on August 1. The place held out and thereby immobilized a large part of his force. During the winter, William, Earl of Pembroke, marshal and regent for the young King, seems to have gathered a body of ships at Rye which interfered very seriously with French communications. In February, 1217, Eustace was able to drive these ships away, but the French and rebels were not making good in the interior and Prince Louis returned to France for re-enforcements with which he recrossed in April, and landing at Sandwich he pressed the siege of Dover. In May a French flotilla with troops was attacked by ships from Dover under Sir Philip d'Aubigny, who guarded that city by sea; but nevertheless, the troops were landed.

BATTLE OF DOVER

The defeat of the northern wing of the French and rebel forces in the city of Lincoln by the royalists, on May 19, 1217, changed the aspect of

---

* Again the number of ships is incredibly large.

FIG. 10.—AN ENGLISH KING'S SHIP OF ABOUT 1200 A.D.

About 36 feet in length and 40 to 45 tons' displacement.
Courtesy of Science Museum, London.

affairs. The siege of Dover was abandoned and Prince Louis fell back to London, where it was necessary to support him with men and supplies, which were collected for him by his wife, Blanche of Castile, and put under Robert of Courtenay who embarked much gear and merchandise and over 900 men on 70 deep-loaded nefs. On the night of August 23-24 they left Calais for the Thames River escorted by 10 large ships fitted out for war, all under the command of Eustace the Monk. When Hubert de Burgh, the King's justiciary and Governor of Dover, became aware of the expedition on foot, he was deeply impressed by the necessity of preventing the re-enforcement from landing and took necessary measures, although the military leaders at Dover were unwilling to commit themselves to a sea battle with Eustace, telling De Burgh that they were not sea soldiers and that he might go and die. But he brought them round, and sent for his chaplain. Taking the sacrament, he appealed to the garrison of Dover to defend their post in his absence, saying, "Ye shall suffer me to be hanged before you surrender the castle, for it is the key of England."

He then prepared to attack the French at sea and probably took his squadron from Dover to Sandwich, which was now held by English Royalists, to await the enemy on his way to London (See La Roncière, *History of the French Navy*). Among his leaders were Sir Philip d'Aubigny and Richard, a natural son of the late King John. On August 24, the English force, consisting of 16 large and well-manned ships, belonging to the Cinque Ports and 20 smaller craft, sighted the much more numerous French ships from Calais standing northerly with a strong southerly or southwesterly breeze to round the North Foreland on their way to London. It is probable that in spite of the French excess of numbers the superiority of strength was with the English, and the main reliance of the French must have been in their 10 large ships equipped for war and probably carrying most of the 900 soldiers.

On getting under way De Burgh did not head to intercept the French, but pointed for Calais, seeing which Eustace is alleged to have exclaimed, "I know that those wretches think to seize Calais like thieves, but in vain, for it is well defended," and continued on his course, for his business was to supply the Prince. When, however, the English were to windward of the enemy, they bore up and approached from the rear. As the English drew within range, Sir Philip d'Aubigny opened the action by a heavy discharge from his crossbowmen, in which he had the advantage; then, when still nearer and about to close, the English threw powdered quick lime in the air, which drifted to leeward and blinded the French. When the ships came in contact, the English threw their grapnels and boarded and cut the French halyards, so that, as Matthew Paris relates, the French were caught under the falling sails "like birds in a net." Recollecting their recent success at Lincoln, the English were in high spirits and victory soon declared itself for them.

To let the other ships get away, Eustace hove his ship to and was surrounded by four enemies. The captain of the first to reach him told his mate to go aloft and cut down the French standard so that the other French ships would disperse. As the French account says, Eustace's ship was heeling so that she could not use her trebuchet (stone-throwing engine).* A battle ensued between the boarders and 36 French knights. Eustace smashed heads with an oar, but was captured with the others. An old comrade asked him if he would prefer the trebuchet or the ship's rail for a beheading block and, without more ceremony, he was immediately slain. Many Frenchmen, disdaining to be taken alive or else fearing the cruelty of their captors, leaped into the sea and were drowned. It is said that only 15 ships escaped. One old chronicler, Roger of Wendover, says that certain "perforated" ships sank. As it does not appear that any galleys took part in the engagement, this statement must be taken to mean that in colliding, planks were sprung or stove in, rather than that the sides were pierced by ram thrusts.

The prizes with the spoils, consisting of money, weapons, and stores, were taken into Dover, where the victors were welcomed by the bishops and clergy in procession with banners. The result of the battle was immediate. Prince Louis could no longer hope for success, for the English Royalists controlled the sea, and he was isolated from his French base. On September 11 the Prince signed a peace and evacuated England with his troops.

Comment on the Battle of Dover

The battle is noteworthy for its difference from contemporary Mediterranean actions. It took place under sail with a fresh breeze and the

---

* The trebuchet was a very unsuitable weapon for ship use. Probably it was carried as cargo for siege work.

English used the breeze to a double advantage. They alone threw lime to leeward and their crossbow bolts ranged farther and struck harder, shooting down wind, than did those of the enemy. The English accounts make much of the advantage of the French in numbers, but the greater part of the French ships were mere transports with very few soldiers. The English ships were not only more serviceable as fighters, but their crews were greatly inspirited by the success at Lincoln and the withdrawal of the French and rebels into London. They knew that their success would end the invasion.

Aside from the use of sails, the battle followed the tactics of the Mediterranean. The action opened with missiles and not until the English had obtained some superiority did they close and board. The battle was a chase, in which neither side seems to have maintained an exact formation, nor could there have been effective ramming even if there had been rams present, for both squadrons were going the same way. It seems probable that Eustace realized that he had lost control of the sea and was anxious only to deliver his supplies in London, avoiding a fight if possible.

THE HUNDRED YEARS WAR

Size of Ships and Crews

During the thirteenth century after the battle of Dover and until the reign of Edward III, there were naval campaigns between the French and English, but no naval battles of note. The fleets escorted armed landing parties and there were raids on merchant shipping, so that commerce was subjected to great risks. Neither nation attempted to control the sea for the sake of ulterior objects. During this time the size of ships continued to increase.

Early in King Edward III's reign, his flagship, the cog *Thomas*, had a crew of 137 men and boys including officers. We may suppose that this was a double crew and that the ship was about 250 to 300 tons burden (90 to 100 feet long), since it was customary to increase the crews when battle was expected (see footnote, p. 89).

In 1376 over 30 English merchant ships were surprised and destroyed in a Breton bay by Spaniards. From a list of these ships which has been preserved, it appears that the largest was of 300 tons and the average size of this squadron about 120 tons' burden (Nicolas, vol. II, p. 510). In

1346 King Edward listed the ships of England for the siege of Calais. The list of these ships has also survived. He levied 738 ships manned by 14,958 men, an average of 20 men per ship (Nicolas, vol. II, p. 510). As ships of 60 tons required 20 men, as already stated, the total tonnage must have been over 45,000.

The ships of the time were high sided with raised poops and forecastles, as may be seen from the seals of various seaports. Few ships of the fourteenth century carried more than one mast, which had a square sail on a yard, for lateen sails were not then generally used in the north, and also a crow's nest at its head for lookout and for archers and crossbowmen in battle.

BATTLE OF SLUYS, 1340

The origin of the Hundred Years War between France and England is to be found in the position of the English Plantagenet Kings, who held Southwestern France as vassals of the French sovereigns. The latter for centuries were making continuous efforts to strengthen royal authority as against the great provincial magnates. In the previous century, the Kings of France had made serious encroachments on the English possessions and early in the fourteenth century it was felt in England that only by war could the remaining British province of Guienne be maintained. An occasion of war was not long delayed.

In 1333, soon after reaching his majority, Edward III invaded Scotland in an endeavor to establish his rule over all Britain. In accordance with French tradition, King Philip IV of France aided the Scottish King. King Edward countered by making alliances with the German Emperor and with several princes of the Netherlands, including the Count of Flanders, for English prosperity depended on the sale of wool to Flanders. The latter was a vassal of France, but his province was much more desirous of good business relations with England than with France. The purpose of the English alliances was to stir up trouble on the northern frontier of France, in order to draw the attention of the French King from Guienne. Philip anticipated Edward and began the war in 1337 by declaring the continental dominions of Edward forfeited to the French crown and by raiding the English coast. The English navy was for the moment quite inadequate and the French fleet destroyed Portsmouth and seems to have been superior on the sea until 1339.

To protect British interests in Flanders, King Edward went there with a considerable army in 1338, but he was so far from controlling the sea that a month before his passage a French squadron was able to land its crews and destroy Southampton. For two years the expensive English campaigns based on Flanders against the French brought no results. Seeing that he could do nothing on the Continent while French ships were operating with much success against his communications with England and were raiding the English coast, King Edward made every effort to levy all ships possible to regain his communications. For this purpose he returned to England in February, 1340, and by June he was ready to go back to Flanders, having assembled a large force of ships.

While the English army was occupied in Flanders, the French fleet had been called out for the purpose of invading England, but hearing that the King was in England and about to return to Flanders, it went to Sluys with orders to intercept him at all costs. Sluys was near the entrance of the Zwyn, which led to Bruges and the center of Flemish trade, but it was a poor place for a hostile fleet to lie in wait, as the shores were unfriendly and it was difficult to get supplies. Consequently, the French fleet was obliged to anchor somewhat off shore, although within the entrance to the bay.

When the King arrived at the port of Orwell (Harwich) about June 10, he had 40 ships and was ready to cross with his retinue, but was met by the news of the great fleet which was lying at Sluys to oppose his passage. The King said he would cross at any hazard, whereupon his Chancellor, the Archbishop of Canterbury, in protest withdrew from the Council and surrendered the Great Seal of England. The King then turned to his Admiral, Sir Robert Morley, and asked him if there would be serious risk. Morley supported the Archbishop, at which the King fell into a great rage and said that all present were agreed to prevent his crossing. Morley replied that he would precede the King even to death. The King then recalled the Archbishop and returned the Great Seal to him, and sent to collect a larger fleet.

Within ten days a force of 200 ships was assembled from London and the west and on June 22, soon after noon, the King sailed for Flanders on board the cog *Thomas*. The next day about noon the fleet arrived at Blankenburgh and was joined there by Sir Robert Morley with the northern squadron of about 50 ships making 250 in all. What was the size and complement of the ships is not exactly known. Nicolas tells us that the seamen of the western ports agreed to furnish 70 ships of 70 tons and upwards. From what was said a little previously, we may assume that the King called for large ships and that his fleet may have averaged 100 tons' burden. A little later, at the siege of Calais, the King had 120 ships with 60 well-armed mariners and 20 archers each. Two hundred and fifty ships of the same average size would take 20,000 men. Froissart says that on this occasion the English fleet embarked 4,000 men-at-arms and 12,000 archers. With ordinary crews of 25 men for each ship, this would give a force of about 22,000 men.

Blankenburgh was about 10 miles west of the mouth of the Zwyn and the French fleet was visible within that arm of the sea. After anchoring, the King landed some knights who rode along the shore and reconnoitered the hostile force. He also communicated with the Flemings asking them to come out to his aid.

The various chroniclers differ in their reports of the size of the French fleet, ranging from 140 large ships to 400 in all. In his letter to his son telling of the battle, King Edward says there were 180 "ships, galleys, and great barges." La Roncière gives a list in detail of the French ships, which numbered 200 in all, among which were 28 royal ships, 3 royal galleys, and 3 Genoese galleys under Barbavera. The rest of the fleet was furnished by the seaports. Their size ran from 200 to 80 tons and the individual crews ran from 200 to less than 60. The total number of men was somewhat over 20,000, of whom 1,200 were in the galleys and 4,000 on the 28 royal ships. There were over 600 crossbowmen, of whom most were in the great *Christopher*, of 300 tons, recently captured from the English. When taken she was armed with three iron guns and a hand gun similar to the *pots de fer* with which some of the French ships had been armed the year before. But the contemporary accounts do not mention firearms at Sluys. The barges, which were numerous in the French fleet, were of a Norse type, enlarged, with two decks, cabins, and two castles. The after castle was the larger of the two and was 30 feet long by 6 feet high (La Roncière, vol. 1). On the whole, we may believe that the British fleet had a few more ships and men, but that there was no great difference in the size of individual ships. The important difference was in the armament. The French fleet seems to have been manned almost wholly by seamen armed chiefly with swords and pikes, and little good armor. There were few crossbowmen. The British had many archers and men-at-arms, the latter with good armor.

After hearing from the reconnoitering party on shore, the English Council of War decided to attack the following morning. The French also held a council at which the Italian Barbavera, commanding the Genoese galleys, advised the two French Admirals, Quieret and Behuchet, to go to sea, as the British would otherwise have wind, sun, and tide in their favor. His advice was not followed, but he himself went out with his galleys. However, the French main body moved to a better position nearer the entrance, and apparently rather to the northern, or Cadzand, side of the channel. The fleet was permanently organized in three divisions according to the home ports of the ships, and was now formed in three corresponding lines. In front of these three lines were placed 4 large ships, among which was the *Christopher*, with nearly 400 crossbowmen on board, and these were no doubt the fourth line to which some chroniclers allude. It is not clear whether the French fleet was under way during the action, but boats were hoisted to the mastheads with men and missiles so that in all probability it was at anchor. English chroniclers say that the French ships were lashed to each other, but Froissart says the French were provided with many grapnels "to see that the English could not get away." Each ship was a fortress with her raised castles at the ends, the top with crossbowmen and stone-throwers, and the boat hoisted half-mast with projectiles.

At sunrise the British fleet was in motion and by six o'clock it was near the entrance. An English nef broke away from the others and attacked *La Riche*, but was overpowered, her crew was killed, and she was sunk. The time did not yet seem right for the English to join battle. The sun in the east shone in their eyes, the current was running to the westward, and high tide was several hours off. So the fleet tacked and stood away until it had gained a position somewhat to windward of the enemy, and the tidal stream had turned. The French mistook the cause of this delay and some accounts say that they broke their formation to chase, but this statement does not agree with the course of the battle. About noon, a half hour after high tide, when the easterly current was strong, the British fleet closed with the enemy. The wind was probably N. or NE. and the course easterly or southeasterly.

The King had arranged his ships to take advantage of the two weapons in which his men excelled. He and many of his leaders had been engaged in one or both of the two great victories over the Scotch a few years before at Dupplin Moor and Halidon Hill. In these battles the English leaders combined the tactical effort of two different arms. Long range archer fire from the wings first shook the Scottish ranks of pikemen and then the charge of mounted men-at-arms broke the hostile line and completed the victory.

This combination of weapons King Edward repeated at Sluys. He put his best ships in the front line and between every two ships with archers he placed another with men-at-arms. The archer ships were to engage at long range and then the men-at-arms would close and board. A second line of archers' ships in rear of the first provided reserves for those in the first line who became exhausted. The King told off a guard of 300 men-at-arms for the protection of the transports which carried a number of ladies who were going to join Queen Philippa in Ghent where she had been left as a hostage for the King's return. It may be strongly suspected that as the English ships drew near they doused sail and took to their oars to take and maintain position. Even the largest sailing men-of-war carried a few great sweeps until after the Napoleonic wars.

As the English drew near, Sir Robert Morley was the first to engage. He attacked the *Christopher* with an overwhelming archer fire. Although most of the Genoese crossbowmen were on board the *Christopher*, their harder hitting bolts did not range as far as the English arrows. The Earls of Huntington and Northampton quickly followed the Admiral into battle and Sir Walter Manny was the fourth to engage. Probably each assailed one of the four great ships composing the first line. Froissart says of Morley's battle, "the English archers firing strongly and all together soon showed these Genoese that they were their lords and masters and entered their ship and conquered them." We must not suppose, however, that the archers boarded the *Christopher* or the other ships. That was work for well-armored men-at-arms with swords and lances, who came up in the other ships when the arrows had weakened the French resistance. Having taken the *Christopher*, her captors killed the remaining French on board; and, as her great size and height made her most effective, she was filled with archers and, once more an English ship, sent against her recent consorts.

The action soon became general. The English concerned themselves only with the van division of the French who, as King Edward said in his letter to his son Prince Edward, "made a noble defence." The King himself, clothed in a long white-leather coat, fought valiantly against two French ships and encouraged all by his valor. It is said that he was wounded by the hand of the French Admiral, Behuchet. After fighting for about eight hours until near sunset, the French front line gave way and the English advanced on the second line which did not put up a determined resistance and flinched soon after it was engaged. A number of crews jumped into their boats, which sank from overweight, so that 2,000 men, as is said, were drowned. About sunset, the Flemings, who had been summoned by King Edward the day before, began to arrive from Bruges, Damme, and Sluys. They attacked the 60 ships of the French third line on the side opposite the English. About 8,000 of them are alleged to have taken part. Presumably their ships were smaller than those of the two main forces. The battle dragged on through the night and towards the morning 24 of the French fleet escaped to sea. Even then, they were not entirely fought out, for the *St. James*, a large Frenchman, grappled a ship of Sandwich and was taking her along when the latter was rescued and the *St. James* captured by the Earl of Huntington. King Edward sent a squadron of 40 ships to pursue the fugitives and it may have accomplished something, for King Edward wrote that some prizes were taken at sea. The French lost about seven-eighths of their ships and, as La Roncière asserts, about three-fourths of their crews. The English loss was "comparatively small," according to King Edward's account, but Flemish estimates run from 4,000 to 9,000.

The interesting tactical point about this action is its similarity to army formation and the very evident application of the newest English army practice, as to combining archery with close fight. As for its results, King Edward wrote in his public bulletin announcing the victory "thus the passage across the sea will hereafter be safer for our faithful people and many other benefits are likely to accrue therefrom to us and our faithful people, whereof the fairest hope already smiles." In short, this victory gave England control of the Narrow Seas for the next 20 years and facilitated the commerce with Flanders, which was so important to both countries. As a recent English historian says (T. F. Tout, *Political History of England*),

> The commercial prosperity of England was very great during the first part
> of King Edward's reign. His wars impoverished him, but his adventurers at
> high pay did well. * * * The English success at Sluys was the fruit of a com-
> mercial activity which enabled the English shipping to deprive the Italians,
> Netherlanders, and Germans of the overwhelming share which they had
> hitherto enjoyed of our foreign trade.

Henceforward Edward could land his armies in France without difficulty
and, above all, he facilitated commerce with the Netherlands, expanded
the British merchant shipping and promoted British prosperity at the
expense of maritime rivals.

SIEGE OF CALAIS

In the continuation of the war against France, in the summer of 1346,
King Edward landed a large army in Normandy and destroyed many
French ships which he seized in that province. After a pillaging march
through Northern France, he was forced to battle at Crécy, about 20 miles
south of Calais. His great victory was followed by the siege of Calais for
the purpose of obtaining a secure port on French territory. The siege lasted
a year and, for at least a part of the time, the English army numbered
32,000 men. This great force was supplied from England under cover of
the fleet which also was necessary to blockade Calais by sea.

To effect this double purpose and also to protect the English coast
from counter raids, King Edward listed, as available (as mentioned on
p. 96) a force of 738 ships manned by 15,000 men, but, as I understand
the account given by Nicolas, only 120 ships, each manned by 60 mariners
and 20 skillful archers, were actually called out and assembled early in
April. Twelve galleys were chartered from Genoese shipping men.

About the midde of April a considerable French squadron entered
Calais port with stores and provisions, but thereafter, until the capitula-
tion in September, the English squadron of 80 ships completely isolated
the city and captured French supply ships. Soon after the seizure of the
city a truce was concluded between France and England, but this did not
put an entire stop to naval operations.

The Battle of Winchelsea or L'Espagnols Sur Mer

The Kingdom of Castile had been giving some support to France and, after the Franco-British truce became effective, the Spanish shipping continued hostilities. In November, 1349, a Spanish squadron of armed merchant vessels under Don Carlos de la Cerda, returning to Spain from the Netherlands, attacked and captured several English merchantmen at Guerande in Brittany and the following summer returned to Sluys on a second voyage. King Edward resolved to attack him on his passage down the Channel. He gathered a force at Winchelsea in Sussex which may have numbered as many as 50 ships with crews running from 30 to 80 mariners each. The King took command of his squadron in person and hoisted his flag on the cog *Thomas* which had borne him at Sluys. He was joined by nearly 400 knights who, with their followers, must have made an addition to the crews of perhaps 2,500 men.

De la Cerda at Sluys became aware of the King's intention and delayed his departure to provide a full complement of fighting men and of weapons. Among other devices, he provided heavy iron bars to throw down from aloft to penetrate the decks and bottoms of the enemy. The King arrived at Winchelsea about the middle of August, accompanied by his wife and two sons and a crowd of noblemen, and embarked on the 28th. His son Edward, Prince of Wales, commanded a ship and was accompanied by his brother, John of Gaunt, who was only 10 years old and too small to wear armor, yet refused to part from his brother. While waiting for sight of the Spaniards the King passed the time with the music of his minstrels. On the afternoon of August 29, Sir John Chandos, one of the most distinguished British soldiers of the day was singing a German tune as the King glanced aloft from time to time at the lookouts in the top.

About 4:00 o'clock the latter reported a sail and then another. The music was silenced and soon the whole Spanish fleet of 40 sail was made out, running free before a fresh NE. breeze. The English fleet got under way and stood out across the course of the enemy. The King called for wine and having drunk with his knights, all put their helmets on their heads and were ready for battle. The Spaniards might have avoided action by sheering off and so have gone by, but they were too confident in their high-sided ships and their strong crews to do so and came straight on.

From the account in Froissart and other contemporaries it does not seem that either fleet was in any precise formation, nor was there any British tactical plan, as at Sluys, to make the archers effective. On account of the speed of the Spaniards, it was a catch-as-catch-can affair, but we have graphic accounts of individual ship actions. The King led his squadron, under sail like the Spaniards, and laid a course to intercept them. He selected a ship to engage, saying to the helmsman, "I wish to tilt with that one." The man placed the ship as ordered and the collision was of great violence. The Spaniard's bowsprit swept away the forecastle of the *Thomas,* and the blow started some planks so that she leaked badly; but his knights started baling and concealed the damage from the King. The Spaniard lost her mast and the men in its top, but she was not held by the *Thomas* and the King sought another antagonist, which he grappled securely and, after a short contest, the English boarded her and threw all on board into the sea.

By the advice of his knights, the King abandoned his own ship and continued the battle in the prize he had made. By this time the battle was general and the Spaniards had an advantage in the height of their ships, and their missiles from aloft.

The Prince of Wales had fortune similar to his father's. His ship also sprung a leak in collision and the effort to save the ship prevented the crew from overcoming the enemy. Fortunately, the Earl of Lancaster came to his rescue on the other side of the Spaniard and she was unable to prolong her resistance. Her crew also, after surrender, was thrown overboard and the Prince and his followers barely had time to leave their own ship before she went down. Late in the day, the *Salle du Roi,* manned by the King's household, having securely grappled a large Spaniard by iron chains, was unable to subdue her and the Spaniard made off under all sail towing the Englishman with him in spite of the latter's effort to get free. Cries for aid were unheard or unheeded by other ships, but at last she was saved by the gallantry of the captain's valet, who leapt on the deck of the enemy and cut her halliards so that her yard and sail fell on deck. Taking advantage of the confusion the English were able to board and take her.

After a severe action, the English squadron was successful in making 14 prizes, and the rest of the Spaniards got away. King Edward caused his trumpets to sound a recall and soon after nightfall his ships anchored at

Rye and Winchelsea. The King landed with his knights and joined the Queen with her ladies, who had been watching the battle from the hills. As Froissart says,

> The night was spent in revelry with the ladies, conversing of love and arms, and the next day, when most of the barons and knights who had shared the honor of the battle waited upon him, he thanked them greatly for their services and, taking their leave, they returned to their homes.

Owing to the recent English truce with France, Peter, the new King of Spain, did not wish to fight the English alone and made peace, so the English were dominant at sea for a number of years.

The battle of Winchelsea shows no grand tactical effort, only hard individual fighting and, although gunpowder had been in use for 25 years, Froissart does not mention it in this battle. In all these battles of the period in the English Channel we see no such attempts, as were the rule in the Mediterranean at the same time, to maneuver ships as a body and to overcome the enemy by attack in the rear and envelopment of the flanks. Knights in armor fought as they knew how to fight on land. Battles were won with weapons rather than with ships as was the tradition of the Mediterranean. It is noteworthy also that in the British Black Book of this time (a book of what now would be called Admiralty Instructions and Regulations) the tactical rules regard landing and raiding on shore rather than ship handling.

AUTHORITIES CHIEFLY CONSULTED IN THIS CHAPTER

BAYEUX TAPESTRY, (At Caen, France).
Cambridge Medieval History, vol. V.
DELBRUECK, H., *Geschichte der Kriegskunst*.
FROISSART, JEAN, *Chronique*.
NICOLAS, N. HARRIS, *History of the Royal Navy*.
OMAN, CHARLES, *History of the Art of War in the Middle Ages*.
PAYNE-GALLWEY, RALPH, *The Cross-bow, Medieval and Modern*.
RONCIÈRE, C. DE LA, *Histoire de la Marine Française*.
TOUT, T. F., *Political History of England*.

APPENDIX TO CHAPTER VII

Long Bows and Cross Bows

In the accounts of battles by sea and land of the twelfth century and later much mention is made of crossbowmen, of whom the best seem to have come from Genoa and Aragon. These were hired by princes of other countries. In England the long bow was considered the national weapon, yet it was never able entirely to supplant the crossbow. English kings hired foreign crossbowmen even when the reputation of the long bow was at its highest. It is therefore worth while to compare the two weapons. The bow was a very early weapon throughout the world. The Northmen were famous bowmen and Norman William owed them much at the battle of Hastings. Two centuries later King Edward the First, in his Welsh wars, learned to value the Welsh archers and developed them to high efficiency.

From old bows in existence, it seems that a long bow was 6 feet or more in length and shot an arrow a cloth yard (37 inches) long. When at rest the string was 7 inches from the middle of the bow and the length of the draw was 28 to 29 inches. The strain on the bow necessary to draw it to the full was technically known as the "weight" and was 60 pounds or more. Only very strong men could draw a bow exceeding 90 pounds. The range of the arrow varied with its own weight and the strength of the bow. From the best information which has come to us, target practice at 200 yards was habitual and the ordinary arrow could attain a range of 250 to 300 yards, according to the strength and skill of the archer. About one-third or one-fourth of each man's supply for war were "flight arrows." These were lighter than the ordinary ones and could attain a range greater by 50 to 60 yards, but had less striking force at all ranges. In popular language the term "bowshot" meant 400 yards and this range could probably be reached by the very best archers, using flight arrows.

As to the accuracy of archery, it was not very great in spite of the wonderful tales of Robin Hood and William Tell. We may be sure of this, for the records of target practice in recent years preserved by the Archery Association of Great Britain show that the best winning score in a long

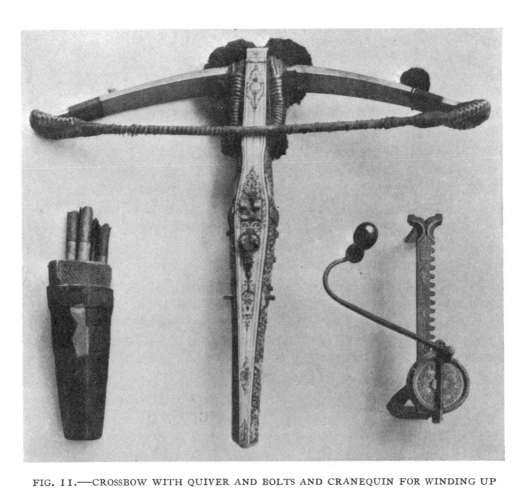

FIG. 11.—CROSSBOW WITH QUIVER AND BOLTS AND CRANEQUIN FOR WINDING UP

The collar at the lower end of the cranequin slips over the butt of bow until stopped by 2 pins. The claw at the upper end of the cranequin hooks the bowstring which is drawn by turning the crank until the sear seen in the middle of the stock can catch it. The cranequin is then removed and the bolt placed on the stock, resting against the bowstring ready for firing when the trigger (underneath) releases the sear. Courtesy of the Metropolitan Museum. See also picture of a crossbowman in action in battle at Constantinople, opposite page 124.

series of annual shooting matches at 100 yards at 4-foot circular targets was 72 per cent of hits. The same champion won in another year with 45 per cent. The lowest winning annual score was 20 per cent of hits. We may therefore believe that 1 hit out of 4 on a target of a man's size (7 square feet) at a measured range of 100 yards would be most remarkable target practice, and at an unknown range of about the same distance under war conditions 3 or 4 per cent of hits would be very high. Of course, the shooting in war would be at a line of men instead of at individuals, but the full allowance of two sheaves of 24 arrows each probably averaged scarcely as much as one enemy casualty.

It is not difficult to calculate the ballistics of a bow,* by drawing a diagram of the stretched bow. From such a diagram it will appear that the accumulated work in drawing the bow is about 50 per cent of the "weight" of the bow multiplied by the length of the draw. When the string is released, part of the accumulated work is expended in moving the string; part in moving the bow itself and the rest goes to the arrow. After weighing each of these three parts of the instrument, the diagram enables us to tell the energy absorbed by each. A 6-foot bow of 80 pounds will develop about 96 pounds on the draw and return about 66 foot-pounds to a war arrow weighing 9 to the pound, giving it an initial velocity of about 196 foot-seconds. A flight arrow weighing 14 to the pound would take up 57 foot-pounds, with an initial velocity of 226 foot-seconds.

The arrow of the long-bow was able to pierce the infantryman's leather coat or "jack," but was not effective against metal armor. So about the twelfth century the crossbow came into use to give heavier blows. At first the crossbow was no more than a heavy wooden bow mounted on a stock at right angles to the length of the bow, making a cross. To draw this bow the archer placed the center of the bow under both feet and drew the string with both hands by the strength of his back muscles, until he could catch the string by a sear and trigger at the rear of the stock. Then the bow was lifted, a bolt was placed in a groove running the length of the stock, and the weapon was ready for discharge. In the course of time crossbows were built stronger; until in the sixteenth century they were of steel, weighing, with the stock, as much as 25 pounds. A heavy bow at the Metropolitan Museum, which I was permitted to examine, had a span of 33 inches with

---

* See article by present writer in *Army Ordnance* for May-June, 1935.

a draw of 5.5 inches and a "weight" of 1,640 pounds. Such bows needed a ratchet or a winch to wind them up. This was a great addition to the burden the crossbowman had to carry. The work accumulated in drawing this crossbow is about 263 foot-pounds, but the machine is not efficient because the bow is heavy and its draw is very short, requiring a very stout bowstring. Thus much of the work is absorbed in the bow and the string. A flight bolt weighing 1.5 ounces is good for a velocity of under 200 foot-seconds and a range of 280 yards. The heads of crossbow bolts at the Metropolitan Museum are of a great variety of shapes to bite on inclined plate armor, to cut ships' rigging, and for other special purposes. Many offer great resistance to the air. A 5-ounce bolt with a 4-pronged head in the above-mentioned crossbow would have a velocity of no more than 160 f.s. and a range of 160 yards. In spite of the comparatively short range of the crossbow, its advantage was that it struck such a hard blow that knights had to wear heavy armor for adequate protection. As a new weapon it was opposed as inhumane and in 1139 the Pope is alleged to have forbidden its use against Christians. Another advantage of the crossbow was that any one could wind it up and weak men were as efficient with it as strong men. It was also more accurate. Its disadvantages were that it was heavy and slow in rewinding.

Although gunpowder was invented early in the fourteenth century and was quickly used for artillery, it was not until the early sixteenth century that a practicable portable fire-arm arquebus (or hackbut) was adopted by infantry and even near the end of that century the advantage of the fire-arm was not very marked. It was the high velocity and long range of the hackbut that compensated for its long time in reloading. There are competent modern authorities who believe that at ranges up to 150 yards the long bow was more efficient than the musket, with which the British infantry was armed until 1840. The musket had a greater range. Although little used at long range of 200 yards, it was more or less effective at such range, at which it was better than the bow.

CHAPTER VIII

ITALIAN NAVAL WARS

THIRTEENTH CENTURY (SEE MAPS I-III-IV-VII)

INTRODUCTORY

THE Christian conquests of the First Crusade in Syria and the reduced strength of the Byzantine Empire gave great commercial opportunities to the three principal maritime cities of Italy, which they all sought to improve, each one for itself, at the expense of the others. The nature of the trade of Asia and Egypt with Europe was much the same as it had been in previous centuries as described in previous chapters. Differences of religion and the warfare arising from the desire of the Christian princes of Syria to extend their dominions by conquest did not check the economic pressure for the exchange of goods between the East and the West. But mercantile jealousies between the great sovereign cities which controlled the rival systems of transportation were a constant source of ill-feeling and frequently of hostilities between themselves.

The cities each obtained mercantile concessions and port privileges in the seaports of the Empire and of Christian Syria as well as in Egypt, but their merchants were not content to enjoy their business in peace. Piracy was always rife and consequently merchant ships were always armed for protection. For additional safety, they sailed in convoy and each year each city sent out its annual "caravan" of a squadron of merchant ships escorted by galleys. When favorable opportunities occurred, the ships of different Italian cities did not hesitate to attack one another and nationalistic riots among the foreign concessionaries in Constantinople were not infrequent. As one or another Italian city acquired preponderance, the Emperor attempted to restore the balance by changes in its trade privileges. Naturally, from time to time, the home governments became involved in support of the commerce on which the municipal prosperity depended and serious wars resulted.

The great prosperity of these maritime cities had much the same basis as that of Athens seventeen centuries earlier. Their sea power rested not only on their shipping, but on the numerous ports scattered about the Mediterranean, which they had managed to secure and which served both to collect the produce of the back countries and as bases to watch and protect the movements of their shipping and attack their enemies. At the same time these outlying bases provided a population of seamen which it was beyond the capabilities of the capital cities to furnish in its entirety. Thus Venice drew seamen from Dalmatia, and Genoa from the Rivieras on both sides of her. In addition to, and supporting, this vast maritime and commercial organization was a far-reaching system of finance and banking. The presence of Italian merchants in business centers extending from England to Syria made it easy for them to control the transfer of money by bills of exchange throughout the civilized world and thus enormously increase the profits derived from trade.

So it was that the city of Venice with never more than 200,000 inhabitants was able through her extended commerce and banking facilities to provide a great income to pay for the protecting fleets, and for the garrisons in outlying bases which made business possible, and moreover accumulate wealth for the state and for individuals.

ITALIAN SHIPS

The men-of-war of the Italians did not follow the Byzantine type with oars on two levels. Italy developed the galley type with oars on one level with one, two, or three men sitting on the same bench, each managing his own oar. Later, the "scaloccio" arrangement with several men working the same long oar became general, and perhaps a few ships of this type may have existed very early in the fleets of the Italian cities. The galley of King Richard Lion Heart, when in the Mediterranean at the end of the twelfth century, is described as being "long, low on the water with a sharp spar at the bow called a spur." The spur was not to pierce the enemy below the water line, but served to break up the hostile "telaro" or great overhanging outrigger frame which carried the oars. (See Fig. (27) of sixteenth century ship). In the thirteenth century the ordinary galleys were about 128 feet long and 17 feet wide with a deep draft of 4.0 to 4.5 feet then they displaced about 130 to 145 tons (Manfroni, vol. 1, p. 453,

Fincati, in *Le Triremi*). Each carried one mast which was usually struck when clearing for action.

The mast's length (according to Fincati) was about four times the ship's beam, or 66 feet. Its position was about one-third of the ship's length from the bow. The mast had a cage at its top for the lookout and in battle slingers or stone throwers were put there. Later, galleys had two masts. The triangular sail was spread on the antenna or yard, which was longer than the mast.

The deck was about 2 feet above the water, with much "crown" or slope from center to side. Higher than the deck was the "telaro" which carried the oars and their tholepins and transmitted the rowers' efforts to drive the ship. The telaro was a rectangular frame of heavy timbers, about 22 feet wide, carrying 60 oars on a side, and was somewhat longer than the rowing chamber which was about 105 feet long. It was composed of two thwartship timbers called "yokes" at opposite ends of the rowing chamber, which were strongly bolted to the ship's deck. The ends of the yokes were joined by longitudinal timbers called "apostis," which carried the oars and themselves rested on a system of knees bolted to the deck and overhanging the side like the outriggers of present racing shells.

Above the deck, along its center ran the "corsia," a vertical longitudinal member of the frame in two parallel webs which stiffened the ship structure and made the principal upper longitudinal girder. Between its two webs there was room for stowing sails and other gear and the grating above it made a runway for passage fore and aft. On each side of the corsia were 30 rowers' benches, each seating two men. They were not at right angles to the keel, but inclined so that on each side the inboard rower with the longer oar sat somewhat farther aft than his companion.

Correspondingly, the tholepins of each pair were separated from each other by a distance of about 7 to 8 inches, and in this way the two rowers on each bench did not interfere. There was often a castle at midlength of the corsia, which gave a high fighting station for slingers and archers. Between each apostis and the side of the ship was a platform on which the soldiers stood between the oars, to repel boarders and from which they could leap to the enemy's deck. A guard rail ran along the apostis, and on it was hung the pavesade. This was a line of square wooden mantlets 2 or 3 inches thick which protected the rowers from hostile missiles.

The mechanical artillery (mangonels and catapults) was installed at the bows with only a small arc of fire ahead. Often a heavy, pointed, iron-shod stake was hung from the end of the antenna to swing over the enemy and drop upon him in the effort to pierce his deck and bilge him. Frequently the sides of the ship were covered with leather or heavy felt to protect them from Greek fire and, when so covered, ships were known as "barbotte." Until the middle of the thirteenth century the method of steering was by two great oars, one over each quarter. Afterwards the present style of rudder slowly replaced the older method.

At this period the crews were all freemen and fought in battle after collision with the enemy. The inboard oarsmen had swords and half pikes. The others were archers and stone throwers. The men lived and slept on deck and were protected from the weather by great tents or awnings which were removed for battle. They were made as tight as possible at the ends and sides to keep out the weather. In cold weather, braziers were placed about the deck; nevertheless neglect about the tents in winter service, which was rare, often caused great losses by illness in the crews. With 60 oars on a side, the crew was 120 rowers and about 40 or 50 soldiers, sailors, and officers.

Another type of galley was the "tarida" of about the same length as the "galea sottila" or ordinary galley but about twice as wide. Such ships had two masts and 150 rowers. Not all the taride had fighters' tops but many were so fitted. They served to transport troops, horses, provisions, and siege machines and were slower than ordinary galleys. In battle they formed the second line or reserve. The merchant galleys (galee di mercanzia) were built for commerce but might be requisitioned for war. They were nearly 170 feet long and 19 to 23 feet wide with few oars. The specifications for merchant galleys of Venice were very precisely drawn by the government, and ships meant for the trade to Flanders differed somewhat from those cruising to the Levant. They had crews of 166 men, including rowers, seamen and pilots (Manfroni, p. 455, vol. 1).

There were smaller rowing craft bearing various names, to act as auxiliaries to the larger ships. The sagitta (sometimes called pamphilo) was a type of dispatch boat similar in design to a galley and having from 48 to 60 oars. Finally may be mentioned the "vacchette" (little cows) which accompanied the larger ships, having as many as 18 or 20 oars, the

FIG. 12.—A VENETIAN MERCHANT GALLEY OF 1420. FROM *Rivista Marittima*, MAY, 1873.

FIG. 13.—SHIPS ON THE LEANING TOWER OF PISA, DATE, ABOUT 1200 A.D.

smallest of which were about 23 feet long and 6 feet wide with 8 oars.

Besides the galleys, the "navi" (English, nefs) or merchant ships driven entirely by sails were sometimes used in battle. We have already heard of them as being used to build "sea harbors" and about this time we hear of corsair "navi" in the maritime wars. Among the nefs there were several varieties. The "usciere" (English, vissier) was so called because it had large ports (usci) in its round stern to ship horses. Uscieri carried soldiers, heavy siege equipment, provisions, and war supplies. They could be used as floating fortresses by erecting castles on them with flying bridges to throw upon the sea walls of fortified cities. For the crusade of King Louis IX of France, in 1268, the Venetians built some "uscieri" whose specifications called for a length of 110 feet (Venetian, of 1.138 American feet), beam of 41 feet, which at a draft of 18 feet would make a displacement of 2,000 to 2,100 tons and a burden of 840 carrache or 1,260 tons. They had two complete decks with a half-deck (paradisum) and quarter-deck (superparadisum) aft and forecastle deck (bannum) and upper forecastle (superbannum) forward. The half-deck and forecastle were joined by two gangways, one on each side above the spar deck. Their masts were two, the mainmast being 120 to 130 feet long (a rule for masts for sailing ships was three times beam). The masts carried cage tops for crossbowmen and antenne for lateen sails which were 20 per cent longer than the masts. Forward the nefs were armed with mangonels and catapults. They carried about 9,000 gallons of water (Guglielmotti, vol. 1, p. 332), enough for 600 men for three weeks. "Cocche" (English, cogs) were even larger. From Genoese sources cogs appear to have had as many as three whole decks with three other partial decks forward and aft, with crews seldom less than 120 sailors and 4 pilots besides soldiers. According to Bartolommeo Crescentio's rule for ascertaining the crews of ships from their tonnage measurement (*Nautica Mediterranea,* pp. 70 and 84) a ship with 120 men would have carried 1,000 tons of grain and displaced about 1,500 tons.

Ships were built along the beach as convenient, until the beginning of the twelfth century, when the state commenced to provide arsenals and storehouses.

PERSONNEL AND ADMINISTRATION

The titles of the various naval grades do not seem to have been very distinct in the early days of the Italian navies. General terms of authority from the Latin were used such as "dux," "præfectus," or a circumlocution as "the fleet was led by X." But about the second half of the eleventh century our present terms began among the Norman Italians with the word "Ammiraglio" derived, it is said, from the Arab "amir" and now in general use in all navies as the commander of a fleet or squadron. Venice began the use of the word "capitaneus" to mark the commander of a fleet, while Genoa applied it by a decree to the commander of a squadron of less than 10 ships and admiral as title of commanders of large squadrons. In Venice the word "admiral" was the title of an officer who accompanied the capitaneus and performed duties comparable to those of a present day chief of staff. Commanders of ships were at first called padroni (from Dominus, patronus) and this word lasted after the word comito (comitus) came into use in the thirteenth century to indicate captains of galleys and other rowing ships. At the end of the fourteenth century the word *comito* began to change its meaning to indicate the master of the rowers and captain began to be applied to the ship master, although Venice called the latter sopracomito. In Southern Italy the *comiti* seem to have held their commands as a hereditary feudal obligation and it is possible they had to maintain their ships at their own expense.

The rowers were freemen who at first gave obligatory free service for a limited time, two to six weeks; later, they began to get payment which varied according to circumstances, but even then the duty was obligatory. In Genoa in the thirteenth century seamen had 18 soldi* ($3.38) a month with rations, or 30 soldi ($5.63) without rations. The ration was biscuit, salt meat, cheese, vegetables, and wine. For clothing the crew wore a doublet and trousers of cotton or linen and woolen cap.

Captains dressed in tunic and trousers of silk and carried a whistle with a purse, inkstand and pen and tablets for writing. In Genoa there was a clear line between those who served by the roster, or without pay, and those who were paid; that is, between those whose service was feudal and those who were mercenary. Besides the rowers there were a number of soldiers, among whom the crossbowmen were the chief. Even the rowers

---

* There were 20 *soldi* to a Genoese lira. In 1244 a lira weighed 64 grams and was worth about $2.70 of money of 1932. In the century previous it was worth a good deal more and later it was worth less (see Manfroni *Storia della Marina Italiana*, vol. 1, p. 466 and F. Donaver, *Storia della Repubblica di Genova*, vol. 1, p. 39. The former gives the value of the lira as more than does the latter).

were all armed and after the ships closed in battle most of them left their oars to use their swords. The captains of sailing ships employed in the fleet were always called "padrone." They had a crew of sailors, all bearing arms, besides the soldiers who were divided into crossbowmen and bellatores, which I take to mean swordsmen and pikemen. The state closely watched the fitting out of galleys, their equipment, the amount of cargo and attended to the protection of the convoy against hostile corsairs. Both in Genoa and in Venice a state commission controlled these matters under severe penalties for offenders. By a Genoese law of 1313, but in practice much earlier, shipowners of large vessels had to put up security of 1,000 Genoese lire (about $2,700) and man their merchant galleys with 12 crossbowmen, 4 pilots (nocchieri), and 162 rowers and seamen, all armed with helmets, cuirasses, darts, swords, maces, and other weapons. They were not to load their ships below a certain water line shown by a cross of iron on the side (an early Plimsoll mark) and finally they had to cruise in squadron under the command of a "captain" chosen by the magistrates and paid by the owners, who was to prevent the breaking up of the squadron, arrange for the stops, and protect the ships from corsairs. In time of war, the merchant galleys were escorted by war galleys, but they were expected always to be able to defend themselves against small forces.

The Venetian rules were much the same. By the end of the fourteenth century the Venetian government owned the merchant galleys and rented them to merchants at public auction for sums which varied according to ages and risks. Sometimes when dangers were very great the state paid the merchants for undertaking the voyage instead of asking for charter money. There were five annual "mude," or squadron voyages out of Venice, to Flanders and England, to Languedoc, to Alexandria, to Syria, and to Rumania (Constantinople and the Black Sea). There was also a small muda along the African coast. Ordinarily, the mude were composed of 3 ships, seldom 4. Besides spices, the exports to France and England were wine, gold-thread woven goods, and timber. The imports were wool and silk goods. The ships went to Alexandria mostly in ballast, but sometimes they took oil, soap, chestnuts, and fruit, returning with spices. Before the fall of the Christian kingdoms in Syria, business there was very prosperous and the Venetian warehouses in the seaports were filled with every kind of merchandise but afterwards business languished. With Constantinople trade was very lively, including wool, silk, velvet, carpets, salt fish, and grain, and slaves from the Black Sea. Genoa had the same type of business but traded more with France and Spain than did Venice.

Tactical Customs

Ordinarily, squadrons moved in column with the admiral leading; in battle the fleet formed in line, sometimes a straight line, sometimes a crescent with the wing ships either advanced or withdrawn. Fleets were maneuvered by signals which were made by flags and sails in day time and by groups of lights at night, but they were few and simple. A common signal was to direct ships to pass within hail and receive instructions by word of mouth. A great use was also made of "fragate" or small rowing boats to carry aids with oral orders before and during battle. (The preceding is chiefly from Manfroni.) Frequently, when the fleet was near shore, the ships were bridled for battle; that is, they stretched cables from one ship to the next, so that the enemy could not break through the line. These cables had to be cast off to retreat or pursue, but it was possible to advance while bridled. I take it that this method of bridling was not the same as that used by the Scandinavians, who seem to have lashed their ships closer together to form a single platform. The medieval battle seems to have made greater use of mechanical artillery than in the early Christian times. The engagement commenced at a distance with flights of arrows, stones, and bolts from the machines. When attacking sailing ships, it was an object to tear the sails with arrows and cut the rigging with scythes. After ships collided the rowers left their oars to fight; divers tried to bore holes under water. Liquid soap was thrown on the hostile decks to make them slippery. Greek fire was thrown in pots and also quick lime, liquid pitch, and boiling oil and incendiary darts. Against all the incendiary devices the ships were protected by movable leather shields and felting which was wet with vinegar. It is noteworthy that few ships were sunk by the ram or otherwise as compared with ancient times. For siege work the ships rigged flying bridges and ladders from the masts to swing against the walls and enable the soldiers to reach their tops. On the other hand, the entrances to harbors were defended by chains drawn across the channel, and on some occasions by piling (lizze) driven to obstruct the channel and by sunken ships.

THE FOURTH CRUSADE
SIEGE OF CONSTANTINOPLE
ORIGIN OF THE EXPEDITION

Although there was much jealously and constant maritime struggles between the Italian cities, there was little noteworthy in the development of naval tactics, yet the Latin conquest of Constantinople affords an interesting picture of the warfare of the day and its delays, so contrary to present efforts. In the latter part of the twelfth century, the Christian Kingdom of Jerusalem was unable to hold its own against the Saracens, and Saladin recovered the Holy City. The Third Crusade led by the French King Philip and Richard Lion Heart of England was unable to regain the city and in 1197 the Fourth Crusade was preached in France by order of the Pope. By the end of 1199 his exhortations took effect and a great number of French nobility assumed the cross. After much discussion lasting through the year 1200 the principal leaders sent an embassy to Venice to arrange for shipping to take them to the East against the infidels. The embassy arrived in Venice in February, 1201, and presented its request, asking for ships both for transport and for battle. A week later the Doge Enrico Dandolo summoned the envoys to say that the city offered to furnish transport for 4,500 knights, 9,000 squires, and 4,500 horses besides 20,000 infantry at the price of 4 marks of silver (1 mark = $10.04 money of 1932) per horse and 2 marks per man; and this price was to include rations for horses and men for nine months. Besides, Venice would furnish an escort of 50 armed galleys on the condition that as long as the French and Venetians acted together the latter were to have one-half of all conquests by sea and land, both in land and money, as the Venetians wished to improve their commercial status in the East, which was yielding to Genoa. The envoys accepted these terms, and paid caution money. The treaty was confirmed by a popular assembly at the Doge's chapel of St. Mark. It was agreed that the ships should be ready at midsummer of the following year, 1202, at which time the crusaders were to arrive at Venice.

DEPARTURE FROM VENICE

At the appointed time the ships were ready but many of the crusaders failed to appear at Venice. Some did not start, some took ship in Flanders or at Marseilles, and others marched into Southern Italy to embark there. The movement was a popular one without supreme authority in any one of the several great noblemen who led their personal followers. After making every effort, those who arrived at Venice (about one-third of the expected number) fell short of being able to complete their payments by 34,000 marks and the expedition was on the point of failure before starting. It is alleged that until they could agree on terms the Doge held the crusaders prisoners on one of the islands of the city (present Lido) where they had been lodged on arrival. However this may be, a compromise as to payments was at length arranged, by which before proceeding against the infidels, the crusaders were to aid the Venetians to subdue an insurrection in Dalmatia by conquering its capital city of Zara, which competed with Venice in business. Much against the wishes of the crusaders, for it was contrary to their crusading oaths to attack any Christian, they accepted this proposition rather than fail altogether. As Geoffrey of Villehardouin, one of the chiefs of the expedition and its historian, says,

> Then were the ships and transports apportioned by the barons. Ah, God, what fine horses were put therein. And when the ships were filled with arms and provisions and knights and sergeants, the shields were ranged round the bulwarks and castles of the ships and banners displayed, many and fair. And be it know unto you that the vessels carried more than 300 mangonels and petraries and all such engines as are needed for the taking of cities in great plenty. Never did finer fleet sail from any port.

But the men were few, less than half the contract called for, perhaps 12,000 to 14,000. The number of ships as given by different chroniclers runs from 50 to 60 galleys, 20 to 120 uscieri, and 40 to 240 square-rigged ships. For 14,000 men, 2,000 horses, and much stores, excluding the galleys, probably a tonnage measurement of 45,000 to 50,000 tons' displacement would be large. Let us say there may have been in all some 300 to 350 transports, great and small, with under 30,000 men in all.

The departure from Venice was on October 8, 1202, three months behind time. As the rowers for the galleys had to be completed from the maritime possessions of Venice in Istria and Dalmatia, the fleet did not arrive off Zara until November 10. It was necessary to land and lay siege to the city, but resistance was slight and the allies occupied and sacked it. The Doge then suggested that the season was late and that it was inadvisable to undertake further operations until spring. He therefore proposed the allies should winter at Zara, as it was in a rich district with accessible supplies. So it was agreed, and the Venetians and crusaders occupied different halves of the city. There was soon a bloody riot between the two allies for the soldiers quarreled as allies will. The leaders pacified the opponents and spring came without any break in the friendly relations of the French and Venetians.

CHANGE OF OBJECTIVE

During the winter much occurred to turn the expedition from its original purpose. Although the contract had not definitely specified the landing point, yet the leaders meant to land either in Syria or Egypt and Villehardouin says the Venetian Council of State was so informed. By going to Egypt the expedition would be easily supplied from Europe and Egypt itself was rich, near the objective of Jerusalem and an excellent base. But a hostile expedition to Egypt was far from pleasing the Venetians who were without crusading zeal and were on excellent terms with that country and doing a thriving business there in spite of a papal interdict against commerce with the unbelievers.

A palace revolution in Constantinople was the occasion for a change in plan. A few years before Alexius, brother of the Emperor Isaac, had deposed and blinded him and thrown his son, the Young Alexius, into prison. The young man escaped and reached Italy about the time the crusaders were arriving at Venice and he besought some whom he met to aid him to regain the throne for his father and himself, saying that if they did this he would then be able to aid their crusade with the resources of the Empire. The barons sent Alexius into Germany to get the support of his brother-in-law, Duke Philip of Swabia, and King of Germany. During the winter Alexius rejoined the expedition at Zara with the warm recommendation of Duke Philip to aid him.

Much debate followed this suggestion. Many held that it was wrong to abandon the crusading aim of the expedition. Nevertheless an agreement was reached with Alexius to take effect in the following spring (1203). But many were displeased at this betrayal of the Christian purpose.

There was much to recommend his proposal both to the French and to the Italians. The desertions from the rendezvous at Venice imperiled the success of any direct French movement against Egypt. The Venetians were much in favor of the change. The Doge Dandolo personally hated the Empire where he had been particularly blinded years before, and all Venice resented the favors which the Emperor was showing to rival Genoese and Pisan commerce. There seemed little hope for Venice to regain her lost privileges in Constantinople and now came an opportunity to revive Venetian trade. Thus the crusading effort was diverted from an attack in Christian zeal upon infidels to one against fellow-Christians (although of a different church) in aid of Venetian profit. It seems that, as yet, there was probably no intention of overthrowing the East Roman Empire. That result was an outcome of the decision to enter imperial internal politics in order to gain support in their own crusading plan. It was not foreseen that the people would resent the presence and burden of a foreign army. By the terms of the agreement, after the allies had expelled the usurper, the restored Emperor was to place the Empire in obedience to the Pope at Rome, give the crusaders a heavy subsidy and an auxiliary army. Besides the Venetians expected their old privileges. Some modern writers believe that the change in purpose was owing entirely to the treachery of the Doge who diverted the crusaders to Venetian ends, but this does not appear from Villehardouin's account, who speaks for the leaders of whom he was one.

THE FLEET SAILS FOR CONSTANTINOPLE

In April the fleet left Zara and stopped 3 weeks at Corfu to disembark the horses for refreshment. From Corfu the expedition sailed on May 24, 1203. Off Abydos, the leading ships waited 8 days for stragglers. Then all went forward in one body and anchored 3 leagues from Constantinople on June 24 (31 days to go 700 miles). The leaders landed and, as the task was great, the Doge advised seizing Princes' Islands as a base for operations. It was so agreed, but the next morning, when the fleet got under way, the French made straight for the mainland on the Asiatic side and landed at Chalcedon where the leaders occupied an imperial palace and all disembarked, including the horses. After two days the ships moved a couple of miles above the city and anchored. The host followed and camped at and above Scutari and remained there, sending out foragers and getting considerable booty in engagements with the enemy.

As for the maritime defense, the imperial fleet was entirely unready.

It is said to have numbered only some 20 worm-eaten ships. As it was not to be feared, the invaders thought it desirable to show the young Alexius to the people of the city and the entire fleet passed in review under the walls with the Doge's flagship at the head of column bearing Alexius in royal apparel. But the populace did not wish to accept him at the hands of foreigners and they shot at him with stones and arrows.

It was then decided to attack on July 5. As Villehardouin, a soldier and a witness, says,

> Our barons were minded to encamp by the port before the tower of Galata* where the chain was fixed that closed the port of Constantinople. And be it known unto you that anyone must perforce pass that chain before he could enter the port. Well did our barons then perceive that if they did not take that tower and break that chain, they were but as dead men and in very evil case. The time fixed was now come and the knights went on board the transports with their war horses and they were fully armed with their helmets laced and the horses covered with their housings and saddled. All the other folk who were of less consequence in battle were on the great ships. The galleys were fully armed and made ready. The morning was fair, a little after the rising of the sun, and the Emperor Alexius stood waiting for them on the other side with great forces and everything in order. And the trumpets sound and every galley takes a transport in tow so as to reach the other side more readily. None ask who shall go first, but each makes the land as soon as he can. The knights issue from the transports and leap into the sea up to their waists, fully armed, with helmets laced and lances in hand and the good archers and the good sergeants and the good crossbowmen, each in his company, land as soon as they touch ground. The Greeks made a gallant show of resistance, but as soon as it came to the lowering of lances they turned their backs and went away flying, abandoning the shore. And be it known unto you that never was port more proudly taken. Then began the mariners to open the ports of the transports and lower the gangways and take out the horses and the knights began to mount and they began to marshal the divisions of the host in due order.

The successful landing above the tower of Galata did not give access to the harbor of the Golden Horn, for the tower and chain were untouched and by boat the city could throw re-enforcements to Galata. For three days the French attacked the tower which was defended by Pisans, by some Englishmen and perhaps by Genoese who did not wish to see their commercial privileges go to the Venetians. At last the tower was taken and in

---

* Not the present Tower of Galata, but one near the water.

the meantime the Aquila, one of the largest uscieri (horse-transports), with her bows strengthened by iron, had charged the chain under a press of sail and helped by the current, had broken through into the Golden Horn, fighting and sinking the small craft behind the chain. She was followed by all the galleys and the other sailing ships and the whole fleet ran up the entire length of the Horn, taking possession of everything afloat. Thus the Venetians gained a secure harbor and the walls of the city were accessible where they were weakest.

For it must be understood that between the wall on the sea front and the water ran a strip of foreshore which served as a quay for handling goods (see the picture opposite p. 126). These walls were so near the water, however, that in places it was possible for the ships to overreach them with flying bridges swung from the masts and antenne, and thus enable the assulting soldiers to gain the top of the wall. After gaining the harbor, a council was held at which the Doge suggested that the French and Italians should all cross the Golden Horn and attack the waterfront together; but the French said they were not sure of themselves, and would prefer to keep their horses and attack by methods they knew and so it was agreed. On the morning of July 10 the French marched up the left bank of the Horn, accompanied by the fleet as far as the stone bridge, which crossed the Horn at its head outside the walls above the imperial palace of Blachernæ. This had been broken down by the Greeks and a day and night were necessary to repair it.

The host then crossed and camped before the city and Villehardouin says of the long land front pierced by ten gateways, that the host was only enough to attack a single section. It was the same double wall that had repelled the early Saracens. The fleet lay on the sea front near the French, and ships raised their ladders and bridges on board and prepared their mangonels and petraries, while the host did the same on shore. Thus they waited for some days under continual threats and frequent attacks by the garrison, so that of the 6 army divisions one was always in front of the camp and all were called to arms several times a day. Nor could they forage more than 4 bowshots (less than 1 mile) from the camp, yet it was necessary to go out, for they had only flour and bacon and fresh meat from slain horses, and of food in general they had only 3 weeks' supply. So the host built a palisaded barrier about the camp which reduced its losses in the daily skirmishes.

On July 17 all was ready and a joint attack was made by land and sea. The French made a desperate effort and a few men reached the top of the wall but they were driven off at last with considerable loss.

At the same time the Venetian fleet was drawn up in a line 3 bowshots long (1,200 yards). The tops were filled with archers and crossbowmen. Mechanical artillery also was aloft in the tops and on the bows. Boarding bridges swung from the masts. These were built upon the antenne (or yards) with rope side guards whose sides were protected by leather. When first beginning the attack, the galleys maintained a missile action, not running themselves on the beach, yet some of the bridges nearly reached to the top of the wall.

After a little, the nearly blind old Doge standing fully armed in the bow of his ship commanded his people to force her on the beach and soon the great standard of St. Mark was seen on the shore. Then the men poured on shore, those in the deep-draft ships taking to their boats, and in a short time scaling ladders were erected and a lodgment was made on one of the towers. At this the defenders took flight and soon the Venetians were holding 25 towers, nearly a mile of wall. The Doge sent a boat to tell the French of his success and with some irony he forwarded a few horses he had seized on the quay. But the Emperor made such a fierce counter-attack on the Venetians that they feared they could not hold their winnings. As the wind blew upon the city the Doge set fire to the quarter between him and the Greek forces and so retained the wall.

The Emperor Alexius now marched his greatly more numerous army through several gates against the French camp. The latter were few,* but they drew themselves up outside their palisades on the defensive, in such a way that they could only be attacked in front. When the Doge heard of the French danger, he withdrew from his hard-won position on the sea wall and went with all his men that could be spared from the ships to live or die with the French. But no battle followed. The French would not move from the support of the palisades and the Emperor did not

---

* The French force of 10,000 to 12,000 men leaving Venice in 1202 had been reduced by desertions on the way. Robert of Clari says that in July, 1203, only 700 knights were in the camp. With their followers there would be about 5,000 and of these more than half were assigned to defend the camp. Against these the Emperor marched out of the city with 17 divisions, of which 9 faced the crusaders, each from 3,000 to 5,000 strong. Villehardouin says there were 40 Greek divisions, but the estimate is evidently much too high in both cases. The imperial troops cannot have numbered more than 2 or 3 times the French force or there would have been a battle.

venture to charge, but slowly withdrew and "none in the French host was so hardy, but he had great joy thereof."

The French had very little food remaining. Their case was serious, but that very night the Emperor Alexius fled from the city with as much treasure as he could take and as many people as wished to follow him. Those remaining were greatly astonished and took the blinded Emperor Isaac from the prison where his brother had confined him, and clothing him royally, they put him on the throne and sent to the host to announce their deed. While the host stood to arms, French envoys went into the city and found the statement to be true. The Emperor confirmed all the promises made by his son Alexius to the crusading host at Venice and at Zara; namely, to put the whole Empire in obedience to the Church of Rome, to give 200,000 marks of silver ($2,000,000) to the host, to send 10,000 horse and foot with the crusaders to the "land of Babylon" at the imperial expense for a year and to send 500 knights permanently to guard the land over sea. When all was settled with oaths and charters with golden seals, the envoys returned and the barons entered the city.

The blind Emperor was recrowned jointly with his son on August 1 and began to make the stipulated payments, while the Latins quartered themselves on the Galata side of the Golden Horn to avoid friction with the citizens. The Emperor was thus in possession of the city, but the burden of the presence of foreigners was too great. The huge payments to be made, the religious question, and the haughtiness of the strangers quickly led to riots.

Perhaps the trouble was fomented by the Genoese and Pisans who saw their rivals, the Venetians, once more supreme in the city's foreign trade. In a riot between the French and the natives, the city again caught fire. It lasted two days, doing much damage, and all the Latins living in the city (about 15,000) felt obliged to cross the Golden Horn to the crusaders' quarters in Galata. By the end of November the Emperor was no longer carrying out his promises, he professed himself unable to pay, and the Latins sent an embassy to the palace to defy him.

Hostilities opened, lasting well into winter, but with little vigor. The principal effort was a Greek attempt with fire ships to destroy the Venetian fleet which was lying in the Golden Horn, under Galata and out of the current. The entire Latin strength was small and the loss of the fleet would have been an irremediable disaster. Above the city the Greeks prepared a number of old ships which they filled with timber, shavings, pitch, and fat. When the wind blew fresh from the south* at midnight, they got the fire ships under sail and, before setting them on fire, directed them towards the hostile fleet. The whole of Galata was alarmed by the sight, the soldiers rushed to arms and the Venetians to their ships and leaping into their boats they threw grapnels into the fire ships and with the galleys towed them, all burning as they were, again into the main current of the Bosphorus, sweeping past the city. The Greeks manned small boats and shot at the rescuing galleys, but did little damage and only one ship, a Pisan, was destroyed by fire. As Villehardouin says, "deadly was the peril that night, for if the fleet had been consumed we should never have been able to get away by land or sea."

The winter wore on and in January, 1204, another palace revolution put a new emperor on the throne, one Mourzouphles, who threw the blind Isaac once more into prison and killed the young Alexius. The war continued fiercer than before, as the national party was now in power and the Treaty of Zara was not of its making. The new revolution gave the Venetians a new pretext for conquering the city. They were now upholding the Catholic Church against the heretical Orthodox Church. The whole of the Latin gains were now at stake, for without Greek help the French were entirely unequal to attacking Egypt, nor could the Venetians regain their former commercial privileges without violence.

In this hostile country boldness was the only salvation for all. Note that the attack on the land front in July had convinced the French that it was impregnable. The water front was their only chance. The Latins prepared for a new attack on the wall by the Golden Horn, and the Greeks, divining their intention, built up the wall and towers with a timber superstructure so that it was at least two or three stages higher than before, in order to prevent the ships from overtopping it with their bridges. While making ready, the Latins sent out foraging expeditions by sea and land and made arrangements for dividing the whole Roman state between the French and Venetians, after the conquest of the city.

On April 8, the soldiers entered the ships and the next day moved to

* Probably the wind against the current made it easier to handle the fireships when shooting into the Golden Horn.

the assault of the wall along the Golden Horn, where the ships extended in a line over a mile long. The tactics was different from that of the summer, for all the forces were now on board the ships. Before, the ships merely landed their men under cover of the ships' mangonels and the infantry climbed the wall; the bridges prepared were not made use of. Although in several places the pilgrims landed and went against the wall to place their ladders, yet elsewhere the ships were able to approach so close to the shore that from their own bridges swinging from the masts, they were able to cross lances with enemies on the towers. The Latins fought from positions as high as the wall. After a very fierce battle, chiefly with projectiles, lasting some hours, the attack was repulsed and all who had landed were driven on board ship. The Latins had suffered by far the greater losses and had abandoned some machines they had put on shore. But not all the ships withdrew out of range; some remained, exchanging stone shots with the enemy.

At vespers that day the leaders met in a Galata church to discuss affairs and many wished to renew the attack on the Bosphorus side where the walls had not been heightened for the occasion. But the Doge said that the current there would make the operation inadvisable, as the ships could not hold their positions. "Many were those," says Villehardouin, "who would have been glad to have the current take them far away, never to return; for the peril was very great."* In the end it was decided to devote two days to repairs and on the third day to renew their effort, but whereas only one ship had been detailed to the attack of each tower, now 40 ships (uscieri) were joined in pairs, each with flying bridges so that each pair of ships could overpower the men in the tower opposed to them.

On April 12 the fleet again moved to the assault, with the coupled ships in the front line and galleys and small craft in rear to bring men and supplies as needed. The main line of ships had wicker work on their sides to break the force of stone missiles. There were hogsheads of vinegar to extinguish Greek fire, and there was further protection to the ships from skins, iron plates, and baled wool. The result of the first engagement had much encouraged the defense and the wall was crowded. When the action had lasted as before for some time, a strong north wind enabled two great

---

* It is probable these malcontents were not cowardly, but felt that they had been betrayed into an attack on Christians.

FIG. 14.—ASSAULT ON CONSTANTINOPLE, BY TINTORETTO

Although this painting is of the sixteenth century, it shows the walls and foreshore of the city. The mode of using the antenne to reach the top of the wall is perhaps in error for Robert de Clari says the antenne carried real bridges with footways and parapets at the sides. Note the crossbow in the foreground, being wound up; its cranequin is of a type differing from that shown in a previous picture of a crossbow.

ships lashed together, the *Pilgrim* and the *Paradise*, to approach so near to a tower, one on each side, that the *Pilgrim* landed her bridge on its top and a bold Venetian and a knight of France entered the tower. Others followed and it was won. Other knights, seeing the initial success, landed and, under the cover of those already on top, placed their ladders directly against the wall and gained four towers. Soon three gates were beaten in and the army entered the city. There was slaughter until dusk and then the victors assembled near the towers they had taken. The Emperor retired to his palace of Bucoleon and escaped by the Golden Gate during the night, but the Latins knew nothing of it and so certain Frenchmen who feared an attack set fire to the buildings in their neighborhood and so caused the third great fire since the arrival of the Latins.

The city was now completely at the mercy of the victors who sacked it most cruelly and seized an enormous amount of booty, the Venetians and French each dividing among themselves 400,000 marks of silver ($4,000,000).* The victors elected an emperor from among their number and divided the Empire among themselves. To Venice fell Epirus, the Ionian Islands, the Peloponnese with the port of Modon, the islands of Crete and Eubœa and others in the Ægean, besides a section of the city as her commercial base. Most of these possessions the Venetian state granted in fief to her principal great families and thus with bases assured throughout the East she was about to enter on a period of unexampled commercial prosperity. But the barrier which for centuries the Empire had maintained against the advance of the Saracens into Europe was destroyed by the crusaders at the demand of Venetian greed.

Strategically, this conquest of Constantinople differs from the Saracen attempts in the seventh and eighth centuries in the complete mastery of the attacking maritime forces. Against the Saracens the Greek navy was sufficiently effective to preserve the sea walls from assault and more or less the water communications of the city. Against the tremendous land walls the Saracens had no chance. Tactically the crusading fleet was used to throw the infantry against the walls in the usual method of assault, with the ships covering the infantry by artillery. In the attack of July the Venetians were successful, but they had no reserve to complete their suc-

---

* The wealth of the city in money, jewels, and portable goods alone has been estimated at 12,000,000 marks ($120,000,000).

cess, for the French were away at Blachernæ and themselves were para-
lyzed by the overwhelming numbers of the Greek army. In April this
fault was corrected. All the Latin force was on shipboard and was directed
against a single section of the wall from the ships themselves. It was easy
to throw the entire army into the city as soon as an entrance had been established.

Naval Situation in the Mediterranean in the Thirteenth Century

The ships and fleets of the three great maritime cities of Italy were in
frequent engagements, some of them very important, but few are so well
described by contemporary accounts that we can clearly see what were their
tactical peculiarities. Besides the maritime rivalry, Italy was much disturbed during the thirteenth century by the disputes between the Papacy
and the Western Empire for the control of Italy. In the wars arising out
of these dissensions, the island of Sicily took a great part, for the fleets of
the Italian commercial cities as well as that of Aragon in Spain were drawn
into the strife of the Emperor and Papacy over Sicily.

War Between Pisa and Genoa, 1282-84 (See Map IV)

In the course of the thirteenth century Genoa slowly developed her
commerce at the expense of Venice and of Pisa. The Latin Empire established at Constantinople in 1204 by France and Venice had not been able
to maintain itself after 1261, and the re-established Greek dynasty was on
the best of terms with Genoa. In consequence, Venetian business in the
East had suffered and the Genoese were prospering. Pisa was allied with
Venice and with the kingdom of Naples and Sicily. She was competing
with Genoa for the control of government and commerce in Corsica and
Sardinia. Although wealthy, Pisa was a city with little back country to
furnish a full quota of sailors and she was not on good terms with her
neighboring cities, which took the opposite side in Italian politics.

In 1282, Venice was disputing with Constantinople about control of
the slave trade of the Black Sea and Naples was embarrassed by the outbreak of the revolution known as the Sicilian Vespers; yet, in spite of the
preoccupation of both her allies, Pisa chose this moment for an effort to
regain territory in Corsica. Genoa was soon convinced that Pisa was looking

for trouble and sent a squadron to the mouth of the Arno in August, 1282, but soon withdrew it. As the season was good, the Genoese might have remained longer intercepting Pisan trade, but many ships were commissioned *ad apodixas;* that is, by a feudal levy for a definite short time, and it was probably necessary to return for the harvest of figs and grapes.

The Genoese government made every preparation for war in 1283. To have the necessary crews at hand, merchant ships were kept from sailing; arrangements were made to have 120 galleys ready, and building was begun at Genoa and on both Rivieras. For this fleet at least 15,000 to 17,000 rowers and seamen were necessary (all freemen and using their arms in battle) besides soldiers who were not so numerous as in later centuries. Half the ships would belong to the state and the rest would be rented or freely loaned by private owners. While Genoa was getting ready, Pisa was guarding against surprise. Petty warfare in every part of the Mediterranean was mantained by a cloud of corsairs, among which were many of the state ships. Both Pisa and Genoa were filled with spies, so that both sides had good intelligence service.

The campaign of 1283 was a lively one, but without any important engagement. The two fleets came together off Porto Vecchio in the peninsula of Piombino, where a part of the Pisan fleet sheltered itself behind a line of piling driven for the purpose and with sunken ships in the main channel. Here it was blockaded by the entire Genoese squadron, but when the other part of the Pisan fleet came up the Genoese gave chase, taking some and driving others on shore. The blockaded part of the Pisan fleet now escaped to Porto Pisano* where it made itself safe behind the chain (a section of which may now be seen in the Campo Santo at Pisa). It was able to get away because the blockading force thought it necessary to renew its water before returning to Porto Vecchio, although it had been out of port only a little over a week. One of the most marked strategic limitations on medieval admirals was the frequent need of watering and good water was not everywhere to be found. After 10 days out, watering was necessarily a primary preoccupation.

The proper strategy for Pisa this year was, as Manfroni says, to weary the enemy by avoiding battle with big forces and to use her bases in Sar-

---

* Porto Pisano was a fortified indentation in the coast immediately north of Leghorn Harbor. The site of the anchorage is now part of Leghorn city.

dinia to issue out to capture single ships, thus obliging Genoa to keep her fleet ready. Then when the latter was obliged to send her crews home for the harvest, the Pisan fleet could strike. Such had been the successful course in previous wars, but now Pisa's pride was averse to it.

BATTLE OF MELORIA, 1284

The year 1284 opened with an attempt by a Genoese fleet to seize Porto Torres and the town of Sassari in the northwest part of Sardinia. A little later the Genoese merchant fleet bound for Romania (the Empire) met with a Pisan force and defeated it. Genoa now felt sure that Venice would not break the peace in spite of her alliance with Pisa, so she tried to profit commercially by her success. A Genoese squadron now blockaded Porto Pisano and captured Pisan ships in Sardinian waters and the Grecian archipelago. In particular, a Genoese squadron of 30 galleys under Benedetto Zaccaria, manned *ad apodixas*, went to Porto Torres in July to send its crews to aid in the siege of Sassari. By this time Pisa had resolved to make her utmost effort, but in secret. However, she could not collect several thousand rowers and soldiers without reports reaching Genoa. The Commander in Chief there, Oberto Doria, became suspicious and recalled Zaccaria, while he assembled at Genoa the crews living along the Riviera in order to be ready for any service.

Suddenly Genoa heard that the Pisan squadron, 72 strong, had put to sea on July 22, under the Podesta Morosini, and Ugolino della Gherardesca, and was bound for Albenga on the western Riviera about 40 miles from Genoa with the probable intention of cutting off Zaccaria whose order to return must have become known in Pisa. Instantly Doria manned all available ships, 58 galleys and 8 pamphylians (rowing craft with 48 to 60 rowers for scouting and dispatch service). On July 31, The Pisan fleet appeared unexpectedly off Genoa. It is not clear why it did so, but perhaps Morosini thought he might secure a battle with the squadron at Genoa and afterwards be able to meet Zaccaria. On sighting the Pisan fleet, Doria left port and formed outside for battle, remaining motionless thereafter. Zaccaria arrived in port that day and probably the lookouts on the hills above the city could see his squadron coming on while it was still invisible to the enemy at sea level. No doubt Doria would have fought to save Zaccaria and was inactive in the hope that he might catch the enemy between two forces, but Zaccaria did not think of fighting and entered port. This junction of the two Genoese squadrons ruined Morosini's plan. The Pisan chronicler explains the failure of Morosini as being due to an unfavorable wind which detained him at the mouth of the Arno, after leaving Pisa, while Genoa learned of his movement.

To take advantage of his assembled and superior strength, Doria came out of port that night and moved to the little roadstead of Sturla, 2 miles east of Genoa, hoping that Morosini would close with the harbor, and finding it empty, would attempt to go in, when Doria would fall on him.

But in the morning only the Pisan sails could be seen far on the western horizon. Doria had to pursue, but several courses were open to Morosini. He might go as far as Nice and then cross to Corsica and ravage Genoese territory and seize shipping there, or he might stop to attack Savona and Porto Maurizio and return again to Genoa, hoping to find the fleet absent in search of him, or he might be going back to Pisa after the failure of the plan of surprise. Of all this Doria must have thought, for, with his ships spreading far to the south, he ran down the coast as far as Porto Maurizio, where he heard that the Pisans had turned toward Cape Corso. He followed them, and learned that the enemy, only a few hours ahead of him, had watered there and headed for Porto Pisano on August 5. On the sixth Doria also appeared off Porto Pisano where the Pisans still were, not yet having gone up to the city.*

In order to be sure that the Pisans would not refuse battle, Doria divided his fleet into two parts. The main body of 63 galleys and 8 pamphylians he placed in the front, formed in a single line with the center somewhat advanced, with the sails loosed (the weather must have been calm). This line was in eight divisions, each under a "protontino" or vice admiral, but not separated from one another. Zaccaria, with 30 vessels, formed the reserve. His masts were down and he was far enough away not to attract attention, or if seen, the enemy might think his ships the usual group of small craft which followed fleets. However, Zaccaria was not too far off to be readily called forward.

In the afternoon the Genoese first line was about 3 miles from Porto Pisano, inside and abreast the tower and shoals of Meloria. The Pisans

---

* There is another account of the battle tactics employed which says that the Pisan fleet came from the city.

were anchored under the protection of the towers of the port and, having counted the masts and seen that the enemy was somewhat inferior in number, the Pisan fleet got under way and, forming a single line, rowed boldly toward the enemy. As the fleets were drawing within range, Morosini identified the second Genoese line under Zaccaria and understood his danger, but Doria was now advancing and it was impossible to retreat without incurring a disorderly flight. There was nothing to do but to see it through. The accounts which have come down to us say nothing of maneuvers and tell only of a bitter struggle, but it is probable that Zaccaria enveloped one of the Pisan wings and cut it off from retreat.

The engagement opened with missile weapons, crossbows, mangonels, and other hurling devices. On coming nearer, they used quick lime, liquid soap, boiling oil, and hand projectiles. According to a Genoese account, the Pisans wore heavy armor, while the Genoese were stripped, whereby the latter were more active and fresh while the former were exhausted by the summer heat. Although the Pisans had the disadvantage of the sun in their eyes, they fought bravely and when the Genoese closed for the boarders' fight, there was great slaughter. The two Commanders in Chief were opposed to each other and the battle was uncertain until Zaccaria brought his ship also against the Pisan flagship and, apparently coming from the rear, cut down the standard flying at her stern. Its disappearance shook the courage of all and marked the moment of Pisan defeat. With the smaller part of the fleet, Gherardesca escaped, to meet a few years later the dreadful fate of which Dante tells us in his *Inferno*.* The Pisans lost 30 ships taken and 7 sunk. Others ran ashore and only about 30 saved themselves with Gherardesca behind the chain of Porto Pisano. The Pisan losses in killed, wounded and prisoners may be estimated as not less than 8,000 men out of 14,000 engaged. Manfroni puts the losses as under 10,000.

Doria wished to surprise Porto Pisano after the battle by a general assault, but the fortifications were good and behind them were the remains of the Pisan fleet. Besides, after the battle, many of the Genoese galleys went off to Porto Venere without waiting for orders, so Doria followed with the rest and had hardly arrived there when a heavy southwest gale came up which would have destroyed his ships had they remained off Porto Pisano. The Tuscan cities, who were Guelph in their sympathies, now

---

* Imprisoned with sons and grandsons, they died of starvation.

tried to induce Genoa to join them in an alliance to destroy Pisa; but, although her commercial rival, Genoa was Ghibelline in Italian politics and did not wish to see Guelph rule established permanently in Pisa. So Ugolino della Gherardesca was able by negotiation to save Pisa from utter ruin, but her greatness had departed.

This campaign is of interest for the strategic movements preceding the battle, and for the use in the battle of the Genoese second line as a reserve thrown on the hostile rear to turn the scale at the height of the battle.

SICILIAN WARS

Toward the end of the thirteenth century there were several naval battles of importance in the development of naval tactics arising out of the situation of Sicily in Italian politics. These showed Ruggiero di Lauria as the greatest admiral of the Middle Ages as well as one of the cruelest of victors.

In the middle of the thirteenth century, after the death of the Emperor Frederick II of Germany, king of the Two Sicilies, the Pope claimed to reassume the suzerainty of the Kingdom of the Two Sicilies which had been a Papal possession in previous centuries, and in 1262 he bestowed the crown on the brother of King Louis of France, Charles, Count of Anjou and of Provence (then independent of France). With a French army Charles gained possession of the Pope's gift, but in 1282 the cruelties of the French rulers in Sicily brought about the insurrection known as the Sicilian Vespers.

The King of Aragon took up the cause of the Sicilians and was chosen King of the island, thus inducing hostilities which lasted for 20 years. Naturally, the warfare for the control of Sicily, fought between Aragonese forces and Angevins working from Naples, depended on the fleets of the two powers. The Aragonese navy is little heard of before the conquest of the Balearic Islands which took place in 1229, when it began to develop under Italian instruction and leadership. By the latter part of the century it was well established with a great dockyard at Barcelona and owed much of its effectiveness to the unusual skill of its Catalan crossbowmen. At this time Catalonia turned toward the sea and her ships spread over the Mediterranean. Thus when Peter, King of Aragon and Count of Catalonia, assumed the crown of Sicily, he had a good fleet

MAP OF SPAIN

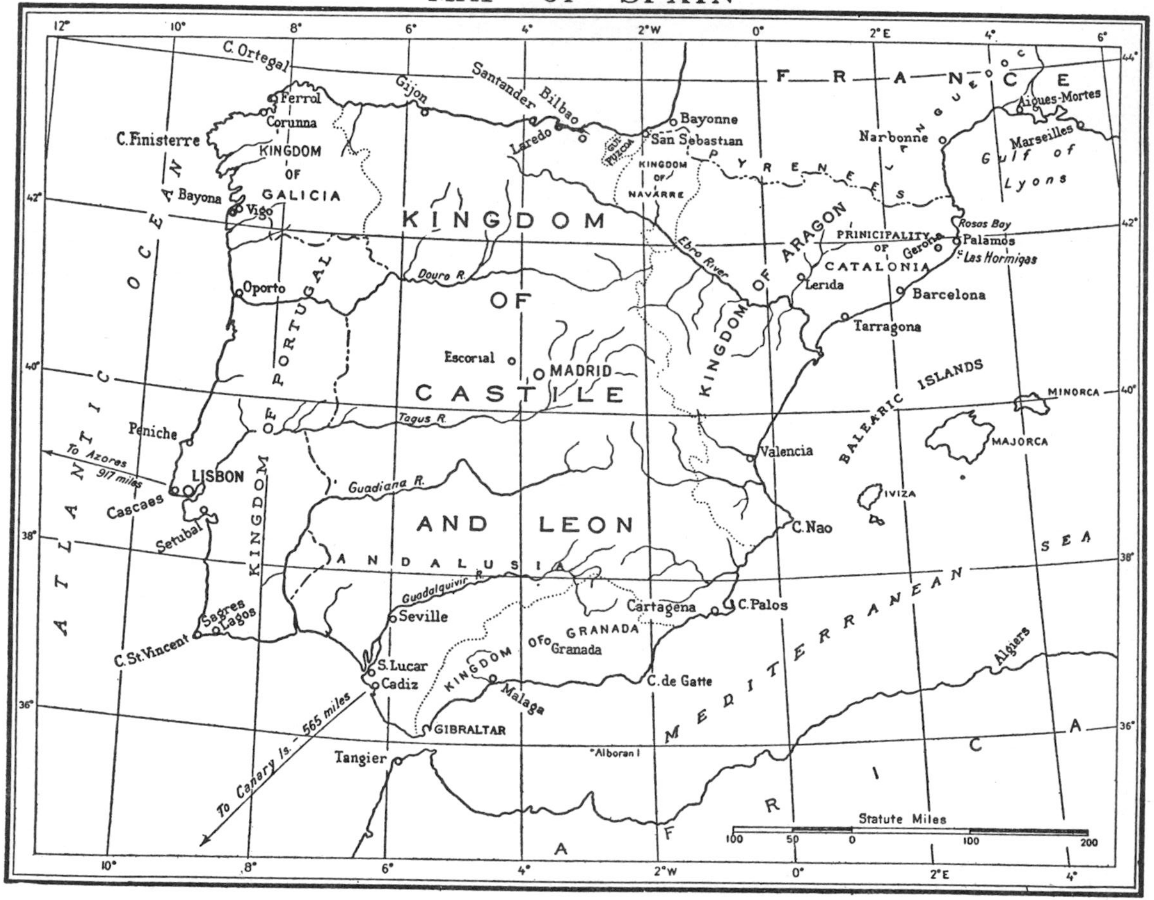

MAP VII

available to bring against the motley and inefficient Angevin fleet at Naples manned by Provençals and Italians.

Ruggiero di Lauria was appointed to command the fleet sent to Sicily by King Peter and he developed a strong and efficient Sicilian squadron. He gained a victory over a Provençal squadron at Malta in 1283 and the next year over an Angevin fleet in the Bay of Naples, and so made the Spanish rule secure in Sicily. By way of creating a diversion for the Angevin cause, the Pope gave the Kingdom of Aragon to the son of King Philip of France.

BATTLE OF ROSAS BAY

In the spring of 1285, while the Spanish-Sicilian squadron was continuing its raids on the coast of Southern Italy, the King of France was preparing a great invasion of Aragon to put his son on its throne. A large army moved toward the Pyrenees, a powerful fleet of 100 galleys was equipped along the shores of France. The King's commissaries enrolled seamen from Pisa to Narbonne and adventurers from all countries were welcomed. The administration and discipline in the fleet left much to be desired.

Against this large force King Peter could oppose only 12 galleys and 4 lyns (a type of round ship). He had no more, for the greater part of the Catalan strength had gone to supplement the Sicilian fleet and was guarding Sicily from the Angevin King of Naples. Although King Peter sent repeated requests for naval aid to his son James, Regent of Sicily, it did not come until late, for the Regent and Lauria seem to have thought it necessary to make Sicily secure before reducing their force there.

Through May and June the great French army invading Catalonia advanced 60 miles, meeting only slight opposition, and besieged Gerona which made prolonged resistance. About 25 miles northeast of Gerona the army advanced base was established on the shore of the Bay of Rosas which the navy occupied to guard the maritime line of supply from French ports. While 25 galleys held the bay, 25 others formed the escort of the supply ships to and from France and others still cruised as far as Barcelona nearly 100 miles southward. For the good fortune of the Spaniards, a pestilence cut down the French rowers, but even so, the danger would have been very great had the French Admiral, Lodeve, been enterprising. As it was, King Peter called Spanish pirates to his aid and they raided the French shipping, going even to French ports, and took prizes, with supplies for the army.

The strategic situation of the French army is worthy of comparison with that of Cæsar in his first Spanish compaign when his army from Gaul was checked before Ilerda (Lerida) and was dependent for supplies coming by sea from the Gulf of Lyons. It will be recollected that, after the victories of Brutus over the Marseilles fleet, the prospect for Cæsar brightened. In his case, as in that of King Philip, the invading army was dependent on supplies by sea.

At first the Catalan squadron at Barcelona did not venture to attack the greatly superior French fleet, but encouraged by the success of the pirates against the French line of supply, it ventured north with 11 galleys. Knowing that on a certain date only 25 ships would be at Rosas, the two Spanish admirals made an attack at dawn on the enemy. They were discovered by the hostile guard ships in time for the French to come out and oppose them; but, although only one-half the French strength, the Catalans lashed their ships together, charged the enemy, and cut through his formation, dividing it into three parts. All the Catalan vessels then surrounded the center group of 7 French ships and, after a hard fight, these surrendered. The Spaniards then turned against the Narbonnese group to the south and these soon drew off, whereupon the Marseilles ships, forming the other French wing, also retired.

The Spaniards then put all their prisoners, except those likely to offer ransom, in 2 of the prizes and sank them and headed towards Barcelona with the remaining 5 prizes. After going about 10 miles, they found themselves pursued by the rest of the French fleet which had been at Palamos (north of San Filiu) only a few miles south of Rosas. As it was impossible to make good speed with their prizes, these were scuttled and abandoned and the Spaniards were able to keep ahead of their pursuers till dark when they shook them off, and returned in triumph to Barcelona.

BATTLE OF LAS HORMIGAS

About August 1 Lauria left Sicily for Spain, going by way of Africa in order not to have too long a stretch at sea. He left behind 10 ships to guard Sicily and took 40 with him. He arrived at Barcelona in the last days of August when Gerona was on the point of surrender. As the contemporary chronicler d'Esclot says, they sailed into port with their banners spread and shields along the gunwales from end to end on both sides, and between every two shields was a crossbow. This latter detail suggests that the proper number of soldiers for any ship was one man to each yard of side (besides reserves), the same as in an infantry line. After 3 days' rest in Barcelona, Lauria joined the Catalan ships to his own Sicilians and set forth the last of August, keeping well out to sea, to attack the French fleet and, if possible, break up the French line of communications and so relieve Gerona.*

The French fleet had not heard of the arrival of Lauria and, on the day after he sailed north, 25 of the best French ships with selected crews started south from Rosas to attack the 10 or 12 Catalan ships which they knew to be at Barcelona. At the close of the day the French squadron anchored for the night with stern lines to the beach in the little bay of San Filiu, about 30 miles from Rosas. The rocks of "Las Hormigas" near by gave the name to the battle. The fleet of Lauria, keeping out of sight of land, would have passed the enemy during the night had it not been for a group of belated ships.

Four of the Sicilian squadron had been delayed on the way from Africa and, on arriving at Barcelona a few hours after Lauria had gone, their commander permitted no one to land. After a short interview with the King, he pressed forward under oars and sail, together with 8 small craft of the city. This detachment, hurrying along close to shore, saw the French fleet and mistook it for its own, while the French took the Sicilians for the small squadron, of which they were in search, and pursued. The Sicilians recognized their error in time and as darkness fell they not only got away, but found their main body near by and brought Lauria back, who did not hesitate to make a night attack, a thing most unusual.

Arriving off the harbor, he sent scouts to examine the situation and then divided his force into two divisions. He took 30 ships under his own command and arranged that the other group of about 20 should wait at one side near the harbor entrance, while Lauria was to alarm the French and withdraw before them until his second squadron could get in their

---

* The contemporary versions of the battle differ widely. This account is based on that of d'Esclot and the modern one of Manfroni.

rear. Thereupon Lauria circled to seaward and, returning, he woke the enemy by sound of trumpet and hoisted a recognition light on each ship. The French ships hastily cleared for battle and chased Lauria, but soon found the other Sicilian squadron in their rear, shouting "Aragon" and "Santa Maria delle Scale," the latter the cry of Messina and used by all from Sicily. The French were much outnumbered, but as the enemy closed on them they answered the cry of Aragon by the same word and similarly they answered the Sicilians by their word, so that Lauria ordered another recognition light for his ships, but the French repeated this also and Lauria then saw that nothing would serve but a boarders' fight, and the fleet closed in. Lauria's own ship struck a Frenchman a glancing blow and swept away its oars. The shock pitched the French crossbowmen along the side into the sea. After a desperate action 12 French galleys, still shouting the hostile war cry and showing enemy's lights, escaped in the dark and reached Aigues Mortes in France.

The 13 prizes were in much danger from a gale on the way to Barcelona, but in the end reached there safely. Here the wounded were fastened to long cables on the beach and the other ends passed on board a galley; the ship rowed seaward and the unhappy prisoners were drowned in the sight of the city. The remaining prisoners who were without ransom value were blinded and under the charge of one of their number who was spared one eye, they were sent to the French King at Gerona.

In the meantime Gerona had surrendered, but an increasing number of Spaniards was confronting the French army and the latter's situation was becoming very difficult. The victorious fleet was now in control of the sea. It went to Rosas, which it seized after destroying the rest of the French fleet. Lauria then sent a part of his command to pursue the French cargo ships into their home waters, while the crews remaining at Rosas entrenched there, repelled an attack of French cavalry sent to recapture the French base, and then marched into the interior and appeared on the flank of the French army, which by this time had abandoned all hope of success and was making a slow and disastrous retreat before the Spanish King.

The Sicilians were anxious to return home and insisted on going in spite of the lateness of the season. Lauria consented to go too in order not to be left alone, but they were overtaken by a severe norther at the end of November and many ships were lost.

The success of the whole invasion of Spain turned on the work of the French fleet in keeping open communications with France, and in this it failed. The night attack at Las Hormigas brought about unusual tactics. Since darkness and uncertainty of recognition made long-distance crossbow battle impossible, the action was a boarders' battle from the first. The use of a reserve force to make an attack from the rear which was common in this century seems to have been unusually well carried out.

BATTLE OF CAPE ORLANDO

In 1286 King Peter of Aragon died and his son and successor, Alphonso, left Sicily to his brother James as regent in a semi-independent status to resist the Pope and the House of Anjou. The Sicilian navy, built up by Aragon, was able to protect the island. Hostilities with Naples continued with more or less vigor for many years, and by 1297 the conditions had much changed. The Angevin navy was not good and made efforts to obtain aid from Genoa. King Alphonso had been succeeded on the throne of Aragon by his brother James who was replaced in Sicily by King Peter's third son, Frederick. James found himself insecure at home and to better himself there he made a disgraceful peace with Charles II of Naples whereby he not only renounced the throne of Sicily but agreed to help Charles recover it. The Regent Frederick, however, refused to surrender his authority to Charles and was crowned King by the Sicilians with the expectation that he would enable them to resist the Angevin attempt at reconquest. Lauria, however, retained his loyalty for King James, and, renouncing the Sicilian navy which he had created, placed his services at the disposal of King Charles.

In 1298 the Catalans and Italians made an effort to reconquer Sicily and renewed the effort in 1299, when King James returned to Italy, accompanied by Lauria. At Naples the King manned 46 Catalan and 10 Angevin galleys, with some cargo ships, apparently meaning to disembark his troops at Patti on the north coast of Sicily about 30 miles west of Messina. Hearing that his brother King Frederick had manned 40 galleys and was at sea to intercept him, he kept a few miles farther to the west and landed at Cape Orlando.

King Frederick understood the advantage of striking an enemy wishing to land and embarrassed by his convoy. He had hastened to leave Messina, but was a little late and he now made the mistake of not attacking immediately on arrival. It is said his delay was incurred for the sake of having the aid of 8 ships coming from the west, which were then at Cefalu 40 miles away. However it was, the delay was unfortunate, for James had time to unload his horses, his sick, and his stores and also to transfer the infantry in the taride* to re-enforce the soldiers on the galleys. Besides it was a mistake for Frederick, having the weaker force, to sacrifice the advantage of surprise for the sake of a small re-enforcement. All the advantage was now on the side of the allies—numbers, position, discipline, efficiency of the crossbowmen, and skill of the commander; for, although King James was present, there can be no doubt that he entrusted the conduct of the battle to Lauria.

On July 4, 1299, Lauria drew up his ships along the shore, with the center ships somewhat advanced and all so closely chained together that, as the chronicler says, not even the Genoese or the Venetians could have broken through the line. It is also probable that flying bridges from the ships' sterns to shore enabled the soldiers already on shore to re-enforce the ships' crews. Against this formation, King Frederick moved with 19 ships to the right of his flagship and 20 to his left. His ships also were chained together. For some time they fought at a distance with crossbows until one of Frederick's captains, anxious to close, cut his cables to his neighbors and pushed forward alone. To help him in his danger, others did the same. The line was broken on both sides and the battle became confused. The first Sicilian ship to break the line had already been taken when 6 of King James' ships which had been held away from the scene by Lauria fell upon the rear of the Sicilians, who now began to lose heart and give way. The Sicilian flagship was the first to withdraw, but it is said that the King was unconscious from heat and exhaustion and that his captain wished to put him in safety. It cannot be believed that this bold and dashing King, who established the independence of Sicily against the

---

* See p. 112 this chapter.

Pope, the Angevins, and Aragon, ran away as his enemies allege. Only 12 Sicilian ships got off. The others were taken by Lauria after vigorous resistance and their crews slaughtered by him to avenge the death of his nephew, killed by King Frederick not long before.

The whole island was now at the mercy of King James but he did nothing. There were discords between him and the Angevins. He returned to Spain and the lieutenants of Charles of Anjou were then defeated in the island. The war dragged on, and in the end King Frederick established his rule in Sicily by the peace of Caltabellotta in 1302.

SUMMARY

Before closing this chapter it is worth while to mention some of the possibilities of galley warfare which may not be described as tactics. With reference to the battle of Meloria where Doria deceived his enemy by letting his sails hang, we may refer to the conduct of the Venetian ships against the Genoese at the battle of Laiazzo in 1294. The Venetians were there superior in numbers and, either through over-confidence or lack of time, they went into battle with their masts standing and antenne hoisted, with sails hanging unfurled. The Genoese masts were down as customary. As the fleets drew near, a head breeze turned the Venetian ships broadside to the Genoese so that the mechanical artillery in the bows no longer bore on them. At the same time the length of formation, which was enough for a line, was not enough for a column of ships and several were obliged to drop out and could not engage the enemy, so that the Genoese had a double advantage and gained a most important victory.

Another incident, worth speaking of foreshadowing future developments of sailing ships as the principal type in war, occurred in 1353 in a war between Venice and Aragon allied against Genoa. The objective of the allies was to seize Alghero in Sardinia, near which the two forces met. The galley fleets were large on both sides and the allies had in addition three large cogs (see p. 113 this chapter) with crews of 300 men each. As the two lines drew near enough for a missile action, the breeze freshened and the 3 heavy cogs, probably 10 times the displacement of the galleys, took advantage of the breeze to make sail and charge into the Genoese line and override as many Genoese galleys. The battle lasted some time longer, but in the end the Genoese were defeated in spite of their greater numbers.

AUTHORITIES CHIEFLY CONSULTED IN THIS CHAPTER

CONSTANTINOPLE

Cambridge Medieval History, vol. IV.

CLARI, ROBERT OF, *Chronicle.*

MANFRONI, C., *Storia della Marina Italiana.*

PEARS, E., *Fall of Constantinople.*

VILLEHARDOUIN, GEOFFROI DE, *Chronicle of the Conquest of Constantinople* (translation).

SICILY AND SPAIN

Cambridge Medieval History, vol. VI.

D'ESCLOT, BERNAT, *Cronica del Rey en Pere* (translation by F. L. Crutchlow).

MANFRONI, C., *Storia della Marina Italiana.*

MUNTANER, RAMON, *Cronica Catalana* (translation by Lady Goodenough).

RONCIÈRE, C., *Histoire de la Marine Française.*

CHAPTER IX

WAR OF CYPRUS
AND CAMPAIGN OF LEPANTO

SEE MAPS IV AND IX-X

THE STATUS OF NAVAL TACTICS

F ROM the fourteenth century till near the end of the sixteenth there
was no great development in naval tactics. Both sailing ships and
rowing ships became somewhat larger and the use of guns increased,
but did not become predominant. The boarders' fight continued to be the
principal phase of battle and was tactically decisive. Early in the sixteenth
century the arquebus, the predecessor of the musket, became serviceable
as an infantry weapon, but it could scarcely be said to replace the bow
and the crossbow for another half-century.

The ram did not develop. The "spur," as it was called by Mediterranean seamen, was a stout spar placed like a present-day bowsprit, and its
purpose was to break up the "telaro," the rectangular rowing frame extending outside the vessel to support the oars. Occasionally, by a direct
thrust against the broadside of a hostile ship, the stem penetrated her hull.
More frequently glancing collisions, in the act of closing in order to board,
caused leaks more or less serious, and sometimes fatal. We may therefore
pass over the great naval wars in the Mediterranean from the fourteenth
century to the time of Lepanto. It is to be remarked, however, that in
this period the tactical methods of battle became more or less stabilized and
there was some formal instruction therein. There are still available for
examination the lectures of one Alonzo de Chaves, under the title of
"Mirror for Seamen." He wrote about 1530 and was the official lecturer
for the Spanish Admiralty of the Indies.

NOTE: A brief synopsis of what Chaves formally taught Spanish seamen will be interesting
to compare with the actual conduct of the battle of Lepanto. These Spanish views are the more
important since they were known in England and no doubt had some influence on British
practice. It should be remembered in reading what follows that, although Chaves was speaking
about sailing ships (nefs), yet the development of sailing-ship tactics had not yet become very

different from that of rowing ships, which was still the norm. Chaves still formed the sailing ships in line and still hoped to board very early in the action.
(From Cesareo Fernandez Duro: *Armada Español,* vol. I, appendix 12.)

CLEARING SHIP FOR ACTION

The captain must keep a good lookout. If a probable enemy is sighted, he must clear the deck, the poop, and the castles. He must put all the bedding along the sides [for armor] and get the ports open and the guns ready. All the "servidores" [the removable chambers for breech-loading guns] must be loaded below deck and brought up to the guns. The arms and shields must be ready, the pavesade [shield wall along the rail] must be rigged. Plenty of stones [ballast for use as missiles] must be brought on deck and two or three sheafs of darts [harpoons]. The tops must have their pavesade of mattresses, and many small boxes of powder or tar with matches,* and others of sifted quick lime and hand grenades with linstocks; also ballistas or escopetas [muskets] with lighted matches. The men below will make a barricade of mattresses behind the pavesade [i.e., across the ship to check the enemy's advance if he should get on board at either end].

The gunners with two helpers for each will make their artillery ready. They will get up a keg of powder and place it on the poop, lashed to the mast, and cover it with a damp cloth. Half-barrels filled with water and wet swabs will be ready to put out fire. Water will be placed about the deck to quench thirst.

The captain will be on the poop to see well.

The carpenter and caulker will have lanterns below deck with planks, sheet lead, and tools to stop leaks. The captain will put safety lashings and "preventer" gear wherever they may be needed for the masts and rigging. He will close all hatches to keep men from running below. If the weather is good, he will hoist out the boat. In it he will put 15 or 16 well-armed men with shields and arquebuses, and a couple of hatchets, some large augers and wedges, and each man will have his oar. These men will keep their boat on the side of the ship away from the enemy.

MANNER OF BATTLE

The captain will fire his bow guns or broadside guns of the side from which he is about to board. The lower guns are to be fired only when the ships are near and then at the water line where they will cause leaks even if not piercing. The upper guns and the small ones fire at the sides and sails and masts and at men on the poop, taking care not to fire blanks, as often happens through haste. At each discharge the "servidor" will be withdrawn, cleaned, and sent below for reloading, for the powder must not be handled on deck; but if there is hurry, the barrel at the mast may be used.

While the artillery is firing at a distance, the crossbows and arquebuses must do nothing, but wait until the enemy is close or in the act of boarding.

If our ship is bigger and more strongly manned, even if with less artillery, she should close after the first broadside, or even before, if she can. She should grapple the enemy, so as not to let the latter fire often.

If you wish to board and the enemy has fired his broadside, let your small-arm men get in action, particularly those in the tops. The "afferrador" [man throwing grappling hook]

---

* A means of preserving fire. Usually a cord wet with a solution of saltpeter and then dried, to use as kindling for firing guns or mines. A slow-match smoldered like a cigar and was available for a long time. A quick-match burned much faster and might be several yards long.

should put the iron in the rigging or the forecastle where it will hold well and the cable must be hauled in so as to keep it taut. Then the small-arms men get busy without losing a shot. The men in the tops will empty their boxes of powder and tar, having lighted their matches and also throw the soap and oil to make the hostile decks slippery. Use stones and arrows also. To repel boarders the greased pikes are good. [The grease was only near the head so the enemy could not grip.] Every one will now fight with steel and with fire-arms. Those with long-handled sickles will cut the enemy's rigging. Those with fire tubes on long handles will try to light the gear of the other ship; and all these efforts must be made with loud cries and all arms must support each other. If the enemy gets fire into our ship, it must be put out with wet swabs.

If the other ship catches fire, we must cut adrift from her. When the two ships have grappled, our boat must go under the other's stern and cut the rudder adrift or jam it with the wedges. If more can be done without discovery, bore holes in her. Or while all the enemy are occupied on one side, our boat's crew should board on the other side or at least cut the shrouds or the rudder, or, if they cannot come close alongside, they should fire the boat gun at the rudder. On the other hand, if the enemy boards us, pikes and swords are the best weapons to repel him. The boarders' netting is an obstacle and, as the boarders try to get over it, we with our pikes from underneath should force them to jump into the sea. Similarly, if we enter the enemy's ship, the broad swords and shields of the corselet men are the best weapons. As soon as our men have entered, some must fight and others must cut the halyards to bring the antenne [yards] down.

If the enemy yields, the men must be told to go below, and the officers must be directed to go on board our ship. Then the men must be called on deck and the ship searched.

FLEET HANDLING

There must be a commander in chief to have unity of action. When battle is near, he will call all the fleet into order, for that is necessary as in other battle [on shore]. He must keep the heavy ships together to close with the enemy and board, and the medium ones are to stand off a little and use their guns and chase those of the enemy who leave the line. The commander in chief will put one-quarter part of the light ships to form on the flanks of the line, to see what is going on. He must tell the boarding ships not to let an enemy get on each side. He must call out one-quarter of the ships' boats to act as has been mentioned against the ships which have been grappled. They must not get between the big ships and be crushed. They must try to pick up the men who fall overboard. Having done all this, with his remaining three-quarters of his fleet, the commander in chief will look about and try for a windward position and see if the enemy is in one body; and also if he is in column or in line, and if the heavy ships are in the middle or at the end, and where the hostile admiral has placed himself. The commander in chief must get his fleet to windward to have the advantage of the drifting smoke; then the enemy may fire on his own ships. If the enemy divides into squadrons, he must do the same, putting the big ships forward to be the first in action. The commander in chief should be in the middle to see what goes on. The fleet should form in line for all to see the enemy, which they could not do in column. The rear guard is the "help" squadron and is the quarter part of the fleet. They should be the fastest ships to see what is going on, and they should be on the flanks rather than in the rear.

If the enemy is in line, we must be the same, with the heavy ships in the middle. If the enemy is in double echelon, we must be in two wings to take him between our lines, making him fight on both sides. If the enemy is in two wings, we must be the same, opening the flanks and closing at the center, so as to catch the enemy on both sides, for we must not be surrounded.

And all must understand the signals.

BATTLE

The commander in chief will sound the trumpets and all will move as ordered. The heavy artillery will begin, firing not too high; and, if we can score, the enemy may go off without waiting to close. Those guns on the off side, which are on carriages, will cross over to the opposite side.

As the fleets close, the smaller guns will fire and then, when about to make contact, use all sorts of fire and let the trumpets sound.

The commander in chief must give an example and make trumpet and visual signals [by upper sails]. He must look out for the conduct of the battle and send help where needed or go himself.

The flagship must not try to close with the enemy, for then the commander in chief could not supervise the battle and, besides, all his own ships would go to his aid and control would be lost.

The reserve should also be slow to close and then should go where aid is needed. The boats are not to approach until the ships are in grapple and then go to the enemy's off side and use their weapons as previously described. Wounded men must be sent below, for they are in the way and intimidate the others. The dead must be quickly thrown overboard to avoid dismay, so that everybody on deck is a fighting man.

If any hostile ship takes to flight, the reserve pursues.

The commander in chief must keep record of all. After battle, having assembled his fleet, he takes care of the wounded and makes a list of dead, and of the distribution of booty. He must make a port and get supplies and repairs.

But I have said enough, and yield to those who know more, for every day there are new things. [Like ourselves, former generations thought themselves quite modern.]

It is said all this attempt at order on the sea is useless, for order can not be preserved. To this I answer that having equal arms, the fleet in the best order will win, for it the wind and sea throw an ordered fleet into confusion, the fleet without order will be more confused. Ships at sea are like horses on land, for if the latter maneuver more readily when alone, yet they are stronger for being together. . . . The most skillful will win over one who does not appreciate times and occasions.

The story of the battle of Lepanto and of the events leading thereto is easily accessible to students. Probably no previous campaign was so thoroughly described by so many participants and historians. In the first place, it was the most renowned battle which had taken place since the invention of printing enabled men widely to spread the knowledge of their deeds. In the second place, the battle relieved the Christian world of an intolerable dread which had oppressed it for centuries. Men had feared that the steady advance of an oriental civilization and a hated religion was uncontrollable, like the rising tide, and, although the material consequences of the battle were slight, the spiritual and psychologic relief to Europe was immeasurable. Two days after the battle, the Papal Commander in Chief expressed the universal exultation of Christendom in a letter to a Venetian correspondent: "It is clear that the Turks are men like ourselves, not to say more in our own honor." They could be defeated, and this great discovery gave prestige to the battle and to all who fought there.

Miguel Cervantes de Saavedra, who was present, commanding a squad of 12 men in the waist of the Genoese *Marquesa*, regarded the day as the high spot of his life, as indeed it was of all, and alludes to it proudly in *Don Quixote*. Even in far-away, heretic England the impression of the Christian victory was so great that 30 years later, when Shakespeare sought a turbulent background for the opening act of his tragedy in Othello, he could find nothing more alarming than the rumors in Venice of the preliminary movement of the Turkish fleet to Rhodes at the outbreak of the "War for Cyprus," of which Lepanto was the culmination.

The War of Cyprus included the last great campaign of rowing men-of-war. In the wealth of detail regarding it we see all the difficulties of ancient administration, of discipline, of weather and of seasons, as well as of tactics and strategy and the astonishing lack of haste, both in politics and military movement. For these reasons I shall take up various side lines of this great adventure, which are scarcely necessary to a straight-forward account of strategy and tactics, but which show us how classic and medieval campaigns were managed.

Political Situation Preliminary to the War

The course of the campaign of Lepanto and even of the battle itself, in which the Papacy, Spain, and Venice allied themselves against the Turk, was much influenced by international politics and the different aims of the three allies. It is therefore important to review the situation leading to the alliance, to understand which we must go back many years.

From the first Venice was a maritime power. Her strength was in commerce and on the sea, and she accumulated commercial outposts on the east side of the Adriatic and throughout the Eastern Mediterranean, but was without any territorial possessions on the mainland of Italy. She had good trade connections with the Orient, but not so good with Europe where the great cities of North Italy were envious of her trade to the north and west. By the fourteenth century Venice began markedly to feel the commercial rivalry of Florence and Milan, and the need of controlling unhampered routes into Central Europe. Her frequent conflicts with Genoa, to gain the mastery of oriental trade, reached their height in the war of Chioggia (1380), in which Venice was blockaded by the fleet of Genoa under Doria and the army of Carrara, Lord of Padua. This blockade, which was so nearly fatal to Venice, showed her the necessity of holding agricultural land in Italy as a measure of economic insurance in time of war, and afforded a second imperative reason for expansion on the mainland. In consequence, Venice entered upon a policy of gaining a foothold in Italy, which introduced her into the major politics of Europe, when France, Spain, and the Western Empire struggled with the Papacy for the sovereignty of the peninsula.

In the East, the rise of the Ottoman Turks in Asia Minor, about 1300 A.D., and their conquest of Constantinople, in 1453, were disastrous to Venice, for the Turks were not favorable to commerce and conquered many of the Venetian possessions in Eastern waters. In addition, the discovery, in 1497, of the rival route to India by way of the Cape of Good Hope was a great blow to the trade and prosperity of Venice, which became less and less able to resist Turkish advances in the Levant. Early in the sixteenth century, the Turkish rule extended along the African shores of the Mediterranean and the maritime power of Turkey became very great. It was not on a legitimate commercial basis, however, like that of Genoa and Venice. It was on a piratical basis, such as the United States knew in the Barbary States in 1789-1815. The Christian shores of the Mediterranean were constantly subject to Turkish piratical raids even when there was no formal war. The Emperor Charles V, in his capacity of King of Spain and of the Two Sicilies, made two great expeditions to Africa against the Mohammedans in the interest of his Italian and Spanish subjects.

Yet, although the Emperor and Venice both found Turkey a most obnoxious neighbor, they did not effectively unite against her for two reasons. Since Venice appeared in the mainland of Italy they had opposite policies. The Emperor ruled Lombardy as well as Naples and Sicily, and wished to extend his power eastward in the Po valley, whereas Venice regarded a hold on Northeastern Italy as essential to her retention of trade with Germany. Besides this broad difference of policy, the two differed as to the special method of fighting the Turk. Venice wanted maritime control of the eastern Mediterranean as a commercial market, while Spain was more concerned with the safety of the western sea from piratical raids. So they could not readily agree on the objective of a joint war; for, if the united fleets went in one direction, the shores were exposed in the other.

Nevertheless, in these differences an intermediary was available. In their general policy of opposition to the Turk, both powers were supported by the Papacy. Crusading against the infidel had been Papal policy since Urban preached the First Crusade in 1097. In the sixteenth century, the Turkish advance in the Balkans and into the territory of the Holy Roman Empire had been a source of preoccupation to the Papacy as well as a woe to the Empire. Besides, as sovereigns of Central Italy, the Popes found it necessary to defend their state against the piratical raids of Turkish and African corsairs. For this purpose they maintained a squadron and many fortified towers along the coast. So during the sixteenth century Pope, King, and Signory of Venice were all hostile in principle to the Sultan. In spite of jealousies, they had been able to join their navies in alliance in 1538.

But at the meeting with the hostile fleet under Khaireddin Barbarossa off Prevesa, the Christian Commander in Chief, Andrea Doria, of Genoa, who was the appointee of the King of Spain, retreated before the Turks, refusing battle, although the latter were weaker. It was then believed, and now seems confirmed by contemporary records, that Doria had orders from Charles V to make arrangements with Barbarossa contrary to the terms of the alliance. The distrust which previously existed between the Spaniards and Venetians was much increased by the encounter off Prevesa and lasted until the following generation, when it had effect upon all the negotiations leading to the triple alliance of 1571 as well as in the conduct of the battle of Lepanto itself.

During the long reign of the Sultan Solyman, about the middle of the sixteenth century, the power and the prestige of the Turks was at its highest. When he died in 1566, his son and successor, Selim, a drunkard and a sensualist, bore no good will to Venice, but a war with Persia and other disturbances eastward occupied the first years of his reign. At the conclusion of the Persian War, Selim thought it time to add to his father's possessions and resolved on the acquisition of the rich island of Cyprus, which he had coveted before coming to the throne and whose position gave it advantage in the Venetian trade with Syria and Egypt. Although Venice had for long submitted to the increasing unfriendliness of Turkey without serious protest, Selim's task proved more difficult than he had hoped. Owing to her growing poverty and the necessity of maintaining her position in Italy against Spain, the Republic had neglected her navy, so that her main reliance had fallen into some inefficiency. Nevertheless, she still had a splendid fleet of unmanned galleys in reserve at her renowned arsenal, whose shipbuilding capacity was noted more than two centuries before as mentioned by Dante in his circuit through the *Inferno*.

The Sultan was encouraged to attempt his venture by a great fire in Venice, in the fall of 1569, which destroyed a part of this same great shipworks. Of this national misfortune the Sultan heard exaggerated accounts and he flattered himself with the false idea that a great part of the Venetian fleet had disappeared in flame. Also Venice was dependent for food on a large quantity of wheat annually imported from the Sultan's dominions, and this, he thought, would make the Republic subservient. Besides, at this moment, Europe was occupied with religious wars and other feuds, so that help for Venice from other Christian powers seemed improbable to the Sultan.

In opposition to the Sultan's proposal, his able Grand Vizier Mehemet Sokolli, who had brilliantly served the great Solyman, pointed out that an attack on Venice might well result in a Christian League and that Venice was so dependent on her trade with Turkey that she was really a natural ally. If, he added, Selim was desirous of military fame, the proper enemy was the House of Austria, whose dominions extended from Spain to the Balkans, and here the existing rebellion of the Moriscoes in Southern Spain offered him a suitable point of attack and the opportunity of aiding those of the Faithful struggling for their religion against King Philip II. The Sultan ignored this suggestion and persisted in his plan. He found a pretext for aggression in the action of a small squadron of the Knights of Malta, which about this time made unneutral use of a Cyprian port as a base from which it issued to seize some Turkish treasure ships.

War for Cyprus

The Sultan sent for Barbaro, the Venetian Ambassador, and told him that, owing to the action of the Maltese Knights, it was necessary to ask Venice to cede Cyprus amicably; otherwise he would be obliged to take it by force. On January 13, 1570, following this communication, the Sultan

MAP VIII.
CAMPAIGNS OF THE HOLY LEAGUE 1570–72

MAP VIII.

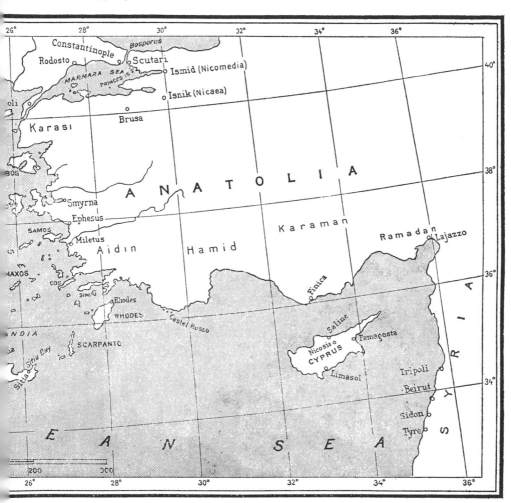

seized two Venetian ships at Constantinople and held Barbaro a prisoner in his house. The question whether it was lawful to break the existing treaty with Venice was referred to the Grand Mufti (chief priest), who decided that it was never necessary to keep faith with infidels. It was given out that Spain was to be attacked, but Barbaro managed to send notice to Venice of the Sultan's real purpose. On February 11, the Sultan sent an envoy to Venice (where he arrived early in April) formally to demand the surrender of Cyprus under penalty of a war in which he would seize all the Venetian possessions. To him the Senate replied that it would never submit to the Sultan's proposal. Already it had taken action to mobilize its fleet in Venice.

TURKISH MOBILIZATION

Selim was resolved upon an expedition of overwhelming strength and was the first to begin operations. The fleet was made ready at Constantinople, but most of the troops were marched overland to the coasts of Anatolia (Karaman) near Cyprus. Piali Pasha was appointed Commander in Chief of the Turkish fleet and he left Constantinople on April 17, 1570, with 80 galleys and 30 galliots, bound for Negropont. By May 15 the remainder of the fleet was ready and Ali Pasha, the Second in Command, sailed from Constantinople the next day with 36 galleys, 12 fuste, and 15 large sailing ships, and many other supply ships. After reprovisioning and cleaning his ships' bottoms at Negropont, Piali left there for Rhodes on May 27 and met Ali with the rest of the fleet and Mustapha Pasha, the Commander in Chief of the army and of the whole expedition. At Rhodes the fleet remained 3 days and sailed June 4 for Finica in Anatolia, where it expected to find horses and ferry them to Cyprus. Here Mustapha remained over 3 weeks and then moved on Cyprus with 160 galleys, 60 galliots and fuste, 40 fregate, 40 horse ships, 30 caramusciali, and 15 sailing ships.* On the first 3 days of July, he landed supplies and a part of his army at Saline. He sent back to Anatolia 100 galleys with 20 horse ships and 12 sailing ships, to bring the rest of the army, which amounted in all to 56,000 men with 50 falconets (small cannon) and 3 large pieces of artillery (Rosell, p. 28).

---

* Galliot, a small galley, without the rembate (platforms) at the bows. Fusta, a still smaller galley with two rowers to a bench and single mast. Caramusciali, light, fast, merchant sailing vessels of from 200 to 300 tons' burden.

Turks Attack Nicosia

Piali and Ali went off in different directions to get more men and returned to Saline on the 22d with 14,000 janissaries. Not until then did Mustapha march to Nicosia, the capital of the island, where he arrived June 24. Nicosia was an inland town about 18 miles from Saline. It was not well fortified and the garrison troops in the island were few. Some recruits were gathered by the Venetian nobles residing in the island, and altogether the city held 10,000 fighting men. A brave defense had been resolved upon and some earthworks had been thrown up. It is a debatable question whether Venice would not have done better to throw a few additional troops into Cyprus in April and May while the sea was free, rather than rely entirely on action by the fleet to hold the island.

The Turks drew their lines around the city, threw up some forts, and began an active siege. On August 15 the Venetian garrison sallied from Nicosia and captured some booty, but were finally driven back with loss. All this time the Turkish operations by sea and land had progressed without the slightest hindrance from Venice.

Venice Asks for Help

From the first Venice knew herself unequal to fighting Turkey alone and already in the winter she began to seek support for the coming struggle. The Republic applied to every power in Christendom and even to Persia for aid, but met with cold replies. She was disliked as a Republic; she was a rival of the other maritime powers; and she was alleged to have been an ally of the Sultan in the past. This charge could be made against many other Christian powers, yet it was true that more than once Venice had been neutral when other Christian states had been at war with the infidel. It was in vain that Venice attempted to justify herself by pointing out that her neighborhood to the powerful Turk compelled her to court his friendship and that all Europe profited by Venetian trade with the East.

Yet Venice found help where she was not accustomed to look for it, at the hand of the Pope. Venice had never been submissive to Papal authority, but Pope Pius V forgot that and rejoiced in his present opportunity. He was of strong character and of singular piety; the last Pope to be canonized, he was called a Saint even during his life. He did much to

FIG. 15.—POPE PIUS V

BY E. PASSEROTTI

Courtesy of Walters Art Gallery, Baltimore.

HE INSPIRED THE HOLY LEAGUE IN 1571

elevate and reform the Church and welcomed the occasion for an enterprise against the Turk, which he regarded as a holy crusade. To his enthusiasm with which he inspired the combatants is chiefly due the Christian victory.

On behalf of Venice he appealed to King Philip II of Spain as a faithful son of the Church to join him in alliance with Venice. The King had no wish to aid Venice for her own sake; rather the contrary, he wished to see her reduced in power, but he knew very well that the conquest of Cyprus would entail bad effects in the western Mediterranean, where the strength of the Barbary States would be much increased and the probability of recovering the lost Spanish holdings in Africa would be diminished, if not quite gone.

Accordingly, after long delay, His Catholic Majesty cheaply acquired the glory of Christian generosity by agreeing, in spite of his bad relations with the Republic, to aid her by sending a squadron to act with that of Venice in Eastern waters. And this he made the more of, since some maritime support was needed in Spain to enable Don John of Austria, his half-brother, to suppress the Morisco rebellion in Southern Spain.

SPANISH MOBILIZATION

However, the King did not at this time accept the formal triple alliance suggested by the Pope. He merely said that he would permit his Sicilian squadron under the command of Gian Andrea Doria, Prince of Melfi, the grand-nephew and heir of the great Andrea Doria, Admiral of Charles V, to act under the orders of the Papal Commander in Chief. It would have been hard to find a man more displeasing to the Venetians as their colleague. For several centuries seamen of his family had led Genoese fleets against Venice, and frequently with success. Above all, it was Gian Andrea's uncle who was thought to have betrayed Venice at Prevesa only 32 years before. Gian Andrea himself, although an accomplished seaman and of great political ability, was thought to have behaved badly on the occasion of the shameful Spanish disaster at Gerbe (or Gelves) near Tripoli, in 1560, when he commanded the fleet at the age of 21 in the name of his very aged uncle, the Admiral of Spain. It was unavoidable that Venetians should be most distrustful of him, and on his part he heartily reciprocated their distrust. The King had not made an auspicious appointment.

The Spanish squadron of 49 vessels was made up of the Royal squadrons of Naples (20 galleys) and of Sicily (10 galleys) with that of Doria himself (11 galleys), which he brought as "assentista," besides 8 other vessels owned by assentiste. An assentista provided and maintained ships and crews, usually without soldiers, as his personal business venture and hired them and his own services in command to some prince for a monthly sum.* Such arrangements were customary and similar to those made by condottieri for supplying troops and even armies to governments which needed military services. It was alleged that assentiste were frequently unwilling to risk their ships in battle, since they were uninsured against loss, and that, therefore, they sometimes avoided battle when they should have fought, in order to avoid consuming their personal fortunes by destruction of their ships. This very charge was made against Doria before the end of the year.

Papal Mobilization

As for the Papal squadron, His Holiness chose as Commander in Chief Marc Antonio Colonna, Duke of Tagliacozzo and Paliano. He was the head of one of the greatest of Roman houses. He was 35 years old and had been a soldier from boyhood, leading cavalry and infantry. He was not without maritime experience, as he had commanded 3 galleys of his own as a young man in a Spanish expedition against the coast of Morocco. He was intelligent, brave, and generous. His diplomatic skill was the principal element in holding the allied fleets together for over 2 years without permitting jealousies, suspicions, and ill-will utterly to wreck its purposes. His personal position exposed him to embarrassment as Papal admiral, or "General at Sea" as his title was. Not only was he a Roman prince, but he possessed great estates in Naples, where, as hereditary Grand Constable of the Kingdom, he owed allegiance to King Philip, who expected him to be ruled by Spanish policies and yet suspected him of undue devotion to Venetian interests and did not entirely trust him. With Venice, Marc Antonio's relations were of the best, for he enjoyed privileges of Venetian nobility and was popular there.

---

* Doria's price was 6,000 scudi ($13,860) per year per ship with crews of rather over 200 sailors and rowers, but the King's own royal galleys cost him 6,700 scudi exclusive of charges for risk and interest.

FIG. 16.—MARC ANTONIO COLONNA, DUKE OF PALIANO
By Scipio Pulzone, from the Colonna Gallery, Rome
Commander in Chief of the Papal Squadron

But as for the fleet which Colonna was to command, it had to be created. The Papal ships which had been lost at the disaster of Gerbe seem not to have been replaced, and the fortifications of the coast were the only defenses against Turkish raids. In the present emergency the Pope had only 2 worn-out craft and was obliged to turn to Venice for the loan of 12 galleys from those lying in reserve at the Arsenal, which he offered to man and maintain at his expense. Venice was careful not to let the Pope have any of her best ships and Colonna had to pay a personal visit to Venice to arrange the best terms he could. Finally, the hulks were taken to Ancona where they were manned and the squadron went to Messina to meet the Spaniards. As for soldiers in time of peace, princes did not maintain more troops than necessary for police duty, and Colonna commissioned 12 noblemen of his choice to recruit companies of 200 soldiers each, paying bounties, etc., very much as happened at the outbreak of our civil war. Rowers were both voluntary, like the soldiers, and impressed. Communities helped Colonna by sending him squads or companies of "forzati" (i.e., convicts and other undesirables) as well as Turkish captives. Falstaff's way of recruiting, as described by Shakespeare, is a picture of the sixteenth century, as applicable to Italy as it was to England.

The Pope lacked money as well as ships and, to supply the former, he created and sold for large sums a number of administrative offices at the Papal Court and put a heavy tax on the monastic orders.

Venetian Mobilization

As soon as the Signory was convinced of the imminence of the Turkish attack, Venice mobilized in great haste the empty hulls lying in reserve at the Arsenal, having already 31 guard ships in Candia and elsewhere, to command which Marco Quirini was detailed. By the middle of April, 42 additional ships, which the arsenal had sent forth, had arrived at Zara, on the Dalmatian coast, which was chosen as the mobilization point. These were under the command of Girolamo Zanne, a citizen of great wealth, who had served with credit in public posts and was now selected as General-at-Sea or Commander in Chief. Sforza Pallavicino was commander of the troops and of land operations. Besides fitting out old ships, the arsenal laid down 66 new keels and, by the time the mobilization was complete at the end of June, Venice had in service 127 galleys, 11 galleasses,* 14 nefs, and other transports. If the galleys were manned by 80 soldiers and full crews of sailors and rowers, and the other ships in proportion there would have been over 45,000 men in the fleet, but probably they were very short-

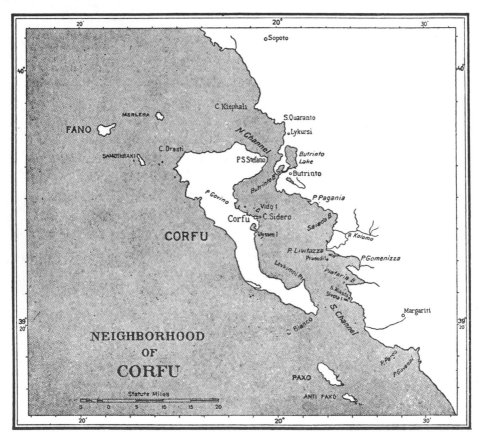

MAP IX

handed so early in the war. Besides, many troops were needed in the garrisons in the Venetian bases in Dalmatia and the islands of Corfu, Cyprus, Zante, Candia, Cerigo, and other places. Two years later, after the loss

---

* Galleasses seem to have been an invention of the moment to carry heavy batteries of guns in broadside. For this purpose, 11 *galee di mercantia*, or merchant galleys, were altered as necessary, but were very slow and had to be towed by other ships. See report made to the Senate in 1593, given in *Le Galere Grosse Veneziane*, by G. Giomo, Venezia, 1895.

of Cyprus, the General at Sea reported over 31,000 troops in foreign garrisons.

The Venetian way of getting men and money was not unlike that of the Pope. The state had some money in hand. There were lotteries and sales of offices, as at Rome; many noblemen subscribed for large sums and others sent or led men at their own expense, from groups of 3 or 4 to 25. The subject cities of Venice sent troops at their expense—Brescia, 1,000; Verona, 500; and so on. Leading men offered to raise from 1,000 to 4,000 men, so that soon the Signory was offered 60,000 soldiers, many of these soldiers were recruited, as usual, in Southern Italy.

Seamen were found along the eastern shore of the Adriatic. The practice of Venice differed from that of all other states in that she employed no "forzati"; all her rowers were freemen and could be trusted with weapons in battle.

We now turn to the fleet movements in the West. Zara was the point of Venetian mobilization convenient for gathering Dalmatian seamen. Unfortunately, the pest broke out and the fleet lost 20,000 men,* so that it was not until June 12 that the fleet moved by several short stages to Corfu (330 miles) to wait for the expected arrival of the Papal and Spanish allies, and for new hands.

EARLY VENETIAN ACTIVITIES

In the meantime, Sebastiano Veniero, the Proveditor (Governor) of Corfu, and Marco Quirini, the Captain of the Gulf (squadron), undertook two of those raids which were so dear to seamen of the time, and yet negligible unless the main fleet battle had occurred. The first with 10 galleys, which were lying at Corfu, attempted a *cup-de-main* against the Turkish hill fort of Sopoto, on the mainland a short march north of Corfu. This he captured in 3 days. Quirini, who had been summoned to bring the Candian squadron of 21 galleys to Corfu, was equally successful in taking Porto Quaglia in the Gulf of Laconia, with only 24 hours' delay, as he came north. He arrived in Corfu July 1.

Early in July, Zanne undertook another purposeless expedition. He sent Pallavicino with 50 galleys and 5,000 soldiers to attack Margariti,

---

* So says Stirling-Maxwell, *Don John of Austria,* vol. 1, p. 315. This would have been fully half the crews and seems high.

another Turkish fortified position a little southeast of Corfu. But the soldiers could not get their artillery in position and nothing was accomplished.

On July 23, the whole Venetian fleet sailed for Candia (310 miles), making frequent stops by the way, and arrived in about 10 days, where Zanne learned the Papal and Spanish squadrons might be expected to join him. The fleet was still very short of men and Zanne sent expeditions among the islands to find recruits to fill vacancies, but the crews of the visiting ships were disorderly and offended the inhabitants, so only 300 new hands were secured and the Commander in Chief had to send out a second time.

On August 7, Quirini with several galleys crossed to Rhodes to get news of the enemy and learned they had landed in Cyprus. About the same time, the middle of August, Piali, Turkish General at Sea, with 100 galleys proceeded west to learn what could be ascertained of the Christians, and in the latter part of August 5 galliots crossed to Candia to "capture tongues," as the Italian phrase is. From natives, these scouts learned the Venetian fleet had arrived alone in Candia and was in bad condition from the pest and was waiting for the Spaniards before going farther.

SPANISH AND PAPAL SQUADRONS

We must now turn back to Italy to see the arrangements made by the Pope to get Spanish assistance. Although he was most enthusiastic in the cause of the war and the alliance, he found progress difficult.

In order that the Venetian Signory might feel assured that the Papal squadron would not fail to be guided according to Venetian interests, it was desirous of having the Pope appoint some Venetian bishop to be commander in chief of the Papal squadron. This the Pope would not do and his choice fortunately fell on Marc Antonio Colonna, as has been said, but he had trouble in manning his ships, which arrived at Otranto on August 6, where they lay to wait for the Spanish squadron.

As for that, the Court of Madrid had heard that Venice was negotiating with the Porte for a settlement of some sort, and did not believe these negotiations would cease unless Spain agreed to a formal treaty of alliance, and this the King was not ready to make.

However, in deference to the urgency of His Holiness, the King at last sent a movement order to Doria at Messina. Yet, as it was known the Venetian fleet was delayed by the need of finding men to fill the plague losses, the King attended to his own needs by telling Doria to visit the Spanish stronghold of Goletta in Tunis, which he was to re-enforce and supply, so that, whatever happened to the allied fleet, Goletta might be able to stand a siege, if the Turkish fleet should go that way. Doria tried to surprise the squadron of Uluch Ali, the Dey of Algiers, on its way to join Piali, but Uluch Ali skillfully avoided the trap set for him and himself fell in with a squadron of 4 Maltese galleys of which he took 3.

Uluch Ali was a notable character, a fierce corsair, and fine seaman, kind and considerate to his Christian slaves. He was a native of Calabria, a fisherman captured by a Turkish corsair and put to hard labor at an oar. Here he lived for several years, suffering (for disease was common on shipboard) from a loathsome itch on his scalp, which caused his fellow rowers to avoid him. At last, a blow from a Turkish soldier made him seek the only avenue open to a Christian slave for obtaining revenge. He forsook his faith and became a freeman. As a Moslem, his abilities brought him rapid advancement. He became a captain of a galley. He helped defeat the Spaniards at Gelves and, after other promotions, he was now, at 60 years of age, ruler of Algiers and Tunis, and was to rise still higher in the Sultan's esteem.

THE ALLIED SQUADRONS AT CANDIA

After his errand to Goletta, Doria met Marc Antonio at Otranto on August 20 and, together, the allied squadrons of 61 vessels moved down the coast of Morea. By the end of August, they were sighted off the coast of Candia, and Quirini issued with a welcoming squadron to meet and escort them into Suda Bay. The three Generals held a council to see what was to be done. The command seemed to be with Colonna. The Venetian General had orders from the Senate

> to show every respect to these captains [Colonna and Doria] and grant them precedence on account of the great Princes they represent, although in the great undertaking they were entering upon they had no duty and authority other than to counsel.

At least, both the Venetian and Papal leaders wished to fight the Turks.

It is doubtful if the Spanish leader had the same purpose. Colonna had received a letter from King Philip which said,

> I am writing to my ambassador at Rome to let you know of the decision I have made that Gian Andrea is to join the galleys of His Holiness and those of the Illustrious Republic with the galleys which he has assembled in Our Kingdom of Sicily and he will obey and follow the standard of His Holiness. And I charge and entreat you that in the battle you will make use in every way of the opinion of Gian Andrea, for I hear you will be pleased to have his help to reach a happy result, on account of his great skill and experience in maritime affairs.

Of this letter Philip wrote to Don Garcia de Toledo:

> As for joining our galleys with those of the Venetians, * * * I have resolved that Gian Andrea shall take those which he has assembled in Our Kingdom of Sicily and join those of His Holiness and of the Venetians and obey Marc Antonio as general of the galleys of His Holiness [not, it will be noted, as commander in chief] and follow his standard as long as they are together.

What orders the King gave Doria are not known, but there is reason to believe that he had secret instructions from the King not to undertake any serious operation. Colonna later wrote to the King,

> Nothing so grieved me in the conduct of Giovanni Andrea as his suggestion that in regard to this matter [the campaign] you had entrusted him with secrets which he [or you] did not reveal to me.

It will be seen that with such vague instructions only the utmost harmony of purpose among the generals could accomplish anything important. However, military decisions through conference, instead of by authority, were customary at that period. The difficulties of reaching agreement among the allies were increased by the necessity each was under of listening to his own council before proceeding to meet his colleagues for a decision. Thus, for example, the Venetian General Zanne had an executive council of four members, himself as General, Pallavicino as General of the soldiers, and Giacomo Celsi and Antonio da Canale as "proveditori" or Vice Admirals. In council, he had merely the advantage of casting an extra vote to decide any tie when the decision was taken.

Besides these small councils there was the great council attended by all the principal officers as well as by those whose birth and distinction afforded them recognition without reference to their actual office. Sometimes as many as 70 were present at one of these large meetings.

It was therefore quite possible to have every proposal for action voted down by a majority.

At Suda Bay, the General Council met on September 1, and two proposals received most attention. Some said it was hopeless to go to Cyprus, for they could not get at the Turkish encampment and the Turkish fleet would retire. This party, therefore, recommended that a diversion should be made by attacking some Ottoman possession which would compensate for the loss of Nicosia.

The other party, led by Zanne, urged that the hostile fleet should be sought and fought wherever found. That, they said, was the object of the expedition and, if they were to advance boldly, it was probable the Turks would retreat rather than engage in doubtful fight.

Doria, who was a skillful diplomat, was cautious by temperament, serene in manner and quick to seize occasion in debate, commended the latter proposal. His personal opinion privately expressed later among his own people was that the Venetian ships were undermanned and "a northerly breeze would knock the soldiers down," meaning they were weak from the plague as well as in numbers. So, he now went on to say, that before undertaking the adventure every ship should be examined to see how all were, for they should not attempt the impossible. He was responsible to his sovereign not to tarnish the glory of the fleet which he led. The King and all Spaniards there present wished to aid Venice and Christianity in general, and their galleys were filled with fine men and abundant munitions and supplies. He wanted to show how capable the Spanish contingent was, and he hoped the others would feel as he did. Zanne and the others understood Doria was not desirous of seeking battle, but they showed themselves as pleased and agreed to submit their ships to inspection before leaving the island.

On September 6, Marco Quirini went out with a few galleys to get information and, on the 8th, others did the same. Some days were now spent in getting supplies and a few more men for the Venetians. On the 13th the fleet got under way with the leaders setting foresails only, so that no vessel could have trouble in keeping position. On the 16th the fleet arrived at Sitia at the east end of Candia where Quirini met it and reported that Nicosia was still holding out. So it was resolved to proceed to its relief. But first the muster and inspection were held, which the Venetians had postponed to the last moment but which Doria required as a *sine qua non*. Doria complained that the Venetians had their boats in the water at inspection and might have used them to transfer men from ship to ship to swell the apparent numbers. He alleged they had not over two-thirds of the rowers and 80 fighting men per ship, including both soldiers and mariners, but this was no doubt an understatement. Rosell, a Spanish authority, says the Venetians had 8,000 soldiers. The Papal ships had over 100 soldiers each and the Spanish about 100. With adventurers, Rosell admits there were 15,000 soldiers. The Italian Contarini says there were 2,000 more. Still, Doria found occasion to wonder how the Venetians dared venture with such ill-manned and ill-equipped vessels. So Zanne stripped the crews from several and left the empty hulls behind. The fleet then numbered 180 galleys,* 11 galleasses, and 15 nefs manned by about 50,000 in all. According to the information of the Christians, the Turks had no more than 150 galleys.

THE SITUATION IN CYPRUS

Since the situation in Cyprus was last mentioned, the siege had progressed faster than the allies knew. During August, Mustapha tried in vain to take the city. He lost many men and the remaining janissaries were discouraged and unwilling. He knew the Venetians in Candia were expecting the other allies and felt the need of haste much more than the Christians. He took one of those risks of which only able commanders are capable, and sent to the Admirals Piali and Ali at Saline asking for 100 soldiers from every galley to make up another assaulting party, for without fresh men the siege would fail. The two admirals deliberated with their council as to the danger from the Christian fleet. They concluded that the Venetians and the Spaniards would not agree any better than they had done in the previous League in 1538 and took the chance. Leaving the ships defenseless, they started for Nicosia before dawn on September 8, with nearly 20,000 men, and arrived there late that day. The great attack was made the next day on every part of the Christian lines, and defenders were too few to hold everywhere. The city was taken and given to pillage, much booty was taken, the men were killed and the women raped. The crews of the fleet marched back the following day with their loot and the

---

* 12 Papal, 49 Spanish, and 119 Venetian galleys.

vessels were again manned and ready for service. Mustapha sent off several ships to Constantinople laden with spoil and captured boys and girls. Not all were contented with their probable fate in Turkish harems and one Venetian lady fired the magazine of her ship and destroyed herself with her fellow captives.

Mustapha now sent 6 galliots to get news from Candia. They soon returned, having taken a Christian vessel from which they learned the allies had joined and were coming to Cyprus. In the meantime Mustapha left a garrison of 5,000 men in Nicosia and with the rest marched 30 miles across the island to Famagosta, the chief seaport of the island, and entered upon its blockade, which lasted 10 months, although defended by a garrison of only 7,000 soldiers.

THE FLEET MOVES EAST AND THEN RETIRES

In ignorance of these events, the Christian fleet watered and provisioned anew at Sitia and on September 17 sailed towards Cyprus. It was organized into a vanguard of 12 galleys followed by 6 more squadrons, then the rear guard and 11 galleasses, 191 vessels in all, besides the nefs and other sailing ships. The organization was strictly national, no leader had ships of other flags in his division under his tactical control. After touching at Rhodes, the fleet arrived at Castel Rosso on the coast of Asia Minor, 65 miles east of Rhodes, on September 22 (200 miles from Cyprus). The weather was bad and most of the fleet sought shelter there, while Doria's squadron remained outside and made a grievance of the matter. The indefatigable Quirini, who had gone out on September 6 to "catch a tongue" (i.e., for information), rejoined at Castel Rosso, saying some Christians, Turkish subjects, had been taken at sea on the 18th, who reported the fall of Nicosia and the overthrow of its walls. Documents captured at the same time confirmed the oral report.

The next day a general council was held. Hitherto, Zanne and Colonna had been anxious to go forward, whereas Doria had been reluctant, but the loss of Nicosia caused Zanne to lose his zeal. In the council it was suggested that the Turks could now double man their ships for battle, and the season was far advanced for operations. So as an alternative, an attack on Negropont was mentioned. Doria had previously announced that he would stay only through the month of September. So that same evening the fleet retired to Scarpanto where it arrived on the 23d and met with bad weather. Doria wished to leave the others and go on, but he delayed for a couple of days and another council was held. Both Colonna and Zanne wished Doria to remain with them, for it was reported that the Turks were about to follow them with 200 sail. Colonna now attempted to ascertain the extent of his authority over the Spanish squadron under his letter from King Philip.

He said to Doria, "if I were to order you to stay, would you do so?" Doria replied that he did not have such latitude under his orders as to stay, unless battle or other serious cause should appear, and that to obey Colonna's order it would be necessary that he should have the same authority as Don John of Austria. The latter had been made High Admiral of Spain the year before, but was then far away overcoming the Morisco rebellion in Spain. A junior Spanish officer in command of troops, a cousin of Colonna, here interposed in the discussion, saying that he had no orders from the Viceroy of Naples to obey Colonna. The latter replied with some heat, and to avoid trouble Doria sent the young man from the council room. It was this incident which led Colonna to complain to the King that Doria had secret instructions which were not known to the former.

It was now plain that harmony was hopeless and the will to accomplish something had disappeared. Doria disapproved the suggestion to recover the former Venetian island of Negropont and said that any attempt at diversion should be made on the west side of the Morea as the fleet returned home. So it was decided to let the separate fleets seek their respective bases. Zanne sent to Famagosta to assure the garrison that men and supplies would be thrown into the city. Doria was the last to leave Scarpanto (September 26) and he said in his report to the King of Spain that the others went out in bad weather and "sowed" the coasts of Candia with galleys "as usual." In fact, the Venetians lost 11 galleys on the way and two Papal vessels broke up in port. The complete lack of mutual support and the total failure of the campaign of 1570 rendered much more remote the prospect of an effective alliance in 1571.

TURKISH OPERATIONS

In the meantime Mustapha heard of the advance of the allied fleet and, believing the Venetians had refilled the vacancies in their crews, the Turkish council decided not to fight a fleet action. Piali landed all slaves and useless people and took his fleet to Limasol on the south side of the island, leaving the transports before Famagosta. But, as time passed and the Christians did not appear, the Pasha realized that the dissensions among them would prevent attack on the Turks and, on October 6, he sent off the fleet to winter in Constantinople and the Archipelago, retaining only 7 galleys to maintain the blockade of Famagosta by sea. The Turkish and Venetian fleets got news of each other through scouts, and the Venetians went to Canea, to be in a good port, and prepared to meet attack. The Turks first thought of attacking the Christians, but were delayed by bad weather and then it seemed too late in the season and they went on, in November, to their winter quarters, leaving only a small squadron in the Archipelago to check dispatch of supplies to Famagosta. In this interval, a chance encounter of 2 Venetian ships with a much superior Turkish force developed such desperate resistance by the vessel commanded by Vicenzo Maria Priuli that, although the ship was destroyed and he was killed, the Turkish Pasha felt that he had done wisely in not going in search of the Venetian fleet.

Doria sailed from Candia for Sicily on October 5. On November 11, Zanne sailed from Canea with the main body of his fleet and arrived at Corfu on the 17th. He was summoned home to answer charges of misconduct and died the next year in prison before trial. Colonna left Candia in company with the Venetians and lost additional ships on his way to the Adriatic. He was delayed and driven about on the Balkan coast by bad weather until November 28 when he crossed to Italy from Cattaro with only 3 vessels, having lost his flagship by lightning stroke, followed by fire. His new flagship was wrecked on the passage. The Papal squadron was destroyed without battle and the suspicion arises that the hulls furnished by the Venetians were unseaworthy.

THE WINTER OF 1570-71

On December 26, Sebastiano Veniero, who had been appointed Proveditor of Cyprus a few months earlier, but had not got farther than Candia, was made "General at Sea" in place of the unfortunate Zanne and he returned to Corfu on March 17, 1571, where he took command of the fleet which he was to lead in the great victory. Veniero was then 75 years old; a man of great and unimpaired energy, passionate and impetuous, with a long record of good service.

During the winter Quirini remained with a guard squadron in Candia, with orders to aid Famagosta in withstanding the Turkish blockade. Quirini had prepared 4 cargo ships carrying stores and 1,600 soldiers to go to Famagosta. He thought they could not get in without an escort, so he decided to go himself, taking 12 galleys. He left on January 16 and was off Famagosta on January 26, where he met the store-ships which had gone independently. The latter went forward alone, the galleys remaining well in the rear. The 7 Turkish blockade galleys advanced upon the Christians, whereupon Quirini came up, but could not get at the Turks effectively, for they beached themselves under cover of their army. Nevertheless he sank 3, while his store-ships entered port. The next day Quirini captured a large Turkish merchant ship and took the Turkish galleys. He then entered the port and, on February 16, he cleared Famagosta with the store-ships which had discharged cargo. On February 21 all were back in Candia.

The news of Quirini's success caused the Sultan to cut off some heads, and the Turkish ships in the Archipelago were immediately assembled. Piali had been relieved of command because he had not gone to Candia to attack the Venetian squadron in November after the allies had separated. Ali Pasha was now made Commander in Chief and went out with 40 galleys and met, at Scio, the Bey of Negropont, with 40 more from Chios and Rhodes. Together they went to Cyprus on April 1 and waited for soldiers and supplies from Tripoli.

By the end of April the rest of the Turkish fleet left Constantinople for Negropont where it cleaned bottoms.

At the beginning of May, Mustapha began active siege operations against Famagosta with the huge army which had merely blockaded the city during the winter. On May 15, Ali left 22 ships in Cyprus to escort troops and supplies from the mainland, and went with 55 galleys to Negropont where he met 100 others from Constantinople and also Uluch Ali from the West and Hassan Pacha. He was ready for a campaign against all the Venetian possessions with 250 vessels. He had not as yet heard of any combination among the Christian powers to oppose his advance and the Venetians themselves were inferior in numbers.

FIG. 17.——SEBASTIANO VENIERO, DOGE OF VENICE, VICTOR AT LEPANTO IN 1571

FORMATION OF THE ALLIANCE

Although Sultan Selim wanted more than the conquest of Cyprus, his Grand Vizier, Mahomet Sokolli, wanted peace with Venice in the winter of 1570-71. Before agreeing to any terms with Turkey the Signory turned to see what the Pope could do for Venice. The Pope was for the moment on bad terms with the Emperor, and thinking that on this account little could be expected, Venice undertook negotiations with the Sultan, hoping that if nothing more came of them, at least she might stir up the Pope and Spain to help her. But the Pope had not lost his crusading zeal. In spite of the fiasco of the joint expedition to Castel Rosso and the bitter international feeling engendered by it, His Holiness had been most earnest all winter in negotiating a formal treaty between himself, the King, and the Republic. The seat of the negotiations was in Rome under the eye of the Pope, but King Philip insisted on managing details from Madrid and the Signory at Venice was suspicious of his aims. So it was necessary at the Convention to produce harmony where the objectives were discordant and confidence where there were suspicions and concealments. After the delegates' agreement, authorization from Madrid and Venice had to be secured. The Pope's high character was an important element in his success, he was austere, zealous, sincere, and obedient to the call of religion to overcome the infidel.

In the Convention the fundamental objective of the Venetians was to humiliate the Turk, by destroying his fleet and checking his expansion, but thereafter Venice wanted to renew good relations, for the Eastern trade was the basis of Venetian existence. Her object was to save Cyprus. The Spanish viewpoint was quite another. Spain was not particularly interested in Mediterranean commerce, she looked to Mexico and Peru as her source of wealth, and her object in the war was to crush Turkey's strength, so that the shores of Italy and Spain might be free from raiders and, to accomplish this, she wanted to hold the states of Tunis and Algiers. She cared little to see Venice retain Cyprus. So King Philip felt small confidence that Venice would see a war through. He wished for some permanent arrangement for opposing Turkey. As the immediate situation was more threatening to Venice, she had to yield on most questions.

Another difficult point in arranging an alliance was the choice of a

Commander in Chief. The Spaniards wanted their man and also the second in command, but this Venice positively refused.

At last, on May 25, 1571, the Treaty of Alliance between the three powers was signed. Its principal provisions were (1) it was to be perpetual; (2) 200 galleys, 100 nefs, 50,000 Spanish, Italian, and German infantry, 4,500 light horse and proper artillery and supplies were to be ready each spring; (3) each year in March or April the objective for the year was to be chosen; (4) when no common enterprise was agreed upon each national contingent was to do as directed by its sovereign; (5) each was to defend the states of the others; (6) Spain was to assume one-half the expenses, Venice one-third, and the Papacy one-sixth, and the two former powers were to give the Pope 12 galleys, which he was to man and maintain; (7) each ally was to supply the stores for which the market price was least in his own territory; (8) the management of the war would be decided by the vote of the three generals and the Commander in Chief would execute the decisions of the majority. Don John of Austria, half-brother of King Philip, was made the Captain General of the League and Marc Antonio Colonna the Lieutenant-General; (9) arrangements for division of spoils in the proportion of costs; (10) all differences were to be decided by the Pope as arbitrator; and (11) no separate peace by any without formal notice to the others. For the current year there were to be 80 Spanish galleys at Otranto to meet those of Venice, Malta, and the Pope.

The Pope now tried to get Portugal and the Emperor to join the League, but they refused.

MOBILIZATION AT MESSINA

The strain of the war was severely felt by Venice. To replace losses, she armed 25 galleys, which for the first time were under the command of nobles from the mainland instead of real Venetians, and, moreover, the scarcity of men led her to break her rule of freemen on her ships and offer safe conducts to bandits and other undesirables to serve either as rowers, seamen, or soldiers. Besides, she impressed 2,000 rowers from her territories on the mainland and hired foreigners to fill her garrisons.

The assembly of the Christian fleet was slow. The King was sending

FIG. 18.—DON JOHN OF AUSTRIA
From his statue at Messina, by Calamech. From Library of Congress.

a squadron from Spain besides those of Naples and Sicily. These together with the Papal squadron were to rendezvous at Messina.

The ships furnished by Venice having been lost, for this campaign the Papal ships were hired from Cosimo de Medici, ruler of Tuscany, who was grateful to the Pope, who had just granted him the title of Grand Duke. The Duke furnished the 12 ships complete with at least 144 rowers. The flagship had over 220 rowers and 60 seamen, but the Pope paid for only 6 ships at 500 scudi ($1,160) a month. However, the Pope supplied the soldiers for all 12 ships and of them Honorato Caetani, commanding the soldiers, wrote to his uncle, the Cardinal of Sermoneta,

> We could only put 100 soldiers per galley in the ships the Grand Duke sent us for they had 60 mariners each and cavaliers and other nobles (adventurers for the crusade) amounting to 30 more per ship. So Colonna said to put no more on board for fear of illness in such a long trip.

The Papal galleys thus averaged not less than 340 souls each. The Papal squadron was ready to sail from Civita Vecchia by the middle of June and left for Messina, stopping at Naples. It is interesting to learn from Caetani's letter home that on leaving Naples the squadron met very light airs ahead and, under oars, made 30 miles the first day in about 15 hours, then anchored for several hours to refresh the rowers and the next day did 55 miles in about 20 hours.

The Venetian fleet was in two parts and undertaking little. A number of galleys had wintered in Candia and were remanned there in the spring. Veniero had the main part of the fleet at Corfu and farther north, and sent 22 of his force to Quirini, in Candia, so 60 were there for local defense. But, later, the Venetian Commander in Chief called all the Candian squadron back to Corfu where he expected to be joined by the Spaniards and Colonna, but all were delayed and Veniero had comparatively few vessels in Corfu when he heard that one of two scouts he had sent south for news had been captured by the Turkish fleet. He perceived that Corfu might soon become untenable for him, and on July 8 he left Corfu for Messina where he arrived in 10 days, having only about 20 soldiers per ship. He explained to the allies in Messina that there were many troops in Corfu that he would draw upon as the fleet went east. As Veniero sailed from Corfu he sent word to Quirini telling him also to go to Messina by way of the Barbary coast, but the order was not received until July 26.

The war was now costing Venice about 300,000 scudi ($696,000) a month.

The Spanish contingent was slow in appearing. After the treaty had been signed, the Pope pressed King Philip to send his ships as had been agreed and at last the King consented. On June 6 Don John of Austria, High Admiral of Spain, left Madrid and, on June 16, was at Barcelona, whence he called up the squadrons from Mallorca and Cartagena. He embarked on July 1, and sailed on July 20, and on the 26th he was at Genoa where he received a great welcome, which took precious time. On August 5 he left and was at Naples on August 9. Here, again, there were rejoicings and ceremonies. There was detention by bad weather and the completion of the ships' stores. He got off on August 21, with 34 galleys, and arrived at Messina on the 25th (200 sea miles in 4 days), where Colonna and Veniero were anxiously waiting. Here, again, there was ceremony and pomp, and the prestige of Don John, both as to birth and as conqueror of the Moriscoes, enabled him to put an end to the street encounters between the Spanish and Italian soldiery which had been menacing to the peace of the town.

The Siege of Famagosta

We must once more turn away to follow Turkish events. During this long campaign the operations of the Turks ran on independently of the endeavors of the Christians on the other side of the Adriatic, from November, 1570, until the fall of 1571, when the great clash occurred.

Mustapha opened the active siege of Famagosta about May 1, 1571, when the season became favorable. He had 80,000 troops at the very least and 74 pieces of artillery to overcome the few thousand men of the garrison. Covered by the great fleet of Ali, he expected no interference from the West.

The early assaults on the city failed, but Mustapha slowly battered down the walls with artillery. On July 8, 5,000 shot were fired in 24 hours. Although Mustapha began to lose confidence, time and the lack of aid began to tell on the garrison. By July 20 the citizens lodged a request with the generals to make terms with the enemy. The Council was divided. Discussion lasted for some days, but on August 4, the surrender was completed on very good terms. The Venetian commanders then went to pay their respects to Mustapha in his tent and were well received. A discussion arose in which Mustapha lost his temper and the Venetians were thrown out of the tent and cut to pieces by Mustapha's order. Bragadino, the Governor, alone was kept alive. His ears were cut off and he was marched around the town most ignominiously for several days and then was flayed alive in the public square. He endured his torture with the utmost constancy, loudly reproaching Mustapha, who was present, for his breach of faith, and died before the excoriation was half-completed. His stuffed skin was hoisted to the yard arm of a galley and sent along the coast to Constantinople. When the news of all this finally came to the Christian fleet, it redoubled the ardor for revenge. The siege cost the Turks 50,000 men. Leaving 22,000 men as a garrison to hold the island, Mustapha went to Constantinople. The other Venetian possessions were now wholly dependent on the success of the League's fleet.

Quirini in Candia with 60 galleys had standing directions from Venice to run the blockade of Famagosta with supplies for the garrison, but after his successful venture in January he accomplished little; for, as was said, the Turkish fleet became active as soon as the season opened.

The Turkish Fleet in the Adriatic

After the assembly of the Turkish fleet at Negropont it went to Melos, June 14, and the night of the 15-16th it was at Cape Meleko near Suda in Candia, where it raided on shore and heard that 30 Venetian galleys were at Canea and as many more at Candia. Bad weather held the Turks at Suda and 4 Venetian ships with supplies passed them within 3 miles. Ali and Uluch Ali, who had come from Algiers, moved about the island and Uluch Ali ran 12 of his ships aground, of which 3 broke up. The navigational losses of the period almost justify Shakespeare's term for a ship-owner as a "putter-forth of five for one." At last the Turkish fleet moved north, and it was most fortunate for the Christians then mobilizing that it had wasted time in Candia.

The Moslems went to Cerigo and landed at Zante and Cephallonia, entered the Corfu Channel on July 1 and spent that month in ravaging on the eastern side of the Adriatic at Valona, Durazzo, Dulcigno, Budua, and Ragusa, but refrained from attacking on the Italian side of the Adriatic, as Ali hoped that if he did not offend King Philip's lands the League might come to nothing. One object of entering the Adriatic was to seize men to replace those lost in raiding ashore in Candia, so many were enslaved, and besides several Venetian galleys were captured as they moved singly or in couples along the coast. On the other hand, Ali lost 8 vessels wrecked at Antivari.

At the middle of July the fleet assembled at Castelnuovo and ships' bottoms were cleaned. A strong squadron went as far as Curzola, after which the fleet reassembled at Saseno in August whence scouts were sent to Italy for news of the Christian fleet.

The presence of the Turks in the Adriatic caused the greatest alarm in Venice, for they were between the city and the allied fleet, of whose movements little could be known owing to slow communications. The city made every preparation to defend the channel entrances. Trenches were dug, traverses thrown up, and the citizens saw themselves at the point of ruin in the absence of their fleet, just as had been the case two centuries earlier when the Genoese came to Chioggia. Messages were sent to Veniero to urge haste in action. While Venice was thus excited by lack of news from its fleet and the nearness of the enemy, Ali himself was rendered cautious by his own ignorance of the movements of the allies. He was unwilling to go as far as Venice until he was sure of not being intercepted. At the end of August he heard of the fall of Famagosta and knew the Christian fleet would no longer be drawn in that direction.

A day or two later the scout vessels from Sicily returned saying the Christian fleets had assembled, whereupon the Turkish fleet moved out of the Adriatic and harried the island of Corfu. Three galleys were driven ashore by the guns of the fortress. The city was surrounded by Turkish troops and suffered much damage, but was not taken, and on September 10, the fleet having arrived at Parga, a galley came from Constantinople with instructions written after the news of the surrender of Famagosta telling Ali to follow up the victory by sea, sparing no one, taking the Venetian Islands and, above all, he was to find the Christian fleet and destroy it. On September 16, Ali left Parga with all his fleet and went to Lepanto to resupply with biscuit and replace casualties among the crews.

THE CHRISTIANS AT MESSINA

As was said, Don John got to Messina August 25 when the news of the Turkish presence in the Adriatic was most disturbing to Veniero. Don

John was young, ardent, and engaging. He had the boldness fitting him for his high post, but the elements of his fleet were discordant, and the mutual distrust was great. The day after arrival Don John called a general council consisting of 70 principal officers and adventurers to see what could be done. There is no doubt that Don John himself wanted to fight from the first instant. But apparently his immediate councilors always were reluctant. In the first place, as was said, King Philip wanted conquests in Africa. Besides, the Spanish councilors felt they had to restrain their young commander's impetuosity. They thoroughly distrusted the Venetians and feared that the latter would make a peace or otherwise leave them in the lurch. They wanted to beat the Turk, but they did not wish to see the Venetians get any advantage from it. Further than this I do not think their caution went. Their feeling was probably not unlike that of certain German-Americans in the late war, who were perfectly loyal to their adopted country, and wished her to win the war, but did not care how much punishment England and France took.

Whatever may have been King Philip's wishes and instructions to Don John's councilors, there can be little doubt that general opinion among the great nobles, of whom so many were in the expedition, was that the hostile fleet was the becoming and creditable objective. The decisive address at the Council was made by Ascanio della Cornia, General of the Allied Infantry, a Spanish subject, who is named by Italians as having been opposed to battle, but in his recorded speech he shows no improper unwillingness. In his address the latter said,

> Your Highness has asked for my opinion as to what we may do, supposing us to have 146 galleys and 6 galleasses, besides transports and 60 galleys expected from Candia, of which we have heard nothing for many days, and supposing the Turks to have 250 rowing ships now in Dalmatia and that the Turks have an army on shore of 40,000 to 50,000 men.

He then went on that they should suppose the Turkish vessels to be well manned and that they should not attempt anything serious without the 60 ships from Candia, whose movements were unknown, but, "we might go to Brindisi, if the seamen think it would not incur danger of meeting the Turkish fleet." His advice was straightforward and without a trace of wishing to avoid battle if on fairly equal terms, but 146 galleys (of which many were not yet in Messina) against 250 Turks was not a reasonable match and the Spaniards did well to say so. So they waited at Messina and prepared their ships. On September 1, Gian Andrea Doria got in with 12 ships of his own and the Marquis of Santa Cruz with 30 Neapolitan ships and also the squadron from Palermo. The next day Quirini arrived from Syracuse with the 60 ships of the Candian squadron, with no soldiers and only 50 seamen per ship. He had delayed leaving Candia in the hope of sending aid to Famagosta, but finally decided not to do so and started west on August 13, although unaware of the loss of Famagosta a few days earlier. As a contemporary historian says, it was fortunate that Quirini renounced his attempt to aid Famagosta, for otherwise the ships needed to turn the scale at Lepanto would have been wanting and there would have been no battle.

The Organization and Instructions at Messina

Thus the fleet was all assembled. The Pope had 12 galleys; the King had 14 Spanish, 30 Neapolitan, and 10 Sicilian royal galleys and hired 12 from Doria and 13 from five other "assentiste." He also had 22 nefs. The Republic had 108 galleys, 6 galleasses, and 2 large nefs (of nearly 2,000 tons' burden). The city of Genoa, the Duke of Savoy, and the Knights of Malta sent 3 galleys each. Altogether there were 208 galleys, 6 galleasses, and 24 nefs carrying supplies. In addition there were some 50 light rowing craft with crews of 40 to 50 men each.*

As for the number of men we have seen that the "ordinary crews," that is, officers, seamen, and rowers, of the Papal ships, were by the contract to be not less than 1,800 rowers and 720 officers and seamen for 12 ships, or 210 men per ship. There is little probability that the contract provision was exceeded. The Venetian ships were somewhat weak. If we take it that the remaining vessels were as strong as the Pope's, we may assume an average of 190 men as a high one for ordinary crews, or a total of not over 39,520 men for galleys. The 6 galleasses probably had no more than 300 men each (they needed 350 rowers to fill their benches). The nefs may have as many as 1,000 seamen and the small craft, 2,000 men. In all, 44,320 men. According to the researches of Rosell and the report of Caetani, the soldiers numbered 29,000. (Rosell omits the 3 Maltese ships which may have had

---

* The various accounts differ as to the precise number of ships at various dates, but we must recollect that reconnaissances and casualties and accessions caused the number available to vary from day to day. Probably there were 72,000 to 73,000 souls.

500 soldiers.) Of these, 1,500 were Papal and 5,000 Venetian, and the King supplied 8,000 Spanish, 5,000 German, and 5,000 Italian troops. There were also 4,000 noble adventurers and their followers, who came for renown in fighting the infidel. Thus we have, as a high estimate, a total of 73,320 souls on board the great fleet assembled in Messina. (However, Rosell says 80,000 in 313 vessels of all types, pp. 79-80.)

The ships were not all in the same condition. The Spaniards were in excellent shape, well provisioned and fully manned. The Spanish infantry were considered the best in the world (although the regiments here were not veterans). The Papal ships were also in excellent condition, but the Venetians were very short of soldiers and even rowers, for they had been hard hit by the plague the year before and discipline was scarcely good. To a friend Don John wrote very disparagingly of the Venetian numbers, discipline, and material. Don John urged Veniero to let him fill up the Venetian ships to at least 100 soldiers each, but Veniero testily refused to let foreigners on board, saying the Venetian rowers were freemen and could be trusted with arms in battle and, indeed, Caetani reported after the battle that they did as well as any soldiers. Don John insisted and, finally, by the diplomacy of Marc Antonio, Veniero very reluctantly accepted 1,500 Spaniards and 2,500 Italians of the King's men. Even with this reassignment of soldiers, the numbers in the squadrons varied much. The Venetians seem to have averaged nearly 75 soldiers, whereas the Papal galleys averaged 130 and the Spaniards about 145 per galley. Some 5,000 soldiers must have been in the galleasses and nefs and as extras in the flagships. In the squadrons the soldiers were not evenly divided among the ships, for the larger flagships had 200 or 300 and Don John had 400 soldiers on his Royal.

The fleet being happily assembled, it was found that opinions had changed. Honorato Caetani wrote, on September 6, "In almost all the private councils della Cornia has been far from fighting, but yesterday in the private council of the royal officials he was very ready. Only Count Santa Fiora was opposed." A general council was called, and Don John said he thought they were now able to seek the enemy, and asked for opinions. After many had spoken, Ascano della Cornia again summed up the situation, saying first that even

if our fleet should be defeated our princes are not so weak that they could not at least take sufficient measures for defense. Whereas, if we are victors we might perhaps expect the rescue of Greece and other great advantages. Besides which, I think, as I have said at other times, we cannot hope much to injure the Turk unless we first destroy his fleet and this we cannot overcome by our inaction, nor hope that it will break up through its own weakness. Rather, it is our own side which is running this risk through caution. So if Your Excellencies have a strength sufficient to hope for victory it appears to me that by all means we should not lose this occasion and so I urge.

This was thoroughly sound strategic reasoning and is far from supporting the contention of those who believe that Don John's councilors were all opposed to fighting (della Cornia was an Italian subject of the King). Della Cornia then compared the two forces.

I confirm what previous gentlemen have said and confess that as for the Spaniards they are new and not very skillful and the Italians are the same and the Germans of little use at sea and are short of arquebuses, but nevertheless I do not see that the enemy can have very good people, nor any better than ours, for we hear that last year there was great mortality and this year they have a great army in Cyprus. As for the number and quality of the Turkish ships our information is conflicting. I am no great judge in maritime affairs * * * and in these matters I defer to gentlemen of more experience at sea, but however it is, it appears to me that Your Excellencies should commit yourselves somewhat to fortune, for in war no one can be so cautious as to exclude luck. So immediately you should get under way and proceed with this fleet as quickly as possible to Brindisi or Corfu where, being so near the enemy, we shall have certain information and shall act as seems best. * * * I warn all that in leaving here it must be with the fixed intention of fighting the enemy on the way, and in conformity, Your Highness must issue the necessary orders for if we go out undecided and as is said "with two hearts," we shall have to make up our minds when action is upon us and we might easily lose if we should unexpectedly meet the Turkish fleet. This is my opinion, with due deference to all better informed than myself.

No advice could have been sounder than that of this distinguished soldier and the Council agreed to it. Don John established the fleet organization and issued the battle instructions.

But not even the decision to fight could put an end to rivalry and jealousies. A dispute arose between the Prior of Messina, commanding the Maltese squadron, and de Leyni, commanding the Savoyard ships, as to which was to have precedence in the assignment of positions in the fleet. Don John decided in favor of Savoy, but the Prior appealed to the Pope as arbitrator under the treaty. Subordination and discipline were then a matter mainly for the lowest ranks, and the subject gave trouble again before the battle.

The year before the squadrons had been formed according to nationality and, as will be recollected, there had been jealousies and suspicions. This year, to make sure that no leader should withdraw his ships, all nationalities were distributed throughout the fleet in every squadron, so that Spanish, Venetian, and Papal ships flanked and supported each other throughout the line.

The fleet was divided into four principal squadrons. The center of 64 galleys was commanded by Don John in person in the Royal with Marc Antonio Colonna in the Papal Capitana on his right and Sebastian Veniero in the Venetian Capitana on his left, all three in the center of the squadron. Thus none of the three commanders could play each other false. The center ships were distinguished by blue pennants at the masthead. The right squadron of 54 galleys carrying green pennants at the peak of the antenne was commanded by Gian Andrea Doria, an Italian serving Spain. His Capitana led the fleet in cruising and was the right ship in line of battle. Augustino Barbarigo, Venetian Proveditor (lieutenant to Veniero), directed the left squadron of 53 vessels which were given by yellow pennants on the vang of the antenna. Barbarigo's own vessel was on the left, in battle formation, and Marco Quirini was on the right. The reserve of 38 ships under Don Alvaro de Bazan, Marquis of Santa Cruz, bore white pennants on staffs at the stern. The reserve squadron was in the rear of the center in battle, and the last in cruising and was to aid stragglers. But from the reserve were detailed 8 vessels to serve as an advance guard, to be 8 to 20 miles ahead of the fleet under Don Juan de Cardona, who also had two fast dispatch boats (fragatine) with him to communicate with the main body. Upon discovery of the enemy, Cardona was to return to the fleet and take his own battle station as left ship of the right wing, while the others were to form as reserve, 4 and 4 in rear of the two wings. In cruising, the squadrons were to move in columns of fours.

In addition, the 6 great Venetian galleasses under Antonio Duodo were divided into groups of two and assigned to the three divisions of the line. In battle they were to take position half-a-mile or more ahead of the main line, each pair in front of its own division and with half-a-mile or more between vessels.

From the first Don John had been much impressed by the tactical possibilities of these new craft. Their distinguishing features were their considerable broadside batteries and the deck covering the rowers, which gave ample room for soldiers.

It was Don John's intention to use their powerful batteries to break up the advancing hostile line and throw it into confusion. Their fire would be efficacious while the enemy passed them and, if some galleys stopped to board, so much the better, the galleasses' high sides and many soldiers would make most effective resistance.

The galleasses were wide and heavy, having 50 oars needing 7 men to each oar.* But they were probably undermanned and they were sluggish, so that the galleys had to take turns in towing them, three, and sometimes more at a time, to each galleass. A flag officer took charge of the towing roster for each galleass. Besides all these rowing ships, the 24 nefs with 3,000 soldiers on board and crews of 1,000 sailors, under the command of Don Cesar Davalos, were to accompany the fleet with supplies of all kinds, including field and siege guns for use if the soldiers should land for operations on shore. In battle, the nefs were to join battle where it would be most advantageous if the wind permitted, but, if it was calm, Davalos was to put his soldiers in boats and send them to report at the sterns of the galleys, who would tell them what to do. The fragatine were to be stationed astern of the galleys in battle to carry messages and were to take two small guns on board and 10 soldiers and fight the small craft of the enemy and render other service as possible.

The instructions for battle were that ships in each squadron were to be as close as possible without interfering with each other's oars, and that the squadrons should be 3 or 4 ship's lengths (150 to 200 yards) apart. As the spread of each ship's oars from tip to tip was 25 yards, we may take it that from mast to mast the distance would be 35 yards or more and that the whole line of 170 vessels was intended to cover about 6,300 to 7,000 yards.** At the signal for battle all vessels would take their assigned posi-

---

* Testimony taken after the war shows that the galleasses had 4 men to the oar and that in order to get them out of the arsenal, the telari or rowing frames were too narrow from thole pin to opposite pin, so that the rowing was very ineffective. See *Le Galere Grosse Veneziane*, by G. Giomo, Venezia, 1895.

** Jurien de la Gravière says that at Rochelle the Duc de Guise put his galleys at 20 toises (128 feet) apart. The same at Lepanto would make a line about 7,500 yards long. But the French ships were probably quinqueremes, needing more space.

tions and fregatine with experienced officers would see that all were in place. Approaching the enemy they would row slowly, to prevent exhaustion, and would take care not to foul each other. The artillery was to be discharged when most effective, but at least two pieces were to be kept loaded until an enemy was actually in contact.

Don Alvaro de Bazan with the reserve was not to hurry into action, but was to help when and where help was needed.

Such were the administrative and tactical arrangements, but also the leaders used every means (now called propaganda) to excite the ardor of the crews. They had much to overcome.

The expedition was made to seem a crusade. The Pope sent a Bishop as special envoy to Messina to take his blessing. Consecrated battle flags were given to Don John and Marc Antonio for display on "The Day."* A jubilee was preached at Messina, and all confessed their sins. His Holiness ordered that all captains of galleys and other vessels should take pains to live, and cause others to live, as good Christians.

Preparations were pushed for sailing. Don John sent to Italy to have additional soldiers assembled at Otranto, and Veniero said he would get many at Corfu. On the 15th the fleet was ready and at vespers the nefs were towed by galleys out to the Faro of Messina with orders to proceed to Corfu, to resupply the fleet there. The fleet knew nothing more of them until it returned to Corfu, after the victory, in some distress for lack of supplies and found the nefs waiting. It then appeared the nefs had anchored in the Gulf of Taranto and waited for orders, expecting to meet the fleet there, as it passed by.

THE ADVANCE TO CORFU

On September 16, the splendid fleet put out from Messina. The Pope's Nuncio stationed himself in a fragatina at the Faro Point and gave the Pope's blessing to each ship as she passed to sea. That night the expedition anchored on the opposite shore of Italy, where the general cruising orders were issued, and the crews "shook down." Here also, Commendador Gil d'Andrada, a distinguished Spanish seaman, returned from a scouting

---

* The Pope's flag for Don Juan was of blue damask with an embroidered crucifix at whose feet were the arms of the Pope, of His Catholic Majesty, and of Venice enlaced by a chain as symbol of the Holy League; and hanging from these were those of Don Juan of Austria, as the executant of the great thought of the united countries (Duro, page 320).

expedition saying that he had left Otranto on the 5th where he learned of the Turks' movement southward out of the Adriatic, and their attack on Corfu.

On the morning of the 17th, being the first day of the expedition, the great ship's tent of Don John's Royal was set up on shore and mass was celebrated, with much ceremony in the presence of the principal leaders, and the fleet moved to Castel Bianco some 40 miles from Messina, anchoring for the night. Here the Capitana of Malta was nearly lost on the beach and after the battle it was understood that this was an omen of her dreadful experience to come. On the 18th the fleet was at Cape Schilazi and the next day at Valle de Crotona where it anchored again; 125 miles in 4 days. Here it stayed 4 days, held by bad weather, and many murmured that Don John wished to give the enemy an opportunity to get away, and that the Council held there was for the purpose of making the Pope and the Doge believe that King Philip wanted battle when such was not the case. It must have been a very trying adventure for the three Commanders in Chief with such suspicions abroad. Don John had sent forward from Messina to assemble infantry here, but only 500 had arrived and unsuccessful effort was made to get 1,500 more at Brindisi and Otranto. Don John now wanted to go direct to Prevesa in search of the enemy, but Veniero persuaded him to go to Corfu, saying he expected to pick up 6,000 infantry there.

On the 24th the fleet got under way again, having good winds, and crossed the Gulf of Taranto the next day and was off Fano (a small island 12 miles west of Corfu) by night. The weather was now bad and a number of ships anchored on the shoals of Fano, but dragged their anchors and had a bad time. The next day, about noon, most of the fleet was off the north point of Corfu, 130 miles in a little over 2 days. Here ships anchored and watered and cut firewood and on the 27th all arrived off the city of Corfu. News of the enemy was verified, and several galleys were sent to scout for further news. Nothing being known of the nefs which were carrying the heavy artillery for siege operations against some strong point, Veniero objected to a proposal to take guns from the fortress as substitutes, but Marc Antonio finally persuaded him to agree, after having directed his attention to the clause in the treaty of the League which required all the parties to supply whatever they had in surplus.

To support his position with his colleagues, it is alleged that Colonna had taken the precaution to provide himself at Rome with a *motu proprio* of the Pope, to use in case of necessity, that under pain of excommunication he was not to consent to any proposal except battle, and now when the Venetians wanted to go direct to Cyprus (not having heard of its loss), Marc Antonio Colonna persuaded Veniero to go on and let time show if they would fight the fleet on the way.

Don John held a general Council (although he personally meant to fight, even if Ali had his whole fleet) (for he did not wish to appear haughty and negligent of others' opinions). It was surprising how many wished to take up some secondary operation. These urged the power of the Turkish Empire and its unity in command, contrary to the divisions among the Christians, who were mostly of little training and far from home.

It is scarcely likely that these half-hearted advisers were either faint-hearted personally or anxious to avoid battle in order to see Venice lose her possessions, as so many Italians affirm to this day. It is more likely that they realized that their chief, the young and gallant Prince, was inclined to be rash and they wished to guard themselves against reproach for their advice in case of disaster, rather than preserve themselves from the dangers of battle.

As the nefs had not arrived, Don John sent the Auditor-General of the League back to Italy, to make arrangements for supplies from other sources and, after completing supplies and taking 500 soldiers from the fortress against Veniero's protest, the fleet moved out of harbor—Don John with the Spanish forces on September 29, Veniero the next day— and they all crossed to Gomenizza, an excellent harbor, on the opposite side of the bay where there was good firewood and water.

The Quarrel at Gomenizza

As they crossed to Gomenizza, a dispatch boat arrived from Gil d'Andrada who was again scouting, and reported that the Turks had arrived at Lepanto a few days previously with less than 200 ships and short of men, due to sickness and casualties of the summer. At Gomenizza ships hauled their sterns to the shore, as if it were friendly country, and sent out watering parties without proper escort. A small party from the neighboring Turkish fort of Margariti killed a few men and horses from the fleet and took 15 prisoners who were sent to Ali Pasha at Lepanto and there examined under torture.

Here the fleet was inspected. His Highness boarded all the capitanas and Marc Antonio and eight other officers, all Spanish subjects, took the others. Several Venetian captains seem to have refused to let Doria set foot on their ships, but allowed Don John to send the Commendador Real of Castile, Don Luis de Requesens, to inspect them. As for Veniero himself, he reported to Venice that he

> was considerably irritated that an Andrea Doria should come to see whether a vessel commanded by one of Your Serenity's generals was in good order after it had already been inspected and praised by Don John himself. Nevertheless, I allowed him to come and see.

Caetani wrote of the inspection to his uncle Cardinal Sermoneta saying,

> The squadron of His Holiness seen by the Commendador Mayor showed up well, some of the Venetians should have had more soldiers but on the average they were good: those of His Majesty were excellent.

As the inspection officers boarded each vessel, she fired a salute and her arquebusiers discharged their pieces, causing many accidents on other ships.

Throughout the entire trip from Messina, salvo firing has caused many casualties in every port, some times as many as 20 deaths; for the soldiers fired carelessly with ball and the galleys were close together. So an order was given providing the death penalty for anybody who fired ball and also for his galley captain and this stopped the losses. As a result of the inspection, 4 Venetian galleys were stripped and their crews distributed among other ships.

A misadventure at Gomenizza nearly ruined the League. Among the Spanish soldiers that Don John had transferred to the Venetian squadron was an Italian captain named Muzio. He was overbearing and rough and enjoyed a row. One of his men infringed some rule of the ship and was called to order by the Comito, the master of the rowers. Muzio took the part of his man; the altercation became a riot which attracted attention on other ships and Veniero sent his provost guard when a man was killed and others wounded. Finally, Veniero's "admiral" (chief of staff) appeared and Muzio was overpowered and made prisoner. Veniero was already annoyed at having subjects of Spain serving on Venetian ships and there had been some friction. He now ordered Muzio and two of his soldiers to be run up to the peak of the antenna and sent to Don John to tell him of the disturbance. Don John politely replied, telling Veniero to act as he thought justice required,* but in a few minutes, when he learned that these Spanish subjects had been executed by a foreigner before his consent had been received, his hot anger, fanned by those about him, knew no bounds at the personal affront to him. He gave no consideration to the fact that discipline in the Venetian fleet was the responsibility of Veniero. He spoke of seizing Veniero and putting him to death or otherwise he would return to Italy with the Spanish ships. The Venetian ships drew out from the others and cleared for action.

Marc Antonio Colonna, ably seconded by the Marquis of Santa Cruz and Barbarigo, the Proveditor of Venice, did their best to quiet matters. Colonna reproved Veniero that at his great age of 75 years he so far forgot his own profession (the law) as to assume authority over a Spanish subject. To Don John the peacemakers said the death of a few men who deserved their fate should not be the means of breaking up the League, and that Don John should not disappoint the Christian world. They assured Don John that Veniero was ashamed of his error and that he could not be punished unless the Spaniards first conquered 112 Venetian ships who would undoubtedly support their General at Sea. In the end, after working the greater part of the night, the diplomatists succeeded in getting Don John to content himself by reporting the whole matter to the King, to the Pope, and to the Signory. While waiting for their decisions, he refused to meet Veniero in Council, where Barbarigo thereafter represented Venice after taking his instructions from Veniero, who retained his command.

When Barbarigo and Marc Antonio Colonna at last were able to tell Veniero of Don John's terms, they feared an outburst of rage, knowing his passionate temperament, but to their great pleasure he received their report with calmness, and preparations for departure continued, in spite of high feeling on both sides.

The Christian Advance on Lepanto

On October 3 Gil d'Andrada himself returned, reporting that the Greeks said victory was certain, but did not know that the Greeks were

* Caracciolo, p. 25.

saying the same to Ali. At this news all was put in order and the fleet
sailed to seek the enemy. The next day, the weather being fine, Don John
made the signal for battle to see that all knew their respective positions.
The three Maltese vessels refused to occupy their assigned stations, but
lay between the right and center divisions in resentment at the decisions
of Don John awarding the ranking position to the Capitana of Savoy. Don
John went personally to beg the Prior of Messina to occupy places assigned him in line, and the latter at last did so, on the understanding that
his compliance was to establish no precedent for the future. This decision
was afterwards confirmed by the Pope.

The fleet now heard of the surrender of Famagosta 2 months previously after having exhausted its supplies in a siege of 10½ months
which cost the death of 50,000 Turks. The ardor of the men for battle
was much increased by desire for revenge. As the pilots did not wish to
reach Cephallonia by night, the fleet furled sail and lay to under oars for
the night, which again caused many to murmur that Don John wished to
give the enemy an opportunity to escape. On which Caracciolo, a partici-
pant and historian of the campaign, comments that this was contrary to
ancient discipline, for soldiers have no right to examine a general's purpose. In the morning of the 5th the fleet ran into a fog, yet it arrived in
the northern part of the channel between Cephallonia and Ithaca, where
it anchored. Later in the day it pushed on to Val d'Alessandria at the
south end of Cephallonia and was held by bad weather, but was able to
use the time in watering.

That night, Caracoggia, a famous Turkish corsair, came among the
fleet in a small boat and counted the ships and returned to Ali Pasha. He
had done the same at Gomenizza. On the 6th the wind from the east prevented movement. Don John's Spanish council showed a preference for
some secondary measure, such as retiring to attack Castel Nuovo. The
prestige of the Turkish fleet was very great and besides, raids and the
seizure of booty and slaves were highly thought of as naval exploits. When
the three generals met a little later, Colonna and Don John are said by
Caetani to have been very ready to fight and Veniero (represented by
Barbarigo) showed that should any diversion on shore be attempted, the
ships were liable to be attacked while the soldiers were away at the siege.
So all were agreed.

At this moment an Albanian appeared, sent by the Governor of Zante. This man had been seized prisoner in the Morea and he alleged that Uluch Ali had been seen a few days before with perhaps 80 galleys and 2 nefs in tow standing southerly towards Modon and they had not returned. (His last statement was incorrect.) So it was resolved to take another step forward, but one which does not show any great expectation of a decisive battle. The fleet was to advance to Petala, a fine port just opposite on the mainland, and from there it would go on and sight the castles guarding the entrance to the Gulf of Corinth, doing this, as we are told, rather for the sake of the generals' reputation than with the idea of attacking the castles. As for the Turkish fleet, few thought it would even be seen, for with 80 vessels absent, as just reported, it would not venture away from the guns of the fortress.

By night the wind had gone down, so with a smooth sea and bright moonlight the Christian fleet got under way under oars about 9 o'clock October 6, with Don Juan of Cardona leading the advance guard with orders to look into Petala. About 6 the next morning the fleet arrived at the Curzolari Islands and Cardona turned northwards towards Petala, but sent one galley southward to look around Point Scropha towards Lepanto, which lay 36 miles eastward beyond the fortresses, guarding the entrance to the Gulf of Lepanto where the enemy was thought to be. The galley was slow in going forward, but landed men to climb the hill and see the prospect.

In the meantime, about 6:30, the fleet passed in among the islands, expecting to anchor there while Cardona was examining Petala. Don John, in the Royal, pushed through the fleet towards the south and Doria leading his squadron was nearly out of the channel between Oxia and the mainland. It was a little after 7 o'clock.

THE TURKS IN COUNCIL AT LEPANTO

The Turkish fleet had reached Lepanto on September 27 and since then had been making every preparation for battle. Mehemet Bey with 60 galleys went up the Gulf of Corinth to get provisions and other supplies and particularly swordsmen. He returned with 10,000 janissaries and 2,000 spahis and as many adventurers. Uluch Ali went to Modon, as the Christians had heard, but his return with many additional men was unknown to them. Ali promptly heard that the Christian fleet had left Corfu for Cephallonia. He knew that the nefs with supplies had not arrived, but he was misinformed as to the Christian strength, for the Spanish prisoners, seized at Gomenizza and tortured, understated its numbers and, by some error, so did Caracoggia. Thus both sides underestimated the strength of the other and both were the more ready to accept battle.

TURKISH STRENGTH

Upon the reassembly of the Turkish fleet, it much outnumbered that of the allies. The primary authorities differ somewhat as to its size, but we may take it that it had about 210 galleys. Many of these were of the largest type with from 28 to 30 banks of oars. Besides, there were about 40 galliots and a number of small craft, possibly twenty. The galliots were rowing vessels with from 16 to 25 banks of oars, but lacked the "rembate" or raised platforms for soldiers at the bows. They were held to be nearly as good as galleys. We do not know the exact number in their crews, but the number of "fanale" (big flagships) was greater in the Turkish fleet. We cannot be far wrong if we allow 200 men each to the galleys and 160 men each to the galliots, giving 48,400 for the ordinary crews. The soldiers were about 25,000. Adding 1,500 for the crews of the small craft, we have a total force of nearly 75,000;* perhaps 5,000 more than the allies, who were now without the nefs manned by nearly 4,000 soldiers and 1,000 mariners, but had picked up an additional 1,000 soldiers.

TURKISH LEADERS

The principal commanders in the Turkish fleet were renowned corsairs, whose names and histories were well known to their adversaries.

Ali Pasha, the Commander in Chief, was a man of low birth, who first found employment as muezzin in the minaret of a mosque to call the faithful to prayer. His powerful and beautiful voice floating over Constantinople attracted and charmed the wife of the Sultan, by whose favor, without any libidinous relations, supported by his own merit, he was raised from post to post to his present great command. Uluch Ali has already been mentioned. Besides these there were Mehemet Sirocco,

---

* Rosell thinks there were 120,000 men in the complements of 315 Turkish galleys and galliots, besides many small craft. I cannot believe the Turks so much outnumbered the allies.

Bey of Alexandria; Carabink, Bey of Caramania; Mehemet, Bey of Negropont; Hassan, son of the famous Barbarossa; Pertau Pasha, commanding the troops, a distinguished soldier of much experience; and many others scarcely less famous in their time.

Comparison of the Fleets

In comparing the two fleets, it may be said that although the Turks had considerably more ships and perhaps a few more men, their great advantage was in prestige. The armies and fleets of Turkey were the terror of Europe. The Christian ships were stronger in artillery, each having five guns firing ahead, whereas the Turks had three only. The Christian galleasses were an unmatched and untried element. The Christian soldiers were better protected, not only by better armor but by pavesades along the ships' sides, whereas the Turks had none of the latter. As for missile weapons, the Christians were mostly armed with arquebuses and these of a better quality than the few that the Turks had. The latter were mostly archers and relied on the rapid discharge of their powerful bows which were superior to the renowned English long bows. The bowman could fire many times as fast as the arquebusier. Good armor would turn both arrows and arquebus shots. But the latter frequently did damage from shock even when not piercing armor, for they had more punch, even with little more range. Arrows were able to do great execution at short ranges and both sides had "trombe" (wooden tubes hooped with iron for throwing fire balls, using small charges of powder).

Turkish Council Before Battle

On October 3d or 4th Ali called a council to consider the Turkish course. Although he had received orders from Constantinople to fight, he asked every one freely to express his opinion. Two Turkish secretaries taken in the battle seem to have given their Christian captors a very good account of the deliberations.*

Hassan led off, urging battle, saying these were the same peoples and organized in the same way as those his great father had defeated 33 years before in the very same waters without drawing his sword (meaning without coming to boarding). He dwelt on the enmity between the Chris-

---

* See Contarini in his dedication, *Cose successe dal Principio della Guerra mossa da Selim.*

tians, so that they had no real strength, and added they were blasphemers of God with much money and munitions to be seized. Nor were their leaders like his own audience "who know no blasphemy and reverence and love each other." He enumerated and praised the Turkish forces and asserted the Christians were inferior in number as well as in spirit, as Caracoggia had reported. The enemy would flee quickly and would be caught in the hand.

Uluch Ali followed in an eloquent address along the same lines, urging the wrath of the Sultan should they refuse battle,* and saying they should not stay to play with the women of Lepanto.

Of contrary opinion were Sirocco of Alexandria, and Carabink, old soldiers experienced in naval war, and Mahomet Bey. The latter attempted to refute Hassan and Uluch Ali. He pointed out the enemy would not have come so far unless he meant to fight, nor without full information of the Turkish strength, and that therefore he would be at least equal in strength. It should not be thought the Christians imagined they were coming to destruction, nor that the gallant Caracoggia had seen all the enemy. They knew, he said, from spies and prisoners, that the Christians meant to fight, and not to show themselves and run away. He denied that the present League was comparable to the former one, as Hassan said, and reminded them that the son of the great Emperor Charles V was in command, young, ardent, burning for glory, loved by the fleet and respected by the Generals, caring neither for gold nor treasure, hoping only to have praise of his valor reach his brother in Spain. He recounted the victories of their own fleet and army in the past year, he named the places raided in the past summer and the glory accruing.

> I say positively and always shall say that there is no less valor and wisdom in knowing how to preserve ourselves and our conquests than in going out to get more by main force and skill.

He alleged that in their present secure position in the Gulf, covered by two strong castles with plenty of munitions and men, they should await the enemy and let him waste his strength against their defenses and, then, if it should seem fit, they could issue from behind the castles and destroy the Christians.

---

* When Uluch Ali returned to Constantinople he seems to have reported that he advised against battle.

In waiting there could be little serious risk, for the Christians would soon lack supplies and the bad season was drawing on to compel them to go back. At last he alluded to the enemies in their own house, meaning the great numbers of Christian rowers. Nevertheless, Mahomet professed himself ready to follow the decision of the Council, whatever it might be.

His opinion pleased Pertau Pasha, Sirocco and many others, but Ali caused the Sultan's order to fight to be read aloud, and summed up the reasons why they might hope for success. He said the Christians would not seek battle without the support of the Spanish nefs and that Veniero could not force the issue if he wished to do so. The Christians would therefore not proceed beyond Val d'Alessandria until the nefs came, and therefore the Turks should hurry. Their many ships would intimidate the Christians and, although many were small, these could go quickly where needed to re-enforce the big vessels. The recruits were good men and would fight well, if mixed with the veterans. The arquebus should not be thought a better weapon than the Turkish bow, for the latter could shoot 30 times while the former was reloading for a second shot. He mentioned the bad feeling in the Christian fleet and the hanging of Muzio.

So Pertau and the other leaders took heart and the Council agreed to seek the Christian fleet at Val d'Alessandria, expecting afterwards to besiege the fortresses of Corfu and Candia during the winter and move to the coast of Dalmatia in the spring, and so proceed slowly against all Christendom, for as yet the gradual advance of the Turks had been continuous for over two centuries with no decisive repulse. Yet that check was now at hand when on October 6 the Turkish fleet left the shelter of the fortresses and, running outside the narrows, it anchored off Galata, about 4 o'clock, to ship additional men. Caracoggia who had gone ahead to spy out the Christian situation, now returned to the fleet at Galata with the news the enemy was at Cephallonia.

On the morning of the 7th, long before daylight, the Turks again got under way, setting their foresails to a fine easterly breeze, expecting to attack the Christians at their anchorage, and were about 10 miles distant as the first of the Christians reached Point Scropha. The encounter equally surprised both parties and, as each believed the other to be weaker in numbers than he really was, both were glad to fight.

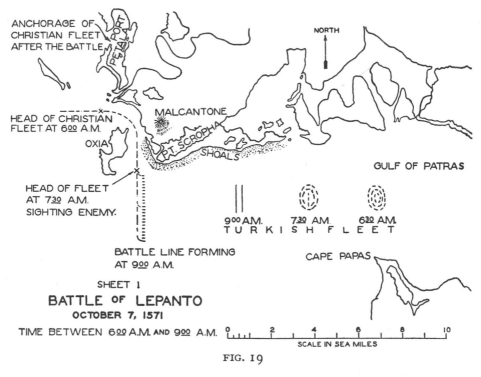

ANCHORAGE OF
CHRISTIAN FLEET
AFTER THE BATTLE

NORTH

HEAD OF CHRISTIAN
FLEET AT 6ºº A.M.

MALCANTONE

OXIA

PT SCROPHA

SHOALS

GULF OF PATRAS

HEAD OF FLEET
AT 7³º A.M.
SIGHTING ENEMY.

9ºº A.M.   7³º A.M.   6³º A.M.
T U R K I S H   F L E E T

BATTLE LINE FORMING
AT 9ºº A.M.

CAPE PAPAS

SHEET 1
BATTLE OF LEPANTO
OCTOBER 7, 1571
TIME BETWEEN 6ºº A.M. AND 9ºº A.M.

SCALE IN SEA MILES

FIG. 19

THE CHRISTIAN PREPARATIONS

As Doria came to Point Scropha about 7:30 o'clock, his masthead
lookout and also the scouts landed from the advance-guard galley who
had climbed the hill, besides the lookout on Don John's Royal simultaneously sighted the Turks. The latter reported a sail, another sail, many
ships and, quickly, the Turkish fleet. Even at this decisive moment there
were Spaniards at the side of Don John, who ventured again to suggest
to him to refuse battle. Although these men fought bravely enough, they
were afraid to take the responsibility of decisive action, and if their advice
to refuse battle at that last moment, had been taken, the result would
probably have been panic and disaster, as at Gerbe 11 years earlier, where
Doria had commanded the Spanish fleet. Fortunately, Don John was
beyond their reach, and answered "It is too late for counsel, it is now
time for battle," and, hailing his neighbors on each side, the Venetian
and Papal generals, they shouted back their agreement, as the treaty
required before action.

Don John fired a gun to call attention and "made a stork," up-ending his main antenna on which he hoisted a green flag as signal for battle. At the same moment he hoisted for the first time the great standard of the League blessed by the saintly Pope, and sent word through the fleet, which was in considerable disorder, to prepare for battle and take assigned stations. Don John himself leapt into a fragatina to move about freely and hustle the laggards. Particularly, he urged the galleasses forward, for they were well in rear and their battle stations were in front of the main line. A group of four galleys eagerly towed each of them.

Doria led the right wing out of the islands, heading south until he was over 4 miles from the land and had left more than enough room for the center and left squadrons to form between himself and the shore. Then his ships headed east and his line faced the approaching enemy, and slowed to mere steerage way. The center and left squadrons followed in order and did the same so that by about 9:30 o'clock the whole main line was formed, and advancing very slowly towards the enemy to permit the galleasses to work to the front and assume their proper position.

In the meantime, while the line was forming, the individual ships were clearing for action, arquebuses, halberds, iron maces, pikes, swords, and stones were distributed about the decks, corselets were put on. The arquebus men assembled on the high "rembate," the swordsmen and pikemen in the waists. The gunners loaded with chainshot and bolts; blunderbusses were brought out; the yards and masts were secured with preventer lashings. Standards and banners were gaily displayed from all parts of the ships. The fetters were struck from Christian convicts, for they were expected to fight when in contact with the enemy, but the Moslems were handcuffed to the oars in addition to the usual leg-irons. All storerooms, except those assigned to take the wounded, were then locked to prevent skulkers hiding there. Rations of bread, cheese, and wine were set forth along the gangways for all to refresh themselves. To give the bow guns good depression upon the enemy, Don John sawed the spur off his Royal and others did the same.

During this time of preparation Don John sent an excellent pilot to examine the enemy more closely, who, returning, made an encouraging report to the Commander in Chief; but, to Colonna, whose ship he afterwards boarded, he said, "sharpen your claws, my lord, for you will be sorely tried." Don John himself was disturbed by the absence of Cardona, who had gone off to Petala with the advance guard, and of the Marquis of Santa Cruz who, with his speedy "Shewolf," was chasing a vessel seen at daylight in the opposit direction. But Don Luis de Requesens, Commendador Real of Castile, told him not to worry about trifles, so Don John again entered a fragatina and ran down one-half the line encouraging the crews to fight bravely, while Colonna as Lieutenant-General of the League did the same on the other side. To the Spaniards the young commander said, "My sons, you are here to conquer or die, do not let the enemy say, 'where is now their God?'"; to the Venetians, "Today you will avenge your injuries"; and to all, "Christianity is at risk today, God will not let those dogs beat us. Both the survivors and the dead will be happy tonight, the former for having fought in this great battle and the others will have their jubilee in heaven." And he promised to watch for merit and reward the bravest. Returning, Don John stopped under the stern of the Venetian Capitana to exchange a few friendly words with Veniero, whom he had refused to see since the affair of Gomenizza. He then boarded his Royal and went forward to view the enemy. After which he called for his pipers and, in his armor in the sight of all, he danced a galliard, with his aide no older than himself, and then retired to the lofty poop, the station of command.

Now Don John again published the indulgence of the Pope which had been promulgated at Messina and there was general confession. Then the trumpets, pipes and drums sounded throughout the fleet,

> There was a universal shout and all devotedly knelt and invoked the Trinity and the Blessed Virgin, then the masters of galleys and the priests with crucifixes in their hands moved throughout each ship urging all with devout speech to fight the enemies of God's Holy Name.

By which, as Contarini ecstatically says,

> There was created a single body, a single will, a single desire without thought or care for death and all wished to fight for Jesus Christ. And immediately was made manifest a great mystery of the supreme power of God, for in an instant all the hates, ill-will, and enmities which had long been harbored for many grave offenses and which neither the efforts of friends nor the fear of justice in any way could reduce, now, these in an instant were extinguished, so that willingly guided by the Great God, Dispenser of every grace, those

who had so cruelly hated each other ran brotherly to embrace each other with fountains of tears. O blessed and merciful power of God over Thy faithful, how marvelous are Thy works!

After their final processional and invocation, the priests themselves went to their battle stations. Some climbed to the tops where they could see the battle and make their exhortations heard; others donned armor and with sword and pike were ready to give examples of Christian zeal in the thickest of the boarders' fight.

At this moment, so it is said, the saintly Pope was discussing business with his treasurer-general. Suddenly he went to the window and opened it, looking up to heaven. After some minutes he closed the window and, turning to the treasurer with an inspired face, he said, "This is not a time for our affair. Go and thank God, for our fleet is about to engage the Turk and God will give it victory." As the treasurer left the room he saw the Pope already on his knees. We may not believe such a story today, but perhaps hit on an explanation by believing that in a state of mental exaltation, the Pope frequently fell on his knees, thinking that instant was perhaps the time of battle and on this occasion it proved afterward he was right.

But let no one think that the work of the priesthood in prayer and battle was an insignificant thing and unworthy of mention in a study of naval tactics. It is the imponderables that win battles. The Pope's holy life and upright enthusiastic character gave him the respect of Catholic Europe and made his diplomacy effective. The incitements of the Pope and his priests on every ship gave the allies strength to face the unbroken prestige of the Turkish Empire. They gradually worked up a desire to fight and a determination to conquer or die, which is the basis of every victory. To-day we have other methods of military propaganda, but at Lepanto the victory belonged to the Pope no less than to the combatants. From him came the psychologic impulse outweighing political differences and reluctances, which animated the souls and strengthened the arms of the fighters.

The lines being perhaps 3 miles apart, Ali Pasha fired a blank charge which was answered by a shot from the Christian Royal. Apparently not recognizing what vessel had replied, Ali fired again and Don John answered again. The two Royals now knew each other, and, to the Christians,

Ali's vessel seemed to leap forward as if she wished single combat with their own flagship. It was now about ten o'clock and the enemy only about 2 miles away, but the Christian formation was not yet complete, for of the unwieldly galleasses only four had been able to reach their positions in front of the center and left squadrons. The two belonging to the right wing were issuing from among the islands, towed by Don Juan de Cardona and the vessels of the advance guard which were thereby kept out of their assigned positions. Nevertheless, Don John decided to delay no longer and somewhat quickened the Royal's stroke.

The Turkish Preparations

When the Turkish Commander first saw Doria's wing issuing from between the islands, it was thought that he was retiring and the Turks shouted "Allah! Allah! the dogs are flying, let us seize them," and much inspirited they made their prayers and ceremonial ablutions as they pushed on, but as the Christian column slowly drew out from the land the Turkish fleet doused sail, for the wind now failed, and formed for battle under oars. When the Christian right center and reserve had appeared, all thought they had before them the entire Christian fleet and praised Caracoggia for his accurate report from Gomenizza, but when the left wing under Barbarigo also issued forth, about 8:30, they understood that they had much to do. They thought well of the western ships (i.e., those of Spain and Sicily) and highly of Gian Andrea; but, as for the Venetians, they said they cared not if they were a thousand, while they marveled that the Christians should let a boy command them.

They went through the same steps as the Christians to prepare for battle, except they had no pavesades to place along the sides; so on coming within range their soldiers were exposed full length to the Christian missiles. The Christian slaves at the oar, whose insurrection in battle was always dreaded, were told to place themselves beneath their rowing thwarts when the enemy was reached and that any one who raised his head would be struck dead. The leaders made the same appeals to revenge, cupidity, and religion as in the Christian fleet. Ali himself was noted for his kindness and humane treatment of his Christian rowers and, striding forward into the middle of the rowing space, he addressed them in a vain hope to secure their sympathy. "If this day is yours," he said, "God gives it to you; but if to me be sure I shall set you free; so do what you owe me in return

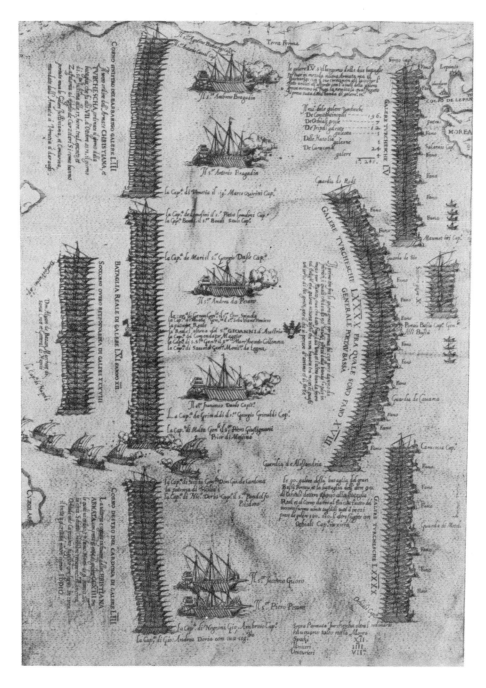

FIG. 20 *(Explanation on bottom of page 195)*

for my favor." He then called his two sons, boys only, and told them to remember that they were his children and do nothing to bring shame upon him. To this they answered with the Turkish formula, "May the bread which thou hast given us be blessed." Thereupon Ali sent them to another ship where they would not be exposed to the utmost fury of battle which would center about his own Royal.

Like the Christians, the Turks organized with three squadrons in the line. Mahomet Sirocco commanded the right wing of 55 galleys with his own Capitana on the right flank in the post of honor. His squadron was somewhat in advance of the center. Ali commanded the center of 90 galleys in line, with 6 more in close support in groups of 3 each. His own Royal was in the middle, supported on both flanks by a group of his most powerful galleys. Uluch Ali had the left wing of 60 galleys and 30 galliots and himself was on the left flank. There was besides a small reserve of 10 galleys and 20 fuste stationed in rear of the center. Thus the Turkish line of 235 vessels overlapped the enemy by 65 vessels, about a mile. All had orders to keep closed and move slowly, preserving the line.

While the two fleets were still far beyond range, Ali Pasha noted the galleasses which were visible in front of the Christian line. He did not wish his advance on the galleys to be diverted by an attack on vessels which were too lofty to be readily entered and overcome. He wished to neglect them as much as possible until the main line had been defeated. So during the approach he ordered that instead of going to meet the enemy in one unbroken line, the formation should divide into groups which should pass between the galleasses and rush upon the opposing line of

FIG. 20.—PLAN OF THE BATTLE OF LEPANTO
Courtesy of Naval Museum, Venice.

There is much information as to the battle written on the sheet. It states that it gives the order of the Christian and Turkish fleets as drawn up for the battle which took place on October 7, 1571, the Day of Santa Justina, at 17 hours (about 10:30 A.M.) between Lepanto and Cephallonia as the news was brought by the galleys of Justiniani and Contarini sent from the fleet to Venice to give account.

Other data: Besides the ordinary crews, the Turks picked up in the Morea 12,000 Spahis, 4,000 Janissaries, and 7,000 volunteers. The Turks had 245 ships, the Christians 205 galleys and 6 galleasses. Such was the haste with which the diagram was prepared that some statements on it are not in accord with others and some figures as to strength seem not to have been inserted in the text, having been left blank.

Venetian hatred for Doria was such that the plan falsely attributes the command of the right wing to Cardona.

galleys as speedily as possible to escape with the least loss from the artillery of the galleasses.

THE BATTLE

When the Christian fleet issued from the islands and formed its line, Barbarigo on the left flank was the guide ship. Being at the head of his wing when he came out, he took considerable sea room before turning

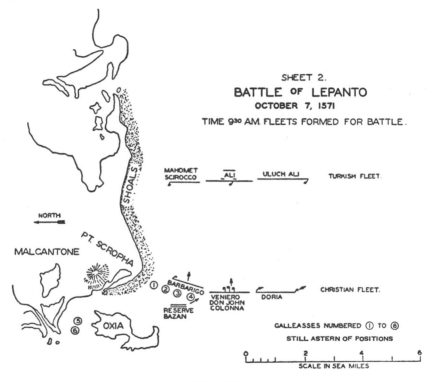

SHEET 2.
BATTLE OF LEPANTO
OCTOBER 7, 1571
TIME 9:30 A.M. FLEETS FORMED FOR BATTLE.

FIG. 21

east, in order to keep well clear of the coastal shoals with which he was not well acquainted. As his other ships followed him and came up on his starboard side, they formed a line of bearing slightly abaft his beam. His entire wing was somewhat in advance of the center with his own ship nearer the enemy than any other in the main line. The center squadron was separated by a couple of hundred yards from the left wing, and farther south, but near the center (when the line first formed about 9 o'clock) was the right wing under Doria.

While the enemy was still several miles off, and before the Royals recognized and headed for each other, the Turkish overlap on both wings became apparent. For the moment the situation had no influence on Barbarigo's movement straight ahead. Doria, on the contrary, was much affected by it. He was opposed by the finest seaman of the enemy, and as he fancied himself as a tactician, he felt obliged to maneuver. Besides, although no doubt a brave man personally, he seems to have dreaded the responsibility of command. He was not anxious to rush to battle and seek

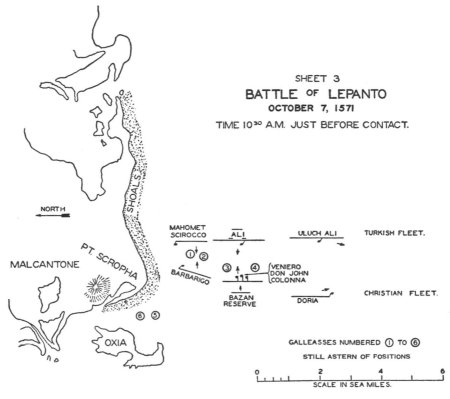

SHEET 3

BATTLE OF LEPANTO
OCTOBER 7, 1571

TIME 10³⁰ A.M. JUST BEFORE CONTACT.

FIG. 22

instant decision. Consequently, when he saw Uluch Ali's vessels reaching south of him, he edged off to his right to avoid envelopment and hoped for a better opportunity. As a result of this movement to the south, Doria naturally fell behind the line of the left and center and, seeing it, Uluch Ali also worked to the south to maintain his overlap and get the sun behind him as the day advanced.

The result was that as the two fleets were about to come within range at 10:30 o'clock, the Christian left wing led; the center was close to it and nearly abreast, while the left ship of the right wing was a mile or more to the right and rear of the Capitana of Malta, the right ship of the center. The 4 galleasses of the left and center were ¾ mile, more or less, in front of their respective squadrons, with from ½ to ¾ mile separating each from his neighbor. The 2 galleasses of the right wing were coming up under tow of the 8 vessels of the advanced guard, but were still behind Barbarigo and far from position. The reserve of 30 galleys was in position half a mile in rear of the center, with Don Alvaro de Bazan keenly observing events and ready to throw re-enforcements into ships needing men, as well as to enter the engagement with his own fine Capitana. He felt it his particular duty to aid and support the Royal. Besides his large vessels, he had 40 or 50 fragatine to transfer men to feed the fight and succor those that needed help.

As the Turkish right wing was slightly in advance of its center and its left was engaging in a game of maneuver with the Christian right, it followed that Barbarigo and Sirocco engaged first; then the two Commanders in Chief less than half an hour later, and Uluch Ali and Doria more than an hour after the centers.

Participants in the battle dwell upon the magnificent and terrible spectacle the two fleets offered each other as they approached. All the ships were covered with gay banners, but the Turks outdid the Christians in liveliness of color, for as their ships had no pavesades, the Turkish soldiers exposed their whole figures with their bright turbans and multicolored clothing. As they drew near on the smooth sea the shining helmets and polished corselets of the soldiers and the metal lanterns of the flagships glittered from afar in the brilliant sunshine, while the foam sparkled from the oars of over 60,000 rowers.

* * * * *

It is convenient to follow the course of the battle separately in each of the three sections.

THE NORTHERN ENGAGEMENT

As the northern wings drew near, the wind rose again but from the west and, although light, it checked the advance of the Turks. One of the center galleasses fired the opening shot of the battle, but she was far out of range. It was about 10:30 o'clock. Immediately the two northern galleasses, commanded by two Bragadino brothers, Ambrosio and Antonio, whose relative had been so cruelly slain at Famagosta and whose vessels led the entire Christian fleet, opened a telling fire on Sirocco's approaching wing, and at the third discharge a vessel began to sink. The Christians cried "Victory," and the Turks were dismayed for an instant. Their drums ceased to beat and even Pertau Pasha far off in the center is said to have torn his beard in disappointment. But the gallant Turks quickly took courage and, at full speed with frightful shouts, the wing of nearly 60 ships inclined to the right, separating from the center, and broke into three groups to pass between the galleasses, disregarding them to fall upon the main line. As Sirocco's pilots were well versed locally, and as Barbarigo was keeping farther from the shoals than was necessary, it was the former's intention to envelop the hostile flank and fight the Christians two to one. But Barbarigo perceived his opponent's plan and realizing that if there was water enough for the Turks, there was enough for him also, he too changed direction with his ships and inclined towards the beach to leave no passage for Sirocco.

At the same time the northern Bragadina,* backing water with her port oars, spun quickly about and continued to fire her heavy bow guns at the passing Turks. She did great execution and, as the disordered Turkish line closed with the Christians, she followed, continuing to fire on the hostile rear with much effect. The other Bragadina remained in position engaged with the enemy's center where she could also protect the right ships of her own wing. A desperate melee followed the collision of the two lines. Only 6 or 7 Turks in all got to the westward of Barbarigo and against these he with his neighboring vessels turned completely about and met them bow to bow. The Turks had succeeded in concentrating on the extreme Christian flank and the boarders' fight was very fierce. Barbarigo at one time had 5 ships against him. But the Proveditor Quirini, who was the right guide of the left wing, recognizing that Sirocco's oblique movement left himself out of action, swung his neighboring ships around "like a door," as Diedo says, and attacked the Turks from their rear. Marino Contarini, Barbarigo's nephew, brought his vessel bravely to his uncle's help and was struck dead on his gangway. So the fight of sword and pike lasted indecisively for an hour with the Turks penned between Barbarigo's ships on one side, Quirini's vessels and the galleass on another, and the swampy shores in the third direction. As Sereno says of

* Besides her given name, a ship was frequently known by the feminine form of her captain's surname.

what he saw himself, "the sky could not be seen for arrows and shot. It was noon and yet it was dark from the smoke of the trombe and the pignatte* of many fire projectiles which were inextinguishable even in the water." Barbarigo was hard pressed; the enemy entered his ship, and he, finding his orders not understood, raised his vizor to speak more distinctly. Those about him remonstrated, but he replied it was better to be wounded than not to be able to command. In that instant an arrow pierced his eye and he fell, speechless, yet conscious, with a mortal wound. There was confusion on board as he was taken below, and the enemy forced their way as far aft as the mast, but Federigo Nani, the flag captain, rallied his men and the Count of Porcia's galley came alongside and drove the Turks out.

Now was exemplified the soundness of the Emperor Leo's maxim that it is well to fight the enemy on his own shores.** After about an hour of bloody fighting, the Turks began to yield. Then on many vessels the Christian slaves rose from under the benches, where their masters had thrust them, cut their chains with the abandoned weapons of the Turks and revenged themselves for the cruelties inflicted on them. Sirocco's ship was taken and he fled wounded to the shore. Caur Ali, a Turkish flag officer, whose ship had followed Sirocco in the envelopment, was also taken with his vessel. Then the neighboring Turkish vessels moved towards the near-by Rock of Villa Marino to save their persons ashore, but not all did so. A number of ships collided and made a sort of bridge to the beach and those whose fortune was favorable reached it and passing through the marshes gained firm ground. But

IRON FIRE BALL 4 ᵀᴼ 5 INCHES IN DIAMETER. THE COMBUSTIBLE WAS PACKED IN THE HOLLOW, AND IGNITED WHEN THE GUN WAS DISCHARGED.

FIG. 23

FOR A TROMBA

many were killed by the Christians, who were looting the prizes, and others leapt overboard too soon and were drowned. Then the victorious ships turned their artillery on the cliff covered with Turks and landed soldiers. Such was the despair of the Turks that some were said to be taken

---

* Pignatta—An earthenware pot filled with a fire-ball and thrown by hand; sometimes it held quick lime or else soft soap to grease the deck.

** He would be the more ready to save himself by getting ashore.

by captors armed with sticks only. Among the prisonerrs made on shore was Sirocco who was badly hurt. He was taken on shipboard and the next day, being in great agony, at his own request his captors mercifully put him to death. The victory of the left wing was complete, not a single Turkish vessel escaped, but all felt that it was dearly purchased by the death of Barbarigo, which occurred the next day after he had thanked God by gestures for the victory. To him was awarded by general consent the prize of valor on that great day. His tact, his gracious manners, his diplomatic skill, and force of character had held the fleet together at Gomenizza, and he crowned his life by his noble death, a worthy example of Venetian nobility at its best.

The Battle in the Center

Ali Pasha and Don John had exchanged recognition shots somewhat before the northern wing engaged. It was about half an hour later (11 o'clock) before they encountered, the two galleasses opening at good range. The first shot from Duodo's vessel brought down Ali's lantern at which he lamented as an evil omen. Upon this evidence of the power of the galleasses, the center ships acted as did those of the right, breaking into three crowded groups rowing furiously to get by and making a brave appearance. Seeing the disorder thus occasioned and that some vessels lost spars and some seemed sinking, the Christians felt confident and, thanking God, rowed on to the strains of pipes and clarions; but until just before contact the three leaders maintained a very slow stroke, that all might keep in good line without fatiguing the rowers, who would soon be using their weapons. Neither did the Christians early reply to the Turkish fire, which was high and negligible as the Turkish spurs prevented horizontal firing. Ali was somewhat ahead of his comrades pointing for the hated flag of the Lion of St. Mark on Veniero's Capitana, but suddenly changing directions at the last moment he headed for His Highness' Royal.

As the lines approached the three Christian Generals each called 2 of their best galleys from the reserve to lie under their quarters and supply fresh men. Ali similarly had 6 galleys in his rear, besides Pertau Pasha and other flag officers on his right and left. The crash of the two Royals came, preceded by terrifying shouts on both sides and accompanied by the discharge of the artillery held loaded in reserve, by the fiery bombs, by the rattle of 300 arquebuses from the Spaniard, and by the hail of arrows from the Turk, which, if not as hard hitting as the bullets, were very rapid shooting and, at that short range, were sufficiently effective. The grappling irons were thrown on both sides. Ali himself was a famous bowman and advanced to the waist of his ship to use his bow. He was probably the last Commander in Chief in Europe personally to employ that weapon.

The two ships engaged in a furious struggle, each attempting to board the other with pikes and swords as the chief weapons and the arquebuses, bows, and pignatte as support to the boarders. The Capitana of Venice ranged alongside the poop of the Turkish Royal and Veniero, too old to engage in the thick of the hand-to-hand fighting, armed in helmet and cuirass with slippered feet (for a good foot-hold), occupied a commanding position amidships with a heavy crossbow and an attendant to wind it up, with which, using iron bullets, he picked off many of the enemy, "thinking himself not unfortunate if his days should end in such a battle, if God so pleased." Similarly, the Papal Capitana fought with Pertau Pasha and other galleys.

The fight became general along the line. A mass of ships closed about the struggle of the Royals as the supporting ships thrust in to help their generals on both sides. Twenty-five or thirty vessels were engaged in a space of perhaps 250 by 150 yards, while the whole center may have extended 1¼ miles. Ali's men more than once entered the Christian Royal and occupied the forecastle. Veniero threw his men aboard his colleague to aid. A Turk coming up to attack Veniero while thus somewhat defenseless presented the broadside to John Baptist Contarini, who rammed and sank her. Don Alvaro de Bazan, who was everywhere feeding the fight, came up and threw 200 fresh men into the Royal and sank by gunfire a Turkish galley at her poop. He then grappled another and put her crew to the sword and passed on to the help of the right wing. Three times the Christians boarded Ali's vessel and three times they were driven out, for her strength was also renewed by fresh men from her supporting vessels. The heat of the fight in the center lasted for 1½ hours.

Soon after noon, Marc Antonio overcame Pertau's vessel and the latter, badly burned by a fire-ball, fled in a caique under pretense of bringing help. Romegasso, Colonna's principal counselor, then said to him, "This galley is ours, shall we look for another or aid the Royal who is still fighting indecisively?" Colonna replied, "Let us aid the Royal." So

Romegasso, who was an expert seaman as well as a fine soldier, took the tiller himself and put the Capitana neatly alongside the Turkish Royal, striking her so hard that the bow ran up as far as the Royal's third thwart. Colonna's arquebusiers had had time to reload and their first discharge swept away many Turks. Then the Spaniards and many of the Italians forced their way through the crowd of Turks, Don John himself leaped on board, though wounded, and in an instant the Royal lost her standards. The Christians had possession and Don John's Royal took her in tow stern first.

As for Ali, there are several versions as to his end. The generally accepted one is that he lay wounded as the Christians overwhelmed his men and he offered his jeweled sword as ransom to a Spanish soldier who instead cut off his head and swam with it to Don John, hoping for great reward, but Don John turned coldly from him, saying "What can I do with it?" So it was exposed on a pike for an hour, and then lost.

Sereno tells a more picturesque story on the authority of "one who saw it."

When Ali saw there was no more hope, overcome by his beastly desperation produced by the valor of those whom he had hoped to overcome by shouting, he took a little iron casket in which he kept the things he most prized, both of superstition and of jewels, and going as far aft as he could to the very tiller, he drew a knife from his belt, thrust it into his throat, and leaped overboard with the casket. Neither he nor the casket were ever seen again.

The disappearance of the great Turkish standard before 1 o'clock marked the turn of battle, but the Turks did not readily give up. It is reported that after the stones and arrows of some of them had been expended, the crews seized oranges and lemons, which stood in crates on deck, and hurled them at the Christians, who threw them back again, half in joke. One after another the Turkish ships surrendered, although some were able to escape. The sea was covered with sinking and burning hulks and broken spars to which swimmers were clinging and crying for help. The sea was reddened with blood.* Little attention was paid to the cries for help and the victorious crews gave themselves over to massacre and pillage, many of them leaving their own ships. Not much was secured by the officers and men of rank, for they had to take care of their ships and

---

* The same was reported off the sea at the Dardanelles in 1915.

consequently men of low degree got most of the Turkish wealth. Such was the loosening of discipline that it was difficult to get ships of the center, where victory was certain, to go to the aid of the right wing where the battle was still in progress.

THE SOUTHERN WINGS

To the action between the two southern wings we must now turn. Owing to the bitterness which so many felt towards Gian Andrea Doria it is difficult to disentangle truth from spitefulness. Some historians allege that King Philip was negotiating with Uluch Ali and that Doria was in the King's confidence and hoped that Uluch Ali would again change his faith and desert. A modern Italian writer, Manfroni, goes so far as to say Doria had orders from King Philip to avoid battle. This charge, the Spaniard Duro says, is unsupported by any evidence. An ill-judged act of Doria's, on the day of battle, which gave support to suspicion, was that, in clearing for action, he took down and placed in safety the great crystal globe which served as his fanale or Admiral's lantern. This splendid and distinctive emblem was known to both fleets and by no one better than by Uluch Ali. His enemies said Doria did it through cowardice. After the battle he explained it was a gift of his wife and he guarded it from sentiment. The matter was not merely one for gossip in later days. In the atmosphere of distrust which already existed, the disappearance of the emblem, which all of that wing were accustomed to follow, increased suspicion and had its influence on the course of battle, perhaps causing the death of many Christians. As example of the way in which Doria was regarded, Sereno, writing long afterwards in the quiet of his monastic cell of the great deeds in which he took part that day, says of certain missing Christian ships, "These were lost by him who was afraid to fight" (p. 216). Another contemporary writer, Diedo, a Venetian, says in his defense, "No one can tell what was in his real mind, which must be held loyal for he joined most heartily in the battle."

Now let us take up the course of affairs in the southern wings.

The Christian line was formed in fairly good shape and headed toward the enemy by about 9 o'clock. Then, as has been said, Doria, whose Capitana was the right flank guide of the entire fleet, appreciated how greatly Uluch Ali's flank overlapped his own, and fearing envelopment he edged off to the south, falling behind the rest of the line as he drew away from it. Besides protecting his flank, this movement in delay, which was no doubt very slow, probably allowed the 2 galleasses of the right an opportunity to overtake him and occupy their proper stations. They were now behind the center hurrying along in tow of 4 galleys each. We have seen how much Don John relied on their opening fire to disorganize the hostile advance, and how he sent to hasten their movement, before going forward himself.

Uluch Ali had a third of the Turkish force, 90 vessels with some 25,000 men, but as he brought many galliots with him from Algiers, the individual ships were, on the whole, inferior to those opposite. Doria with 54 galleys and 2 galleasses had about a fourth of the Christian strength, or, say, 18,000 men. As Uluch Ali was distinguished for seamanlike skill, he, like Doria, preferred maneuvering to immediate battle. If he could get to the southward of Doria, he could make his numbers tell by enveloping the hostile flank and he would further have the advantage of the sun in the eyes of the enemy as the day wore on. Besides, the westerly wind which had sprung up would be less disadvantageous to him if moving north to the encounter. It might also seem to him that if he could maneuver Doria away from the main body, he could choose whether to fight him or attack the Christian center. Tactically, this latter reason seems adequate for Uluch Ali's delay. The alleged political reason, already mentioned, seems rather far-fetched.

While the two were contesting for advantage of position, and moving slowly to preserve the strength of the rowers, the two belated galleasses were gaining on Doria. By 12 o'clock the leading one was not far from Doria's northern flank, and the other one perhaps ½ or ¾ mile northerly.*

Uluch Ali was probably over a mile away from Doria and nearer the Christian center than the latter, whose attempt to guard his own right had exposed the right of the Christian center. This exposure had led Don

---

* (See the plan.) The positions of the various units are based on comparison of the primary statements of contemporary accounts that soon after 7 o'clock Doria was off Cape Scropha, that the battle opened about 3 hours later, was decided in nearly 3 hours more, and fighting continued (near Cape Scropha) almost another 3 hours, and the fleet and prizes were secure in Petala about dusk (6:30). There is also some information as to speeds, and the most southerly vessels, at about noon, reached perhaps nearly 6 miles from Pt. Scropha. So the various positions may be worked up to approximate truth.

John before the battle opened to send a boat to Doria to recall him. As the two opponents thus hung in observation and hesitation, the suspicions held by many in regard to Doria's loyalty developed into action about 12 o'clock or a little earlier. About 15 or more vessels, forming the left of Doria's command, resolved to share in the glory and the victory and parted company from the rest in a disorderly manner. Rowing hard, they directed their course towards the battle of the centers where the struggle seemed still at its height and the outcome uncertain. Doria with 35 or more vessels continued to face Uluch Ali.

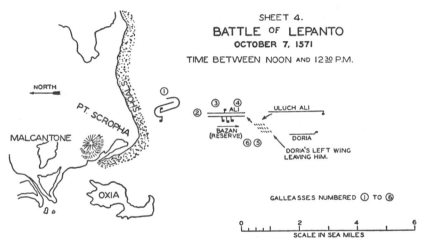

SHEET 4.
BATTLE OF LEPANTO
OCTOBER 7, 1571
TIME BETWEEN NOON AND 12:30 P.M.

FIG. 24

No sooner had the purpose of the stragglers made itself apparent than Uluch Ali saw that his long-awaited opportunity had come. He had the lead of Doria, being nearer the two centers. Instead of enveloping Doria's right flank, his new tactical objective was, if possible, to leave Doria and the 35 vessels with him out of action. He therefore threw his whole command towards the 15 stragglers and quickly attacked them 3, 4, and 5 ships to 1. These imprudent and eager seekers of renown found more than they had bargained for. In spite of a most gallant defense and the aid of the left galleass, together with that of the galleys which had been towing her, it was not long before the Turks had overwhelmed and taken 11 Venetian, 2 Sicilian, 1 Savoyard, and 1 Papal galley. Among these unfortunates was the vessel of Benedetto Soranzo, Venetian, which was boarded and nearly all the crew killed. Then although he had 3 arrows in his face, Soranzo fired the magazine and destroyed his enemies with himself. His own ship burned to the water's edge and the upward explosion did great damage to the Turkish vessels lying against her. Cardona's Capitana also suffered severely. She was boarded by the Turks, who penetrated as far as the mainmast, and Cardona himself was badly burned by a fire-ball. But help came to him, for Doria now arrived, furious at having been outwitted, and burning for revenge.

When Doria had grasped the danger of the ships which had deserted him, he instantly led his remaining vessels in front of his right galleass in order to fall on Uluch Ali's rear while he was busy with the others. This renunciation of the artillery support of the galleass makes plain that Doria's delaying maneuvers had been merely for tactical advantage and not from disloyalty. He was now eager to redeem his error by battle.

Very soon his squadron struck the victorious Turks and regained the captured vessels, except 1 sunk and 1 burned, and besides made several Turkish captures. His own Capitana made 5 prizes, it is said, and he showed personal courage. Other vessels also did well. But Uluch Ali did not wait for close action with Doria. After some exchange of long range shots, the former hastened with about 30 ships to attack the right of the Christian center where he made a vigorous assault at about or soon after the time the Turkish Royal was taken. Here the Capitana of Malta, a superb ship, was prominent on the flank. The utmost enmity existed between the Order of Malta and the Algerine corsair, who had captured 3 Maltese galleys the year before, much to the discredit of the order. Of course Uluch Ali selected the Maltese for his opponent. She was already embarrassed by enemies, having nearly overcome 3 Turks, when Uluch Ali arrived with 3 more. So she was taken after nearly all on board were killed. Fra Giustiniano, Prior of Messina, her commander, saved himself by offering money, and was thrust below, wounded, with five others, while Uluch Ali transferred her proud standard to his own Capitana and took her in tow, stern first, with 300 dead Turks on board.

This astonishing reversal of the course of the battle proved only local and temporary, for it came too late. Already Don Alvaro de Bazan had satisfied himself as to the safety of Don John and now started to reseize the Capitana of Malta. But it was hard for him to get other aid, for the victorious crews of the center were not ready to abandon their prizes, and many men were out of their ships, looting. Nevertheless, two other galleys of Malta and some Spanish vessels came up, so that Uluch Ali was forced to release his prize, and think rather of escape than of further battle. Rowing his best, with 20 or 30 other vessels, he hoisted the great standard of

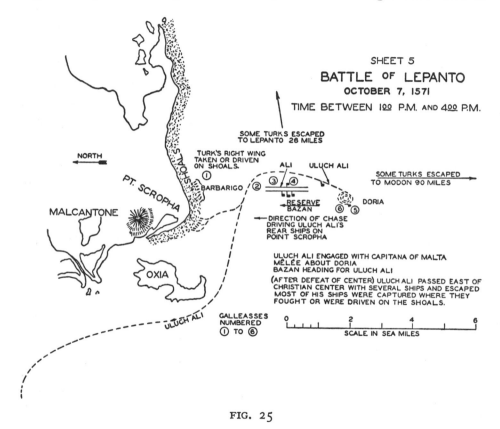

SHEET 5

BATTLE OF LEPANTO

OCTOBER 7, 1571

TIME BETWEEN 1.00 P.M. AND 4.00 P.M.

SOME TURKS ESCAPED
TO LEPANTO 28 MILES

NORTH

TURK'S RIGHT WING
TAKEN OR DRIVEN
ON SHOALS.

ALI   ULUCH ALI

SOME TURKS ESCAPED
TO MODON 90 MILES

BARBARIGO

PT. SCROPHA

MALCANTONE

RESERVE
BAZAN   DORIA

DIRECTION OF CHASE
DRIVING ULUCH ALI'S
REAR SHIPS ON
POINT SCROPHA

OXIA

ULUCH ALI ENGAGED WITH CAPITANA OF MALTA
MÊLÉE ABOUT DORIA
BAZAN HEADING FOR ULUCH ALI

(AFTER DEFEAT OF CENTER) ULUCH ALI PASSED EAST OF
CHRISTIAN CENTER WITH SEVERAL SHIPS AND ESCAPED
MOST OF HIS SHIPS WERE CAPTURED WHERE THEY
FOUGHT OR WERE DRIVEN ON THE SHOALS.

ULUCH ALI

GALLEASSES
NUMBERED
① TO ⑥

0   2   4   6
SCALE IN SEA MILES

FIG. 25

Malta and passed in front of the bows of the Christian center, making them think he was going to the aid of the Turks who had been so mishandled by the allied right wing.*

Don John, Colonna, and Veniero were now disengaged and they, with others of the best disciplined vessels of the center, dropped their prizes,

* So says Sereno. Another version of this movement, confirmed by a contemporary plan of the battle (Fig. 20), says Aluch Ali passed behind (west of the center), but if this is right it is hard to see how the rear ships of his groups were forced on shore near Point Scropha.

thinking that Uluch Ali had conquered the right wing and that they would have to fight again.

Caetani and Sereno tell disgustedly of the experience of their "Grifona" at this period of the battle. The former says in his letter to Cardinal Sermoneta, written two days after the battle,

> After gaining the day in the center, His Highness went that way [to the right] with Colonna, and I dropped the galleys I had taken and had in tow to go where help was needed. Some Venetian galleys coming behind boarded my prizes and had much booty, for these corsairs were very rich. I do not care, for I did not come to rob but to fight and serve Our God.

And Sereno adds, "Although the hulls and guns were delivered to us by order of Don John, we got nothing but the honor and fatigue of towing them to Messina." The same happened to several others.

It proved impossible to bring Uluch Ali again to action. He set his foresail to a light breeze which sprang up from eastward and, still rowing, his flight became apparent. At first he hoped only to run his ships ashore and save the crews by flight, but he did better than he hoped. The Christian ships were slow in following him towards Malcantone (Cape Scropha), for they had broken many oars and the rowers were tired and wounded. Besides there were many absent in prizes. Uluch Ali soon made additional sail and with a Corfiote galley as prize, he and others passed through the Christian line, where there were few ships (probably near the interval between the center and left wing) and made off to the north, still rowing hard. Although the corsair himself was able to clear Point Scropha and get safely away with seven others, the rest of his squadron was less fortunate, for the pursuit was sufficiently effective to cut many of them off at the Point and drive them ashore, where so many of Sirocco's vessels had been lost. The crews were able to escape to the shore.

Don John wished to follow Uluch Ali, but was dissuaded by Romegasso, who said the certain victory ought not to be put in doubt. It was now approaching 4:00 o'clock. The weather was showing some signs of breaking up and the efforts of all were turned to getting into port with the prizes. These were full of provisions much needed by the Christians, who were almost running out of stores owing to absence of their supply ships for three weeks. The prizes that were clearly unseaworthy and some on the beach were burned and, as darkness came on, the flames made a fine illumination for the triumphal entry of the fleet into Petala. An effort was made to preserve some of the injured Christian ships. Among these was the Papal Fiorenza, which had lost nearly all her crew in the last phase of the battle. She was brought in by Caetani, who, as Sereno tells us, was too good

> to wish to see the wounded die, and he towed her as far as Sta. Maura, where, being useless, her artillery was removed, and she was burnt by order of Don John in the "fiesta" for the victory.

By 7 o'clock the fleet was at anchor with 170 prizes and safe against the approaching storm.

The Survey After the Battle and Return to Base

No sooner were their vessels secure than all the chief officers of note, still armed as in battle, poured on board the Royal to congratulate Don John and each other. Nothing was seen but embraces and kisses. Veniero was hesitant about visiting Don John but, upon an intimation from the latter, he too appeared and was met at the ladder by the Prince, who, calling him "most excellent father," said, "I rejoice with your Excellency over this great victory." Whereupon they fell into each other's arms and wept for joy as did many others in sympathy.

Don John took occasion particularly to thank Antonio Duodo, commanding the 6 Venetian galleasses, for their great good service which, he said, had been a principal factor in the victory and later he gave him a certificate to show to all the world.

His Highness sent for the two sons of Ali, who had been captured, and treated them with the utmost courtesy, condoling with them over the loss of their father.

Then was exchanged talk of the incidents of battle. Above all, it was a subject of pious remark that the great standard of the League, blessed by the saintly Pope, had gone through the battle untouched by shot or arrow, although all other standards had many marks of the fierce contest. All seem to have found time to mourn most sincerely the loss of Barbarigo.

Among the heroes of the day was Alexander Farnese, Prince of Parma, grandson of the Emperor Charles, and afterwards the greatest general of his day. Somewhat older than his uncle, the Commander in Chief, he was

FIG. 26.—BATTLE OF LEPANTO

By Vasari. In Sala Regia, Vatican.

The scene shown is the map of Greece and the positions of the fleets before joining battle. The Latin inscription partially visible below the painting reads

CLASSES OPPOSITAE TURCARUM UNA CHRISTIANAE SOCIETATIS ALIERA
INTER PIUM PONT MAX PHILIPPUM REGEM VENETAM REMP
INITO IAM FOEDERE INGENTIBUS UTRIM Q ANIMIS CONCURRENT.

Noteworthy as contemporary picture of the galleass squadron at Lepanto.

merely one of the band of noble adventurers who had joined the expedition for glory and personal renown. Of him it was reported that he had leaped on board a Turkish galley and, supported by a single Spanish soldier, Alonzo Davalos, the two, unaided, had gone from end to end of her and subdued her by the might of their arms. Then, too, it was told of the priest, who, after having duly performed the rites of the church before battle, bound his crucifix firmly to a halberd and, heading the boarders of his ship, did great execution with his heavy weapon on the deck of the enemy.

Sergeant Martin Muñoz, lying ill below on board the San Giovanni of Sicily, hearing that the enemy was on board, leaped from his cot, ran on deck saying he did not wish to die of fever, snatched up a weapon and fell upon the Turks with such fury that he killed 4 and drove the rest beyond the mast. Then, pierced by 9 arrows and with a leg nearly severed, he sank upon a thwart, exclaiming to his mates, "Gentlemen, let each of you do as much," and bled to death.

But not all the tales were creditable. There was much boasting, for so many claimed to have captured several ships each, that it seemed that the Turkish fleet must have numbered 800 sail. There were some, as Sereno says, who were known to have behaved badly, yet to put on a good appearance "bought trophies from those who had gained them with their blood and, clothed in Turkish jackets, showed themselves walking pompously." Of one he does not name (Doria?) he says,

> I know a great captain whom I saw, who to counterbalance the testimony which his own conscience gave, went about purchasing praise from writers and asked for false accounts hoping to conceal his vileness by such glory.

The storm broke that night, and blew hard with thunder and lightning, but the fleet rode it out safely and the next morning Don John, with Colonna and Doria, went to view the place of battle with an escort of 8 galleys. They saw a group of galleys which they thought they would have to fight, but soon they perceived they were abandoned. One had been burned and one jammed in the rocks so that it was in vain Colonna tried to drag her off. So the artillery was salvaged and all the wrecks given to plunder and then burned.

On this day the drowned began to rise to the surface and boats put out to strip the bodies and much booty was so obtained. All men who had seized over 100 ducats were ordered to turn in their booty. Don John gave a lunch party to the leaders on this day, but it was necessary to do so on board Doria's Capitana, as it was the only one whose table service was not ruined. This was alleged to prove Doria's slight share in the fighting.

The next day, October 9, the fleet moved 8 miles to Dregomestre on the coast of Albania, where a muster and survey were held. It was found that 117 galleys and 13 galliots worth preserving with 388 guns had been taken. Some 40 others were destroyed as worthless, and another 40 were lost in the battle. About 50 or 60 ships escaped to Lepanto and Modon. It was difficult to get an account of prisoners, for captors naturally wished to retain them as personal prize; so parties were sent to every ship at midnight to count prisoners and some 3,500 were discovered. A later count raised the official number to 7,200. It was thought perhaps nearly as many more were not accounted for.

Nearly 30,000 Turks were held to have been killed, 8,000 to have escaped to shore, and 12,000 Christian rowers were rescued from slavery. Perhaps some 10,000 to 12,000 men got off unhurt in the 60 ships which escaped, and which probably were mostly of small size.

The Christian losses were 12 ships, 8 Venetians* (of which 1 captured), 1 of Doria's, 1 Sicilian, 1 Piedmontese, and the Florentine destroyed after salvaging. The lives lost were about 7,700, of which 800 were Papalini, 2,000 Spaniards, and over 4,800 Venetians. The wounded were about twice as many.

Don John's head was not turned by his great success, and he remained most attentive to his duties. He knew what each had done and congratulated all the great ones. He caused the wounded on his own ship to be placed in the best quarters, and he inquired as to the care of all the others. When he lunched with Doria, he visited the wounded on board and spoke particularly with a man whose courage had been noteworthy.

THE RETURN

From Dregomestre the fleet moved slowly to Santa Maura on the way to Corfu, where the wounded were to be landed. At Sta. Maura a recon-

---

* In his report to the Doge and Senate on the campaign, Veniero says 7 Venetian vessels were "mal menate" (roughly handled), apparently meaning they were abandoned as not worth keeping, or sunk in battle. Contarini uses a similar locution for all the losses whose number he does not state.

naissance was made of the fortress with a view to taking it, but it was thought too much time would be needed, for the fleet lacked provisions; and the wounded needed attention at Corfu, for wounds began to be infected and many died. Contrary winds delayed the fleet there. Some ships would have been near starvation, had not the supplies on the captured vessels been available. The prizes were divided and a council was held which decided nothing more could be done within the short remaining season, on account of the many wounded and the great shortage of oars. While at Santa Maura 3 galleasses and 4 galleys arrived, which had been delayed at Paxo by bad weather and these brought word that all the nefs were at Corfu and that more Venetian galleys and soldiers would soon arrive there. There was complaint in the fleet that if the nefs had only come on, some expedition might have been undertaken.

On Sunday, October 21, the fleet sailed for Corfu and met a squall that night which obliged many galleys to cut the lines to their prizes, but the fleet arrived safely on October 23 and was welcomed by a salute of shotted guns. The political animosity which had for an instant disappeared before success was not long in showing itself. The very night of the victory, after the reconciliation of Don John and Veniero, the latter gave offense again. He was sending a galley with dispatches to Venice and offered to send those of Don John by her. The offer was accepted and then by some error the galley sailed with only the Venetian letters. Don John was furious. Colonna, the peacemaker, assured Don John that Veniero had another galley waiting specially for letters to King Philip and the matter passed over, but at Sta. Maura, when the prizes were divided, Veniero refused to sign the Spanish version of the record, saying he did not understand Spanish and did not know if it agreed with the Italian version. Again Colonna intervened successfully by giving Veniero his certificate in the name of the Pope, that he had compared the two and found them in agreement.

It is evident from these little incidents how difficult it was for political opponents like Spain and Venice to work together against the Turk, and how marvelous the great victory was. For on The Day every one seems to have done his best, even the maligned Doria.

In a few days the Papal and Spanish squadrons sailed for Messina in several divisions, as it was thought more seamanlike not to cruise in large bodies when no enemy was apprehended, as thus harbor facilities were not embarrassed. Of Don John's departure Veniero reported to Venice, "On the 28th, after the expressions of civility and of confidence, in which there was little truth, either public or private, I accompanied His Highness to sea until he sent more than once to tell me to put back." Very different was Don John's welcome at Messina. He arrived on November 1 with 12 vessels and gradually others came in. Don John at once went to church to return thanks to God. The next day all the galleys went to sea and returned in two columns in precise order with standards and banners displayed. In the middle were the Royal of Don John and the Capitana of Marc Antonio Colonna. Don John towed the Turkish Royal and the other galleys their own prizes, all sterns first, with the antenne reversed* and banners trailing in the water. In entering the port the galleys fired a fine salvo to which the Castle and other forts replied. Then the two Generals at Sea landed and were received with much pomp and in a procession of the clergy they went to the Cathedral where the archbishop of Messina said mass and then the Generals went to the Palace accompanied by all the nobility. It was very appropriate that the adventure should terminate in church, for it was the Pope's holy zeal that provided the fiery courage that won the battle, against the ever victorious Turks.

The rejoicings all over Christendom were very great. In Rome, Naples, and Venice ceremonies of notable character were observed. The Pope instituted a perpetual festival in honor of the day which is annually observed at the Church of Santa Maria Maggiore in Rome. On the tercentenary of the battle in 1871, as an additional ceremony, the body of the canonized Pope was exposed in remembrance. In Spain the popular delight was as great as in Italy. The King's secretary wrote to Don John, "It seems to us a dream for never was such a naval victory seen or heard of and tonight the houses are lit up and the streets have bonfires." Don John's own messenger wrote, "I thought they would have torn me into relics in Italy and in France as a man sent by Your Highness." But the King received the first news at vespers with the same impassibility which he afterwards showed at the loss of the Armada.

The fleet was dispersed to winter ports. The colonels and most of the

---

* The peaks of the antenne were made to point forward.

people of importance returned home and the soldiers were quartered about Sicily and the Kingdom of Naples. But, in spite of public joy, the adventurers and private soldiers were much dissatisfied at the lack of liberality shown them, reminding us of the old adage

> Our God and soldiers we alike adore
> But only when in danger, not before,
> After deliverance both alike requited,
> Our God forgotten and our soldiers slighted.

The principal tactical interest in this great battle lies in showing a transitional stage in the use of artillery. In the main Lepanto was a boarders' fight of the old style with efforts of the Turks to employ their greater number of ships by enveloping both flanks. That on the north was accomplished; that on the south developed into an alternative movement. The new feature was the use of the artillery of the galleasses to play a major rôle for the first time in naval warfare on a plan which, if not originated by the young Commander in Chief, certainly was warmly advocated by him. These heavy ships were not readily open to assault by boarders and the use of their guns to break up the charge of the galleys was successful as well as novel. Not less worthy of note than the tactics is the development under the Pope's influence of the resolution to fight.

CAMPAIGN OF 1572

The war of Cyprus continued in 1572, but Christendom was disappointed in seeing no major battle and the campaign proved an anti-climax. Nevertheless, it has its place in naval history, on account of the efforts to develop the lesson of Lepanto as to the employment of artillery by using it in sailing ships and also on account of the unsuccessful attempt to utilize sailing ships in the same tactical formation with rowing ships.

It was the hope of Europe that the destruction of the Turkish fleet at Lepanto would make operations easy in 1572. The Sultan declared, however, that the loss of his fleet was no more than the singeing of his beard; both would grow again. After Uluch Ali made his escape from the battle, he returned to the Bosphorus in December, bringing with him the remains of the fleet and such other ships as could be found in the ports of the Levant. He was able to show the captured standard of Malta as evidence of his own valor and so won the confidence of the Sultan that he was made

High Admiral. Under him and the Grand Vizier, the work of renewing the fleet went on with every resource of the Empire. New building slips were erected, even in the Sultan's gardens. Old hulls thought unseaworthy were repaired and put in service and new galleys built. One hundred and fifty ships were fitted for sea during the winter. When Uluch Ali expressed the fear that the anchors for these new ships could not be provided, the Vizier replied, "the wealth of the Empire can supply you, if needful, with anchors of silver and cables of silk. You have only to ask for what you want."

Nevertheless, the new vessels were of green timber, the guns were of poor metal, the seamen and oarsmen were recruits, and the soldiers were trembling at the stories of Lepanto. Uluch Ali provided 20,000 arquebusses to replace as many bows. Lepanto marked the last great battle of archers, although the weapon lasted for a long time still. By early summer the Christians heard that the fleet was at sea with 200 ships, great and small, with abundance of soldiers, although short of seamen and rowers. Such an accomplishment was possible only under a unified government and was a great surprise to the allies.

Christian Preparations

For the allies, although they really were more powerful on the sea, arrangements were more difficult. When he heard of the victory, the enthusiastic Pope pushed his preparations and urged his allies to do the same for the coming season. Spain offered 100 galleys and 18,000 infantry; Venice, 100 galleys and 15,000 infantry; and the Pope 14 galleys and 3,000 infantry, the Grand Duke of Tuscany having agreed to renew his rental of galleys to the Pope. Besides, the allies were to furnish 500 horses (for reconnaissance when the troops landed), 40 nefs with supplies for six months, powder and shot for 20,000 cannon rounds, and also to pay pro rata for 10,000 soldiers to be stationed at Cape Otranto, ready for transportation where needed. In the spring the Pope fell ill and the warmth of the allies fell off in consequence. He died on May 1 and his death took the fire out of the combatants and the life out of the League.

The new Pope, Gregory XIII, was favorable to the policy of Pius V. He confirmed Colonna in the command and carried out other arrangements of his predecessor. Don John, as Admiral of Spain, continued in command of the Royal fleet and was reappointed General of the League. During the winter he freely expressed his determination not to serve with Veniero as a colleague, whose haughty temper and overbearing manners he pronounced intolerable. Accordingly, but not until Veniero made the request himself, the Signory appointed the latter to command in the northern Adriatic with the soothing proviso that should he fall in with the main Venetian fleet he was to command that also. His grateful countrymen by no means forgot his great services, and in 1577 they elected him Doge of Venice at the great age of 82. His successor as General at Sea was Jacopo Foscarini, a leading senator, whose appointment was pleasing to Don John.

MOBILIZATION AT MESSINA

By early June the Papal and Spanish squadrons began to assemble at Messina, two months earlier in the season than the year before. The Grand Duke of Tuscany provided 2 galleasses, which he had built during the winter after the Venetian model, and for the hire of these he asked 1,000 scudi ($2,300) a month for each, or double the price of a galley. But delay soon appeared, and the Venetian proveditor (vice admiral) went to Messina with the squadron, nominally to act as an escort of honor to Don John but really to hurry him. Colonna and Foscarini were anxious to go in search of Uluch Ali, who was harrying the Venetian islands in the Archipelago with 200 vessels. Don John wished to go too, but his authority was restricted by the King. At last, on June 14, Don John issued the movement order, but revoked it the same day.

The reason was not then apparent, but it is now known that it was on account of the traditional opposition of France to Spain and the Empire in Italy. At this time France was fomenting the insurrection in the Spanish Netherlands and sent an ambassador to the Sultan by way of Venice to mediate between him and the Republic. France also wished to have Algiers placed under her control to avoid danger of having Spain take it as the result of the war. So the Spanish King held up his fleet, in order to be able to oppose the French designs in Africa. The situation was not understood by Philip's allies; his false and secretive character prevented his making them a frank explanation and the lack of it caused suspicion and distrust on both sides, which extended to all ranks.

Although Don John was thus refused permission to go east, it was arranged soon after at a general council at Messina to send the Papal fleet with a considerable Spanish squadron, under Gil d'Andrada as Don John's lieutenant, to Corfu to join the main Venetian fleet, and seek the enemy under the lead of Colonna as Lieutenant-General of the League, while Don John, with the rest of the Spanish vessels went to Palermo in readiness to oppose any French hostilities. Accordingly, Colonna sailed from Messina on July 7 and arrived in Corfu on the 15th with 58 allied vessels. At this moment internal French politics brought a new party to power which favored Spain. Philip felt that the French would now do nothing to embarrass him and gave Don John permission to go east and join the main body of the League fleet. On July 16 Don John sent a dispatch to Colonna saying he was coming and telling the fleet to wait for him. Still King Philip required Don John to leave a strong squadron of 39 galleys and 9,000 soldiers in Sicily, under Doria, to guard the situation in Africa and the western Mediterranean, and prevent any incursions from Africa.

Don John arrived in Corfu on August 9 with a squadron of 55 galleys, 2 Tuscan galleasses, and 40 nefs, besides many small supply ships, and 15,000 soldiers.* He was very angry to find that Colonna and the rest had gone south and that a battle might be fought, in which he would gain no credit. So he cleaned ships' bottoms while waiting for news, declaring that he would find a way to punish Colonna and that he would have Andrada's head.

The First Encounter of 1572

On arrival at Corfu, Colonna found the main Venetian fleet and made preparations to proceed. His orders from Don John were to bring the Turkish fleet to action, but not to besiege any fortress which might allow the ships to be surprised without soldiers. The force he had was composed of 13 Papal, 22 Spanish, and 105 Venetian galleys: 6 Venetian galleasses and 24 nefs, with perhaps about 21,000 soldiers and about 30,000 seamen and rowers.** Of these about 16,000 soldiers and 27,500 others would be on the galleys and galleasses. On July 29, just as the fleet was getting under way, Colonna received Don John's letter of detention. There

---

* Rosell, p. 141.
** Guglielmotti, vol. 6, p. 321, says that on July 23 there were 25,000 troops at Corfu belonging to the fleet.

was an ambiguous clause in it which Colonna and Andrada, under pressure from Foscarini, interpreted to mean that they might go forward, if necessary, to prevent damage to the Venetian islands, and so they did without delay.

The Christians arrived at Cerigo on August 4 and heard that the Turkish fleet was at the fortress of Malvasia 35 miles away. Foscarini re-

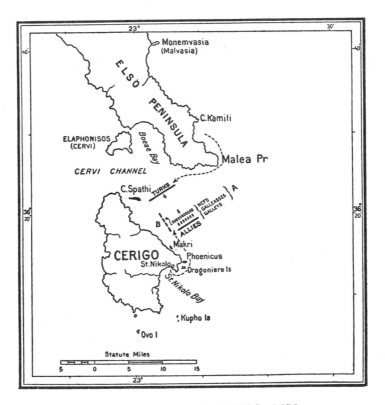

MAP X.—FLEETS ON AUGUST 7, 1572

The Christians first formed as at *A*. Afterward the nefs were shifted to *B*.

ported to Venice that the Turks had 210 sail of which 70 or 80 were galliots only. There were plenty of soldiers, but they lacked confidence and the seamen and rowers were few and poor. In the aggregate the Turkish ships probably had a good many more soldiers and perhaps a few more seamen and rowers than the Christians,* but individually they were

* Possibly 2,000 more soldiers and 500 more seamen and rowers.

much inferior in artillery and in speed. Above all, the Christians were exalted and the Turks depressed by the recent battle.

Although it seems that Colonna would have been justified in fighting without the nefs, as he had informed Don John he was willing to do, yet in the face of the enemy the three leaders resolved not to fight unless they could have the sailing nefs with their guns in support of the battle line of row-galleys. Uluch Ali was equally determined not to encounter the nefs and hence much maneuvering followed, whose interest to us lies in its showing that sailing ships and rowing ships could not work together. It was an important moment in tactical development.

On hearing of each other's vicinity, the Christians drew out from the fortress of St. Nikolo and anchored off the Dragoniere islets where they covered the routes to Candia and to Corfu. The Turks ran down to Malea. On August 7 the Christians sighted the Turkish fleet hugging the shore after rounding the Cape. The allies formed battle with the different nationalities mixed as the year before, with three divisions in the front line of galleys and a small reserve in rear. In front of all were the galleasses and the nefs to break up the Turkish* line. It was a repetition of the plan of Lepanto, with the addition of the nefs.

Uluch·Ali then crossed towards Cerigo and his long line almost filled the channel between that island and Cervi. Apparently, he meant to take advantage of the westerly breeze, which was due every day about noon, and run down on the allies when their nefs could not head toward him. So Colonna moved all his nefs (they must have been towed) to the left of his line of galleys with their line making an angle with the galleys.** So that as the Turks approached the Christian galleys, the nefs, heading north, could enfilade the Turkish line; or running off the wind, they could charge upon them. But the usual breeze did not spring up. Instead, there were light airs from the ESE., so Colonna improved his opportunity by putting his whole fleet under sail in its original order and ran toward the enemy. This did not suit Uluch Ali, who backed away toward the west, thus keeping to windward. About 4 o'clock, before the fleets came very near,

---

* I think the nefs were in a first line, then the galleasses, and the galleys in the third or rear line, but Guglielmotti's account is not clear, and possibly the nefs and galleasses were in a single line.

** Guglielmotti's account, which is full, does not say positively that the nefs' line was at an angle with that of the other ships, but it seems it must have been so, to act as Colonna intended.

the wind failed. As the nefs could no longer move, the Turks stood fast and were willing to fight the galleys alone. Colonna refused to leave the nefs behind, for he said public opinion in the fleet would not allow it. However, he towed the nefs with two galleys each and advanced slowly in the prescribed order. Uluch Ali retreated, backing water until dusk when he fired blank salvos to form a smoke screen and disappeared without showing any lights to indicate his course. The allies then returned to their anchorage to take in water. Here a number of captains showed much indiscipline but neither Colonna nor Andrada ventured to punish them for some of the principal offenders belonged to great Spanish families, and Colonna could only tell Don John about it.

On the 9th the Christians got under way to search for the enemy towards the west. During the night a council decided to return to Corfu, fearing the Turks might catch Don John's smaller force, but in the morning of the 10th, after searching the Gulf of Laconia, as the fleet was approaching Cape Matapan under sail with an easterly breeze, the enemy was seen ahead also under sail. Challenge shots were exchanged, the two fleets approached in formation as on the 7th with the nefs leading the Christians, and then the wind failed.

The Turks lay on their oars and the Christians slowed in order not to overrun their nefs, but the two fleets continued to approach and soon exchanged fire. That of the Christians was effective and several Turks were disabled and several drew back. Uluch Ali thought it wise to withdraw his whole line. The Venetian Soranzo commanding the right pushed on and Colonna in the center passed his nefs and both wanted to fight with the galleys only.

But this was an unexpected change in plan. Only a few ships in the center and right and none in the left wing imitated the leaders and passed beyond the nefs. By this time the Turks were retiring in some confusion; but seeing the check in the Christian advance, the Turks reformed and stood fast. Colonna with Foscarini, Andrada, and Soranzo and a few others, refused to retire for fear of starting a panic and remained facing the enemy until the rest of the rowing ships and the nefs slowly came up, and about noon the Christian line was also reformed. Uluch Ali refused to meet the whole Christian fleet and backed off until about dusk when the Turks fired a smoke screen, turned their ships about, and made sail toward

Quaglia. Their damaged ships were beached on the way and destroyed by the local people. The wind was not favorable for going westward and the allies bore up for Cerigo with exhausted rowers but no crippled ships. On both sides many individual ships had done badly and both commanders were displeased, but only the Turk ventured to punish his captains.

The maneuvers of the past few days had convinced Colonna that the nefs were no asset in battle. The enemy could refuse to fight them by taking a position to windward, and, if there was no breeze, the galleys' rowers were exhausted by towing them. Colonna was now convinced that the hope of victory was in joining Don John's squadron. As it was dangerous to have it run the risk of meeting the whole Turkish fleet, the allies resolved to go north and meet Don John under the guns of some Christian fortress. On August 14 the fleet sailed for Zante with an easterly wind and arrived there in 36 hours.

Don John made a couple of false starts from Corfu to join the others in the south, but in the end he required them to join him in Corfu where all were assembled on September 1. There was much saluting and ceremony in public, but Don John was very angry because the fleet had gone south without waiting for him and in private he showed Foscarini and Colonna little honor. Foscarini was the servant of an independent state, whom Don John could not reprove, but Colonna's position was a false one since he was a subject and hereditary officer of the King of Spain while commanding the independent fleet of the Pope. So there was a bitter quarrel in which Don John behaved childishly and most unworthily. As for Gil d'Andrada, he was Don John's lieutenant and directly answerable to him. He boldly gave his sound reasons for his actions and said he was willing to lose his head if he had done wrong.

After a day or two of quarreling Don John had worked off his spleen and he agreed to please the Venetians and move against the Turkish fleet, for the advanced season allowed no time for operations on shore.

The whole episode is a remarkable example of the style of discipline and co-ordination of the time. Don John behaved like a spoiled child at having lost an opportunity of personal distinction and took improper advantage of his royal birth. Yet no one thought of telling him that under the terms of the treaty Colonna and Foscarini, being a majority of the League Council, were fully authorized to act as they pleased when leaving Corfu in August.

The Second Campaign of 1572

At Corfu the ships cleaned bottoms, for after 30 days the loss of speed from grass was noticeable. On September 6 the Council decided to seek the hostile fleet and the next day most of the nefs left for Zante with heavy artillery, horses, and siege material, and there they were parked under the guns of the fortress, for they were not to go farther until the fleet battle had been fought. On September 11 the fleet sailed. There were 13 Papal, 76 Spanish, and 105 Venetian galleys, 194 in all, including two Tuscan galleys hired by the King and 6 hired Venetian ones; 24 Spanish nefs and 7 Venetian ones. Among the Venetian galleys there was one manned by French gentlemen adventurers; also there were 2 (hired) Tuscan and 6 Venetian galleasses. Besides, there were 60 small rowing vessels of which 20 carried adventurers. In all, there were not less than 32,000 soldiers (see Guglielmotti, vol. 6, p. 386), and perhaps 42,000 seamen and rowers in the force leaving Corfu, of which nearly 25,000 soldiers and 37,000 others were on the galleys and galleasses. The nefs at Zante had about 7,000 soldiers available for landing and perhaps 3,000 seamen.

On the way the allies heard the enemy had arrived at Modon and Navarino 7 miles apart where he had received some guns and supplies and a few soldiers, but was still very short-handed with much sickness. At Cephallonia the allies took 8 days' water and 2 boat loads of throwing stones for each galley. At Zante a Council was held, at which Colonna and Foscarini wished to hasten on and surprise the Turkish fleet divided between two ports, but Don John's own Spanish Council persuaded him to move slowly, so that the fleet was just in time to see the last of the squadron at Navarino leaving for Modon on the morning of the 16th.

After arriving off Modon, the Council resolved to go to Corone to water again, although they had done so within the week. As the fleet moved off, a part of the hostile fleet, probably with re-enforced crews, came out of port. The Christians faced about, causing much confusion, for the position of honor was on the right and some ships turned where they were, while others started to go to the opposite flank to take place according to precedence. The enemy did not seek action and withdrew to port. So then the fleet went to Corone and watered with some fighting on the part of the escort on shore protecting the watering parties. On the 19th the fleet was again off Modon.

FIG. 27.—MAP OF MODON, PUBLISHED AT VENICE IN 1572

From Library of Congress.

The big General Council boarded a capitana and all went to reconnoiter. Over 200 Turkish ships were anchored along a stretch of beach about 3,000 yards long, with stern lines running to the shore and the heavy bow batteries pointing seaward. On one flank was the fortress of Modon and on the other was a rocky hill occupied by artillery and infantry. The ships were scarcely 15 yards from mainmast to mainmast and were in far closer order than it was possible for the Christians to maintain while under way. Besides, a large island (Sapienza) in front of the harbor would oblige the Christian fleet to approach in column and then turn into line under fire of the fortress. The position was impregnable and the Christians decided to go to Navarino (the ancient Pylos) and wait for supply ships and troops to come from Zante.

In this ample harbor the fleet could lie beyond the guns of the castle at the upper end, and ships immediately began to renew their water under protection of a landing party. Nothing could be done till the siege artillery arrived from Zante. On September 27 the nefs arrived, bringing only 2,000 soldiers and 5 days' provisions instead of 7,000 soldiers and 60 days' supplies as expected.

Uluch Ali had meant to land his soldiers and attack the Christian parties on shore during this interval, leaving his ships under the shore batteries, but an on-shore gale obliged him to shift his anchorage to a position not covered by the castle and he could not take the soldiers from ships thus exposed. On their part the Christians also wished to do something and, as the Turkish galleys could not be directly attacked, Colonna proposed to form a strong line of defense at Navarino by anchoring the galleasses and nefs across the harbor mouth, adding passive obstructions and, with the galleys safe behind them, he suggested landing 12,000 soldiers from the galleys to march the 7 miles to Modon and occupy the hills behind the fortress, cut off all supplies and bombard the ships from the land. The Council rejected the proposal. Neither would the Council agree to let a strong body of troops march along the shore, escorted by the fleet, to attack Modon. As the 194 Christian galleys alone were more than a match for the 200 sickly and under-manned Turkish galleys, it is evident that the spirit and dash of the previous year had gone. A last half-hearted attempt was made against the castle of Navarino with a landing force of 5,000 men. Personal jealousies of the leaders brought it to nothing, and the party re-embarked on October 6. The Council resolved to return to Italy, as only a week's provisions were on hand.

On October 7 the fragata on scouting duty outside the harbor reported that 2 Christian supply ships coming to Navarino were attacked by 15 Turkish galleys and were defending themselves with artillery. Instantly Don John put to sea in his Royal and other ships followed, the fastest leading, all heading along the shore to cut the enemy off from Modon. The Turks abandoned their prey and raced for port with several Christian ships in hot pursuit. At last the Capitana of Naples, the "Loba" (She-wolf), bearing the Marquis of Santa Cruz, drew near that of Mamut, son of Dragut and nephew of Barbarossa, both famous corsairs of the previous generation. Mamut was a young man of 22 years, noted for his cruelty to his Christian slaves, of whom he had 200 on board. He stepped forward from his station on the poop to urge the efforts of the chained rowers, and, after killing several in his fury, the stroke oarsman, always a most powerful man, seized him and dragged him into the midst of the rowers, who dropped their oars and fell on him like wild animals. Mamut was thrown from bench to bench, every man taking a bite from his carcass as he passed forward and he was a corpse before he reached the bows. (See the slightly variant account in Don Quixote, Part 1, Chap. 37.) Terrified by the fate of their captain, the Turks made little resistance to Santa Cruz, who took the ship in tow. The Christian nefs which brought about the encounter were saved. On the anniversary of Lepanto, Mamut's vessel became the sole prize of the entire campaign and the reward of the labors of 70,000 men. She was a fine vessel and was taken into the royal squadron of Naples under the name of "Prize." The Christian fleet followed the chase and lined up in front of Modon, but Uluch Ali made no movement and the Christian fleet withdrew.

Such was the anticlimax of the campaign of 1572. The campaign was finished; for the advanced season and the lack of supplies made a longer stay inadvisable, and the Christians retired to Zante. It was learned from the Christian slaves rescued from Mamut's vessel that the Sultan had ordered Uluch Ali to return to Constantinople at all risks. Knowing he could not avoid a battle on the way, the latter remained under the guns of Modon. He contemplated saving his men by a retreat overland, abandoning his ships, but his resolution was rewarded by the failure of the Christians to attack the fleet or Modon in any way. The Turks asserted that in thus maintaining their position, in the face of a much superior enemy and so preventing any loss of territory, their glory was no less than that of the Christians the year before.

It is difficult not to agree with them. The Turks were well led by an able Admiral and there was unity in command. The maneuvering on both sides about Cerigo was very skillful, although without result. But in the second campaign Don John behaved foolishly about his personal share in the credit for command, discipline was poor, and the allies distrustful of each other; from all of which Uluch Ali drew full advantage.

At Zante the fleet received very necessary supplies and on October 16 it arrived at Corfu, after towing the nefs part of the way.

At Corfu a quarrel broke out between Don John and Foscarini over the matter of salutes from the fortress on arrival, but the peacemaker, Colonna, was able to persuade Don John that the neglect was an error rather than willful and, although Don John felt obliged to return at once to Italy, he offered to let 2,000 King's troops remain to help the Venetians in any coastal attack they might wish to make. But the officers and men concerned refused to stay, saying they were not well treated. None was punished and Don John departed immediately for Messina where he arrived October 25. The King's soldiers returned later than Don John and met bad weather in which they suffered greatly and many died. The remainder were discharged and, with many complaints of their treatment, they took to beggary and, as Sereno says, gave an ugly view of the badly ordered soldiery of the time.

VENICE MAKES PEACE WITH THE SULTAN

Although Foscarini gained a small success at Cattaro after the allies had left him, Venice felt nothing of importance had been accomplished in the campaign and there was much resentment at the ill support which it was thought the allies had given to Foscarini. The city was in distress with loss of business and high taxes and the Signory now thought of peace with the Turk.

So through the winter of 1572-73, without notifying her allies, Venice sought peace with Turkey; yet she did not cease hostilities and sent out several small expeditions. On April 4, 1573, the Doge declared that a peace had been signed.

It was for the term of 30 years, and by it Venice regained her trade, although at a considerable price. There was to be free business for merchants on both sides; goods were to be freely carried and the commerce of all the Venetian possessions was to be free. Alexandria was to be open to supply Venice with spices (although most of this commodity was now going to Portugal by the Cape route). The Sultan would release all prisoners upon ransom and Venice would release hers without ransom. Venice was to pay 300,000 sequins ($693,000) as reparations and an annual tribute of 2,500 sequins ($5,775) for retention of Zante and Cephallonia. She was not to man more than 60 galleys each year, although Turkey might man 300. Should her late allies attack Venice, Turkey would defend her.

The treaty was kept secret as long as possible and the Pope was looking forward to a renewal of the war when he heard of the peace. He was very angry and threatened to excommunicate Venice. Don John hauled down the Standard of the Holy League at the mole of Naples where he had hoisted it with high hopes in 1571. King Philip said to the Venetian ambassador who announced the peace that he had no cause of quarrel with the Sultan and had entered the League in his zeal for religion at the request of the Pope. So ended the last of medieval naval wars.* In the name of holy religion it was a war to retain commercial advantage on the part of Venice and a war to check the advance of Mohammedan power on the part of Spain. Only Pope Pius V was actuated strongly by religious motives.

SUMMARY

The campaign of 1572 illustrates the power of the "fleet in being," as Mahan terms it. Each fleet protected its own territories, for neither could be attacked under the guns of its own fortress. Each fleet feared to land its soldiers for an enterprise on shore, except when the ships were secure without them. As for tactics, the success of the heavy gunfire of the galleasses at Lepanto had been so great in breaking up the hostile line that the next year at Cerigo, Uluch Ali refused to face the batteries of the nefs and ably avoided the equally able efforts of Colonna to bring them into action.

---

* There were some fleet galley actions in the next century, but of no great tactical importance.

In the August encounters, although Colonna had less than three-quarters as many galleys as Uluch Ali, it seems probable that he did not make sufficient allowance for his heavier artillery and the individually weak crews of the Turks. A resolute attack at Cerigo with only the galleys and galleasses might well have overpowered the Turks. But Colonna's position as Lieutenant-General of the League, fighting against the wishes of the Commander in Chief and without the main Spanish squadron, made him unduly cautious.

The war shows an undue desire on both sides to make territorial gains with the fleet, instead of destroying the hostile fleet first. Supplies and men were hard to find for the ships available. The great nobles who took part on the Christian side, particularly Spaniards, were unruly and animated by unbecoming personal jealousies. The soldiers were much neglected, yet nevertheless it was possible to work the latter up by suitable appeals to their emotions and get most excellent service from them on the day of battle.

PRINCIPAL AUTHORITIES CONSULTED IN THIS CHAPTER

CAETANI, ONORATO, *Battaglia di Lepanto* Lettere, pubblicate da G. B. Carinci.

CARACCIOLO, FERRANTE, Conte di Biccari, *I Commentarii delle Guerre Fatte co' Turchi da Don Giovanni D'Austria.*

CONTARINI, GIOVANNI PIETRO, *Historia delle Cose Successe dal Principio della Guerra mossa da Selim Ottomano.*

DIEDO, GIROLAMO, *La Battaglia di Lepanto.*

DURO, CESAREO FERNANDEZ, *La Armada Española.*

GUGLIELMOTTI, ALBERTO, *Storia della Marina Ponteficia.*

JURIEN DE LA GRAVIÈRE, J. B. E., *La Guerre de Chypre et la Bataille de Lepante.*

MANFRONI, CAMILLO, *Storia della Marina Italiana.*

MARTEILHE, JEAN, *Memoirs of a Protestant Condemned to the Galleys of France.** Translated by Oliver Goldsmith.

ROSELL, CAYETANO, *Historia del Combate Naval de Lepanto.*

SERENO, BARTOLOMEO, *Commentari della Guerra di Cipro.*

---

* Although written in the 18th century, this book throws much light on galleys and service on board.

APPENDIX TO CHAPTER IX

About the middle of the sixteenth century the ordinary galley, as described by contemporary writers quoted by Admiral Fincati in his book *Le Triremi,* was of the same general type as those of the fourteenth century previously described, but was larger. The displacement was about 170 tons, the length 131 feet at the water line, and 165 from the tip of the spur to the extremity of the poop. The beam at the water line was 18 feet and the draft about 4.5 feet. The whole crew numbered about 225 men. There were 25 benches on each side with 3 rowers on each, so that the telaro was 26 feet across and the oars were longer (being 36.5 to 31.5 feet) and the stroke a slow one, only about 26 a minute at racing speed. The oars weighed about 125 pounds each and, as only one-third of the length was inboard of the pin, that portion was of much greater diameter than strength required in order to make the oar balance at the tholepin, and if necessary, a lead weight was added near the handle. The stroke was a very long

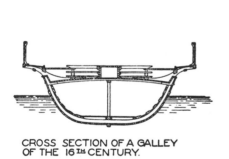

CROSS SECTION OF A GALLEY OF THE 16ᵀᴴ CENTURY.

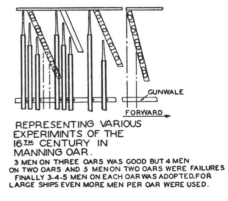

GUNWALE

FORWARD

REPRESENTING VARIOUS EXPERIMINTS OF THE 16ᵀᴴ CENTURY IN MANNING OAR.
3 MEN ON THREE OARS WAS GOOD BUT 4 MEN ON TWO OARS AND 5 MEN ON TWO OARS WERE FAILURES FINALLY 3-4-5 MEN ON EACH OAR WAS ADOPTED.FOR LARGE SHIPS EVEN MORE MEN PER OAR WERE USED.

FIG. 28

one known as "rise and fall" or "royal." That is to say, to begin the rower rose from his seat and put his inboard unchained foot on the bench in front of him, thrusting the handle of the oar as far as possible towards the stern, and, dipping his oar, he fell back on the bench with all his weight. With 150 oars a speed might be reached somewhat short of 7 knots for a brief

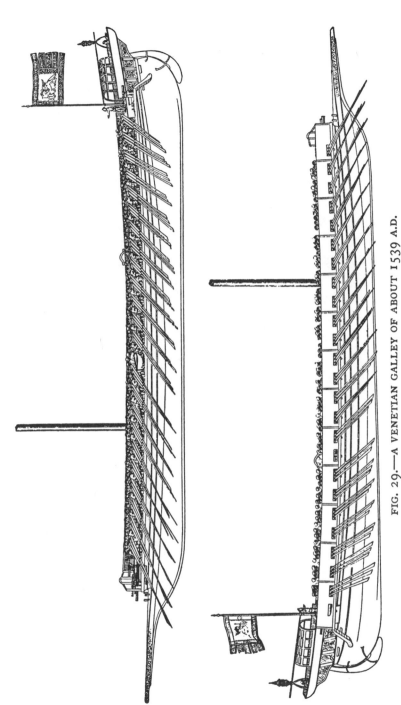

FIG. 29.—A VENETIAN GALLEY OF ABOUT 1539 A.D.

From Paris, *Souvenirs de Marine.* Broadside views of the starboard side, showing the pavesades in place for battle; the port side is without them. On one side the boat occupies the space of one bench; on the other side is the kitchen.

period of perhaps no more than 20 minutes before exhausting the rowers, who each developed about ⅛ horsepower.* For longer distances than a couple of miles the speed had to be reduced and the full crew might make 4.3 knots for a watch of 2 hours. As the bottom was uncoppered, it needed frequent cleaning and greasing to prevent serious loss of speed. Under sail with favoring conditions, with a quartering wind and little sea, the galley might reach a speed of 12 knots (See Guglielmotti).

The "spur" was very different from the classic ram which was at or below the water line. The galley spur was in the position of a bowsprit of today and inclined very slightly upward. Its length was about 18 feet and it was strongly secured to the ship. When collision occurred, it was the purpose of the spur to break up the rowing system of the enemy by shearing away his apostis. It sometimes offered a bridge for boarding. It was also serviceable in managing the sails. The hold of the ship was divided into several compartments by thwartship bulkheads which increased safety and served to store supplies, equipment, and ammunition. The largest compartment was the breadroom, which would hold about 40 days' supply in the galleys of the end of the seventeenth century. The water was carried on deck in breakers and seems to have been enough for only about 20 days. So after 10 days out of port the amount of water remaining on board influenced the decision as to what was possible to do. The principal change in these ships from those of two centuries before was in the adoption of the battery. This consisted of 5 (sometimes 3) guns mounted forward, all firing directly ahead without any arc of train, so that they had to be pointed by the helm, as was the case with some small English gunboats with a single heavy bow gun 40 or 50 years ago. There was one heavy gun in the center on the keel line, weighing 2 or 3 tons and firing a shot of 30 or 40 pounds. On each side of it were a 12-pounder and a 3- or 6-pounder. None of the five could be altered in elevation and all recoiled between parallel longitudinal timber guides. Several more 3- and 1-pounder guns were placed on pivot mounts on each side of the apostis.**

---

* See *Greek and Roman Naval Warfare*, by present author, for fuller discussion of speed and power. The ancient ships were somewhat faster than medieval ones for they had more rowers per ton of displacement.

** At Lepanto the Christian galleys had 5 bow guns each, one a 36-pdr., two 9-pdrs., and two 4½-pdrs. and besides three 4½-pdrs. on each broadside. The Turks usually had only 3 bow guns; a 36-pdr. and two 9-pdrs. So that at Lepanto the Christians had a total weight of

FIG. 30.—VENETIAN GALLEY OF SEVENTEENTH CENTURY

From Museo Civico Venice. There are 3 masts instead of 1 as in the early part of the previous century and the oars are of the "scaloccio" type with 5 men per oar.

By the middle of the sixteenth century the arquebus or hackbut had not entirely replaced archery, as each ship carried 50 bows with 100 bow-strings and 3,000 arrows but only 40 arquebuses and muskets. A few years later at Lepanto the infantrymen were almost all hackbuteers. By this time most of the Mediterranean maritime states had substituted convicts and Turkish slaves for freemen at the oars, and Venice was the only one which retained freemen, who took up weapons when alongside the enemy. Consequently, Venetian ships carried fewer soldiers than those of the other states. The inboard Venetian rower on each bench had a sword and half-pike, the middle one a bow, and the outer one threw stones. All had breast plates and almost all shields and head-pieces (Fincati, *Le Triremi*, p. 32). In the early part of the century the whole crew numbered about 150 rowers and 70 soldiers and seamen with a few officers. At the time of Lepanto, when the archers had mostly gone, the soldiers were increased to 100 or more and the whole crew, when full, exceeded 300. The oars were then increased slightly in length and the three men on each bench were all on one large oar. Gian Andrea Doria explained that with 3 men on one big oar it was easy to increase the rowers by adding a man to each bench. As was previously mentioned, flagships were usually somewhat larger and had 5 men on the after half of the oars and 4 on the other half. In this way it was easy for the flagship to maintain the lead in a voyage and set the speed. For a similar reason, in each ship the stroke oar had an extra rower to make it easy to set an even stroke for the others.

In spite of some important galley battles between the Venetians and Turks in the seventeenth century, the battle of Lepanto marked the end of the great days of rowing ships, for the great development of oceanic trade consequent upon the discovery of the Americas and the ocean route to the Indies made the sailing ship predominant. Nevertheless, at the time, people did not realize that the rowing man-of-war was doomed and not only did galleys continue to be built, but they increased in size. It was not until 1748 that the French Navy abolished the galley fleet and in Italy the type lasted a half century longer. It must be noted that during this period of

---

fire for 205 galleys 18,450 pounds besides the 6 galleasses each with an all-round fire of 326 pounds each. The Turks had a total fire of about 13,500 pounds, bow fire, in about 250 vessels. (Guglielmotti, vol. 6, p. 29.) But the galleys seldom fired their large guns more than once or twice.

decadence galley service was valuable as a coast guard to check piratical raids by the Barbary corsairs.

A word may be said as to the development of rowing craft after Lepanto. The best easily accessible information is to be found in the works of Admiral Jurien de la Gravière and Admiral Paris of the French Navy. From these it appears that in 1691 the French Naval Ministry standardized galley construction. The length at the water line was 146 feet, beam 19 feet 8 inches, and load draft 7 feet 9 inches. The displacement was 298 tons. There were 5 men on each oar and 26 oars on a side with about 150 soldiers and sailors making a crew of 400 or more men. The "capitanes" (1st flagships) and "patronnes" (2d flagships) were larger, the former having 30 or 31 oars on a side and the latter 28 or 29, with 6 and 7 men per oar. Their displacement ran as high as 500 tons. There are in the Louvre beautiful contemporary models of all three types of galley.

In Chapman's *Naval Architecture* are drawings of a capitana of Malta having 30 oars on a side. She was 179.5 feet long, 25 feet wide at the water line, and her draft to the bottom of the keel was 8.33 feet, giving a displacement of 525 tons. With 7 men on the after oars and 6 on the forward ones (390 rowers), she could probably make about 6.55 knots, nearly the same speed as an ordinary galley. The whole crew of such a ship, with officers, amounted to nearly 800 men.

All galleys, and especially the flagships, were richly ornamented with painting and gilded wood sculpture, sometimes by great artists. The stern was most highly decorated and vessels carried many flags, tapestries, and silken hangings to display on festive occasions. The accounts show that these ornaments made a large part of the cost of the ship.

The life on board was very trying for the officers, worse for the free soldiers and sailors, and still more miserable for the rowers, who were captured Turkish slaves or the scouring of the local jails. The slaves had a small clothing allowance and a ration of bread and beans and as much water as they wished. They worked at such small industries, as their chains permitted, to earn a trifle for additional food and debauchery. As they were chained permanently to their rowing positions, their personal condition was filthy and it was said that the odor of a galley could be perceived a mile or more to leeward. It is alleged that the habit of using very strong perfumes on the person, which still endures to a certain extent in Latin

FIG. 31 (*Explanation on page 235*)

countries, established itself in galley times to overpower the ship's stench and became popular as a suggestion that a man had served his King and religion against the Turk.

*   *   *   *   *

The galleass type had a very short period of life as compared with that of the galley. The galleass squadron did good service at Lepanto where it made its first appearance, and a Spanish squadron was seen in the Channel in 1588, but this made no mark. Nevertheless the galleass did not disappear during the seventeenth century. The tactical purpose of the galleass was to develop a heavy battery on the rowing ship, and the load of the guns made the ship heavy and sluggish under the limited power available by oars. Instead of a few small guns in broadside which the galley carried, the galleass had a considerable broadside battery as well as heavy guns in bow and stern. There is a large model of a Venetian galleass of the very late sixteenth century in the naval museum in the Arsenal at Venice, whose photograph is here reproduced. The data therewith in regard to her are drawn from the inscription on the case, from a letter to me of the Curator of the Museum, and from a letter written to

FIG. 31.——GALLEASS

Courtesy of the Naval Museum, Venice.

Model in the Arsenal at Venice—Scale 1/10. Length, 165.5 feet, beam at water line; 27.68 feet; draft, 10.37 feet; displacement, about 700 tons. She had 49 oars manned by 343 rowers and with officers, seamen, and soldiers carried about 700 in her crew. Her racing speed under oars was about 6.5 with an E.H.P. of 27.0*, and under sail over 12 knots in favorable conditions, but seldom was the wind strong enough for such speed. This model is not the galleass of Lepanto, which, as Duodo stated in his previously mentioned letter to the Senate, was rather shorter and had a narrow apostis (36.5 feet) instead of 42 feet as in the model. The guns of the model are 30 in number and probably the same as those mentioned by Duodo in his letter, that is, 2 heavy bow guns, firing shot of 40 libbre (26.5 American pounds) and 28 lighter ones, culverins (long guns), cannon (medium length), and periers (short guns) whose projectiles varied from 30 to 6 libbre in weight. Six guns fired astern, and 6 others ahead and 18 on the broadsides. The total weight of one discharge was 492 libbre or 326 pounds. Besides, the model mounts two 20-barrel machine guns firing bullets on the break of the poop and two more on the forecastle where they command the ship's waist, presumably for use against hostile boarders, should they gain possession of that part of the ship. To account for the great effect of these rather light guns at Lepanto, we must recollect that the planking of galleys was only 3 or 4 inches thick, that the crews were all on the open deck and that, unlike the Christians, the Turkish vessels had no pavesades (temporary wooden mantlets along the side for protection of the crews).

---

* For a discussion of speed and horsepower of rowing ships, see my previous volume, *Greek and Roman Naval Warfare.*

the Senate in 1593 by Francesco Duodo who commanded the galleasses at Lepanto.

An essential difference between the galley and the galleass was that the latter had a deck over the rowers (much of it a grating only) which protected them from the weather and from injury in battle and gave ample room for the soldiers to fight and the seamen to handle the sails. The 3 masts were lateen rigged and carried in all about 8,000 square feet of sail area.

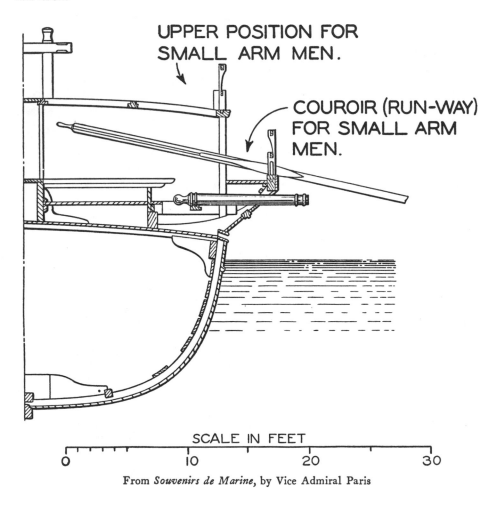

UPPER POSITION FOR SMALL ARM MEN.

COUROIR (RUN-WAY) FOR SMALL ARM MEN.

SCALE IN FEET

0   10   20   30

From *Souvenirs de Marine*, by Vice Admiral Paris

FIG. 33.—SECTION OF A FRENCH GALLEASS END OF LOUIS XIV REIGN SHOWING THE BROADSIDE GUNS AMONG THE ROWERS BENCHES

FIG. 32.—GALLEASS UNDER SAIL. FLAG AT MAINMAST SHOWS LION OF ST. MARK

By permission of the Royal United Service Institution. This drawing is of a somewhat later date than the model in the Arsenal. Note that there is a gun mounted between every pair of oars besides those on the poop and forecastle; and also, that, unlike the galleys, the rowers are placed beneath the upper deck.

For the general appearance of these galleasses at Lepanto we have a contemporary painting by Vasari in the Sala Regia of the Vatican, commemorating the victory. It shows stumpy vessels with high forecastles and poops and 2 side steering oars to each ship.

Of the galleasses of the next century when they grew larger, but had survived their brief day of importance we have more knowledge from the researches of Vice Admiral Paris of the French Navy, for many years in charge of the Naval Museum in the Louvre. The drawings and text published by him show that the "Royale" built in the latter part of the reign of Louis XIV was somewhat larger than the Venetian one whose photograph is here given, being of about 1,000 tons. A few additional particulars may be given of this biggest of rowing ships. A manuscript of 1690 gives the crew as 1,001 men, including 450 rowers for 49 oars and nearly 400 soldiers and gunners. The rest were officers, seamen, mechanics, convict guards, and medical and religious staffs. The model in the Louvre shows only 42 oars which, with 8 men on one half and 9 men on the other half, would give about 5.5 knots at full speed and 3.5 knots for 2 hours, with all the rowers, and 2.4 knots when in 3 watches. There were 3 masts with a sail area of 9,100 feet, which would give a speed of 12 knots or more under good conditions. Not only did the soldiers have the deck over the rowers for their station, a platform (couroir) running above the oars between the apostis and the side gave a low level position for a part of the soldiers. The heaviest part of the battery was on and under the forecastle where 6 guns (36-pdrs.) fired directly ahead and 3 more (24-pdrs.) on each beam. Four guns under the poop fired directly aft and on each broadside seven 8-pdrs., placed among the rowers and benches, fired under the oars which had to be peaked (their blades raised high). On the couroir, and the side of the upper deck were eleven 2-pdrs. on each side. The entire weight of one discharge was about 732 pounds (788 pounds American). The heavy guns firing ahead and astern were always pointed level without any arc of train, and it is apparent that one discharge, about the time of closing with the enemy, was all that was expected. A second round was a matter of good fortune.

The merchant ships (nefs) and the sailing men-of-war of the campaign of Lepanto differed little except in the armament. The tomb of Alexander Contarini, a Venetian admiral, who died in 1553, in a church in Padua, gives a fine representation of a sailing man-of-war of the time. The drawing herewith from Paris (*Souvenirs de Marine*) shows her gen-

From *Souvenirs de Marine,* by Vice Admiral Paris

FIG. 34.—SHOWING A DOUBLE RANK OF ROWERS ON EACH GREAT OAR

For simplicity in the drawing only two rowers are shown to each oar. Note the handles fastened to each oar for the rowers. The oar did not feather. The rowers stripped naked to row.

eral arrangements. The same work gives also a drawing of a merchant nef, somewhat smaller, of 278 tons' displacement with a fourth mast aft with a lateen sail, and with an upper and lower forecastle but only 2 partial decks aft. Such a ship employed as a transport could carry nearly 300 men in addition to the crew but would need some changes in internal fittings as will be mentioned in the next chapter.

FIG. 35.—NEF, SAILING MAN-OF-WAR, MIDDLE OF SIXTEENTH CENTURY
From the monument of Alessandro Contarini, died in 1553, by Michele San Micheli,
in the Church of San Antonio, Padua.

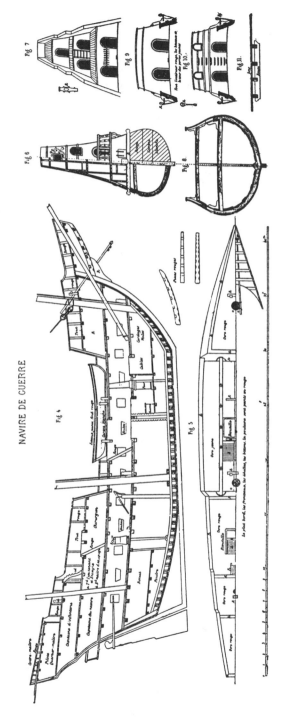

FIG. 36.—A NEF

Drawing from the model of a Venetian man-of-war of the sixteenth century from *Souvenirs de Marine*, by Vice Admiral Paris. The model has been redesigned by the draftsman with the aid of manuscripts of the period, and shows the same type of vessel as that sculptured on Contarini's monument previously illustrated. This vessel is about 96 feet long on the water line and of 30 feet beam. At 10.5 feet draft she would displace about 450 tons. Note the half-deck, quarter-deck, and poop above the upper complete deck, in which she was similar to the Spanish ships engaged in the Great Armada mentioned in the next chapter. She carries 5 sails, a lateen sail on the mizzen and square main topsail, mainsail, foresail, and a spritsail under the bowsprit. The total sail area was about 10,000 square feet (fairly large). She carried a main battery of 12 guns in broadside on the main, or covered, deck (probably demi-culverins, or long 9-pounders). Probably other small guns were mounted on the upper rail.

CHAPTER X

THE WAR OF ELIZABETH OF ENGLAND WITH PHILIP II OF SPAIN AND THE CAMPAIGN OF THE GREAT ARMADA

THE voyage and defeat of the Spanish Armada by the English fleet in 1588 was the culmination of a diplomatic and belligerent struggle between the two countries which lasted the entire reign of Queen Elizabeth and almost all of that of Philip II of Spain. Peace was signed only after the death of both sovereigns. During the struggle the power of Spain sank and that of England rose. The campaign of 1588 is noteworthy as the origin of English reliance on sea power for national defense, for previously she had depended on her armies and had thrown them on the Continent. Tactically, the campaign marks the beginning of the sailing ship as the primary tactical unit on the sea instead of the rowing ship. On the Spanish side many of the leaders had served in the victorious fleet at Lepanto 17 years before and expected to conquer the English by the same tactical methods that had been successful against the Turks. But the English introduced a new type of battle, relying on great guns in sailing ships rather than on boarders in rowing ships, so that in this year we see the birth of a system of tactics which developed and lasted until the advent of steam as motive power rendered it obsolete.

POLITICAL SITUATION UNDERLYING THE WAR

As political situations underlie wars and their strategy, we must undertake a brief examination of European economics and politics which led to the expedition of the Great Armada. France and Spain had long been the leading powers in Europe, striving for predominance. Under the Emperor Charles V, King of Spain, and Francis I, King of France, the two nations had fought for control of Italy and Charles had been successful. As Lord of Burgundy and the Low Countries he was further desirous of preventing France from expanding northwards and he needed contentment in those rich provinces, as well as the friendship of England, in order to complete the encirclement of France. To secure England, towards the end of his reign he married Philip, his son and heir, to his cousin Queen Mary of England. The protestant English nation did not approve of the Spanish marriage, although the Queen herself was a most devoted wife to Philip and anxious for England to conform to her husband's Spanish policies. After a year in England as titular King, but without any real authority, Philip was called to throne of Spain, in January, 1556, by the abdication of his father.

Less than three years later, the death of Queen Mary severed the bond between England and Spain to the general content of Englishmen. The new Queen Elizabeth, sister to Mary, did not follow her policies: she was of the new religion and no friend of Spain whose new king had most ambitious views. He was deeply religious and desired to re-establish the unity of the church, which heresy had so affected in his own provinces of the Netherlands and in the neighboring nations, England, France, and Germany. He hoped that after uniting the Catholic elements in all these countries he might attain the hegemony of Europe. As a military foundation for his attempt he relied on the unrivaled soldiery of Spain, who came chiefly from Castile and in the previous two generations had been developed into the finest body of mercenary troops in Europe.

On the economic side Spain was not so well off as her contemporaries thought. The industrial situation in Spain was bad and from her own resources she was not capable of great belligerent effort. Her population was about 8,500,000, but the royal revenues were small, for the principal tax was a very high one on sales which ruined industry. Although much bullion came from America, much of it passed out of the country in return for necessary imports. From his possessions in Italy Philip drew little revenue for the Spanish crown, and after the revolution broke out in the Netherlands, these wealthy provinces were a drain on his purse. From Aragon and Catalonia, he got little. A larger sum came from Castile, which habitually voted 450,000,000 maravedis triennially (little over $900,000 per year, money of 1932).

NOTE: The Spanish crown of 10 reales and of 340 maravedis contained 52.2 grains of gold, 11/12 fine. It was therefore equivalent to $2.061 of American money. A Castilian ducat had 375 maravedis, worth $2.273. The peso or dollar of 8 reales, the celebrated piece-of-eight, contained 423.7 grains of silver, 17/18 fine and was worth $1.65 American money. The Spanish coinage ratio of gold to silver was therefore at the rate of 10.45.

The principal income of the King of Spain came from the mines of America, whose average annual production at the time of the Armada was about 350 tons of silver besides several tons of gold. The whole value varied from year to year from 25 to 30 million dollars of 1932. The winter before the Armada the American fleet was said to have brought to Spain as much as 14 million ducats (of 375 maravedis, $31,822,000). Of this the Crown was entitled to 20 per cent, but such was the corruption of officials that the King lost much of what was due him.

The industrial weakness of Spain provoked international disputes. The American provinces, like other colonies, needed manufactured goods which they did not produce themselves, but as the King feared that the presence of foreign traders might increase heresy he closed America to foreign trade, in spite of Spain's inability to supply colonial requirements. The situation induced friction with England, which, in that century, was growing rapidly in population, industry, and wealth. The Portuguese discovery of the route to the East by way of the Cape of Good Hope, in the previous century, had inflicted a very serious blow on the business and shipping of the Mediterranean maritime powers and their trade with England and the Low Countries. Thus long distance maritime transportation passed out of the Mediterranean into the Atlantic Ocean, and the vigorous and expanding British nation was determined to seize its share. Spanish America needed English goods and in the face of the demand Spanish officials not only failed to suppress British smuggling, but frequently aided it.

In Spain, where the royal authority was more effective, the British traders often complained of being annoyed by the inquisition and, in America, they were sometimes very severely dealt with.

So it came that many English seamen believed themselves unjustly treated by Spanish authorities and they sought redress. Under the international law of the time, redress frequently took the way of "reprisals." When complainants went to their sovereigns with grievances against a foreign power, it was then the practice for the latter to authorize "reprisal" as a means of righting the wrong. In such a case, the sovereign issued letters of marque granting permission to the aggrieved party to cruise against the shipping of the offending nation until he had recouped his losses. Among the most noted of such corsairs were Sir Francis Drake and Sir John

FIG. 37.——PHILIP II, KING OF SPAIN
By P. De La Cruz. Library of Congress.

Hawkins, who, in early life, engaged in the illicit Spanish trade and after an ill-fortuned adventure of the two at Vera Cruz in 1567, Drake conceived he had received a wrong which justified his subsequent attacks upon Spanish trade and shipping. Of course, to Spain such reprisals seemed merely piracy and the harsh treatment of English prisoners taken in these adventures accentuated ill-feeling between the two countries. But the so-called piratical cruises of Drake and others were not the only cause of war.

Revolt in the Netherlands

The English relations with the rebellious Netherlands were most offensive to Philip. His father, Charles V, had treated these extremely wealthy provinces with great consideration and drawn large revenues from them, amounting to about 1,500,000 livres annually or about as many dollars of our money of 1932. But Philip's policy was very different. He wished to draw revenues from these provinces which Spain could not furnish, but he also wished to subdue heresy there as the first step towards putting it down elsewhere. The result was a growing unrest which broke into open rebellion against the King's Governor, the Duke of Alva, in 1568. The war thus started lasted over 40 years. The King soon gained control of the southern provinces, now Belgium, but the northern provinces he was not able to hold and they ultimately became the present Kingdom of Holland.

Protestant England sympathized with the rebels on the point of religious persecution and deeply felt the distress brought upon English commerce by Alva's destruction of life and property in Flanders, for the commercial relations between the two countries had been close and important for centuries. After the insurrection broke out under the Prince of Orange, many English volunteers went to Flanders to offer their aid, although Queen Elizabeth gave no open countenance to the revolt. She did find a pretext for seizing a large sum of money which the King was sending by sea from Spain to Flanders in 1568 for the support of his army. Thereupon Alva made reprisals upon English property in the Netherlands and the Queen made counter reprisals which initiated unfriendly proceedings between the two governments, although formal war was still some years distant in the future.

In the beginning of the insurrection, while Alva was still in substantial control of the country, the rebels set up a flotilla of 18 vessels to prey upon Spanish commerce supplying the army from Spain and elsewhere, and early in 1570 there were 80 of these rebel ships which had taken 300 prizes, under authority of letters of marque issued by William of Orange as sovereign of his principality. But although the sea-rovers were a great annoyance to the Spanish rulers of the disaffected provinces, they had no seaport which they could use as a base and were consequently under little control by the Prince whose letters they bore. A base where they could replenish stores and dispose of their prizes was an absolute necessity for continuous operations and the freebooters (sea-beggars as they were known) found that Queen Elizabeth winked at their use of southeastern English ports for these purposes.

Early in 1572 the diplomatic relations between Elizabeth and Alva became better than they had been for several years, and the Queen forbade her subjects to supply the Dutch vessels with food or beer. The latter was a very important part of the seamens rations for centuries. Without a base, and in a condition approaching starvation, the flotilla appeared on the coast of Holland and seized the town of Brill on an island at the mouth of the Meuse River by an act of great audacity. Soon the flotilla seized Flushing also and by a general uprising of the people the rebels rapidly gained successes and territory in Holland, Zealand, and the north.

From the seizure of Brill dates the birth of the independent states of Holland and 6 other Dutch provinces, under the fostering care of the Prince of Orange. The Spanish army was able to hold the southern provinces and beggared them by its presence, but the free north prospered in spite of constant war. Its commerce greatly developed under the protection of its fleet which lived on Spanish prizes. In the decisive campaign of 1588, the Dutch flotilla, thus founded, played an important, though inconspicuous, part.

England and Spain Become Unfriendly

For several years the Prince of Orange tried to get France and England to aid him in the struggle against Spain. The wars of religion in France prevented that country from taking effective foreign action and Philip played upon its two religious parties to keep the country weak. As for

England, the Prince of Orange tendered the Queen the sovereignty of the Netherlands if she would declare war on Spain and offered several cities in pledge. But the Queen long refused open help, although many English volunteers were fighting the Spaniards in the Low Countries. As each year passed, it became more apparent to Philip's advisers, if not to himself that the northern provinces could not be conquered unless England was subdued, but although not yet ready to make war, for many years he practiced a diplomatic diversion by entering into many conspiracies to arouse the Catholics in England and Scotland and put the imprisoned Mary Queen of Scots on the throne of England to which she was the next heir.

There were two parties among Elizabeth's ministers. One, headed by Sir Francis Walsingham, wished war with Spain; the other, of which William Cecil, Lord Burleigh, was chief, wished to preserve peace. For years, the Queen followed a vacillating policy, sometimes favoring Spain and sometimes not. In 1577, when the Queen was opposing Philip, she sent Drake on his famous cruise around the world. The Queen was one of the shareholders who financed the expedition, and when he came back in 1580 he was welcomed by the whole country and knighted by the Queen. He had taken immense booty from Spanish treasure ships, getting 26 tons of silver (then worth 2.5 tons of gold or over $1,680,000 money of 1932) from a single vessel. Tension grew very much after this incident. In the next year, 1581, Philip marched an army into Portugal and seized the sovereignty as heir to the childless King who had just died. This acquisition brought the Spanish monarchy about 1,500,000 new subjects and greatly increased its maritime strength, for Portugal held the trade to the East Indies and possessed a great fleet of merchantmen, based principally on Lisbon. Thereby, the prospect of war became greater.

In order to complete his occupation of Portugal, the King sent a fleet to the Azores to put down an insurrection, where it defeated a superior fleet of French adventurers who were supporting Don Antonio, claimant to the throne of Portugal. The Admiral of the Spanish fleet was Don Alvaro de Bazan, Marquis of Santa Cruz, who had commanded the reserve at the battle of Lepanto with the greatest skill and efficiency. After the battle at the Azores he was considered the best Admiral of Spain and took advantage of his prestige to urge further service.

In a letter to the King, Santa Cruz said that his recent victory should be followed by the conquest of England and that he was ready to undertake it with the fine fleet and army which had overcome Don Antonio. Having possession of England, there would be good hope of victory in the Low Countries. He said Queen Elizabeth was much in fear of such an attack, that there was little preparation in England and many Catholics (who would favor intervention). He added that there were those who would not fail to say to the King that money was lacking and that aid to the Queen would come from Flanders and France, to which he answered that the French had lost standing with him (on account of their poor defense in the Azores battle) and, as for money, such a great King would never fail to find it, the more so as it was for the service of God and the public good. The King replied thanking Santa Cruz and saying he would bear the matter in mind. Nothing was undertaken at that time, for the King had little money and he had great trouble in paying his soldiers in Flanders.

In the meantime many exiled Antwerp merchants in London sent aid to the Prince of Orange; the English volunteers serving in the rebel armies grew to 5,000 men, and English seamen found enough profit in the forbidden trade with the Spanish colonies to overlook its dangers.

In 1584 the Duke of Anjou died. He was heir to the French throne and the protestant King Henry of Navarre now became next in succession. The event changed the politics of Europe. The Catholic party in France now had enough to occupy it at home without undertaking foreign adventures in Flanders or elsewhere. Philip supplied money to aid it against the Protestants and, with France thus divided against herself, he began to think of undertaking the conquest of England with the help of money from the Pope. In the summer of 1584 Alexander Farnese, Prince of Parma and Governor of the Netherlands, was able to accomplish the murder of the Prince of Orange, and the subsequent progress of the Spanish army under Farnese seemed to promise the speedy recovery of the Low Countries.

In despair at the prospect, the Provinces turned both to France and England for aid.

Elizabeth was aroused by their situation and became convinced that if Philip was successful he would attempt the conquest of England. Although she did not wish to undertake their relief by her own power alone, yet she could not permit the increased strength which would come to

FIG. 38.—SIR FRANCIS DRAKE
Courtesy of the Library of Congress

France were that country to rescue them. So the Queen was for a joint protectorate. The party in Holland and Zealand favoring the English alliance began to gain, and the Queen was told that the provinces could support 15,000 foot and 3,000 horse and would give her Sluys and Ostend as pledges if she would take on one-third of the strength. In view of these offers, a great council was held in the fall of 1584. Burghley, head of the peace party, now said it was better to make war outside the Kingdom with the help of the people of Holland rather than after the King of Spain should have consummated his conquests there. The Queen was willing to take action but did not wish to break the formal state of peace. Throughout all these years preceding the war the Queen showed a preference for actions showing her resentment but which were not serious enough to provoke Philip beyond endurance. So now she would not go further than "reprisal."

DRAKE'S RAID TO AMERICA

An occasion was found in Philip's recent step. A bad crop in Spain induced Philip to invite a number of English vessels to bring grain under promise of safe conduct. No sooner had they arrived than an embargo was laid on them, their crews thrown into prison, and the ships, guns, and cargoes confiscated for the "enterprise of England." The King could not evade responsibility, for one ship escaped with papers which were conclusive. The indignation in English commercial circles was very great and thereafter no party was opposed to war. The Queen felt with her people and laid a retaliatory embargo on Spanish goods; letters of general reprisal were issued to merchants and, in June, 1585, Drake was authorized to requisition ships for an expedition to the Caribbean to attack the seaports there.

Territorial possessions of a sovereign were not subject to the maritime law of reprisal within which the Queen meant to act. But a pretext was found to evade the law. In order to prevent the spread of heresy, the King had forbidden foreign shipping to enter the American Colonies, yet old treaties permitted Englishmen to trade with Spanish territorial possessions. Elizabeth therefore held that, if trade were not permitted with the Colonies, they could not be territories and consequently were subject to the maritime law of reprisal.

Drake's proposed expedition was very popular in London and other cities followed its example in offering ships. The enterprise was to be carried out in the usual way by a fleet of merchantmen, with a few additions from the Royal Navy, and was to be financed by a joint stock company among whose subscribers was the Queen. By August, Drake had assembled a fleet of 29 vessels including 2 of the Queen's. The rest were all private vessels and included 8 pinnaces. The entire number of men were about 2,300, of whom about half were mariners and the rest soldiers under Christopher Carleill, son-in-law of Secretary Sir Francis Walsingham. It was the strongest private expedition that had ever left England. Every one understood how much turned upon its success, and even Burghley was eager for its departure. But the Queen now fell into indecision and thought of making terms with Spain. At last, on September 14, Drake sailed with insufficient water, having left stores on the quays in order to get away before receiving royal orders delaying him. He appeared at Bayona and Vigo on the coast of Spain and remained there a week, getting water and booty, and went on his way to America, while Santa Cruz slowly assembled a squadron to pursue him to America (see Map No. XI).

On the outward voyage Drake stopped at the Canary and Cape de Verde Islands and did some looting in the latter, where the crews picked up an epidemic which decimated them before arriving in America. Nevertheless, Drake captured San Domingo and Cartagena, both fortified ports and important colonial centers, where he inflicted much damage. At Cartagena Drake held a council to discuss whether he should retain it as a base for operating against Spanish trade in America, and particularly against the treasure fleets which annually departed thence for Spain via the Straits of Florida and brought the principal income of the King. It was decided that the battle losses and the pestilence made this bold step undesirable. Had Cartagena been securely held and a strong fleet sent out, it is quite possible the whole course of the war might have been changed by transferring the main operations to America, but, besides the military difficulties, the Queen was not then desirous of pressing matters to an open war. No doubt Drake knew of her preference for bringing Philip to terms by an effective demonstration and feared that he might not be supported at home, if he were to hold a station in America. So he returned home, arriving in the summer of 1586.

The booty was not enough to recoup the stockholders, but the expedition was a great success. The losses to Spain in ships and stores was very great and, above all, it was of great moral effect all over Europe. The very sources of Philip's revenues seemed threatened; Parma could no longer get money from bankers to pay his troops; and it was thought that Philip himself might be forced into bankruptcy. Above all, Spanish prestige was ruined and that of the English exalted, greatly affecting the spirit of the combatants and the outcome in the decisive campaign two years later. The King, however, was little discouraged by his losses.

King Philip Resolves on War

During the period of Drake's voyage negotiations were current between Elizabeth and the United Provinces. In spite of Parma's lack of money, he was so successful in the field during 1585 that, in order to secure the Queen's aid, the Dutch government again offered her the sovereignty of the Low Countries. She declined the offer with much courtesy, but agreed to send 5,000 foot and 1,000 horse to act against Parma and, as a pledge of good faith, the Provinces allowed English garrisons to be placed in four cities. At the end of 1585 the Queen's favorite courtier, the Earl of Leicester, went to the Continent as her Commander in Chief. A royal manifesto cited the Queen's reasons for hostilities, naming religious persecution, the Papal expedition to Ireland in 1579 which Philip had aided, and the attempt of the Spanish ambassador in London to arrange a plot for an invasion of England.

In sending troops to the Provinces, the manifesto avowed three objectives: peace founded upon recognition of religious freedom in the Netherlands, restoration of their ancient political liberties, and security for England. The document was equivalent to a declaration of war, and Philip replied by ordering the seizure of Dutch and English ships, the arrest of persons, and confiscation of property within his reach. As Drake had already insulted Vigo and was known to be on his way to America, the King now turned resolutely to undertake the conquest of England. By the end of 1585 he was writing to Parma "as Antwerp is taken, I want your advice about the invasion of England." He did not wish Parma to delay the English adventure in order to conquer the Dutch sea-islands, but recognized that seizure of a good seaport in Holland would be necessary before attempting to cross the channel.

Santa Cruz Submits a Plan for War on England

Santa Cruz, as Captain General of the Ocean Sea and of the army of the Kingdom of Portugal, was greatly disturbed by Drake's raid, and early in 1586 he repeated his recommendation to make war on England. As his reasons he assigned the great damage of Drake's raid, the English aid to the revolted provinces, which prolonged the war there, and the loss of business, so that the cost of the existing state of affairs was, as he thought, four times the cost of an effective expedition. The King replied telling the Marquis to submit a detailed plan, which he did at great length in March, 1586. It differed from that of the King, who had thought of sending Parma to England with the field army of Flanders. Santa Cruz proposed to mobilize both fleet and army in Spain and Portugal and expected to command the whole himself. Philip did not accept the plan for it was too vast for the royal revenues, but it was the basis for the naval mobilization of 1588.*

The King thanked Santa Cruz for his plan of campaign, but wrote to

---

* As such basis it is worth while to consider some of its items as showing the economic side of war at that time. The document gave the number of ships, their tonnage and home ports, the nationality of each regiment, the total of provisions, stores, and ammunition, and whence each item could be supplied and its cost. The estimate called for 510 requisitioned ships, great and small, to make up a tonnage of 110,750 at a charter price of 6 reales ($1.25) per ton per month.

The Spanish ton (tonelada) was equivalent to 2 pipes of wine or 250 gallons. In cubic space it was about 53 feet. In ship measurement the tonnage was reached by multiplying length, beam, and depth of hold and dividing by a factor; it was not much different from the tonnage reached by the English rule.

The law required these vessels to carry crews at the rate of 20 men per 100 tons, but Santa Cruz said so many seamen could not be found and the presence on board of the army would make 15 per 100 tons a satisfactory allowance, giving in all 16,612 officers, seamen and boys. The pay for seamen would be at the rate of 1,000 maravedis ($6.07) per month. In addition to the sailing ships, there would be 40 galleys and 6 galleasses with crews of 13,720 seamen and rowers. The army was to number 55,000 infantry, 1,200 cavalry, 4,290 artillerymen, and 3,400 adventurers and people of distinction. The pay of privates was at the rate of 28 to 30 reales ($5,76 to $6.17) per month, according to nationality. The whole number of souls was 94,222. Provisions and supplies for 8 months were to be taken, among which the principal item was hard bread at the rate of 1½ pounds per ration, amounting to about 15,000 tons, and also bacon, dried meat, dried fish, cheese, beans, peas, rice, garlic, oil, and vinegar, making about 7,000 tons more. The wine ration was about a quart per head per day, but none for the rowers, and came to 20,000 tons. The whole cost of the expedition was placed at 44,895,656 reales, or about $9,257,000, after making some deduction for deaths and desertions such as were to be expected. It may be noted as of interest that the cost of the expedition was estimated at twice the pay of the private soldiers and sailors, that is, at about 60 reales per man per month.

FIG. 39.——QUEEN ELIZABETH OF ENGLAND

Courtesy of Library of Congress

him the same day that he wished him to take a squadron to the Americas to defeat Drake and repair the damages which the latter had inflicted in the islands. The same letter assured the Marquis that the King was by no means renouncing the idea of the English campaign. From information received from Bayona, Santa Cruz believed that Drake had about 14,000 men with him and told the King that he would try to raise 10,000 infantry for the expedition.

The work of Spanish authorities was always slow and, in fact, this relief fleet, such as it was, did not leave Spain until long after Drake was back in England. In the meantime Philip began to mobilize his forces for the invasion of England, but on a scale much smaller than Santa Cruz had suggested. He directed the latter to assemble a fleet at Lisbon from all the Spanish possessions, and told Parma to subordinate his other operations to that of invading England when the fleet of Santa Cruz should appear in the Channel.

The Queen Neglects Preparations

Although Secretary Walsingham kept the Queen well informed of the intentions of King Philip, she was not inclined to make adequate defense against the invasion which he was preparing. Her income was under half a million pounds ($3,445,000),*
and she was averse to spending money in the Netherlands, as she was always very close-fisted. Soon after Leicester and his army were sent to the Continent the Queen seemed to regret her action. She wrangled bitterly with Leicester about finances and sent him little money, so that he exhausted his private fortune in unsuccessful efforts to pay and feed his soldiers. Using her army in the Netherlands as a threat only, she was now willing to entertain a suggestion from Parma that she should negotiate with him for peace. Thereupon ensued fictitious negotiations which lasted for two years. The Queen was honestly desirous of closing the war on condition that the Provinces should be guaranteed civil and religious liberties, but, as she did not take them into her confidence, their relations with her became strained. King Philip and Parma were only anxious to

---

* The pound troy of gold of 11/12 fineness was at that time coined into 33 sovereigns and the same weight of silver (0.925 fine) was made into 66 shillings. The value of the pound in money of 1932 was thus $6.89. The ratio of gold to silver in the English coinage was therefore 10.09 to 1 and differed slightly from that of Spain.

spin out the discussion, in order to gain time to mobilize the forces for invasion while the Queen slowed down her military and naval preparations.

It is quite possible that if the Dutch and English armies had pushed a sharp campaign at this time, Parma might have been driven out of the country, in spite of his great military ability, for he had no money to make war. The Queen's attempted economy was really wasteful, for she lost the opportunity offered by Spanish poverty.

In the summer of 1586 the famous Babington conspiracy was discovered. This was a plot in which Mary Queen of Scots and Philip were concerned for the assassination of Elizabeth. The Queen and her counselors were convinced by it that her throne and her life were incompatible with Philip's designs, and, in consequence, Mary was executed early in 1587. Although Mary's death had made terms impossible, yet the Queen continued to negotiate with Parma while he persevered in preparations for invasion. He thought that flat boats could be assembled at Dunkirk, Gravelines, and Newport to take 30,000 soldiers and that an escort of 25 or 30 large ships would be enough. The passage might take 8 to 10 hours and the cost he estimated at 300,000 dollars ($493,500) a month, while the garrison remaining in Flanders would cost half as much more. He hoped to make the attempt in the fall of 1586, but money was unavailable to recruit troops and nothing was then done. At the same time Leicester was writing home that

> No doubt the King of Spain's preparations be great, but I know that he and all his friends are not able to match with her Majesty's forces, if it please her to use the means that God hath given her. But besides her own, I will undertake to furnish her from hence, upon two months' warning a navy for tall and strong ships with their furniture and mariners that the King of Spain and all he can make shall not be able to encounter them. And in this country they esteem no more of his power by sea than I do of six fisher boats off Rye.

Philip Assembles the Armada at Lisbon and Drake Raids the Spanish Coast

During these years, while Parma was hoping to invade England, the King was slowly assembling a great fleet in Spain. When Babington's plot came to light, the English fleet was mobilized to make a reconnaissance on the coast of Spain and ascertain the state of the preparations there, but it was held in the channel during the winter of 1586-87 to prevent the Guises from making any attempt to rescue their niece, Queen Mary of Scotland. After the latter's execution, it was decided that Drake should sail as early as possible in the spring, in order "to impeach the provisions of Spain." By the end of March Drake had assembled at Plymouth a force of 23 sail of 5,000 tons, including 4 ships and 2 pinnaces of the Queen. Drake's instructions were to

> impeach the joining together of the King of Spain's fleets out of their several ports, to keep victuals from them, to follow them in case they should come forward towards England or Ireland and cut off as many of them as he could and impeach their landing, as also to set upon such as should either come out of the East or West Indies, or go out of Spain thither.

And he was particularly directed "to distress the ships within the havens themselves." Probably these orders were drafted under Drake's supervision and are of much strategic value, indicating an objective far beyond the usual views of that day when local looting and prize taking was chief purpose of purely naval expeditions.

Drake's assigned task was to prevent the invasion of England. He arrived at Plymouth on March 23/April 2 and found that the ships of the Levant Company from London were detained by contrary winds and did not arrive till April 1/11.* Drake feared he might be delayed by advices from London and next day he wrote to Secretary Francis Walsingham,

> The wind commands me away. Our ship is under sail. God grant that we may so live in his fear as the enemy may have cause to say that God doth fight for her Majesty, as well abroad as at home, and give her long and happy life, and ever victory against God's enemies and her Majesty's. And let me beseech your honor to pray unto God for us that he will direct us in the right way. Then we shall not doubt our enemies, for they are the sons of men. Haste; from aboard her Majesty's good ship *Elizabeth Bonaventure*.

Drake had no sooner hoisted his flag than Elizabeth began to hesitate. The Spanish influence about her was growing and she returned again to the belief that an understanding with Philip might be reached if she did

---

* At this time the Spaniards had adopted the new calendar but the English had not. Consequently the contemporary English and Spanish records differ by 10 days in their dates. Hereafter the new calendar is used in this account.

not press him too far. So formal orders were sent from London telling the Admiral to "forbear to enter forcibly into any of the King's ports or havens or to offer any violence to any of his towns or shipping within harboring, or to do any hostility upon the land." When these orders reached Plymouth, Drake had gone. A pinnace took them in pursuit but met bad weather, and then took a valuable prize, with which it returned to port; so the restraining order was never delivered. It is probable that the effort to do so was not strenuous.

The first day out of Plymouth, Drake chased 2 ships which proved to be English and by virtue of his commission he ordered them to follow him. With his force now raised to 25 vessels he reached Finisterre in 5 days, but his fleet was then scattered by a gale and it was not until the 26th that all were assembled off Lisbon. Here he heard from some Flemish ships that at Cadiz there was a great accumulation of stores and shipping soon to be sent to Lisbon and he resolved to destroy it. He ran down the coast with his large ships well at sea and the smaller ones sweeping the coast to pick up small prizes and arrived off Cadiz on April 29. While still out of sight of port, the signal convening the council was hoisted, although several ships were much astern. Drake listened to his officers' opinions, although the meeting was not a formal council, after which he gave the order to follow him into the harbor, and at four in the afternoon he entered with a leading wind.

The harbor was formed by a spit of land about 5 miles long running parallel to the coast, with the city standing on a rocky plateau at the end of the point. The bay was wider than the range of the guns in the protecting forts, and was divided in half by a tongue of land running into it. Obstructing shoals near the entrance threw the channel close to the guns of the castle at the seaward side of the town. Abreast the city were some 60 vessels of many types and nationalities, almost all of which were in some way connected with the "enterprise of England." Many of them had no sails on board, as it was the custom to remove them from requisitioned ships (to prevent their unauthorized departure) until about to leave port. There were beside 12 galleys for local defense.

On seeing the approach of the English fleet, two of these galleys ran out from St. Mary port on the mainland side of the harbor to reconnoiter, and the English fire upon them alarmed the entire town and shipping.

Every vessel that could move cut her cables and sought shelter, some at St. Mary and others at Port Royal at the head of the bay. Ten galleys put out from the town to cover the shipping, but could accomplish little. Their battery arrangement with the heaviest guns pointing ahead and their tactical purpose of boarding required them to approach Drake's squadron of 4 Queen's ships head-on, and they met a raking fire which drove them off. One was beached, 2 ran to the head of the bay, and 7 placed themselves under the guns of the castle. The English then were free to take possession of the merchantmen that had not gone off. Those that had sails were kept and those without motive power were plundered and burned. The English vessels then took positions near the inner bay beyond range of the forts, with the Queen's ships covering the rest from the galleys. They lay quietly all night and at daylight Drake organized a flotilla of pinnaces and ships' boats to take a large craft belonging to Santa Cruz himself. By 11 A.M. the work was done and Drake began to move out, but the wind failed; he had to anchor. Troops were now pouring into the city, guns were dragged out on the point, fire-ships were set adrift on the ebb tide, and the galleys attacked repeatedly and were as often driven off.

The next morning the wind was favorable and the fleet departed, at dawn, with only one man injured and five captured in a small boat. In two nights and a day Drake had destroyed 18 Spanish vessels with supplies for the expedition, had taken 6 prizes and had revictualed his own ships. The official Spanish estimate of their losses was 172,000 ducats ($391,000). Besides the material damage wrought, and the consequent dislocation to the enterprise, the English learned an important tactical lesson from the galley attacks. These vessels had fought with the English under way and at anchor and they had been badly defeated under both conditions, and again the prestige of the English was exalted and the spirit of the Spaniards depressed. Drake wrote,

> We have now tried by experience these galleys' fight and I assure you that these her Majesty's 4 ships will make no account of 20 of them in case they might act alone, there were never galleys that had more fit place for advantage in fight.

During his stay at Cadiz Drake had gained full information as to Spanish shipping. Lisbon was the point of concentration for the fleet and the ships that were to compose it were scattered from Guipuscoa in the

North to Cartagena in the Mediterranean, numbering at least 100 great and small. It was Drake's intention to interrupt the assembly and he disappeared from Cadiz on May 1 heading west. While at sea Drake wrote home explaining his purpose.

> Now being well furnished with necessary provision, our intent is (God willing) to impeach the fleet which is come out of the straits and divers other places before it join with the King's forces; in the accomplishment, neither willing minds nor industry shall be wanting.

On hearing Drake was at sea, the King ordered Santa Cruz to put out to protect the treasure ships on the way from America, but the latter replied he was without men and could not move. In a few days Drake appeared north of Cape St. Vincent where he had gone to seek the guard squadron of Don Juan Martinez de Recalde which was stationed there to escort the American fleet to Seville upon its arrival. But Recalde had already withdrawn to Lisbon upon receipt of an urgent order from the Indies Office at Seville, so Drake occupied his station and blocked the concentration of ships at Lisbon, in conformity with the orders he was obeying. This was a strategic conception beyond the usual military ideas of the time.

Under Cape St. Vincent, between it and Sagres, about 2 miles away, was a small but important anchorage where vessels were in the habit of lying when the wind did not favor rounding the point, and on account of its usefulness the capes on each side were fortified. Drake resolved to capture these forts, to have access to fresh water for drink, and to secure a base enabling him to stop all maritime movement. On May 14 he landed to seize Lagos, a few miles east of St. Vincent, but found the works on the land side were too strong and re-embarked without the loss of a man. He then attacked the Cape itself. The landing force gallantly assaulted the castle of Sagres, which stood on a high precipitous point overlooking the anchorage about 2 miles from St. Vincent. The English had no artillery, but Drake led a party which placed fire against the gate and the castle soon surrendered. Two other fortified points then yielded and Drake had his necessary harbor and watering place. From St. Vincent eastward for several miles the seamen swept the shores of caravels and barks with supplies for Lisbon and burned them.

Then, leaving a garrison at Sagres, Drake took his ships to Lisbon for reconnaissance. He came to the conclusion that the place was too well fortified for him to enter the river, but he lay off the port for some days and made some prizes. Santa Cruz was at Cascaes, outside the forts, with 7 galleys, but would not risk them against the English ships and the latter withdrew to Sagres. Apparently about this time sickness became serious in the English fleet and it was necessary to land the crews of many ships for refreshment on shore and cleanse the ships by changing foul ballast, washing, and disinfecting.

By this time the alarm had spread all over Spain and, by order of the King, nothing put to sea, while he planned important assemblies of ships to drive Drake off. But nothing came of these efforts. Of the situation Captain Fenner wrote,

> We hold this cape so greatly to our benefit and so much to their disadvantage as it is a great blessing the obtaining thereof, for the rendezvous is at Lisbon, where we understand of some 25 ships and 7 galleys. As for the rest we lie between home and them * * * and they cannot come together.

It soon became apparent to Drake that traffic had stopped and that he would make no more prizes on the coast. He heard of a great carrack coming to Lisbon from the East and resolved to catch it.

He disappeared from Sagres on June 1 to go to the Azores where the carrack would make her first landfall. Owing to the epidemic he sent several ships home with the sick and as he did so the *Golden Lion*, flagship of the Vice Admiral William Borough, also departed for England with a mutinous crew, taking the Vice Admiral along. The story of the relations of Drake and Borough is a curious example of the conditions of command at the time. Borough was a skillful seaman and hydrographer, but personally cautious and an adherent of tradition. His character did not permit him to work harmoniously with his bold and impetuous admiral. The first difference occurred at the entrance to Cadiz. When Drake told his captains to follow him into port, Borough was greatly shocked by this summary order. He had been brought up in the old military school where the Commander in Chief was the executor of the council's decision and it was wholly irregular and unprecedented to act as Drake was doing. Henry VIII had issued a standing regulation that "the admiral shall not take in hand any exploit to land or enter any harbor of the enemy but he call a council and make the captains privy to his advice." When inside the harbor and the shipping had been destroyed, Borough was anxious to get quickly out again and he incurred Drake's displeasure.

Later, when Drake proposed to seize the forts at St. Vincent, Borough was again shocked by the rashness of the deed. He was deeply conscious of the importance of his own office as Vice Admiral. He sent a letter of remonstrance to Drake, on May 14, reciting that when the latter called a council he did not ask for advice but stated what was to be done;—that he found all advice offensive;—that he did not have a proper sense of the writer's position as the Lord Admiral of England always had;—Borough asked Drake for his own sake to be more careful;—when Borough came on board the flagship he heard Drake's intention to land already under discussion about decks;—this was unseemly;—besides, the Lord High Admiral had told Drake not to land and, above all, Borough disapproved of landing, for it is always a risky proceeding. Two days after the remonstrance, so Borough wrote to Burghley, Drake sent for him and, when on board the *Elizabeth Bonaventure*, Captain Fenner charged Borough with accusing Drake of negligence and of tutoring him. Just what Drake said to Borough we do not know, but two days afterwards Borough wrote another letter, regretting the first and promising to burn it. For several days the matter was quiescent, but then something unknown brought it to a head. Drake wrote to Lord Burghley that "for his persistence" he had deprived Borough of his command. It is not clear just what this persistence was, but a new captain was sent to the *Golden Lion* and the fleet stood away for the Azores.

After some bad weather, most of the merchant vessels were missing at the rendezvous but the *Golden Lion,* although present, went off and soon her new captain appeared in a pinnace to say that the crew had mutinied, alleging as reasons that the ship was short-handed and lacked food and water. He had abandoned the ship as he refused to take her to England. Drake called the council of war and a jury tried the mutineers, by which Borough and the principal officers of the *Golden Lion* were sentenced to death in their absence. On board the *Golden Lion,* at the request of the crew, Borough resumed his authority to navigate her home. Although Drake endeavored to push proceedings against Borough after he arrived home, the latter was acquitted of the charges of desertion and mutiny and was later made Comptroller of the Navy.

In the meantime the loss of the *Golden Lion* and the damage from the weather prevented Drake from attempting any large operation, but on June 18 he was fortunate enough to sight the *San Felipe*, the great prize he was looking for, under the land of the easternmost of the Azores. He attacked and she surrendered after little resistance. Drake went home with the prize, where he arrived July 6, 1587. The *San Felipe* proved to be loaded with spices and silks, which were sold in London for £114,000 ($785,460), of which sum the Queen received over a third and haggled for more. What was in the end as important as the cargo of the *San Felipe* were her papers, which revealed the long-kept secrets of the India trade and English commerce soon profited by their revelation.

Not the least important effect of Drake's raid was the moral one, increasing that of the cruise to the West Indies. Spanish mothers quieted their screaming children with the terror of his name. It was alleged that he had a magic mirror in which he looked to see where he would find the treasure ships and, if he needed more of his own, he merely cut chips from a twig and threw them into the sea where they turned to tall ships. At home the English told stories no less marvelous. A couple of years later, when he laid a conduit in the hills outside Plymouth to bring water to the city, it was stated that he rode out to the spring and when he turned and galloped back the spring foamed at his horse's heels, cutting its own channel. These foolish tales are not unworthy of attention. That they were credited by both nations affected the resolution and confidence with which combatants went into battle and weighed heavily in the balance of defeat and victory.

It was the general opinion in England that the damage Drake had done would prevent the Spaniards from sailing that year, but Drake came back convinced of the magnitude of King's preparations for invading England and wished to go out again that summer, once more to raid along the coasts of Spain, but he could not gain the Queen's consent. She clung to her plan of damaging the King's shipping only as a threat of worse to come, but was not ready to offend him deeply. So while welcoming the £40,000 ($275,600) which Drake brought as her dividend, she disavowed his action in landing at Sagres, saying he had done so without authority, paid off her ships, and continued her negotiations for peace with Parma. In fact, the parsimonious Queen was appalled by the expense of her army in Flanders. The cost was certified to her as £579,360 ($3,991,790), of which she had paid only £146,386 ($1,008,600) and the rest had been paid by, or was owing to, the States. It was little wonder that relations between the Queen and the States were strained and that Parma was able to gain some success in spite of his own poverty.

The King Wishes to Invade England in 1587

During the summer of 1587 Farnese (now sovereign Duke of Parma) had been able to capture the important seaport of Sluys and he thereafter held a suitable point from which to embark for England. The King believed that in September the army in Flanders available for the English enterprise numbered 30,000 men. Besides Farnese had begun an intrigue with Scottish Catholics to have them invade England from the north. As to this the King warned Parma that he could send no Spanish soldiers to help the Scots, as that would weaken the Armada too much. In the fall of 1587 the King was more resolved on war than ever. When Santa Cruz at last got off to the Azores in search of Drake, the King recalled him and insisted on hastening the concentration at Lisbon, but as the ships of Santa Cruz had been damaged by gales, some time elapsed before they were fit for service. For all this the King made no allowance. He wished Santa Cruz to set off at once and anchor off Margate to cover the passage of the flotilla carrying the army of Flanders. Santa Cruz told the King that the fleet could not be repaired before winter and that the enterprise would have to wait for the spring season, but the latter directed Parma to be ready to cross before the end of the year, in order that money might be saved by promptness.

Parma did not believe that operations in Flanders should be suspended in order to conquer England, but nevertheless he replied in December that he would cross in a cockboat, if His Majesty so ordered, but he did not think the crossing could be made. In spite of his lack of money, Parma pushed the building of vessels, the assembly of supplies and recruitment of troops, and reported in December that 74 warships and 220 light craft, sufficient to carry all the army and its train, were ready between Newport and Dunkirk. But, in the face of the Dutch blockade, this shipping could not get to sea before the arrival to Santa Cruz.

The financial question was at the root of the Spanish difficulties. The expense of the fleet and army was running at between 400 and 500 thousand ducats ($909,600-$1,137,000) a month. The King's income available for war was chiefly from his American mines, whose annual output was 12 or 14 million ducats. If the King were able to collect the whole of the 20 per cent which was his due, which he could not, it was less than one-half of the current war expenses, but he had accumulated a reserve of 6,800,000 ducats ($15,463,200) and this he wished to preserve as far as he could. In spite of the King's urgency, Parma did not attempt the impossible, and the winter of 1587-88 was a hard one for him, as he had little money and his soldiers fell away by disease and poverty. The English Governor in the United Provinces, the Earl of Leicester, had been called home, but as relations were not good between England and the Provinces, Parma felt little pressure from the enemy.

In April, 1588, the army in Flanders received large re-enforcements from Italy, so that Parma had 60,000 men, of which he expected to take half to England, leaving the other half to garrison the Low Countries; but disease and desertion soon reduced his numbers, so that in July he had only 17,000 available for the "enterprise." In his correspondence with the King, he therefore insisted all through the spring that he must have 6,000 soldiers come from Spain in the Armada to make part of the army of invasion. He said that if 30,000 were proper for a surprise, now that England was alert, 50,000 was too few. In the spring his intrigue with Scotland failed, as King James was won by superior offers of money from Queen Elizabeth who, as Parma said, "was now a confirmed heretic." So Parma waited with diminishing numbers during the spring and summer of 1588 for the fleet to appear, and in the meantime he did not neglect to maintain negotiations with the English commissioners in Holland in order to check the English preparations ashore and afloat.

The storms which Santa Cruz encountered off the Azores had saved England from attack in 1587, and on his return he suffered from jealousy at court and from the desire of Parma to have supreme command of fleet and army, which the King intended to confer on him. In reference to the command, Philip said that if Santa Cruz did not wish to be under the orders of Farnese, he had only to decide whether he would accept the situation or stay at home. Then the King sent an inspector to see if the Marquis was earnest in his effort to get the fleet ready, and the mortification of the latter was so great that he took to his bed and died in February, 1588.

SPANISH ARMADA* IS MADE READY IN 1588

The death of the Marquis of Santa Cruz had left King Philip without any one suitable to replace him, for he was not only an able admiral and soldier, but also a member of the great nobility whose position in command was acceptable to all of lesser birth. Although there were many capable seamen in the royal service, none of them had sufficient prestige, either through rank or performance, to put him entirely above the jealousy of those who would be his subordinates. The King therefore chose, as his new "Captain General of the Ocean Sea," Don Alonzo de Guzman, the Good, Duke of Medina-Sidonia, then serving as Captain General of the Coast of Andalusia, in which province he held one of the greatest estates in Spain. Don Alonzo was a grandee of the highest rank, about 38 years of age, and was reputed very rich. As Captain General of Andalusia he had not pleased the people of Cadiz in his effort to repulse Drake the year before, but the King told him not to be worried by that, for he (the King) was quite satisfied. When Santa Cruz was on his death bed, Medina was notified that the King had him in mind for the former's successor, whereupon he wrote to Court saying,

> I kiss his Majesty's hands and feet for thinking of me for so great a task and wish I had the strength for it, but I have not the necessary health and have been little at sea. I am seasick and rheumy. Besides, you know I am poor and my house owes 900,000 ducats ($2,047,000), so I have not a real (20.6c) to spend for the campaign. Besides, neither my conscience nor my duty requires me to assume this task, for the force is so great and the service so important that no one without experience at sea or in war should accept it. * * * I am sure I should do badly.

Nevertheless, the King insisted and told him to hasten to Lisbon and take command, giving the fleet, as was said at the time, a general of gold to replace one of iron. Perhaps an additional reason for his choice was that Don Alonzo was not a sufficiently forceful character to dispute the wishes of the Duke of Parma after reaching Flanders. Medina accepted the

---

* Captain Duro notes with emphasis that this great fleet was never formally called "Invincible Armada." It was officially known as "the Armada," the "Great Armada" and sometimes "Most Fortunate (Felisisima) Armada."

King's order saying, "May Our Lord be pleased to help the good intentions of your Majesty, and as it is His cause, I hope of His Mercy he will do so." The Duke did not err by promising too much.

Before Medina arrived at Lisbon, the King sent him a wordy order saying that, although all were engaged in God's work, they could not expect His countenance unless they did right by Him. Particularly he wished the men of the Armada to lead Christian lives without blasphemy or other sins, for otherwise they could not expect success. So all were to confess themselves and ask a blessing. The Duke was also directed to see that neither public nor private loose women embarked in the fleet, and on this point he was to give particular instructions to all admirals, campmasters, captains of infantry, and captains of ships. The religious observances were the same as those prescribed before Lepanto, but in this campaign there was no saintly Pope to arouse enthusiasm and Christian zeal as the source of victory. As for the light ladies who were forbidden to lend their encouragement to the gallant campaigners, they chartered ships at their own expense and accompanied the fleet, but their good will was not rewarded, for one was cast on the coast of France in the Channel and none had opportunity to see their friends until the return to Spain.

On arriving in Lisbon about the middle of March, the Duke found royal instructions awaiting him, saying that as the necessary alterations and repairs were finished, the troops were to be inspected and put on shipboard without delay. As the expedition would fail if it were not to sail promptly, he could make up deficiencies by taking soldiers from the local garrisons, and if a few ships chanced to be in bad order he was to leave them and distribute their men among other ships. The fleet was to sail at the end of March.

After inspection the Duke found a great fleet assembled indeed, yet far from ready to sail as the King hoped. All the artillery needed to be changed, for it could not be used as then placed. The soldiers were short in numbers, not being over 10,000 and perhaps only 9,000 instead of 15,000 as the King believed. The Portuguese levy could not be counted on because the gentlemen who had been asked to raise companies had declined. The local garrisons were short of assumed strength and could spare few and the sick and absentees were more than had been thought. The Duke called on his principal officers for reports and the most serious matter was the shortage of weapons and ammunition. There was only 3,000 hundredweight of powder and all thought that was less than half enough, for, at the Azores, Santa Cruz expended 1,800 hundredweight in a single day, using only a part of the artillery. There were 30 shot for each gun and there should be 50, but money was lacking to buy them. Lead for the small arms was wanted. He inspected the fleet, ship by ship, and the water supply was smaller than had been reported. The Duke, therefore, would leave it to the King whether it was wise to start, and would do as he was told. Money was very scanty. The Duke asked for enough to make three payments (of a month's wages) to all. The sailors of the pataches were 17 months in arrears.

By return letter, the King would not authorize more than two payments, for the ships from Italy were also in arrears. And, because if the money was paid on shore some soldiers would amuse themselves and not go on board, he directed only one payment should be made before and the other after embarkation. After that none but a few of the most reliable men were to be allowed on shore, but the Duke was ordered to arrange with the civil authorities to send on board refreshments and other things the men most needed, so that they could spend their money. The King then continued his letter saying that the Armada was costing him 116,000 ducats of 10 reales ($238,496) a month and, as the paymaster had only 433,787 ducats ($986,432), two payments would leave only 200,000 ducats ($454,800) as reserve which was not to be touched. As it was understood that more sailors would be needed, half of the men on all French and other foreign ships at Lisbon and Setubal were to be impressed with great secrecy the day before sailing and the other half were to be left on their ships for navigation. The King now countermanded his order that ships in bad order might be left behind, as numbers would impress the enemy.

On March 21 the King signed the Duke's commission giving him full powers of life and death in civil and military offenses, with authority to delegate the same to be exercised in accordance with justice. He could requisition ships and assume authority over Spaniards and foreigners on board. His pay was fixed at 12,000 ducats of 11 reales ($27,288) per year.

In the instructions accompanying his commission, Don Alonzo was ordered to see that all the men lived righteously; that inspectors and paymasters made proper musters of seamen and soldiers so that the treasury would suffer no loss through false payments; that the men were paid properly; that all stores and provisions were in abundance and of good quality; and that the ships' tonnage measurements were correctly taken (so as not to overpay for the charter). Captains, pilots, and officers were not to be absent from their ships unless upon permit. The King had heard from Santa Cruz before his death that many of the cavaliers and persons of distinction wished to build staterooms and apartments on board ship and that this would interfere with space necessary for battle and with the work of the seamen, so he now repeated his order that no such encumbrances were to be allowed.

To all this Don Alonzo replied that he had directed that every man be ordered to turn in a certificate of confession, each was to pray faithfully for success; no man was to take a mistress and only married women living with their husbands would be allowed. He was taking steps to have correct muster rolls, but the Inspector General and paymasters were to give out that the number of men was greater than reality for the sake of moral effect. They would only tell the real numbers to His Majesty and the Governor of Portugal. He regretted he could not fully carry out the order to permit no staterooms, for there were so many important people that he had to allow a few, but they could easily be knocked down for battle. Again Medina asked for money to make another payment to troops who were suffering and discontented; adding that the decoration of the flagship of galleys would be done according to the royal orders, yet "will not be excessive, for the lack of money makes me careful about it and other things not very necessary."

On April 4 Medina wrote that the next day the shipment of stores would be completed, but the companies "are short of their numbers and many officers and old soldiers say they will not leave their houses unless they get the extras beyond the common pay" (longevity, rank, and other allowances). But on the same day the King made a present to Medina of 20,000 ducats ($45,480) "in view of his expenses" and hoped that he would be able to find this sum within the amount of two months' pay already allotted for the fleet.

In April the King sent instructions to Medina about his military objectives. First, he repeated the order about blasphemy "because God gives and takes away victories as he will and we must deserve them." There were many other details which the King mentioned which any one of experience would attend to without orders and there were many good leaders in the fleet. The Armada was ordered to go directly up the Channel as far as Margate and there join with Parma and make it easy for him to cross according to "my plan which you both have." If Drake were to appear to embarrass the fleet by a diversion, Medina was to pay no attention to him but go on, fighting him only if Drake followed. In case of dispersion by bad weather, Vigo or Corunna was to be the rendezvous if near Spain; otherwise at the Scilly Islands.

> If you meet no enemy until at Margate and find only the Admiral of England with his fleet or if Drake is with him you will be so superior to him in quality that you may gain the wind of him and give battle and I hope God will give the victory. For the day of battle I have little to suggest. I charge you to lose no advantage and arrange the fleet so that all fight and aid each other without confusion. The enemy will fight at long range to get the advantage of his artillery and artificial fires and you must close and grapple, taking them in your hand. This you must be sure to do. After victory do not let the fleet break up in pursuit but keep it together, and do not land troops until sure of victory.

When the Duke crossed, Medina was to give him 6,000 soldiers from the Armada and then go to the Thames estuary and keep the channel open for supplies. A sea battle was the only thing Medina was to undertake without the advice and help of the Duke. It is noteworthy these instructions correctly told Medina what the English tactics would be. Their error lies in assuming that knowing the British intentions would be enough to frustrate them. Besides these tactical suggestions, Medina carried a letter to Parma saying that in case of a drawn campaign the latter might employ the renown of the fleet to make peace on three conditions—free worship for Catholics in England, surrender of the places in the Netherlands held by the English, a money indemnity. But as the English would not carry out the terms without collateral security, Parma was to take hostages and hold places in England; the Isle of Wight would be suitable.

General Orders to the Spanish Fleet

In April the Commander in Chief issued general orders to the fleet, opening with the preface that as they were going against heretics to the faith, all should be good and make confession. The punishment for blasphemy was set at losing the wine ration and, as "swearing occurs mostly when gambling," there was to be little of the latter and none at night. No women were to be in the fleet. Every morning at daylight the pages were to sing Matins at the mast and Ave Maria at night. Then came the more worldly matters. The Duke suspended all quarrels and challenges until a month after the close of the campaign; no one might carry a dagger nor quarrel. Aggressors were to be severely punished. Disputes between soldiers and sailors (i.e., corps quarrels) were forbidden. The soldiers were not to interfere with the issuing of victuals nor take them by force nor go down to the storerooms. They were to keep their quarters clean and have no hammocks. Officers would see that the soldiers keep their weapons bright and exercise them twice a week. As the sailors had to work ship, they were to be berthed on the quarter-deck and castles forward and aft throughout the voyage (i.e., without being displaced by soldiers). The soldiers considered themselves of a class superior to the sailors and it was necessary to see that they did not abuse and bully their shipmates. (As will be seen, little attention was paid to these last orders by the soldiers.)

Once at sea, all vessels were to pass under the flagship's lee to salute and take orders and the password. Neither by day nor night was any ship to pass in advance of the flagship, but reduce sail as necessary. All vessels were to take night orders and the password every night; but, as the fleet was so large, the subordinate flagships only would approach the Captain General and then repeat to their own commands. The fleet was to go to Finisterre and after passing it the rendezvous was to be off Scilly. Each ship was to be provided with two boat loads of hurling stones to be distributed conveniently about the decks and in the tops, and half-barrels of water were to be placed where needed for use of artillery and for fighting fire. Pikes were to be distributed and greased at their ends. Seamen who knew the management of arquebuses were to be issued the spare ones and the others were to have pikes.

RATIONS

The allowance of water was to be not over 3 cuartillos (1.59 quarts) for cooking and drinking. Of sherry wine the allowance was 0.71 quart but of wine of Crete only 0.53 quart. The daily ration consisted of 1½ pounds of biscuit or 2 pounds of fresh bread and on different days of the week 6 ounces either of bacon or cheese, with beans and peas, or fish with 3 ounces of beans and 1½ ounces of oil. It was substantially the same as that of the other Mediterranean navies then and until the nineteenth century and, although lacking in fresh vegetables, otherwise was large enough. At the beginning of April the fleet had shipped in all 110,000 hundredweight of biscuit and other provisions in proportion, enough for 30,000 men for 8 months, but the 11,000 pipes of water was enough for 115 days only.

CHIEF OFFICERS OF THE FLEET

By May 14 the Armada was ready to sail. Under Medina there were many officers of experience. Juan Martinez de Recalde was selected by Medina as Admiral of the Fleet and confirmed by the King. He was knight of Santiago and a good seaman. He had supervised the construction of the King's ships in several places and had been of much assistance to Santa Cruz in the campaign to the Azores. In the campaign of England he was a leader in council and in battle, always recommending the bolder course to Medina. He commanded the Squadron of Viscaya. Alonso de Leyva was a soldier who had seen much service. He had served with credit as Captain General of the galleys of Sicily and had left them to command the Milanese cavalry and came to Spain in 1587 to assist in the English enterprise. The King appointed him Captain General of the Armada to rank next to Medina and assume his duties in case of his death or disablement. After Parma's landing in England he was to command the contingent of soldiers landed from the fleet. He sailed in the *Rata*. Miguel de Oquendo was one of the most renowned seamen of Spain who had distinguished himself in the Azores and elsewhere. He commanded the Squadron of Guipuscoa. Diego Flores de Valdes was a distinguished seaman of a cross-grained and disagreeable temper. He commanded the Castilian galleons but embarked on board the flagship *San Martin* as naval adviser to the Duke. Don Pedro de Valdes commanded the Andalusian Squadron. He, too, had fought under Santa Cruz. Martin de Bertendona, who had a high reputation at sea and in battle, commanded the Levantisca Squadron, so-called as coming from Italy. Don Francisco de Bobadilla, Campmaster-General and a man of much experience ashore and afloat, went in the *San Martin* with the Commander in Chief as military adviser.

Numbers and Strength of the Armada

When ready to leave Lisbon, the fleet numbered 130 sail in 10 squadrons. The main fighting force included 64 galleons and large ships of from 1,250 to 350 tons, besides 4 Neapolitan galleasses of great size and 4 Portuguese galleys much smaller. There were 23 urcas or storeships of considerable size (300 to 700 tons), which had artillery of no great strength and 33 pataches and zabras (small craft built for fishing and as corsairs) of from 36 to 96 tons. These latter were of no combatant strength, but had important fleet duties as dispatch boats for reconnaissance and to give aid to ships in distress. These vessels made up a total of 57,868 tons' burden with 8,050 sailors, 18,973 soldiers, 2,088 rowers (for the galley craft) and 1,279 adventurers, servants, hospital men, and clergy, amounting in all to 30,712 souls.

The men were of poor quality. Many of the sailors were boys or foreigners from Italy and Greece. Some were Hollanders who had served on Dutch ships and were now drawn out of prison. Although some ships had more than enough seamen, the average number on board was only about two-thirds of the proper complement. The soldiers were formed into 5 regiments of Spanish veterans, whose ranks were swollen by recruits, of whom nearly 4,000 were peasants from Castile who saw the sea for the first time on May 30. There was a Portuguese contingent of recruits about 2,000 strong.

Types of Ships

As for the ships, there was not great difference in the build of merchantmen and men-of-war at that time. They could be changed from one class to the other by adding or removing a few pieces of artillery and this at first thought might seem an advantage for the sovereign, as he did not need to maintain a permanent navy, having only to requisition ships and man them with his own subjects or any foreigners who happened to be in port. Really the advantage was not great. In these merchant ships impressed for the royal service it was necessary to make many alterations to fit them for war. The guns had to be placed aboard and emplacements built for them and many fittings and sometimes an extra temporary deck had to be built in to accommodate the soldiers. Storerooms for powder and shot were also built in and there was loss of charter money while the ships were fitting out.

The general proportions of these vessels were of the one, two, three, type; that is, two drafts in the beam and three beams in the length. There were two decks, the first near the deep-water load line and the second about 6 feet above. If the ship was large, the hold space was divided by a row of beams with no deck on them. Above the upper deck was a half-deck extending from the stern nearly to amidships and a quarter-deck above the after part of the half-deck, and above this a poop. A forecastle covered the forward part of the main deck.

The heavy guns were on the lower deck and lighter ones above. Very light guns were in the cage tops. In order to provide against the entrance of hostile boarders, the space under the half-deck and forecastle was cut off from the waist of the ship by bulkheads in which were gun ports and light guns,* so that if the enemy got on board the crew might retreat to the deck above, while these guns swept the main deck. The half-deck was similarly guarded by a bulkhead under the quarter-deck. In case of boarding a hostile vessel, the light guns in the tops and on the upper decks, using dice shot (i.e., handfuls of iron cubes), prepared the way and supported the boarders after they had entered.

The largest ships had three or four masts with square sails on the two forward ones and lateen sails aft. The smaller ships, such as the pataches, had only one deck and were provided with oars as well as sails. They had 6 to 12 guns of small size, 2-pounders and smaller. Although these vessels did excellent work as auxiliaries, they were too low to board big ships and their small guns were of use only against equally small craft.

Owing to their lofty sterns and the weight of the temporary deck and other fittings, the Spanish ships were cranky under sail and made much leeway. The records published by Duro tell us that the Armada was equipped with 2,431 guns, but their caliber does not appear. Nevertheless there are a number of details given both by Duro and, in regard to captured Spanish ships, by Laughton, which enable us to make an approximation of the artillery strength of the different ships.** The 14 flagships

---

* See Fig. 36.

** In the *Armada Invencible*, vol. 2, p. 83, it appears that 123,790 projectiles were provided for 2,431 guns, making 50.92 rounds per gun. The powder weighed 5,175 quintals (hundredweight), all arquebus powder, which was somewhat stronger than cannon powder.

presumably had broadside weights of about 200 pounds; the rest of the fighting ships, from 105 to 25 pounds; the urcas from 58 to 8 pounds; and the dispatch boats from 28 to 4 pounds. Taking the 14 flagships with 473 guns at 2,611 pounds and the 31 other vessels with the heaviest batteries with 875 guns and 1,761 pounds broadside, the total weight of broadsides would be about 4,373 pounds for the best 45 ships in the Spanish fleet. The galleases' heaviest fire was ahead, about 300 pounds and half as much on each broadside and 50 pounds astern.

There was also 1,238 quintals of lead for arquebuses. From vol. 1, p. 292, we learn that each pound of lead needed half a pound of powder. So the powder reserved for arquebuses was 619 quintals, leaving 4,556 quintals for artillery. On p. 389, vol. 1, the armament of the galleasses is given in detail and on p. 293 their allowance of powder is placed at 200 barrels (quintals of 100 lbs.) while the galleys, with 5 guns each, had 30 barrels. Consequently, the powder remaining for the sailing ships' artillery was 3,636 quintals. The 4 galleasses' guns numbered 200 (vol. 2, p. 65) in all, and a single discharge weighed about 650 pounds, more or less. At 50.92 rounds per gun each galleass had 33,100 pounds of projectiles, for which she had 20,000 pounds of powder. Applying this ratio to the 3,636 quintals of powder for the sailing ships they had 601,758 pounds of projectiles. The galleasses and galleys together had 220 guns and at 50.92 rounds they had 11,202 projectiles and the sailing ships had a remainder of 112,588 projectiles. The 33 light craft carried 198 guns whose average weight was 6 quintals (vol. 1, p. 292) and the projectiles for such guns may be taken as 2 pounds. So they had 10,082 projectiles weighing 20,164 pounds. The remainder for the 87 large ships and urcas is 102,506 projectiles weighing 581,594 pounds. This is an average weight of 5.674 pounds per shot, and a total weight of 11,422 pounds for one round and 5,711 pounds for one broadside. But we can not apply this average weight to the number of guns to get the weight of each ship's broadside, for we know that the principal ships were more heavily armed. Two Spanish flagships, the *Nuestra Señora del Rosario* and *San Salvador*, were made prizes and the inventories of their batteries have been preserved, although some of the smaller pieces were missing. These are given in Laughton's *Defeat of the Spanish Armada*, and the two were nearly alike in weight of battery, although the *Rosario* had many more small guns. At capture she had 3 demi-cannon (30-pdrs.), 6 cannons pedro (short 24-pdrs.), 4 culverins (long 18-pdrs.), 1 basilisk (long 15-pdr.), 1 demi-culverin (long 9-pdr.), 1 minion (4-pdr.), 2 fowlers (short 5-pdrs.), 1 falconet (2-pdr.), and 22 bases and other small pieces (2-pdrs.). Besides, several small pieces were removed by the Spaniards to arm small craft, thus accounting for 46 given in Duro's table. The total weight of one round for the 71 guns in the two ships would be about 784 pounds. Or the broadside of each would be about 196 pounds with a mean weight of 11.04 pounds per projectile. Making the assumption that the other 12 flagships fired the same average weight of shot per gun, we find that the 14 flagships with 473 guns had 24,085 projectiles weighing 265,900 pounds. The remainder for the 73 galleons and urcas is 78,421 projectiles weighing 315,694 pounds, an average of 4.026 pounds per shot. We can now make an approximation to the weight of each ship's discharge by multiplying her guns in broadside by 4.026. Omitting the 2 flagships, the urca squadron had 21 ships with 322 guns in all, with broadsides running from 58 to 8 pounds. So the remaining 52 vessels which were expected to assume the burden of battle with the flagships and galleasses had a battery of 1,218 guns and a total weight of broadside of 2,452 pounds, running from 105 pounds for the heaviest, on the *Florencia* galleon to the *Santa Barbara*, lightest, with 23 pounds.

The Armada Leaves Lisbon

The soldiers were slow in assembling and many complaints were made by them as to lack of pay, but by May 14 the fleet had dropped down the river and was ready to put out as soon as the wind would permit. On this day an officer arrived by sea from Parma, 50 days out of Flanders, saying the latter had only 17,000 infantry and 1,000 light horse, with 300 small ships for crossing to England. It was a great reduction in the intended strength. At the mouth of the Tagus the Armada was delayed by winds which did not allow it to cross the bar and it was not until the 30th that it got to sea, when Medina wrote to the King, saying that he had accomplished marvels in preparing the fleet considering the many difficulties and the lack at Lisbon of officials who were serving the King "with love and in accordance with law"—a probable allusion to peculation which was very rife.

The Armada's progress as it worked up the coast was slow, as the urcas were poor sailers and detained the others. By June 10 the Duke was telling the King of spoiling provisions. He sent ahead to have fish, dried meat, and bacon sent out to him on passing Corunna, and on June 18 he reported to the King that he was abreast Corunna and held there by north winds. The pilots urged him to enter port, but he declined as he feared desertions "as usual" would break up the expedition. If the provisions did not come out that day, Medina said he would go forward although much in want of them, for "we did not take any meat and the sardines and cuttle-fish we have thrown overboard and the bacon is spoiling fast. This and the water give the most trouble." The water casks were leaking.

The Armada Enters Corunna

The next day the Duke changed his mind. After passing the night under short sail, he sent for the Generals and thereupon, the weather being bad, the water very short, and provisions spoiling, he entered Corunna with as much of the fleet as saw his movement and could get in before dark. He had neglected to send word what he was about to do. The weather turned bad during the night and the ships outside were scattered. Most made various ports on the north coast of Spain, but more than a dozen, including one with women, ran up to the rendezvous off the Scilly

Islands, thick weather having prevented their seeing the others entering port. Here they were seen and reported to the English fleet in Plymouth, but no harm came to them for Medina suspected what had happened and sent two patches under oars and sail to recall them, so they withdrew in good time, without meeting an enemy.

The King wrote immediately urging Medina to pursue his voyage without delay; but besides lack of provisions, many ships needed more or less extensive repairs and clean bottoms. For example, the Girona galleass took out 400 hundredweight of wet biscuit and then calked all her decks and was hove down (made to heel over) so as to calk below the water line. Stiffening knees were put in the bow and the rudder was strengthened. All this damage was done in weather which was not severe, for large vessels were not then so strongly built as they were in the next century. On this point Duro remarks that the hull was not firmly braced and there was no inside planking, so that the water-tightness depended chiefly on the calking. The two principal masts were so heavy that they strained the ship when she rolled in a seaway, causing play of the members which worked the calking from the seams until the sea tore it out, and this explains the condition in which so many vessels entered Corunna.*

After a few days in port, Medina wrote that he had examined the condition of the fleet, that the weather continued as bad as in December, that the provisions were few and bad so that they would not last over 2 months, that the fleet was weakened and so was Parma's army; the Armada's officers did not know their business and, in view of all, he recommended honorable terms with the enemy instead of war. On June 27 the Duke called a council to ask whether it was better to cruise along the coast to pick up the missing ships or wait for them to assemble there. He was answered that it was better to stay there and send for the others. He then asked if they should start for England with the vessels then present, lacking 28 ships with 6,000 men. To this Don Jorge Manrique, Inspector General, replied that the whole number of men was only 27,884, of whom

---

* The larger the ship the weaker she was and the most experienced seamen held that ships over 400 tons (say 90 feet long on the keel and 30 feet wide) were not as seaworthy as smaller ones and in very rough seas a still smaller size was best. The small craft, the patches of 60 tons or less (not over 50 feet on the keel) were far stronger boats and more seaworthy. As we have seen, the Duke did not hesitate to send two dispatch boats to England, when the larger ships were damaged and seeking shelter.

22,000 were effective, after allowing for boys, clergy, rowers, and other non-combatants, so that without the 6,000 in the absent ships they had only 16,000 remaining, of whom some were sick, so that the Armada was short a third of its strength. Therefore, Don Jorge advised not to go and the council agreed to wait until all were assembled, for this was the whole force of Spain and the English were strong.

Against this opinion Pedro de Valdes was alone. He held that as the English force was in two or three parts, they should go with the ships of the fleet then near by. He discussed the amount of provisions and said his own vessel had 3 months' supply and that he thought it was enough, if they did not waste time in port. Don Jorge answered that considering all that had been consumed since April 13 he did not think that there could be more than 80 days' supply left and everything was spoiled except bread, dried vegetables, and wine.

Of this council, Valdes wrote to the King that Medina looked on him unfavorably for having said that the fleet should proceed and added that he had advised a short ration of bread and fresh meat with which the crews would be satisfied and healthy. Under date of July 5 the King replied telling Don Alonzo to press forward as soon as possible, and he ordered supplies from Lisbon, but it is hard to see why he retained such a pessimist in command. On July 6 Don Alonzo reported to the King that all the fleet except two or three had arrived at or near Corunna, but that some needed repairs and were without a drop of water. He said he had established guards everywhere to prevent desertion. He was feeding the crews on fresh meat and would soon have fresh bread. It was a great luxury and the crews were much pleased. There were not many sick and these had been placed in hospital on shore where the archbishop of Santiago was taking care of them with very scanty means.

On July 15 the Duke reported that everything was ready and that, although it was calm, he was directing several squadrons to use their boats to tow themselves to the harbor entrance. Certain Germans who had supplied powder complained that the Duke's order for payment was not honored at Seville and he asked the King to see that they were promptly paid. Fresh bread had not been procured, but they had biscuit to last until September 10; of other provisions there was not much. He was reducing the rations a little to make them last a few days more. The number of men was little under what he had hoped to have. In order that all might confess and communicate with least trouble he had sent all the monks in the fleet to an island where some tents had been spread and altars erected. The island had been well guarded to prevent desertion and he was sending all by companies to the island, and already 8,000 had confessed to date and this gave him more joy than anything else in the expedition. He then informed the King that 400 Galician soldiers secured at Corunna were useless on account of age and otherwise. They did not know what an arquebus was, and their wives made so much noise at losing them that their captains did not want them. Some had not eaten for two days and so he had sent them to their homes.

By July 19 all was ready and as they were consuming ships' provisions it was desirable to go, but the weather delayed departure until the 22d, when the fleet got out but anchored a few leagues outside owing to a calm. On the 23d it was away with a fine quartering breeze.

Numbers and Formation

The fleet included all but 8 of the ships that had left Lisbon and to these and Duke had added 9 water barges and 7 faluas (small scouting and dispatch vessels), so that he now had 137 sail. The numbers on board were reduced to 7,050 seamen, 17,017 soldiers, and 1,388 officers, servants, adventurers, etc., making in all 27,500 souls. The rowers were about 2,000 but are not named in the second list. Out of the whole number, 60 carrying 6,000 men were cargo vessels and pataches of little combatant strength although they carried their share of soldiers. The remainder, with the 8 rowing vessels, were the battle strength with some 21,000 men.

As for the formation in which it cruised and fought, the official papers compiled by Duro give no information, but we have some information of the matter from a publication by a certain Filippo Pigafetta issued in Rome in August while the Armada was at sea. There is no reason to doubt that he was well acquainted with decisions which had been reached in council at Lisbon as to the way in which the fleet was to be handled. It was a soldier's formation rather than that of seamen. Pigafetta says that, in order to avoid confusion and delay on sighting the enemy, the battle formation would also be the cruising formation. As the leaders wished to board the enemy and settle the outcome by a hand-to-hand struggle, they adopted the line abreast, as was the practice for rowing ships having the same tactical purpose and wishing to charge the enemy while preserving a free field of fire ahead. Pigafetta gives the arrangement the name of "eagle formation," comparing its squadrons to the head, body, wings, and tail of a bird, and says the rate of travel "will be two miles an hour."

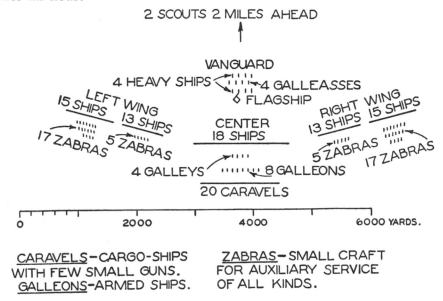

CARAVELS—CARGO-SHIPS WITH FEW SMALL GUNS. GALLEONS—ARMED SHIPS.

ZABRAS—SMALL CRAFT FOR AUXILIARY SERVICE OF ALL KINDS.

INTENDED BATTLE ᴀɴᴅ CRUISING FORMATION
OF
SPANISH FLEET ɪɴ 1588.
(ACCOUNT OF FILIPPO PIGAFETTA)

FIG. 40

The "faluas will be ahead to get news and signal by fire and guns." The first group was the vanguard (or head) consisting of 12 vessels in three ranks of 4 each. The first and third ranks were of large galleons with the Commander in Chief in the second ship of the third rank where he could see and direct the whole force in his rear. Alfonso de Leyva, the second in command, was in the first rank. The second rank was made by the 4 great galleasses of Naples, which had the heaviest batteries in the Armada and could go to aid any part of the line at pleasure, owing to their oars. In each rank the ships were 42 paces (70 yards) apart and the ranks 50 paces (83 yards) apart. The advantage of this arrangement, as we are told, was that the front line could attack along with others in support, or one or both the other lines could come forward to make a single line in close order. It is plain that the formation was based on army usage. The main battle consisted of 30 vessels in line, half a mile in rear of the vanguard, with 18 in a first rank at the same intervals as in the vanguard. Then came a second line of 4 galleys followed by a third line of 8 large galleons. Behind these was fourth line of 20 cargo caravels which had some artillery and would not be entirely negligible in the scuffle.

The two wings were each composed of two squadrons. Those next the center were separated from it by 300 paces (500 yards) and contained 13 ships. With an interval of 100 paces (167 yards) came the outer squadron of 15 ships with a distance of 40 paces (67 yards) between ships. The line of the wings was slightly inclined to the direction of advance, so that each ship was about half a length ahead of her neighbor next towards the center. Behind the outer squadrons came 17 hulks, pataches, and zabras in three lines and behind the inner squadrons were 5 zabras. Don Juan Martinez de Recalde in the *San Juan* commanded the right wing and was on the extreme flank. Francisco de Bobadilla commanded the left wing and was stationed on its left flank in the flagship *San Marco*. The whole front covered 3,594 paces (5,990 yards).

To an approaching stranger the fleet would undoubtedly appear to have the shape of a crescent with the points advanced, although Pigafetta denies it, saying it is fantastic to talk of a semi-lune formation. The advantage of the plan is that the fleet cannot be surrounded, and if charged in the middle the wings will surround the enemy. Although the fleet as described by Pigafetta numbers 27 more vessels than Medina had with him, there is every probability that its formation actually followed his general plan, although flag officers were not in the ships he named. A letter Medina sent to the King, in which he explained his tactical intention, shows it was in consonance with Pigafetta's account. Medina told the King that he would not divide his fleet nor follow the enemy before joining Parma and added:

> If Drake fortifies himself in Plymouth or elsewhere to let me pass and then comes out to catch me between his squadron and that which is lying opposite Parma, for that I am well prepared by the form of main battle.

(Vol. 2, p. 103, Duro.) In that case he would attack one of the hostile squadrons with one wing supported by half the vanguard, including two galleasses; and with the rest of the Armada and the other two galleasses which the Duke himself would command, he would meet the other enemy, and "so without altering my plan in order to meet this situation we shall navigate, if it shall please God."

VOYAGE TO THE LIZARD

For two days after departure the weather was excellent and, although the speed of the fleet was limited to that of the poorest sailers, it reached latitude 48°–30', a run of 350 miles, in 2½ days. On Tuesday the 26th the weather was calm at daylight, but at noon the wind came out ahead and the sea grew rough. The Diana galley was missing and the Duke learned from the flagship of the galley squadron that during the night her captain had sent to say she was making too much water to hold her position and that he would have to seek the nearest Spanish port. The Duke replied that it was heavy weather for the galleys and that, if necessary, they might run for some French port. Two pataches were sent to keep company with, and aid them, and all that day they were in sight but at dark they disappeared and were not seen again. (It may be said here that they reached a port of Southern France where the Diana was lost and the others returned to Spain.)

On the 27th the weather was very bad and the fleet in danger. On the morning of July 28 Don Pedro de Valdes and 40 other vessels were not in sight. Medina sent 3 pataches in different directions to find them and to sound and pick up the land. On the 29th the pataches returned, saying that the ships which had gone ahead were waiting off the Lizard and those which had fallen astern were coming up. On that day, the Armada was off the Lizard and at 2:00 P.M. it was seen from shore, where many smoke signals were made, whereupon the flagship *San Martin* hoisted a standard bearing a crucifix with Mary the Virgin and Mary Magdalen on each side; three guns were fired and every one prayed and returned thanks for a good voyage.

The fleet is all united and will make sail as soon as the capitana galleass has repaired her broken rudder for assuredly these craft are very frail in these seas. The galleys have not been seen. All the rest are present and doing very well with the crews very content.

The following morning the fleet was near land and noticed many fires and smokes along the shore.

On Saturday the 30th the Duke wrote to the King he meant to go no farther than the Isle of Wight until he should hear from Parma that he was ready to cross, for, said Medina, there is no port on the coast of Flanders where the Armada can lie if bad weather comes up while it waits for the army to make ready. But this resolution he did not execute. That afternoon about 4:00 P.M. the English fleet was seen working out of Plymouth.

The Queen is Reluctant to Make War

During the winter and spring while the King was making his preparations the Queen fully trusted Parma, whose instructions from Philip were to deceive her and delay English mobilization. But delay worked against Parma too. At the very time that the King flattered himself that Parma might be in Greenwich Palace (November, 1587) the Duke had lost many men by sickness and was without money to get more. Perhaps the Queen's parsimony was not entirely objectionable, so far as it concerned the navy. She kept a small squadron in the channel for blockade duty and it must be remembered that in those times to keep a fleet mobilized in winter exposed their crews to great losses by epidemics, and it was well to keep them well-housed on shore as long as possible before service. It was necessary, too, to dock ships before sending them out on a cruise, as they had no copper sheathing.

English Preparations in Spring and Summer of 1588

In December, 1587, the government and the public began to realize that Parma was making great preparations and that the fleet at Lisbon was mobilizing, although the Queen was scarcely convinced. The threat of the army in Flanders seemed very dangerous. People did not clearly understand that it could not venture to sea in the face of the efficient blockade which the Dutch fleet under Justinus of Orange was maintaining, since the Spanish vessels were flat-bottomed transports and not fighting ships. So England feared an invasion should the Channel be un-guarded even for a brief time.

There was as yet no regular army in England nor was there an estab-lishment of officers. It was the business of every able-bodied man to defend his country. For this occasion there was levy of the armed men of the counties under the Lords-lieutenant. The levies were undisciplined without annual training, but there was a law that men should practice at archery and some were good at it, although the arquebus was in general use abroad and the Queen had a reserve of these weapons in the Tower. In London and other cities there were organized companies of "trained bands" with pikemen, arquebusiers, and archers. It would not be difficult to obtain volunteers in the pay of the Queen to assemble and train when the danger of invasion should become imminent. Yet they would be of little use, for war had become a profession. Nevertheless, Queen Eliza-beth refused to have a standing army which would have maintained order at home and given England double weight in foreign affairs. In all this perilous period the Queen was relying chiefly on her diplomacy, in which Parma outplayed her. As Fortescue says of her in his *History of the British Army*, "she hated straight dealing for its simplicity, she hated conviction for its certainty, and above all she hated war for its expense."

NAVAL PREPARATIONS

During the fall of 1587 a small English blockading squadron under Sir Henry Palmer, in conjunction with the Dutch squadron, maintained a watch on the Spanish army under Parma, but the Queen's 34 ships lay at Chatham, unready for service. They were her personal possession. It was not until the Commonwealth that the Royal Navy became national. About November 11 it was decided to mobilize (see Laughton, *Spanish Armada*, p. 3) and, on December 31, Charles, Baron Howard of Effingham, a cousin of the Queen and Lord High Admiral of England, was commis-sioned as High Admiral and Lieutenant General at Sea. Howard, no doubt, owed his appointment to his noble rank, as did Medina-Sidonia, but he was far better qualified both by native character and by experience. Although not a seaman by profession, he had commanded a squadron 18 years before and in this campaign he was wise enough to be guided chiefly

FIG. 41.—CHARLES, LORD HOWARD OF EFFINGHAM

By Mytens

by the great seamen on his council, Drake, Hawkins, Frobiser, and Thomas Fenner.

On January 1, 1588, Howard reported that in 2 or 3 days the Queen's ships would be ready. The English fleet had mobilized in less than 2 months; the Spanish fleet took 2 years. Two days after the issuance of Howard's commission another was conferred upon Drake to command 30 ships to cruise on the coast of Spain and repeat his operations of the previous summer. On January 13 he went down to Plymouth to organize his squadron where were 13 of his squadron of 1587. He expected 7 Queen's ships and 5 Londoners and had to find 5 more. Howard retained 16 ships in the Medway under his own command, sent 9 to Sir Henry Palmer in the Narrows, and 6 to Drake at Plymouth. At Plymouth Drake learned that the work in Spain was proceeding, but the English Ambassador in Paris informed Elizabeth that sickness and desertion were ruining the Spanish force, so everything was held up by an order from London to reduce crews by one-half. Comptroller Croft, who was in Spanish pay, even urged the Queen to sacrifice Drake and confiscate his property.

This delay is usually attributed solely to the Queen's parsimony which was always excessive, but it must be remembered that Philip had resolved to postpone his enterprise until spring and this was probably known in England, for transmission of intelligence was fairly reliable both ways, although not very prompt. The effect of the royal order was, of course, to check any voyage by Drake, and by the end of February he had orders not to leave the coast. Besides, the death of Santa Cruz seemed to reduce the prospects of war, so the Queen again sent her Commissioners to the Duke of Parma to treat of peace, while his object was only to delay her preparations. It was an unwise pause, for Drake could have done much, even if Lisbon had proved unassailable. So all that was done during the winter was an effort to impress Parma by a demonstration of the fleet off Flushing where the Peace Commissioners were sitting.

In March the Queen's Council hatched a plan of campaign, entirely defensive, by which the fleet was to be divided into two parts. The eastern squadron was to be stationed in the Narrows of the Channel to watch Parma, and the western one was to be towards Ireland and Spain, so that if the Armada were to enter the Channel it would be caught between the two. A detachment was to be sent to raid Portugal and perhaps it might land the Pretender Don Antonio after the Spanish fleet had put to sea. Perhaps, also, another detachment might be sent to the Azores to intercept the Spanish treasure fleet. It is probable that King Philip heard something of this plan, since he wrote to Medina to warn him about being caught between two fleets. But the King's strategy and psychology also failed him, for he told Medina that if he met the western fleet he was to push for the Narrows, instead of defeating the immediate enemy. As it happened, this order had a most unfortunate effect on the spirits of the Spanish forces.

On the other hand, the English Council's plan was as bad as the King's, and Drake replied to it on April 9, saying that the proper thing was to make the fleet at Plymouth as strong as possible and then

> seek God's enemies and her Majesty's where they may be found. . . . My very good Lords, next under God's mighty protection the advantage and gain of time and place will be the only and chief means for our good, wherein I most humbly beseech your good Lordships to persevere as you have begun, for that with 50 sail of shipping we shall do more good upon their own coast than a great many more will do here at home and the sooner we are gone, the better we shall be able to impeach them.

In this letter Drake added that his ships had only one-third of the powder he thought necessary and on April 23 he wrote to the Queen asking for 4 more Queen's ships and 16 others then at London.

> Then shall your Majesty stand assured, with God's assistance, that if the fleet come out of Lisbon as long as we have victual to live withal upon that coast, they shall be fought with, and I hope through the goodness of our merciful God, in such sort as shall hinder his quiet passage into England; for I assure your Majesty, I have not in my lifetime known better men and possessed with gallanter minds than your Majesty's people are for the most part which are here gathered together, voluntarily to put their hands and hearts to the finishing of this great piece of work, wherein we are all persuaded that God, the giver of all victories, will in mercy look upon your most excellent Majesty and us your poor subjects, who for the defence of your Majesty, our religion, and native country have resolutely vowed the hazard of our lives.
>
> The advantage of time and place in all martial affairs is half a victory, which being lost, all is irrecoverable. Wherefore, if your Majesty will command me away with those ships which are here already, and the rest to follow with all

expedition, I hold it in my poor opinion the surest and best course, and that they bring with them victuals sufficient for themselves and us, to the intent the service be not utterly lost for want thereof. Whereof, I most humbly beseech your most excellent Majesty to have such consideration as the weightiness of the cause requireth; for an Englishman, being far from his country and seeing a present want of victuals to ensue and perceiving no benefit to be looked for, but only blows, will hardly be brought to stay. I have order but for two months' victuals beginning the 24th of April (4th of May) whereof one whole month may be spent before we come there; the other month's victual will be thought with the least to bring us back again. Here may the whole service and honor be lost for the sparing of a few crowns.

As a result of this letter Drake seems to have been summoned to London and apparently he won the Queen over to his view, for on May 20 the Privy Council resolved

to refer the employment of the navy that is to repair to the west parts of this realm to the Lord Admiral's consideration; to be employed as by his Lordship shall be thought meet upon such intelligence as he shall receive from time to time.

The resolution also provided for the issue of money to provide reserves of victual.

It was the practice to supply the ships for a month of four weeks and then issue another supply a few days before that on hand was gone. There was constant complaint from all the admirals that by this limitation they were never prepared for service of more than few days and that if the enemy should appear as supplies were running short they could not undertake effective operations. But Elizabeth persisted in the policy, partly because she did not wish the fleet to run away on offensive operations, but also because she hated to spend money.

In spite of the new decision in Council, Drake did not get authority to seek out the Spanish fleet; but as the news of its approaching readiness and its strength became more conclusive, Howard was directed to move to Plymouth. On May 31 he left Lord Henry Seymour, his nephew, to maintain the blockade of Flanders with 13 Queen's ships, 3 large ones and the rest small, and 21 merchantmen, of which 8 were pinnaces and small hoys. Howard himself made sail for Plymouth with 16 Queen's ships and some 20 others, where he arrived on June 2 and was met outside Plymouth by Sir Francis Drake with 30 ships drawn up in three ranks and the light craft thrown ahead as in reconnoitering would be done. Thus the two squadrons entered port together.

Howard now made Drake his Vice Admiral, and wrote to Burghley that after two days in port to water his vessels he would go to Spain by the first favorable wind with the intention of lying off shore to wait for the Spanish fleet. It was known that the latter was on the point of sailing and it seemed rather too late to go to Spain with any certainty of finding the enemy still in port. On June 7 Howard reported to Burghley that he had only 18 days' provisions with him and none to be had from the countryside and "what that is to go to sea with your Lordship may judge, and to tarry, that we must not. God send us a wind to put us out, for go we will though we starve." Howard meant to leave a bark to bring the victualing ships after him upon their arrival at Plymouth and would stay in the Sleeve (between Ushant and Scilly) as long as possible.

> I believe surely that if the wind hold here but six days [i.e., till June 13] they will knock at our door. * * * Therefore I pray you, good my Lord, to cause our victuals to be hastened after us with all speed and to speak to Mr. Quarles that there may be made some supply again against anything that may happen and so I bid your Lordship heartily farewell.

The same day Howard wrote again to Burghley,

> My good Lord, there is here the gallantest company of captains, soldiers, and mariners that I think ever was seen in England. It were pity that they should lack meat when they are so desirous to spend their lives in her Majesty's service. * * * And God send us the happiness to meet with them before our men on the land discover them for I fear me a little sight of the enemy will fear the land men much.

Howard's trust in his men is very different from that of Medina, who put guards from the garrison of the town about his men when they went to confession.

The fleet did go out on June 9 and met with severe southerly and southwesterly gales. After a week, the wind shifted to the west and the fleet returned to port with only 9 days' supplies. On June 23 Howard wrote that he had been held in port by strong west and southwest winds which had then lasted two weeks, and victual had not arrived from the east, but that from time to time they had been refreshed with some 12 or

14 days' supply, so that at all times they had had enough for 15 or 16 days.

> Sir, I will never go again to such a place of service, but I will carry my victuals with me and not trust to careless men behind me. * * * We think it should be marveled at how we keep our men from running away, for the worst men in the fleet knoweth for how long they are victualed; but I thank God as yet we are not troubled with any mutinies, nor I hope shall not, for I see men kindly handled will bear want and run through fire and water, and I doubt not but if this month's victual come to us from London before we depart, we will make it to serve us to continue very near three months. And if it does not come, yet assure yourself we will not lose any opportunity, nor we will not lack: there is good fishing in the seas. * * * God send us wind. And if the wind had favored us when we went out from hence which was the 8th of June they should not have needed to come thus far to have sought us.

By this time it was known to Howard that the Spanish fleet had left Lisbon on May 30. He reflected that it had had time to get to Ireland or Scotland. "Sir, if you can by any means learn, or if we can, that they are in the Groyne (Corunna), I doubt not but by God's grace we will make sport with them." (They had arrived there 4 days previously.) But the Queen became disturbed by the idea that her fleet might go to Spain and leave the coast unprotected, in case of missing the enemy, so on June 19 she sent an order forbidding Howard to go to Spain or beyond such a point as should enable him to meet any "attempt against this realm, Ireland, or Scotland." It was hard to find any such commanding position and, in fact, the lack of victual was the limiting condition.

Howard received the order on the 23d and the next day replied to Walsingham,

> * * * which letter I do not a little marvel at. Sir, for the meaning we had to go on the coast of Spain, it was deeply debated on by those which I think the world doth judge to be men of greatest experience which this realm hath; which are these Sir Francis Drake, Mr. Hawkins, Mr. Frobiser, and Mr. Thomas Fenner, and I hope her Majesty will not think that we went rashly to work, or without a principal or choice care and respect for the safety of this realm. * * * And if we were tomorrow on the coast of Spain, I would not land in any place to offend any but they should well perceive that we came not to spoil but to seek out the great force to fight with them and so should they have known by message, which should have been the surest way and most honorable to her Majesty. * * * But I must and will obey, and am glad there

be such there [i.e., in London] as are able to judge what is fitter for us to do than we here, but by my instructions I did think it otherwise. But I shall put them up in a bag, and I shall most humbly pray her Majesty to think that that which we meant to do was not rashly determined, and that which shall be done shall be most carefully used by us and we will follow and obey her Majesty's commandment. * * * But Sir, I will persuade no more but do as I am directed, and God send the wind do not force us thither; otherwise, upon my duty, we will not go thither, now we know her Majesty's pleasure. And so I bid you heartily farewell. From aboard her Majesty's good ship the *Ark*.

On July 1 the presence off Scilly of the Spanish ships that had gone there when Medina entered Corunna became known at Plymouth and the same day the provision ships arrived there with a change of wind. Howard wrote that he was working night and day to transfer the supplies and would get off on the 4th to seek the enemy; but it was too late, the Spaniards were recalled. The fleet then proceeded to sea with victual to last till July 30 and went to the coast of France, sending pinnaces to search the ports, as it was feared that the Duke of Guise might unite his forces with the Spaniards. Afterwards the fleet lay in three widely separated squadrons between Ushant and Scilly with pinnaces maintaining communications, thus closing the entrance to the Channel. While thus placed it was learned from various sources that the enemy had gone into Corunna and, as no news of them came from elsewhere, Drake and the rest became convinced they really were there and in bad condition, unready for an early departure. Drake objected to waiting longer, as it would be necessary to reduce rations, which would raise discontent.

Contrary to the Queen's orders, upon the advice of his Council, Howard now decided to run for Corunna and destroy the Spanish fleet in port. Accordingly, on July 17, with a good northerly breeze the fleet laid a course for Spain. Two days later, when a day's run, more or less, from Spain, the wind came out ahead and, as many of the smaller ships had short supplies, all turned back to Plymouth, where they arrived on the 22d, the day the Armada left Corunna.

The strategy involved in the attempt to go to Spain is worthy of consideration. As Drake knew from his examination of the Tagus the year before, there was little chance of getting at the main body at Lisbon. Howard proposed, as we saw, to wait outside for the enemy to come forth. This could only be done if the ships were supplied for a long cruise, which the Queen would not permit. The movement southward in July, when the English knew the Armada was at Corunna, failed for lack of supplies and was rash and a grave risk, for it was based on the mistaken assumption that the Spaniards were seriously crippled. The Spaniards might well have got to sea a few days earlier and gone up the Channel unopposed. The more cautious policy of the Queen of waiting for the enemy was made effective by her limitation of supplies and consequent limitation of the fleet to short cruises. Therefore it was unwise in her admirals to attempt a bolder course without adequate means.

The fleet got home in time to revictual for the coming battle, and in a few days Howard learned that the Armada was soon to come. Besides a shortage of provisions and ammunition, the health of the crews was not good. Already in June, the *Elizabeth Jonas* at Plymouth had broken out with illness, losing 200 out of 500 men and, as Howard reported,

> I was driven to set all the rest of her men on shore, to take out her ballast and make fires in her of wet broom, three or four days together; and so hoped thereby to have cleansed her of her infection; and thereupon I got new men, very tall and able as ever I saw, and put them into her.

But this did not end the matter, and of the July cruise he wrote on his return to Plymouth, "We must now man ourselves again, for we have cast many overboard, and a number in great extremity which we have discharged. I have sent with great expedition a prest for more men." Again, two days before the Armada appeared at the Lizard, "Some four or five ships have discharged their men, for the sickness is very great so that we are fain to discharge some ships to have their men to furnish the others."

While busy renewing supplies and replacing men, the *Golden Hind*, Captain Fleming, a small bark which had been left in the Sleeve as lookout, arrived at Plymouth, saying that the Spaniards were at hand. The story is that he found Drake and other leaders playing bowls on the Green and that Drake merrily cried out that there would be time to finish the game and beat the Spaniards afterwards. It is not unlikely that Drake was playing bowls and possibly may have made the remark as alleged, but if so, it was a word of confidence to raise morale rather than one of action. In fact, the situation was one of difficulty. The southwest wind bringing the Spaniards was very scant for working the fleet out of harbor, yet it had to be speedily done that night to avoid being closed in port by the enemy. In Howard's *Relation* he says,

> Although the greater part of the ships of the English army, being then in Plymouth, with that wind, were very hard to be gotten out of harbor, yet the same was done with such diligence and good will that many of them got aboard as though it had been with a fair wind. Whereupon the 30th of July, his Lordship accompanied with 54 sail of his fleet, with that southwest wind plied out of the Sound and being gotten scarce so far as Eddystone, the Spanish army was discovered and were apparently seen of the whole fleet to the westward as far as Fowey.

Most of the ships were provisioned until August 20, but some had not completed.

DATA AS TO THE ENGLISH FLEET

The list of ships in service during the campaign is given in *Defeat of the Spanish Armada,* by Laughton. There were 197 ships in all of a tonnage measurement of 29,716 tons, with 15,925 men. Of this total the Queen's navy provided 34 vessels of 13,470 tons with 6,705 men. This force was in two parts. The smaller one under Lord Henry Seymour was at the Narrows, maintaining a joint watch with the Dutch squadron under Justin of Nassau upon the Spanish flotilla, which Parma had provided to transport his army to England. Seymour's force included 13 Queen's ships and 23 coasters. In addition, 23 voluntary ships came out of various English ports when the enemy appeared, bringing supplies and men anxious to serve. The larger force at Plymouth under Howard and Drake, which was now about to meet the enemy, included 20 Queen's ships, 33 merchantmen, and 20 coasters working under the Lord Admiral, 34 merchantmen under Drake, and 30 ships set forth and paid by the city of London. Many ships in this list were engaged only in the service of supply and took no part in the fighting. Others did not serve throughout all the campaign. Of the small craft which were present at the fights, most were of use only in reconnaissance, in message-bearing between ships and shore, and in bringing off men and supplies of food and powder. Of the 117 vessels serving in the west, Howard states that

FIG. 42.—BRITISH SHIP OF THE LINE IN THE CAMPAIGN OF 1588
AGAINST THE SPANISH ARMADA

Courtesy the Science Museum

Model built from recently discovered drawings, original drawings, Science Museum, South Kensington. Believed to be the plans of the *Elizabeth Jonas*. Length of keel, 100 feet; rake forward, 36 feet; rake aft, 6 feet; beam, 38 feet; depth of hold, 18 feet; tonnage, 684; ton and tonnage, 912; displacement, about 1,500 tons. Approximate armament: 2 demi-cannon (32-pdrs.), 2 cannon-periers (24-pdrs.), 18 culverins (18-pdrs.), 14 demi-culverins (9-pdrs.), 10 sakers (6-pdrs.), and smaller guns. Total weight of one round about 600 pounds, but some guns were chasers and could not be fired on the broadside.

only some 90 were in Plymouth when the enemy appeared. From a memorandum by Lord Burghley it appears on August 19, when the fighting was over, the total force in service was 117 ships with 11,120 men. The difference in the gross figures is chiefly in the smaller ships.

Contemporary accounts of the campaign generally state that the Spanish ships were far larger than their opponents, but this belief probably arose from the fact that the Spaniards were higher out of water and carried loftier poops, giving a false idea of their size. Really, the difference was not excessive; the largest Spanish ship, the *Regazona,* was of 1,249 tons and the largest English was the *Triumph* of 1,100 tons. There were 7 Spaniards over 1,000 tons, aggregating 7,709 tons, and 2 English aggregating 2,100 tons. It is said, on the other hand, that the English mode of reckoning gave a smaller result than the Spanish, but neither does this seem to be true.*

As for the gunpower of the English fleet we are more uncertain, but it may be believed that the best 45 English ships had about 1,600 guns firing a broadside of nearly 7,000 pounds.** They carried about 8,171 men

---

* The 12 largest Queen's ships aggregated 8,400 tons by the official list. In Oppenheim's *Administration of the Royal Navy,* he gives the dimensions of these ships and also the Spanish rule for calculating tonnage. The same rule is given in Artiñano's *Arquitectura Española.* The English rule is given in *Spanish War,* 1585-87, published by the Navy Records Society. Both rules reach a "solid number," length multiplied by beam and the product by depth of hold. Dividing by a factor, the quotient gives the carrying capacity in wine-casks, or tuns. To get the load capacity, or "ton and tonnage" the English rule added one-third to the tonnage, and the Spanish rule added one-fifth to get what was called "armada tonnage," As Artiñano tells us (pp. 118-411), the unit of the Spanish measurement was the "royal codo" of 1.885 feet. The essential difference of the two rules is that the English was based on keel length and the Spanish on deck length. "Ton and tonnage" and "armada tonnage" agree precisely when keel and deck lengths are in the ratio 100 to 128.9. This ratio seems to have been a not unusual one. Working out the measurement of the above 12 English ships by the English rule for "ton and tonnage," it comes to 8,572 tons and by the Spanish rule for "armada tonnage" it is 8,487 tons. Comparing these figures with the official record of 8,400 tons, it is apparent that the two fleets are fairly compared as to size by the official figures, although the recorded measurement of the English ships seems to be in round numbers.

** It seems that just before the campaign the batteries of the English ships were being altered. There are battery records before and after 1588, but it is not known how far the changes had gone that year on individual ships. There is comparative certainty about the *Vanguard* and *Rainbow* of 500 tons each, which had 32 large guns and 20 small ones, giving a broadside of 286 pounds. Two tables of batteries in Oppenheim and Clowes give the *White Bear* a broadside of 500 and 350 pounds, respectively. We may take it that the 5 largest Queen's ships of from 800 to 1,100 tons had broadsides weighing 350 to 450 pounds, the 8 ships of 500 to 600 tons broadsides of 230 to 286 pounds, and 8 ships of 200 to 400 tons broadsides of 96 to 200 pounds, giving a total for the 21 largest ships of about 5,000 pounds. The 10 re-

and their tonnage was 17,110. We may compare this with the best 45 Spanish sailing ships of 35,508 tons, 15,235 men, and about 1,350 guns with a broadside of under 4,500 pounds, and poorer shooting.

While this estimate cannot pretend to accuracy, it is enough to show how far superior the principal English ships were in battery strength, and also in their smaller size, which helped their nimbleness in the quiet summer weather. As for the smaller ships on both sides, they were negligible in battle. Besides, the English were far more expert in the use of their batteries. Drake held target practice at Plymouth. From the first the English meant to make a gun fight, whereas the Spaniards regarded the guns as auxiliaries. So we have another example of the great tactical advantage of so managing the battle as to make the victory turn on the superiority of the weapon in which the victor is strongest.

---

maining Queen's ships of 30 to 50 tons had broadsides of 15 to 40 pounds, say 250 pounds in all.

The batteries of the merchant ships are still more uncertain. In Laughton's *Spanish Armada*, vol. 1, p. 339, is a list of 10 London ships with their burden, crews, and guns. From this it appears that they fired a broadside of 280 pounds, or 0.25 pound per ton of burden. Applying this factor to the other merchant ships we find that the 14 ships with Drake (vol. 2, p. 326) of over 200 tons, may have had an aggregate broadside of about 875 pounds, and the whole 34 ships about 1,307 pounds. The 10 London ships over 200 tons would have had an aggregate broadside of 550 pounds and the whole 30 (vol. 2, p. 327) would have had a broadside of about 1,130 pounds. It is probably a small estimate, as it is based on small ships. Larger ships had proportionately heavier batteries.

Another approximation may be made from a letter of Drake, dated April 9, in which he says that the *Revenge, Nonpareil, Hope, Swiftsure,* and *Aid,* then at Plymouth, had 6 lasts 8 hundredweight (15,296 lbs.) of powder, enough for a day and a half, and that 23 merchantmen there had 5 lasts (12,000 lbs.), enough for a day. It follows that the broadsides of the 5 Queen's ships were to those of the 23 merchant ships as 6.33 to 7.5. Taking the fire of the Queen's ships as 1,020 pounds, the merchantmen fired 1,208 pounds. It is not clear from the data in Laughton which were the 23 ships to which Drake alluded, but assuming them to be those named on p. 31, vol. 1, in *Defeat of the Spanish Armada*, it appears that their crews numbered 1,780 men and as the tonnage of all is not given, we must distribute the weight of metal according to the size of crews. This would give the largest ship, the *Merchant Royal,* a broadside of 120 pounds, and the 9 smallest craft 20 to 40 pounds each. This method gives a broadside weight about 16 per cent greater than that derived from the given weights of the 10 London ships. Taking the mean of the two, we may say that the 14 merchant ships over 200 tons, which were with Drake, had an aggregate broadside of about 1,000 pounds, with possibly 425 guns, and the 10 largest ships of the city of London, 630 pounds, with possibly about 275 guns.

As for the guns themselves, they fell into four classes (See *Spanish War,* 1585-87, by J. R. Corbett). There were cannon of about 18 to 28 calibers in length, weighing 4,000 to 6,000 pounds and throwing shot of 30 to 60 pounds in weight, but at this time the 6-inch 30-pdr. was the only one retained in service, as the others were thought too heavy for ships' use. The culverins formed the second class; they were longer and higher powered, 32 to 34 calibers in

The English ships were of the same general type as the Spaniards, but were better designed for the type of battle which occurred. They were not so lofty, being apparently without the poop deck, and therefore exposed less hull surface to drive them to leeward and carried their sail better without heeling over so much. Some English vessels were of the type known as "race-built"; that is, they were also without a quarter-deck, having only a "half-deck" above the upper complete deck known as spar deck, and in this way gained an additional advantage in sailing, for the omission of the poop and quarter-decks enabled these ships to carry heavier batteries without danger from overload. Besides the English ships were longer in proportion to their beam and so were more speedy as well as more weatherly.

The Battles in the Channel

At the same time that the Duke hoisted the battle flag on July 30 he called a council of the squadron chiefs to discuss the coming battle. Know-

---

length and consisted of the culverin (18-pdr.), basilisk (15-pdr.), demi-culverin (9-pdr.), saker (5 to 6-pdr.), minion (4-pdr.), falcon (3-pdr.). The third class were the periers, short guns of 6 to 8 calibers in length, originally for stone balls, case shot, and fire balls. The largest were cannon-periers, muzzle loaders of about 6 inches and called 24-pdrs., although a stone ball of their size would weigh only 9 or 10 pounds. Port-pieces, fowlers, and slings were breech loaders with two or three separate powder chambers for each, which were cleaned and sent below after each discharge and loaded there. These periers were smaller, running from $5\frac{1}{2}$ inches in caliber down to 2 inches and less. The fourth class of guns were the mortar pieces of about $1\frac{1}{2}$ calibers in length. The largest was 6 inches in caliber. Besides the guns on deck a number of the small breech-loaders were mounted in the tops and on the superstructure decks for use against boarders. It is said that some of these small breech-loaders could fire 300 times a day.

The English ships were not well provided with ammunition. How much they had is not clearly stated in the published records, but an estimate may be made from allusions. In Appendix C of *Defeat of the Spanish Armada* is a table of the period telling the weights of powder and projectiles for British guns of all sizes. From this it appears that in a broadside of various calibers 100 pounds of projectiles called for about 70 pounds of powder, more or less. Referring again to Drake's letter and taking the broadsides of the 5 Queen's ships as 1,020 pounds, they would need 714 pounds of powder per broadside and, as they had 15,296 pounds, it was enough for 21 broadsides or between 10 and 11 rounds. So Drake thought 14 broadsides enough for one day's fighting and wanted over 60 in the magazines. A day or two after the last battle Sir William Wynter, who served on the *Vanguard*, wrote a letter saying that on the last day the *Vanguard* fired 500 shot of demi-cannon, culverins, and demi-culverins in 9 hours. Now the *Vanguard* carried 32 guns of these calibers; so in a long day of battle she expended under 16 rounds, about $3\frac{1}{2}$ broadsides an hour, or at about twice the rate which Drake foresaw. As will be seen later, we may conjecture that while at Plymouth Drake got perhaps half as much powder as he asked for and that the entire consumption in the whole campaign was between 40 and 50 rounds for the most eager ships.

ing that the English fleet was in Plymouth, 14 leagues away, it seemed to de Leyva and others that it would be well to enter and fight while the English were at anchor and unprepared; for the local castles could not fire without hitting their own ships. The Duke answered there were two objections. The King had ordered him not to enter any port and there were shoals in the entrance so that the fleet could not go in with more than two or three abreast and the castles could do them much damage. In the meantime the English fleet could shelter itself toward shore and after its defeat there would not be time to carry out the Armada's purpose. So all agreed to the Duke's proposal to go forward and fight the enemy as they might be found.

At sundown the lookouts on the *S. Martin* saw a great number of ships to leeward, but it was too hazy to count them. The Duke did not wish to let the enemy get a windward position for a battle in the morning, and so he sent word around how he wished the Armada to form for battle and anchored overnight. At the same time he sent Juan Gil in a rowing zabra to get news. Somewhat after midnight the latter returned with four fishermen who were examined separately and agreed in saying that the Lord Admiral and Drake had both sailed that day from Plymouth.

On the morning of July 31 the breeze was at WNW and the Spaniards saw the English fleet to windward of them, reported as about 60 strong, while another group of 11, 3 of them large, was working to windward along shore and, after some exchange of shots, they joined their main body. The formation taken up at this time by the Spanish fleet is not clearly described either by English or Spanish participants. A Spanish account says it was in three main squadrons: the center under Medina-Sidonia, the vanguard (or right) under Alonzo de Leyva, and the rearguard (or left) under Juan Martinez de Recalde. An Englishman present says they were in squadrons of 12 vessels each. Both may be correct, with about 24 ships in each of the three grand divisions. The contemporary charts made by Adams show the Spaniards in a line convex to the east and about 7 miles across. In the center, the line is three ships deep, and on the flanks two deep, with small craft to leeward in a fourth line. From a study of these diagrams, it seems probable that when the enemy was seen to the westward, the Armada took up a formation approximately the inverse of that laid down by Pigafetta. That is to say, the urcas and light craft passed through the intervals of the fighting ships and were to leeward heading up Channel, while the 60 or 70 fighting ships interposed between them and the enemy, with the flanks trailing somewhat behind the center so as to enfold the enemy when he should close for battle.

After sighting the enemy late in the afternoon of July 30 the English fleet had crossed the front of the Armada, while it was at anchor during the night; had passed around it; and, when the two fleets sighted each other at daylight, was well to windward with the Spaniards probably bearing near ENE.

ACTION OF JULY 31

After getting under way, to induce the enemy to close, Medina made a show of meaning to enter Plymouth. In reply, as Howard's *Relation* says,

> The Lord Admiral sent his pinnace, the *Disdain*, to give the Duke of Medina defiance [i.e., she closed and fired a shot] and afterwards the *Ark* bare up with the admiral of the Spaniards wherein the Duke was supposed to be.*

Calderon, who was aboard the *S. Salvador*, Almiranta of the cargo ships, agrees with Howard that the English closed, having the wind aft. As for the English formation, it is not apparent that there was any. The fleet seems to have been in two groups led by Howard and Drake, respectively, and ships seem to have followed the two admirals somewhat as each pleased.**

According to the Spanish accounts, which are fuller than the English, the English fleet ran down on a course a little more northerly than that of the Spaniards, who were heading up Channel, so that they crossed the Spanish rear obliquely and some of their ships exchanged fire at long

---

* At that period the word admiral was the title of a flag officer and also indicated the ship which carried him. In Spanish custom the word Capitana was applied to the admiral's ship and Almiranta to that of the vice admiral. In the Armada there was an admiral and vice admiral to each squadron besides the Admiral and Vice Admiral of the Fleet who were in the Capitana Real and the Almiranta Real.

** Sir Julian S. Corbett, in his *Drake and the Tudor Navy*, asserts that at this time and place the English leaders invented the battle formation for sailing ships of the close-hauled line ahead, or as we now say, "the column." Two Spanish witnesses say that when they sighted the English fleet it was in line (ala) and one of them says it was in very good order. I cannot see the slightest foundation for Corbett's belief, either on this day or any other time of this campaign.

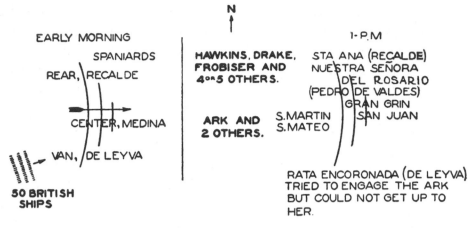

SUNDAY JULY 31 1588.
OFF PLYMOUTH.

FIG. 43

range with the ships of the Spanish vanguard (southern flank) as they ran toward the center and rearguard (northern flank). Medina now seems to have tacked and headed south to meet the English and was engaged by Lord Howard in the *Ark* with two other ships. The *S. Mateo* of the Portuguese squadron commanded by Don Diego Pimentel, who was most ardent in every encounter, stood bravely by the *S. Martin,* close by the wind without firing a shot and waited with disdain but in vain to be boarded, for it was not the English policy to accept his challenge. De Leyva, in the *Rata Encoronada* left his position with the vanguard and worked across to the center in hope of engaging Howard but could not do so, for the wind shifted, so he could not get up, and he, as well as *S. Mateo,* came under fire of other ships. The *Gran Grin* of the rearguard also seems to have been in action here. (Some say she was with Recalde.)

The action of the other English group on the northern flank seems to have been more important. There, as Howard tells us, Drake, Hawkins, and Frobiser were engaged. The Spanish account says that the English came down in "ala," extended, or in a line, and in good order. Two ships from the direction of the shore came to reconnoiter and then rejoined their flagship, which hauled up his foresail and sent 4 ships, one of which bore a flag, to skirmish with the Spanish rearguard. The Spanish use of the word "skirmish" means the English refused decisive action by keeping beyond grappling distance and declined to be boarded. Recalde in *Sta. Ana,* the "almiranta real," distinguished himself and won the honors of the day. With his single ship he engaged 7 or 8 enemies and received considerable damage aloft, including two shot in the foremast. Although Don Pedro de Valdes, commanding the Andalusian squadron, stood by him in *Nuestra Señora del Rosario,* he was not well supported by his squadron, most of which retreated into the center and the Duke sent word to these vessels to turn their bows to the enemy.

About 1:00 o'clock the English Commander in Chief made signal to withdraw, for 40 ships had not yet been able to join him out of Plymouth, and those with him he was unwilling to hazard too far. The Duke then pursued his course up Channel and Howard called a council, after which an order was sent to each captain how to pursue the fleet of Spain.

The action was a trifling one, for the Spaniards seem to have brought only 7 vessels into action and the English not more than 10 or 12.* Vanegas, who commanded a company of soldiers on board *S. Martin,* and was no doubt aware of the reports made to Medina, says that the Spanish loss on this occasion was 7 killed and 31 wounded and that Recalde's vessel took until noon next day to repair damages aloft. She fired 120 shot and the rest of the Armada, 600, not much for 4 hours' battle. The English expenditure of ammunition he estimates at 2,000 shot.

At the close of the day Howard wrote to Walsingham telling him of the encounter:

> In this fight we made some of them to bear room [run to leeward] to stop their leaks; notwithstanding we durst not adventure to put in among them, their fleet being so strong. Sir, the captains in her Majesty's ships have behaved themselves most bravely and like men hitherto, and I doubt not will continue to their great commendation.

It is noteworthy that he praises only Her Majesty's captains. But the principal item was in a postscript. "Sir, for the love of God and our country, let us have with some speed some great shot sent us of all bigness, for this service will continue long, and some powder with it." By

---

* Spanish accounts say the Duke fought against 3 ships and Recalde against 8. There may have been some other English which engaged. Medina's diary says the *Gran Grin, S. Mateo,* and *S. Juan* fought near Recalde. Other Spanish accounts make it possible they were near the Duke.

request of Howard, Drake wrote that same night to Lord Henry Seymour at the Narrows, telling him of the approach of the two fleets and to be in readiness. The note arrived by water in 48 hours, the distance being about 240 miles, and Seymour instantly wrote to the Council asking for ammunition, saying he was short.

Already the policy of not coming to close quarters with the Spaniards had been decided upon. Sir Walter Raleigh says of this resolve that it was principally due to Lord Howard.

> He was better advised than many malignant fools were that found fault with his demeanor. The Spaniards had an army aboard them and he had none. They had more ships than he had, and of higher building and charging; so that had he entangled himself with these great and powerful vessels he had greatly endangered this Kingdom of England. But our Admiral knew his advantage and held it; which had he not done, he would not have been worthy to have held his head.

The battle was only the beginning of the day's misfortunes for the Spaniards. *Nuestra Señora del Rosario,* flagship of the Andalusian Squadron of the rearguard, under Don Pedro de Valdes, attempted by Recalde's request to approach the damaged *Sta. Ana.* As she luffed to do so, she fouled the *Catalina* of her own squadron, losing a couple of spars and before she was under control again, another ship fouled her doing further damage. She sent word of her condition to the Duke and managed to run in advance of the fleet for protection, where she hove to for repairs. The sea now rose and her foremast fell and injured the mainmast whereupon Valdes fired distress signals.

Notwithstanding, the Armada passed on, abandoning Don Pedro, who, as he wrote to King Philip, was left "comfortless in the sight of the whole fleet." The Duke's own story was that he tried to aid her with his own vessel, but not being able to do so, he left several ships and a galleass to help her, either to take her in tow or to remove her crew, but neither was possible and so he proceeded, collecting his fleet for what might happen the next day. The current gossip in the Armada was that Diego Flores de Valdes, who was on board the Capitana as nautical adviser to the Duke, was jealous of his cousin and did not give the Duke such advice as he should; telling the Duke that if he stayed to aid Don Pedro, the Armada would run on and be scattered in the darkness.

FIG. 44.—*Ark Royal*, BRITISH FLAGSHIP IN CAMPAIGN OF 1588.
By Visscher
Courtesy of Nederlandsch Historisch Scheepvaart Museum

About the same time, another vessel, the *S. Salvador*, A'miranta of the Guipuscoan Squadron, suddenly exploded a barrel of powder which had been brought up for service, much damaging two decks and the poop and killing and injuring a great number. A Flemish gunner who "had been given the stick" by his captain was said to have applied his lighted linstock to the powder in revenge. The Duke immediately turned to her aid, fired an alarm gun, and sent pataches to help. The fire was extinguished and the hostile fleet, which was running down, kept its distance when it saw the "Real" interpose. Thus the *S. Salvador* was able to take cover in the body of the fleet.

In the afternoon the English Commander in Chief organized the pursuit by telling Drake to precede the fleet as guide, showing the usual guide lantern at night. This was done, but during the night Drake saw some sail abeam and feared the enemy was doubling back. To ascertain the fact, he extinguished his guide light and with the *Roebuck* ran southwards and found several German merchantmen which he allowed to proceed after examination. At daylight, as he was returning to the fleet, Drake met the disabled *Rosario* and sent a pinnace to demand her surrender. Valdes asked for terms and it is said that Drake replied "tell him that I am Francis Drake and my matches are burning." According to the manner of the time it was an honor rather than a disgrace to surrender to a man of such renown, and Valdes promptly yielded. He was received on board the *Revenge* with every honor and given a place at Drake's table, while the *Rosario* was sent with the *Roebuck* into Torbay and her powder and shot sent forward to the English fleet.

In the meantime, the *Ark*, with the *White Bear* and the *Mary Rose*, followed the enemy through the night within gunshot, but the rest of the fleet, having no guide light, lagged behind and at daylight was hull down beyond the horizon and did not get up to the *Ark* till late; so there was no battle that day. Still the Spaniards had another misfortune. Early on the morning of August 1 the captain of the *S. Salvador* arrived at the *Royal* to say she was sinking. The Duke immediately ordered the wounded and the treasure to be removed and the ship to be sunk. The order was not well obeyed and she was deserted without being sunk. The English took possession of her and brought her to Portland, whence her powder and shot also were sent to the English fleet.

Spanish Loss of Morale

Sunday's action and the subsequent loss of two great ships was taken as a bad omen throughout the Spanish fleet and was far more important for its effect upon the spirits of the adversaries than for the material damage given and received. The English found that their vessels were speedier and more manageable than the Spaniards and that the initiative was theirs, so that they were confirmed in their resolve to make victory turn on gunfire and refuse the boarders' fight which the Spaniards preferred. The latter were greatly depressed by their failure to board. Several ships had given evidence of timidity. These had no gentleman of distinction on board whom the sailors would respect. So the Duke thought it necessary to call the sergeant-majors of the six regiments to the *S. Martin* where he gave each a written order to take a patache and go through the fleet, putting every ship in its assigned position. Should any ship leave her station the sergeant-majors had further written orders to hang summarily the captain of the faulty ship. For this purpose each was to be accompanied by his provost-marshal and executioners and three were to go with one-half the fleet and three with the other half. But this stern order could not restore morale which had been greatly shaken by the loss of the two ships.

Writing on board the *S. Martin*, Vanegas says,

The abandonment of this ship [*S. Salvador*] and the loss of Don Pedro broke the spirit of the people and timid minds justified their fears, saying they did not wish to expose themselves to the risk of dismasting and then be abandoned to the enemy as these ships had been; for the enemy would not get the better of them if things were well managed.

The fighting of Sunday seems to have convinced the Duke that he should divide his combatant vessels into two parts, an escort for the cargo ships, and a fighting squadron. So on Monday he ordered de Leyva to pass over with the vanguard to join the rearguard making one body under his command, while Recalde was repairing his *Sta. Ana*. To this force the Duke added 3 galleasses and *S. Mateo*, *S. Luis*, *Santiago*, and *Florencia*. In all there were 43 of the best ships to confront the enemy and prevent all hindrance to joining the Duke of Parma. Medina took charge of the rest of the fleet which became the van. This day the Duke also sent Juan Gil in a pinnace to the Duke of Parma to report progress.

Action of August 2

On Tuesday August 2 at about 1:00 A.M., the moon was bright, the wind and sea at rest. At this time de Leyva, Oquendo, and Recalde ap-

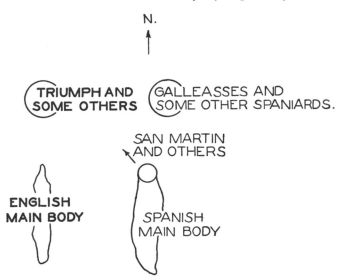

N.

TRIUMPH AND SOME OTHERS

GALLEASSES AND SOME OTHER SPANIARDS.

SAN MARTIN AND OTHERS

ENGLISH MAIN BODY

SPANISH MAIN BODY

CALM AT FIRST, LATER WIND CAME UP FROM N.E. BRITISH MAIN BODY FIRST MOVED N.W. AND THEN TACKED TO EASTWARD. SPANISH MAIN BODY ATTACKED IT AND THE ENGLISH RAN OFF THE WIND, FIGHTING. MEDINA, WITH OTHER SHIPS FROM MAIN BODY AND THE GALLEASSES ATTACKED THE TRIUMPH GROUP, WHICH ALSO BORE UP, DECLINING CLOSE ACTION. AFTER THE WIND SHIFTED TO S.E. AND LATER TO S.S.W., A CONFUSED ACTION FOLLOWED ON THE PART OF ALL WITH RECALDE'S SANTA ANA (STILL UNDER REPAIR) AS THE CENTER.

TUESDAY AUGUST 2 1588.
OFF PORTLAND.

FIG. 45

peared on board the "Real" to point out that certain ships of the enemy towards the land were isolated from the others and that if the galleasses were to attack the former at once, no matter from what direction the wind might later spring up, the Spaniards would be able to force a general close action on the rescuing English squadrons. The Duke, "who wanted a close action more than many in the fleet," sent Oquendo to Don Hugo Moncada, commanding the galleasses, to fire on the detached ships and to promise him an estate of 3,000 ducats a year if he did well. Oquendo gave the message but the galleasses did not carry out the order and at daybreak they were inshore and half a league from the enemy and from their own vessels.*

It is hard to make out the details of the action on August 2 from the accounts of participants; largely, as I believe, because the individual ships did not adhere to fixed positions with regard to each other. There was no binding fleet formation. At daylight both fleets had detached portions near the land, the English being to the westward. The wind rose in the NE. and the English took the starboard tack heading towards shore hoping to get to windward. But it was soon apparent to Lord Howard that he could not accomplish it and the fleet went about, heading east. Thereupon Bertendona in the *Regazona*, commanding the Levant Squadron, with several ships of his own and the Portuguese Squadron bore down on the English, running free. The *Ark, Nonpareil, Elizabeth Jonas, Victory*, and several others awaited them and a brisk exchange of fire took place, but the Spaniards were unable to close and board as they wished, for the English bore up and the Spaniards fell astern. The Spaniards thought Bertendona might have boarded an English vessel but he refused to assail any but the *Ark*. This phase of the battle ended about 10 o'clock.

In the meantime the Duke sent an aid to Moncada to say to him "certain words which were not complimentary" and directed him to use every effort of oars and sail to close with the *Triumph* and other detached ships. The Duke himself, in the *S. Martin*, also went that way (NW.). This time the galleasses got into action, although preceded by several ships, *Rata Encoronada, Santiago, Begoña*, and others which were trying to board. The English kept away and put up a very strong resistance for an

---

* In his *Drake and the Tudor Navy*, Corbett suggests that Moncada refused to obey because the day before, when the *Ark Royal* had outrun the English fleet and was close to the Spaniards, Moncada asked to be allowed to attack her and was refused permission, and so was too sulky to undertake a less honorable task. The story of the request and its refusal is told by Meteren in his history (translated in Hakluyt), but he says nothing to authorize Corbett's surmise which, however, is in accord with Spanish mentality.

hour and a half, when they were aided by some vessels which came from the main body and the galleasses left them.

About 10 o'clock the wind began to veer, first to SE. and then to SSW. The English group with the *Triumph* now returned towards the enemy with the wind and tide and fell upon Don Juan Martinez de Recalde in the *Sta. Ana,* still under repairs. De Leyva and Medina-Sidonia both supported him. Thereupon Lord Howard in the *Ark* with *Elizabeth Jonas, Galleon of Leicester, Golden Lion, Victory, Mary Rose, Dreadnought,* and *Swallow* (the Spaniards say about 50 in all) bore down (heading NE.) to aid their detached ships. The *S. Martin* shortened sail and the English ships ran by her, discharging their broadsides in succession while she made a furious reply. For some time *S. Martin* and *Sta. Ana* were alone, for of the rest of the Spaniards, some were pursuing other enemies and some were avoiding action. Medina sent an aid in a boat to summon assistance and gradually it came. Oquendo interposed his ship, *Santa Ana,** between his chief and the enemy, conning his ship from a position above the nettings and directing himself the fire of the principal guns. Then Don Augustin de Mejia in the *S. Luis* and the Marquis of Peñafiel in the *S. Marcos* and other ships (Howard says there were 16 in all) came to her support and after a hard fight of about 3 hours the two fleets separated, each claiming that the other gave way.

However it was, late in the day the "Capitana Real" fired a gun to assemble the Armada and it resumed its course up Channel. The Spaniards lost 50 killed and 70 wounded. Medina's vessel was hit about 50 times. Much of her rigging was cut and she had several leaks, which were closed by sending divers overboard to apply sheet lead. She fired 120 times and the two fleets, 5,000 times. (So Vanegas, who was estimating as to the English but was in a position to know the reports made to his Commander in Chief.)

The Spanish accounts insist that the English fled before them and call the day's work a skirmish. They could not resist this conclusion because the English tactics were Parthian. They struck while they withdrew and suffered very little, although the Spaniards flattered themselves they had inflicted much damage.

---

* There were several *Sta. Anas.*

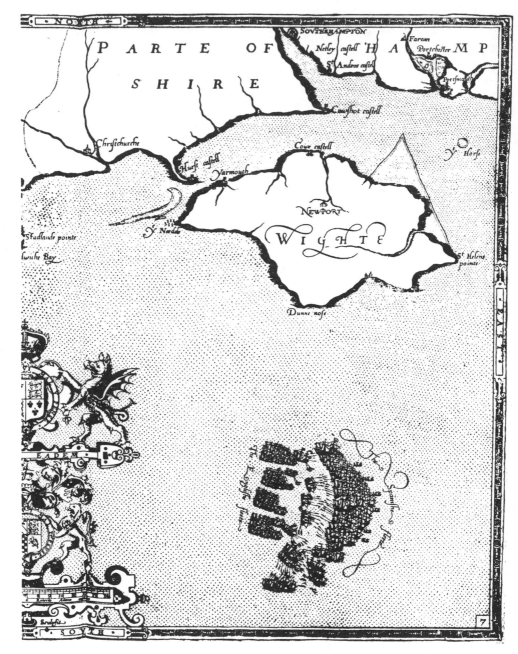

FROM RYTHER'S DRAWINGS FOR LORD HOWARD OF EFFINGHAM
Library of Congress
FIG. 46 (*Explanation on opposite page*)

From the very first appearance of the Spanish fleet on the coast of England the southern ports began to pour out men, victual, and ammunition for the English fleet, but on Wednesday August 3 very little powder, if any, had come and Lord Howard found he had not enough for another action like the day before. Consequently, the principal English effort of the day was replenishment of the magazines by barks and pinnaces which were sent to the shore for that purpose. The day of rest was further utilized to organize the fleet into four squadrons, one under Howard himself, the others under Drake, Hawkins, and Frobiser. This seems strongly to suggest that many ships had not been anxious to get under fire and the division into squadrons was to increase the control of the admirals. Indeed, Sir William Wynter wrote of the final engagement that the merchantmen did little but "make a show" (letter to Walsingham August 17, 1588). Lord Henry Seymour also wrote slightingly to Walsingham of many ships' services (letter of August 18).

The Spanish accounts of this day differ from the English, saying that on Wednesday at daylight they were near the Isle of Wight and that Recalde, having repaired his vessel, resumed command of the rearguard, which he thenceforward shared with de Leyva, each having 20 vessels. There was an hour's cannonade in which apparently only 10 Spaniards were engaged. These did not leave their stations in the formation and the galleasses fired only their stern guns. The English then withdrew and repaired damages for some hours. The Duke even shortened sail, but the English kept clear. Thereupon the Duke called a council which concluded that the English only wished to offer check until a storm should damage the Armada. So it was decided to delay no more, for the English were so quick that it was impossible to grapple and make them fight. As

---

FIG. 46.—FLEETS ON THURSDAY, AUGUST 4

British and Spanish fleets in action off the Isle of Wight on Thursday, August 4, 1588. The plan shows the first attempt of the British fleet to form a tactical organization. The day before Howard had divided the fleet into 4 squadrons under Hawkins, Frobiser, Howard, and Drake, and seemingly they were in the order given from north to south. A proper organization for battle was not found until the time of the Commonwealth, by the soldiers commanding the fleet. It may be noted that each of the 4 British squadrons was composed of a mass of ships with boats towing a number of them. Only the leading ships of each squadron were in action. Similarly with the Spaniards; the mass of transports was pursuing its course, while the fighting ships fought a rearguard action.

Luis de Miranda wrote home by a dispatch boat, "All their ships are more nimble than ours and more responsive than a well-trained horse." Vanegas states that this day the Armada lost 60 killed and 70 wounded. The *Santa Ana* fired 130 shots and both fleets 5,000. The flagship of the Spanish cargo squadron received 40 hits and the English flagship had her main-yard broken by a shot from the *Santa Ana*. So the Spaniards found the day not so negligible as Howard reported. But the losses seem out of proportion for an hour's fight.

On this day Howard had the satisfaction of hearing that the French party under the Duke of Guise, which was subsidized by King Philip, would send no raiders against the English fleet.

Battle off the Isle of Wight

On August 4 the two fleets were a few miles south of the Isle of Wight. It was the day of St. Dominic, who in his life was of the Duke's family. The latter therefore hoped that the anniversary would be propitious, so he was glad to fight and the fleet displayed all its standards. The day opened with no wind and two Spanish ships were astern of the others. One of them was the *Santa Ana* which had been so hammered both on Sunday and Tuesday. The center English squadron under command of Hawkins was nearest and his own *Victory* and several other ships got out their boats and towed within range of the detached Spaniards until the latters' small-arm fire became too much for the men in the boats. De Leyva in the *Rata* and two galleasses of the rearguard came up in support. Presumably the *Rata* was towed by one of the galleasses. At this, Lord Howard in the *Ark Royal* with his cousin Lord Thomas Howard in the *Golden Lion* also towed within range and met the *S. Martin* and the *Girona*, galleass. There was a brisk engagement, of which Lord Howard says that he did the galleasses much damage and one of them went off "on the careen" (meaning she was heeled over to keep a shot hole above water). The *S. Martin* confessed to losing some men in a very close action. A little breeze now arose, others of the Spanish fleet came up and, under their cover, the galleasses and the ships with them were able to withdraw.

The direction of the wind is not mentioned by the participants, but was probably in the SW. quadrant. In the meantime, when the wind came,

N

PROBABLE GENERAL POSITIONS OF
SQUADRONS EARLY IN THE DAY.

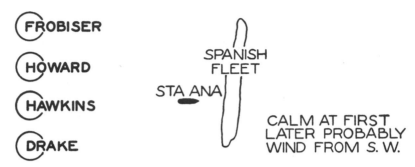

FROBISER

HOWARD   SPANISH
                          FLEET
HAWKINS   STA ANA

                          CALM AT FIRST
DRAKE   LATER PROBABLY
                          WIND FROM S. W.

PROBABLE POSITIONS OF PRINCIPAL SHIPS ENGAGED.

FROBISER	**TRIUMPH** **WHITE BEAR** **ELIZABETH JONAS** **AND OTHERS**	SAN JUAN DE FERNANDOME SAN LUIS SAN JUAN DE SICILIA OQUENDO RECALDE & OTHERS
HOWARD	**ARK ROYAL** **GOLDEN LION** **AND OTHERS**	SAN MARTIN GIRONA (GALLEASS)
HAWKINS	**VICTORY** **AND OTHERS**	STA ANA RATA ENCORONADA 2 GALLEASSES
DRAKE	**REVENGE** **AND OTHERS**	

BATTLE OFF ISLE OF WIGHT
THURSDAY AUGUST 4 1588

FIG. 47

a large part of the English fleet, apparently the northern squadron under
Frobiser, attacked the northern wing of the Spaniards. Here the *S. Luis,*
S. Juan de Sicilia, Oquendo, Recalde, one of the galleasses, and others
became engaged. Even the *S. Martin* worked over to that quarter, where
Oquendo interposed between her and the enemy as he had done two days

before. The *Triumph* was to the northward and in some danger from damage to spars. She was supported by the *White Bear* and *Elizabeth Jonas,* and was towed out of danger by 11 boats sent to her aid, so that as a Spaniard wrote "it was a marvel to see." Thus she got away from the fastest Spanish vessel, the *San Juan de Fernandome,* and the Spanish lost their hope of boarding her which was their only way to victory. The English accounts make no mention of Drake on this day, but it seems probable that it was his squadron with that of Hawkins which attacked the southern part of the Spanish line causing it to retire on its center.

The Duke saw that with the escape of the *Triumph* he no longer had the advantage of the wind and fired a gun to assemble the fleet and proceeded on his course, sending a pinnace ahead to ask Parma to be ready. The damaged *Sta. Ana* drifted out of the fleet and to Havre de Grace where she was wrecked. It does not appear why Medina changed his mind about waiting at the Isle of Wight for a message from Parma, but we may presume that it was because he could not grapple the enemy and did not wish to give them an opportunity to annoy him at anchor.

This day the Spaniards lost 50 killed and 70 wounded. The English losses are not mentioned, but the expenditure of ammunition was so great that Lord Howard found that he had not enough for another day and resolved to postpone battle until off Dover, where he could get a further supply. Since the first day men and ships had been coming from the ports, joining up as the fleets passed and the enemy noted how the number of English ships was increasing. The next two days, Friday and Saturday, the two fleets ran quietly along, a few miles apart, while Howard sent pinnaces and barks to the shore where they picked up ammunition. Yet such was the niggardliness of the authorities that when a messenger from Dover galloped to the Tower of London, which was the chief magazine, to ask for ammunition, the reply was for the Lord Admiral to specify his needs, in form.

Both Fleets Anchor off Calais

On Friday it was calm and both fleets towed their laggards into their midst, while the Duke sent another dispatch to Parma asking him for 4-, 6-, and 10-lb. shot. On the afternoon of Saturday the Armada was off Calais and, as the pilots said it would not be well to get into the currents farther on which would sweep them too far, the Duke anchored the Armada off Calais, 20 miles from the nearest Flemish port. Shortly afterwards the English fleet also anchored, west of the Spaniards beyond gunshot, and were joined by 36 vessels from Dover under Lord Henry Seymour, which Howard had called out by a message in advance. The number of English ships now present, great and small, was said to be 140. Probably many of these were small craft only, which had come to see the sport. A Spanish count put the English ships at 130 only.

The Duke of Medina immediately sent his secretary to Parma urging haste and also to the Governor of Calais to say he was waiting for Parma and would do no harm. The Governor sent refreshments for the Duke and said the Armada was in a bad anchorage. Finding the Governor friendly, the Duke sent purchasing officers ashore to buy victual. On the morning of Sunday, August 7, an aid of Medina, who had been sent forward 13 days before, returned from Parma, saying that latter was at Bruges and that on Saturday neither men nor supplies had commenced to embark. Sunday night Secretary Arceo got back and reported it seemed to him impossible for the army to be ready within a fortnight.

To the Duke of Parma it looked differently. A letter of his to the Spanish Consul at Venice said that he received Medina's successive messengers and when Juan Gil arrived with news the fleet was off Plymouth, he ordered the troops to move to the points of embarkation. Sanitary reasons made it undesirable to put the troops aboard too early. It was apparently late on Saturday, August 6, when the last messenger found Parma at Bruges. The next morning he had a letter from Medina saying he was at Calais and, on Monday, he again heard from Medina that the enemy was very threatening. Parma much regretted that his small, low ships could do nothing to aid the Armada. Parma could do nothing on account of the blockade of the coast which had been long maintained by the Dutch fleet of Justinus of Orange, as mentioned on page 279. This unspectacular work of the Dutch played a great part in saving Britain from invasion, but British historians pay little attention to it. Had the Dutch fleet not been present it is conceivable although not probable that Parma might have crossed to Margate while the British fleet was in the north, after the last battle. On August 16, the States of Zealand wrote to the Queen, drawing attention to the great part played by the Dutch

COURSE OF SPANISH ARMADA

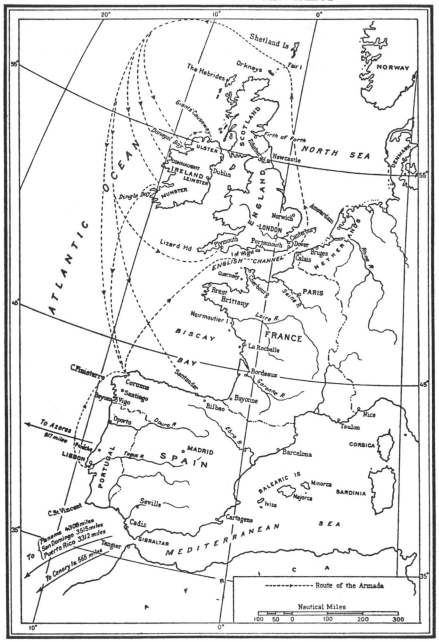

MAP XI.—VOYAGE OF SPANISH ARMADA

fleet, before Medina's arrival. On Monday night the Duke of Parma was at Newport, where he found the embarkation was almost finished, 17,000 afloat, and at Dunkirk all were ready to go on board at an instant.

A message arrived at this instant from Medina saying the Armada was in danger and asking Parma to come out with local ships and men and fight the enemy, or try to gain a port at Wight. This Parma thought improper to attempt, for the King's orders were to wait at the Narrows and it was Medina's business to protect the passage of the small army transports. The embarkation was nearly complete on August 10, when Parma heard that the Armada had been driven off. He seems to have done his best, in spite of Medina's complaint.

THE ENGLISH FIRE-SHIPS

In the meantime, while Medina had been waiting for Parma's help to defeat the English fleet, the latter had been busy. Early on the morning of Sunday, a council was called which decided to send fire-ships against the Armada, and Sir Henry Palmer went to Dover to bring the combustibles which had been assembled there. After his departure, it was resolved not to wait for his return but to make the attack that night, and 8 ships were filled with inflammables. In the meantime, about 4:00 P.M., an English pinnace saucily ran close to the Capitana Real and discharged 4 shot at her, and returned to the fleet. The *S. Lorenzo*, capitana of galleasses, "returned thanks" with a couple of shot which merely cut her topsail, while all the Armada wondered at her daring and her marvelous readiness in handling. At midnight, when wind and tide were both favorable, the fire-ships were let drive under sail. Medina had suspected there might be such an attack and had stationed a pinnace with grapple and cable to tow any fire-ship to the shore. All vessels were warned to have their own boats ready to tow them out of danger.

When the Duke saw 8 fires coming down on the anchorage and that they were not diverted, he feared they carried explosives and gave orders for his own ship to get under way, making signal to the rest to do the same, meaning to reoccupy the anchorage after the fire-ships had passed But this did not happen. Although the Capitana and some others anchored, the rest did not see her and were carried off Dunkirk by the strong tide, while the fire-ships burned out harmlessly on the beach. Medina himself behaved with courage, refusing advice to leave his ship, and stayed on board and directed matters in an honorable manner, but the panic was very great, for the soldiers feared the fire-ships were a repetition of the terrible explosion ship at Antwerp, three years before, which the Dutch had sent against an important bridge, destroying it with the loss of many lives, and inflicting serious injury to the Duke of Parma himself. In the great confusion of the night, the Capitana galleass injured her rudder by fouling another ship's cable and was obliged to anchor near Calais, where she remained.

BATTLE OF GRAVELINES MONDAY

At dawn of Monday the situation seems to have been that the *S. Martin*, the *S. Marcos*, and a few others had anchored as soon as possible after they were clear of the fire-ships. As for the rest, many had had two anchors down and in their hurry they cut their cables, so that before they could get their spare anchors ready, and drop them, they drifted far away from the Capitana. At daybreak (sunrise at 4:37) all got under way and the Duke hoped to occupy his former berth. The breeze is variously stated, but Medina says it was fresh from the NW. and nearly directly on shore, so he could not take the starboard tack without drawing ashore.

The English fleet was under way also. As Lord Henry Seymour wrote, it was the English plan to make three onsets, the first by Howard's squadron, next by Drake, and then by Lord Henry. But when Howard saw the galleass alone under the town castle, he stayed to attack her. For a commander in chief to turn aside from the main action to attend to such a detail is quite contrary to present ideas of duty, but then the medieval rôle of champion was not unbecoming to any noble gentleman and the galleass had the heaviest battery in the Spanish fleet to make the encounter creditable. So the *Ark* turned from pursuit of the enemy to deal with the *S. Lorenzo*, but could not approach her for lack of water, yet several smaller craft opened fire on her and she slipped her cable and ran ashore close to the town. The *Margaret and John* of 200 tons got nearer, but also grounded, whereupon the *Ark* and the *Margaret and John* sent their boats, which went close alongside and opened small-arm fire. Richard Tomson, a lieutenant in the *Margaret and John's* boat, wrote to Walsingham,

These two boats came hard under the galleass's sides, being aground, where we continued a pretty skirmish with our small shot against theirs, they being ensconced within their ship and very high over us, we in our open pinnaces and far under them, having nothing to shroud and cover us, they being 300 soldiers besides 450 slaves, and we not, at the instant, 100 persons. Within one-half hour, it pleased God, by killing the captain with a musket shot to give us victory beyond all hope or expectation, for the soldiers leaped overboard by heaps on the other side and fled to the shore, swimming and wading. Other English boats now approached and the few remaining soldiers put up handkerchiefs on the points of their rapiers in sign of surrender and the English entered and pillaged her for an hour and a half.

When the English occupied the prize the Governor of Calais sent officers to compliment the victors and tell them that he granted pillage freely to them which they well deserved, but that the hull lay on French soil and he claimed it with the guns for himself. Tomson returned polite answer, but asked the Frenchmen to refer the point to the Lord Admiral who was present in person. With this answer they were going off well satisfied, but as Tomson wrote,

Some of our rude men, making no account of friend or foe, fell to pillaging the Frenchmen, taking away their rings and jewels as from enemies. Whereupon these going ashore and complaining, all the bulwarks and ports were bent against us and shot so vehemently that we received several shot dangerously through us.

So the English had to abandon their prize,* and at last the *Ark* followed the fleet.

While the Commander in Chief was lagging with the galleass, the rest of the English fleet was in pursuit of the enemy. When Medina got under way about daylight his fleet was several miles away and somewhat to leeward. The wind did not permit it to stand back directly to Calais. When the Duke saw Drake, Hawkins, and Frobiser bearing down on him with their squadrons, he realized that if he ran down to join his fleet, all would be so close to the shoals off Dunkirk that it could not reform. Therefore, supported by the Marquis de Peñafiel in the *S. Marcos,* he showed his port broadside to the enemy and sent pataches to tell the fleet to keep close hauled to draw away from the shoals lying off shore. At

---

* The 300 Turkish slaves of the galleass were sent to Constantinople by the King of France, whose traditional policy was favorable to the Sultan as an enemy of Spain.

this time it appeared to Sir William Wynter that the main Spanish body was in two wings of 16 ships each with the rest in the center. The latter must have included the cargo ships.

As Howard tells us, Drake's squadron was the first to close; later came Hawkins. These two seem to have attacked Medina and the *S. Juan* and *S. Marcos,* who were with him about 8:00 o'clock, and the Duke soon had 17 enemies on his port side and 7 on the other. It must not be supposed that all these ships were firing at *S. Martin* at any one moment.

We get an idea of the method of attack from an interview held by Sir Martin Frobiser with a follower of Drake in a room at Harwich a few days after the battle. From his language, Frobiser was probably under the influence of liquor and very jealous of Drake. He said Drake "came bragging up at the first and gave them his prow and his broadside and then kept his luff, like a cowardly knave or traitor." From this we may conclude that the accepted mode of attack was to close with the Spaniard, having the wind free and fire the bow guns, then luff and fire the broadside. The charge made by Frobiser apparently is that Drake held his luff instead of wearing and firing the other broadside. We may understand, then, that this swarm of English ships about the small group of Spaniards fired in succession and made way for each other, whereas a single ship would have gone about to fire the other broadside.

S. Martin with *S. Marcos* and *S. Juan* held out for some hours against a heavy fire, which they returned at the short range of 200 yards and less, using musketry as well as great guns, after which they were able to join the rest of the fleet. Apparently Hawkins did not stay long with Medina, but passed on to attack the center group of Spaniards of about a dozen ships. Medina mentions those of De Leyva, Recalde, the 5 camp-masters, the two Enriquez, and the Capitanas of Diego Flores and Bertendona, as having fought well. The Spaniards tried to board, but all the English kept clear in spite of the short range. At the same time, Lord Henry Seymour with Sir William Wynter and the rest of the Dover Squadron charged on the "tail" of the enemy (Wynter says "starboard part").

About 3 hours after Drake first engaged the Commander in Chief came up and a confused fight followed until about 5:00 P.M., in which the English by their speed and handiness avoided every attempt of the

Spaniards to board. Although it would appear from Wynter's accounts that there were three Spanish groups in battle, the two ships which Seymour claims to have injured so that they left the fleet (*S. Mateo* and *S. Felipe*) are expressly stated by Medina to have been in the second group whose ships he names. So Seymour probably joined Hawkins' squadron. By 5:00 o'clock both sides were fatigued and had nearly exhausted their ammunition. A light drizzle had begun and the sea was rising, so the action ceased with the Spaniards in much confusion.

The fight is well pictured in a letter of Wynter to Walsingham.

The fight continued from 9 of the clock until 6 of the clock at night, in the which time the Spanish army bare away NNE. and N. by E. as much as they could, keeping company one with another, I assure your Honour in very good order. Great was the spoil and harm that was done unto them, no doubt. I deliver it to your Honour upon the credit of a poor gentleman that out of my ship there was shot 500 shot of demi-cannon, culverin, and demi-culverin, and when I was farthest off discharging any of the pieces I was not out of shot of their harquebus and most times within speech one of another. And surely every man did well, and as I have said, no doubt the slaughter and hurt they received was great, and time will discover it; and when every man was weary and our cartridges spent and munitions wasted (expended)—I think in some altogether —we ceased and followed the enemy, he bearing hence still in the course as I have said before.*

When the action closed no English ships were much injured and the total loss of life in the whole 10 days was put at 60 only. But the Spanish fleet was in bad plight. Several ships were in worse condition than the *S. Martin.* Among these the *S. Mateo, S. Felipe, S. Marcos,* and *S. Juan*

---

* From Wynter's statement about his expenditure we may gain some idea of the amount of ammunition provided by the English authorities. The fleet left Plymouth with a supply which was almost exhausted by a short action on Sunday and one on Tuesday which lasted most of the day. Wednesday there was a trifling engagement and ammunition was received. Thursday there was fighting which used up that received the day before. No fighting was undertaken until further supplies came Sunday at Calais, after which the big battle on Monday exhausted the magazines. The 500 shot fired by Wynter, in his one engagement, made 32 broadsides in 9 hours. It was nearly all he had and was a heavy day's work. The other fighting included 2 half days and 2 whole days, but not such hard work as the last day. We may take it, then, that the English fleet was scantily fitted out with perhaps 20 rounds when the enemy appeared; was supplied from shore during the week with an additional 30 rounds or more, which was nearly all expended. The Spanish fleet had 50 rounds and the best ships expended all they had. So the rate of consumption was about the same for the two. The English fire was, no doubt, more accurate.

de Sicilia had been most hotly engaged and had suffered most, so that only the *S. Marcos* was able to keep with the fleet. The *S. Juan* may have gone down during the night. She did not get home. The Duke sent boats (patches) to take the crews out of *S. Felipe* and *S. Mateo,* but Don Diego Pimentel in *S. Mateo* would not leave his ship and asked for help to save her. So the Duke risked the *San Martin* by sending her diver to stop the *San Mateo's* leaks, but could not reach her. She drifted out of sight during the night. *S. Felipe* went alongside the hulk *Doncella* to transfer the crew when a cry was raised that the latter was sinking, whereupon the captain and Don Francisco de Toledo, who said he preferred to drown in his own galleon, leaped back on the *S. Felipe* and she too was missing in the morning.

Both vessels drifted towards the coast. *S. Mateo* hailed a fisherman to pilot her to Newport, but when she was between Ostend and Sluys three Dutch men-of-war lying off Flushing came out and she surrendered after a 2-hour fight. "The best sort were saved and the rest were cast overboard and slain at the entry." The banner of the *S. Mateo* was a prized trophy which hung for many years in the great church of Leyden. *S. Felipe* drifted towards Newport where a feeble effort at rescue was made and the camp-master, Don Francisco de Toledo, and others escaped in boats sent from Newport, but some vessels of the Dutch fleet seized the ship and took her into Flushing. Here the captors found much wine on board and as they sat drinking it, the leaks she had incurred in battle overcame her and she sank with 300 of her prize crew.

This final and decisive battle on August 8 cannot be called a severe one by the standards of the eighteenth century. The *San Martin* was continuously engaged for about 9 hours and fired 300 shot (roughly, about one broadside in 43 minutes), receiving in return 107 shots in the hull, masts, and sails. At the close, she was leaking badly from holes below her water line, yet they were stopped by her divers, and she lost only 12 killed and 20 wounded. The whole fleet lost only 600 killed and 800 wounded. Out of about 250 ships present in the 2 fleets, probably not so many as 30 were seriously engaged on the English side and less than 25 Spaniards. (Duro says, vol. 1, p. 99, that not over 40 Spanish ships fired at all). The Spanish morale had been destroyed by their inability to force a boarders' fight on any day during the passage up the Channel. At the same time, the

English policy of long-range battle (at 200 yards or so) was ill-supported by their shortage of ammunition and inaccurate shooting. There were few good gunners in the English fleet and Lord Howard discouraged target practice as is shown by his letter to Walsingham of January 27 in regard to Drake's practice.

THE CHASE

On the morning of Tuesday, August 9, the wind increased so that it was impossible for the Duke to think of returning to the Channel. At daybreak the Capitana Real with several others of the best ships was about a mile away from the pursuing English and the rest of the Spanish fleet was much to leeward and in danger from the shoals. The enemy approached and the group with Medina hove to.

> There were those who told the Duke that he should surrender, but he replied that he would trust in God and His glorious Mother for safety and, if His will was otherwise, he would not disgrace his ancestors, and so he and many others confessed their sins and were ready to die.

When the English came near, they did nothing, and the Spaniards thought it was fear. It looked as if the fleet would be lost on the shoals when the wind hauled and every Spanish ship was able to clear the shoals. By 11 o'clock the Spanish fleet was united, standing northward, and the English followed, keeping beyond range.

The weather was not too rough to prevent assembling a council at which the Duke asked what was to be done. Every moment ships were asking for ammunition, for even the spare supplies on the urcas had gone. Oquendo had been given 80 shot, for he had none, the provisions were scant, and the wind not good to return to the Channel. De Leyva, the second in command, answered that all had seen how he had tried to close with the enemy, that his ship had only 30 shot, and was leaking badly from shot holes, but that he wished to do his duty and did not think that they should go north. Those were not lacking who said that the King's business should be done and that the enemy must be short of ammunition too. It was discussed whether they should winter in Norway or Germany and get supplies, but the Duke held it was not well to winter in hostile country with the enemy fleet near by and the coast of Spain undefended. So it was resolved to go back to Flanders, if the wind would permit;

otherwise, to Spain.* The Duke issued an order cutting the rations very short—only 8 ounces of biscuit, a cuartillo (0.53 quart) of water, and half as much wine without anything else. Many died of hunger and thirst before getting back to Spain. The Duke ordered the King's mules and his own horses to be thrown overboard in order to save water. "We passed many swimming, and it was a great pity, for they came to the ships to see if we would help them." On Tuesday, August 9, Captain Robert Crosse of the *Hope* was offering terms to one of the largest Spaniards when she sank before his eyes. She may have been the *San Juan de Sicilia*, so punished the day before. It is told of her that she refused to surrender, but an officer attempted to haul down her flag. The captain thrust him through with his sword, and the man's brother then killed the captain. In this quarrel the ship sank. The story was told by the 4 or 5 survivors who were picked up by Crosse.

Late on Tuesday the Lord Admiral sent Lord Henry Seymour back to Dover to resume the blockade, fearing that the army of Parma might attempt to cross. Seymour was very indignant at his uncle's order, attributing it to jealousy, but, as the squadron was almost without food, there was nothing else possible. The other squadrons were also short and Sir William Wynter says, "Truly we had much ado with the staying (preventing) of many ships that would have returned with us besides our own company." The English leaders scarcely realized how thoroughly the Armada was worn out. On Monday evening, when all was over, Howard sent an urgent message asking for ammunition and food, adding, "Their force is wonderful great and strong and yet we pluck their feathers, little by little. I pray God the forces on the land be strong enough to answer so present a force." The defeat of the Armada was more in the minds of the men than in the actual damage suffered. They had lost only about 1,800 killed and wounded, in addition to those on the ships which had been taken or sunk. This in itself was not enough to discourage the finest

---

* Duro states (p. 108, vol. 1) that after the fleet left Calais the Duke of Parma sent a confidential messenger to Don Alonzo with a copy of the latest royal instructions, whereby the latter was ordered to do whatever Parma should direct and that accordingly the Duke should winter at the free cities of the Empire and repair there. Thus Parma would have the fleet in the spring to help in the execution of his own plan to pacify the Low Countries before undertaking the "Enterprise of England." But the Duke did not acknowledge the communication in any way except by showing ill-humor to the messenger.

soldiery in Europe, but they were in despair at not being able to make the English fight on their terms. It was useless, as it seemed, to try to grapple the swift and handy English ships. Men were hungry and sickness was growing. The wind stayed in the SW. quadrant. It was this that caused the Duke to attempt no more, but go home by the north of Scotland. So the English fleet (not over 70 strong by Spanish count) followed the Armada, both being out of ammunition, until Friday, August 12, when the fleets were in the latitude of Newcastle.*

As the English fleet was provisioned for only a few days more, Howard resolved to enter the Firth of Forth where he thought a naval demonstration would encourage King James to resist any Spanish landing in his kingdom. At noon two pinnaces were directed to follow and observe the enemy and the English fleet turned west to make the land and run down the coast to the Forth. The next morning the wind came out at NW. and the fleet was obliged to head towards the North Foreland to renew supplies. About August 17 it arrived at various anchorages, Yarmouth, Harwich, and the Downs. From Harwich, Howard wrote to Walsingham:

> Sir, In our last fight with the enemy before Gravelines, the 29th of July, (August 8) we sank three** of their ships and made four go room with the shore so leak as they were not able to live at sea. After that fight, notwithstanding that our powder and shot was well nigh all spent, we set on a brag countenance and gave them chase as though we wanted nothing until we had cleared our own coast and some part of Scotland of them. And then, as well to refresh our ships with victuals of which we stood in wonderful need, as also in respect to our want of shot, we made for the Firth and sent certain pinnaces to dog the fleet until they should be past the Isles of Scotland, which I verily do believe they are left at their sterns ere this.

The English Crippled by Pestilence

The English losses in this remarkable campaign are not formally stated in any official record. No ships were taken or seriously hurt. Captain Thomas Fenner wrote to Walsingham,

> God hath mightily protected her Majesty's forces with the least losses that ever hath been heard of, being within the compass of so great volleys of shot both

---

* Had the Spaniards only realized the British lack of ammunition and turned against the enemy, either they would have been able to make their way back to Flanders upon any change of wind or they would have secured the boarders' fight which they so much desired.

** One sank after the action off Gravelines unknown to the English.

great and small. I verily believe there is not three score lost of all her Majesty's forces.

In the same letter he estimated the Spanish losses at eight of their best ships besides sickness and slaughter, and prophesied they would go home by Scotland and Ireland.

The English fleet got to port only to be struck with pestilence, which, if it had come a few days earlier, might have cost England dearly. On September 1 Howard wrote to the Queen,

> My most gracious Lady, With great grief I must write unto you in what state I find your fleet here. The infection is grown very great and in many ships and now very dangerous; and those that come in fresh are soonest infected. They sicken the one day and die the next. It is a thing that ever followeth such great services and I doubt not but that with good care and God's goodness it will quench again.

On August 20 Howard wrote to Burghley,

> My good Lord, Sickness and mortality begin wonderfully to grow amongst us; and it is a most pitful sight to see, here at Margate, how the men, having no place to receive them, die in the streets. I am driven myself, of force, to come aland to see them bestowed in some lodging, and the best I can get is barns and such outhouses; and the relief is small that I can provide for them here. It would grieve any man's heart to see them that have served so valiantly to die so miserably. The *Elizabeth Jonas,* which has done as well as any ship did in any service, hath had a great infection in her from the beginning [while based on Plymouth]. * * * Now the infection is broken out in greater extremity than ever it did before and the men die and sicken faster than ever they did, so as I am driven of force to send her to Chatham. We all think and judge that the infection remaineth in the pitch.

Besides the infection, the crews, like the Spaniards, were very discontented at lack of pay. On September 1, the same day he told of the infection, Howard wrote to the council,

> My Lords, I must deliver unto your Lordships the great discontentment of the men, which I and the rest do perceive to be amongst them who well hoped after this so good service to have received their whole pay, and finding it to come but scantly unto them it breeds a marvelous discontent among them.

The fleet was so weakened that on September 2 Howard wrote, "Many of our ships are so weakly manned that they have not mariners to weigh their anchors." The fighting crews were almost three times as large as those needed for handling the ships. One would think that they must have lost over 50 per cent. Other ships were no doubt better off. We may put the English loss by pestilence at 3,000 to 6,000. At all events, the fleet was completely incapacitated for perhaps 6 weeks after its return to England.

MILITARY SITUATION IN ENGLAND

It is proper here to mention the perilous state of England if the Armada had not been driven off. It was Parma's instructions to march directly upon London from whichever side of the Thames he made his landing. There were no fortresses on either side of the river to oppose the veteran army of the first general in Europe. The English army enrolled early in 1588 amounted to 100,000 horse and foot, but it had not been mobilized and only half had even slight training. Leicester was the Commander in Chief and was to have a force of 30,000 men to guard London, but at midsummer little of it had appeared. Lord Hunsdon was to protect the Queen's person with 36,000 men, but this force was an imaginary one only. The militia was to be used, but it was quite worthless. The Queen promised to visit Leicester in his camp at Tilbury, 25 miles below London Bridge, and he wrote to express his pleasure.

On August 4, when the fleets were fighting off the Isle of Wight, and invasion was possible within a week, only 4,000 poor troops had been assembled at Tilbury on the main road to London. On August 19, when the Queen made her famous visit to the camp and dined with Leicester to review the army and make a noble and inspiring address, there were not over 10,000 men there. The Queen then knew that the Armada had been driven beyond the Firth of Forth and had good reason to believe that it would not again threaten England. Yet she was angry that no prizes had been made to recoup her expenditures. Only the day before her great speech, she had caused Walsingham to write to Lord Howard about reducing the ships in commission, so that she must have felt that her words smacked somewhat of buncombe, although of the highest class.

Howard still urged caution, although he did not greatly fear the return of the Armada. On August 17, he wrote to Walsingham, then with the Queen, "Good Mr. Secretary, let not her Majesty be too hasty in dissolving her forces by sea and land." And the next day with the same idea, "Sir, sure bind is sure find. A kingdom is a great wager. Sir, you know security is dangerous." Drake was more confident that the Spanish fleet would not be seen again, but he still feared Parma might try to cross, and he too was not in a hurry to see the fleet reduced. It was fortunate for the Kingdom that the wretched assembly at Tilbury was not called on to confront Parma's veterans.

THE ENGLISH THANKSGIVING

The reduction of the fleet had already begun when a report arrived that the Armada was returning through the North Sea to Flanders. This caused Howard some anxiety, yet he hoped to fill up his weak crews with soldiers. Drake gave little credit to the report.

On August 26 Count Justinus of Nassau arrived at Dover with 40 Dutch men-of-war and wrote to Walsingham that the Duke of Parma had disembarked his soldiers, but that he (Nassau) was ready to oppose Parma if the latter should use his flat boats to make an attempt to take Ostend. Information was also received that the Spaniards were north of Scotland on their way home, so the danger of invasion seemed wholly past. Gradually fears ceased and the Queen caused November 29 to be proclaimed a day of national thanksgiving. On this day she went to St. Paul's in great ceremony, riding a white horse, carrying a marshal's baton, and attended by all her principal Officers of State. In the church the captured ensigns were displayed, a solemn service of prayer was offered, and all the public rejoiced.

THE SPANISH VOYAGE HOME

We return to the Armada. The change of wind on August 9, which preserved the Armada from the shoals, made impossible any immediate return to Flanders, so the course was perforce northerly. On August 10, late in the day, the English drew closer to the Spaniards and, as there were few ships in the Spanish rear-guard, the Duke made signal by gunfire for the rest of the fleet to wait for and support the rear. The Duke had given orders to the sergeant-majors to inform him of the captains who behaved badly or were cowardly. On this occasion two vessels, the *Sta. Barbara* and the *S. Pedro*, did not heed the Duke's signal, but ran on a couple of miles and then shortened sail to repair damages received in battle. A patache summoned their captains to appear on board the flagship and, on arrival, they found that they had already been sentenced to death.

Don Francesco Cuellar, captain of the *S. Pedro,* who tells the story, called attention to his valiant service in the past week and demanded to see the Duke. But the latter was in his cabin, overcome with distress, and refused to see any one or transact business. Bobadilla, the Duke's adviser for military affairs, was in complete charge and consented to refer Cuellar to the Auditor General (Judge) Aranda, who was in another ship. After a hearing, the latter sent word to the *S. Martin* that he would not hang Cuellar without a written order and, as this did not come, Cuellar remained under the charge of the Auditor to write a remarkable tale of his adventures in shipwreck and captivity. Avila, the captain of the *Sta. Barbara,* was not so fortunate: he was hung at the yard arm of a patache and his dangling body exhibited through the fleet as a warning against disobedience. A considerable number were named to the Duke for similar offenses and about 20 were condemned to death, but Avila was the only one who suffered the extreme penalty; the rest were deprived of their commands.

After the English abandoned their pursuit, the weather is described by the Spaniards as very bad, but it was not so continuously, for apparently communication from ship to ship by pataches was common and even supplies were transferred on occasion. While still east of Scotland, on August 18, Don Luis de Miranda, a gentleman on the staff of the Duke, wrote that

> We must have lost 2,800 infantry between killed and missing [in the missing ships]. God save those who are left. If this Armada could be strengthened by 50 galleys we might do something. There is no other way of having suitable vessels, for the ships here are superior to anything Spain has. I am well, and that is not a little at this time. I have seen three or four taken off at my side and as many more lost their arms and God be thanked who took us through the strongest and heaviest gunfire that was ever seen or written about. We thought to come rich out of this campaign and we shall have only our shirts, for our baggage has gone overboard.

The fleet passed between the Orkney and the Shetland Islands and lost the *Gran Grifon* on Fair Island at that time. She was the first of the ship wrecks.

The Duke was fortunate enough to capture some Scotch pilots who took him around the Orkneys, which he passed 12 days after leaving Calais. He told the fleet to keep close to the *Royal* and issued a circular letter for the return to Spain, saying that ships would go as far north as 60°–30'* and then keep well to the west before taking a southerly course. The weather turned thick after clearing the Orkneys and the negroes in particular suffered much from cold.

From Marcos de Aramburu, an officer on the Almiranta of Castile, we learn that on August 30 he took the sun in Latitude 58° and also a sounding which tells us that he was on Rockall Bank about 250 miles west of Scotland, but he thought he was 95 leagues west of Ireland. For several days afterward, westerly winds helped by the currents caused his reckoning to fall in error and on September 11 he sighted Ireland, probably the Blaskets Island, when his reckoning showed him to be about 200 miles off. Although Aramburu's ship got home, a similar error, combined with defective outfits, was probably the cause of the loss of many of the others.

In appraising the conduct of the Spanish seamen at this time, we must remember that the ships were considerably injured by gunfire. The masts had been shot through, the shot holes were badly stopped, and the crews were weak with hunger. On September 3 the Duke wrote to the King that he had passed 4 dreadful nights during which he had lost sight of 17 vessels, among which were those of de Leyva and Recalde and that he then had 95 sail and was in 58°, with many sick. Thereafter ships continued to drop away from the main body. Many were never heard of. Others stood north and then south, as the wind shifted, drifting all the time towards the Scotch and Irish coasts until they met disaster. De Leyva, who was prized by the King more than any other in the expedition, kept his *Rata Encoronada* afloat until driven ashore on the coast of County Mayo in Ireland. He transferred himself to the Patrona galleass, which had accompanied him, and, putting to sea again, they hoped to reach Scotland, but she was driven ashore near the Giant's Causeway in the north of Ireland and all but 5 men were lost. Some, like Recalde's group of ships at the Shannon River, landed and supplied themselves with water by force of arms, but many were miserably wrecked.

Cuellar tells of his shipwreck in most graphic terms. His ship with 2 others anchored on the coast of Ireland and remained for 4 days, when the wind so increased that neither could their anchors hold nor the sails

---

* It appears from Vanegas' account that the S. *Martin* reached as high as 62° latitude.

be used. They dragged ashore and the ships were broken on a rocky shore. Only 300 reached shore out of 1,300. Don Diego Enriquez, who had been one of the most gallant in the fighting, went into the closed compartment of his ship's boat with 3 others, and 16,000 scudos in gold and jewels. The hatch was then calked and, as the boat pushed off, 70 more leaped into her. She capsized and drowned all on deck. Thirty-six hours later the natives found the boat on the beach. Enriquez died as he was removed, and the savages plundered the treasure.

On another ship of this group Cuellar was on the poop talking to Aranda, watching the natives plunder and maltreat the survivors as they crawled from the sea. As Cuellar could not swim, he got a hatch cover and jumped overboard with it. Aranda followed and reached the hatch cover also, but in an instant a wave tore him from it. His shirt and drawers were sewn full of gold; the weight was too much for him and he disappeared. Cuellar was finally thrown on the beach and, after many adventures in Ireland and Scotland, he reached Antwerp in October, 1589. His record is still an authority for conditions in Ireland in that century.

After plundering the shipwrecked Spaniards, the native Irish were not ill-disposed to them, but the English rulers had little mercy. Sir Richard Bingham, Governor of Connaught, who had served in the Spanish fleet at Lepanto, wrote to the Lord Deputy of Ireland October 1,

> The 700 Spaniards in Ulster were dispatched, which I know your Lordship heareth before this time. And this I dare assure your Lordship that in 15 or 16 ships cast away on the coast of this province [Connaught] which I can say of my own knowledge to be so many, there hath perished at least a 6,000 or 7,000 men, of which there hath been put to the sword, first and last, by my brother George and in Mayo, Thomond [Clare], and Galway, and executed one way and another about 700 or 800 or upwards, besides those that be yet alive, of which Don Luis de Cordoba is supposed to be the best, for Pedro Mendoza was slain in Clare Island by Dowdaraugh O'Mayle before he would yield in time of the execution. So as now—God be thanked—this province stands clear and rid of all these foreign enemies, save a silly (pitiable) poor prisoners.

Ten days later Bingham reported to Walsingham, "The Spanish losses were three ships in each of Sligo, Mayo, Galway, and Thomond,* and three or four more on the outward islands."

---

* Counties in Connaught. Thomond is now Clare.

In December Bingham wrote directly to the Queen, telling her with much satisfaction of the wrecks in his province and of the slaughter he had done upon the Spaniards who came ashore and added that "Other wrecks they had both in Munster and Ulster, which, being out of my charge, I have not so good notice of." Don Alonzo de Luzon, camp-master of the Neapolitan regiment, was wrecked in Ulster and his soldiers massacred. Under examination he testified,

> They landed by shipwreck as many of them as they could in a broken boat of their own, some swam to shore; the rest were landed in a boat of O'Doherty's country, for the use of which they gave in money and apparel 200 ducats. Touching their entertainment when they came on land, he saith that he and five more of the best of his company landed first only with their rapiers in their hands, where they found four or five savage people—as he termeth them—who bade them welcome and well used them until some twenty more wild men came unto them, after which time they took away a bag of money containing 1,000 reals of plate and a cloak of blue rash, richly laid with gold lace. They were about two days in landing all their men, and being landed, had very ill entertainment, finding no other relief of victual in the country than of certain garrans (horses) which they bought of poor men for their money, which garrans they killed and did eat, and some small quantity of butter that the country people brought also to sell. * * * He * * * saith that before he and the rest of the gentlemen of the company yielded themselves none were slain by the common people. Item, he saith that the killing by the soldiers and the savage people was the same night that he and the rest of the gentlemen had yielded at which he was not, and therefore knoweth not how many were slain.

It is apparent that the English treatment of prisoners was on a par with that of Alva in the Low Countries, both being in accordance with the practice of the time.

While the Armada was making its disastrous round of the British Islands, the King of Spain was getting favorable news of its progress. Ten days after the battle off Gravelines King Philip wrote to Medina,

> A dispatch has come from Rouen that the Armada fought with that of Drake on the 2d and that God gave you victory, having gotten to windward of them, and that you sank 15 ships of the enemy, including the almiranta, and that the rest of them have retired to Dover. In France the news is thought certain and at Havre de Grace there are those who saw it. I hope in God that it is so, and that you have known how to follow up the victory.

Even after the action at Gravelines the rumors of Spanish success were prevalent. On August 13 it was reported in Calais from Harwich that Drake had boarded the *S. Martin* and they had grappled, bringing about a general battle in which Drake and many other ships were taken and many sunk and that 15 vessels got to Harwich very much knocked about. This report was published in Spain as a news bulletin on September 5 with the addition that the Armada was on the way to Scotland.

On September 21 the *S. Martin* arrived off Santander unaccompanied. The Duke fired guns to call out some pilots and when two boats arrived the Duke made an excuse of his wretched health to go at once ashore and most of the cavaliers went also. The *S. Martin* anchored outside the bar and that night she was struck by a violent squall. The anchor dragged and she shipped some hundreds of tons of water. She nearly went on the rocks and cut her cable and got to Laredo, where she found a number of other vessels from Santander.

Oquendo and Recalde got to port a few days after Medina, suffering from exposure and even more from mortification. Of Oquendo, it is said that on reaching the shore he took to his bed and, turning his face to the wall, he refused to speak even to his wife and died in a few days after landing. Recalde lasted very little longer. Ships continued to straggle into port through the month of October.

The condition of the ships as they got in is told by a letter from Father Geronimo de la Torre, serving on board one of them.

> We reached the height (latitude) of 62° where in the middle of summer we found gloomy weather, the strangest clouds, such as we do not know, rains every day, many thick squalls, cold never known since birth, nobody ventured on deck where the pilot was, for all sought shelter; and beside all this, hunger and thirst, for we had only a cuartillo (0.53 quart) of water and half as much wine and half a pound of rotten biscuit. We swam in the water and it rained continually. The ship was leaking and the people perishing with thirst. The squalls were heavy and the sea very rough so that no human being could suffer it. The tempests and the power of the sea were such that scarcely any one said good morning * * * and often, not only I, but every one lost hope of seeing the land. And when we cheered up, the mainmast was about to fall or the ship would roll her yardarm under water. God be thanked for having taken us out of such dangers, for the ship was opening in different places so that it was necessary to gird her with stout cables to keep her together, one near and

one within the poop cabin, one near the mainmast, for with these blows [of the sea] striking us one side and the other the ship was opening.

The day before St. Matthew,* God was pleased to show us land and the rejoicing was so great that men seemed going crazy with delight. That day we could not reach port, for we did not know where we were, although we thought off Corunna, so we were at sea that night and the next day because we could not place ourselves. That day was calm but in the night one of the heaviest storms came up that we had met in the voyage. Others had lasted a half or a third of the night but this was all night long, and with such tremendous wind that although the sails were furled we thought the ship would break up, and neither mariner nor soldier slept during the night. I was dying with fever and dysentery, and captains, cavaliers, and everybody came to my bed, all trembling with fear to confess to me, and so I had no lack of company. On this most dreadful and laborious night several ships lost a mast and ours was in danger of going also.

The next day we heard that the Duke had entered port in a felucca** and that day we saw grapes from the shore and it gave us much pleasure, and we got into Santander and saw bread, fruits, and water in plenty and meat so that it seemed a paradise on earth, and truly the land compared to the sea is a garden and a paradise, for what is more of a desert than the sea where is to be seen neither bread nor fruit, nor meat nor even fish for they are found in harbor? Only the sky and water at sea, with bad days and worse nights, much labor. Well is it called "sea" for it is full of "bitterness" [a Spanish pun on sea and bitterness]. Blessed be God who saved us from it, and I say no more but that I shall go to Madrid when I can travel. I forgot to say * * * that in all more than thirty-five died of shot wounds and many died of sickness during the campaign and almost all arrived sick and injured. I have said nothing of myself. Many confessed each day of battle as I went about with a crucifix and they came running to kiss it with great confidence in victory and they confessed from captains, cavaliers, and ensigns to the poorest soldiers in the ship and every day we said litany to which they came. The soldiers who were disturbed in mind came to the father to have him recommend them to God and if I did not go to them they came to my bedside, many made their wills, and put their affairs in my hands and it seemed to them that having a churchman at hand they would take his advice, and so I think my time well spent and so no more. From Santander September 30, 1588.

The Duke wrote pitiful letters to the King telling of the failure; complaining much of his own bad health and suffering; that he knew

---

* St. Matthew's day is September 21.
** Small lateen-rigged craft.

nothing of the sea or of war, and must go home. He added that he had left Diego Flores de Valdes in charge when he came ashore. He said that *S. Martin* had lost 180 dead of sickness (besides 20 killed in battle) out of 477 in all. Of his own staff, all but two were dead or sick. The ships lacked everything and he had no money to procure necessaries.

The King had received a few days earlier the bad news sent in advance by the Duke on August 21, and replied by a most kind and sympathetic letter to Medina, expressing much solicitude for his health, telling him to appoint a deputy, and giving many particulars of what was to be done for the ships already in port. The Duke was told to send small craft to sea with supplies to give them to approaching ships at the earliest moment. The infantry was to be taken out of the ships and cared for in every way by local officials without making them a nuisance to the local inhabitants. When the troops came ashore for refreshment, guards were to be established to prevent desertion and they were to be told they would be well paid and fed, but desertion would be punished. Hospitals were to be established for the sick and the local bishops would take charge of all medical and religious arrangements falling within their dioceses. But with all these humane directions the King did not fail to send his accountant to take inventory of all equipments and supplies and Medina was told to provide him with assistants. The ships were to be distributed to the greater ports of the Kingdom for easy maintenance. And this having been done, the Duke of Medina-Sidonia was authorized to go home.

Yet, in spite of all the good intentions of the King, from first to last his orders were much neglected. The province of Guipuscoa filed a complaint with the King, of which the principal items were that ship-owners and crews were short paid; that the sailors were dispossessed of their quarters by the soldiers; that when the short rations were ordered the soldiers seized control of them and the sailors suffered distress and loss of life thereby; and that the soldiers took control out of the seamen's hands in time of danger and that ships were lost thereby. All of which shows that in a military force, good order depends on good treatment and steady pay.

In October the King issued a circular to bishops directing them to cease prayers for the success of the Armada and substitute thanks to God that matters were no worse.

Spanish Losses

We may close the account of the campaign with an estimate of losses. Duro states that the total Spanish loss in ships was 63, which he distributes as galleons and ships, 26; hulks, 13; patches, 20; galleasses, 3; galleys, 1. Of these he says that 2 were lost to the enemy, 3 were lost in France, but property was recovered; 2 were lost in Holland; 2 were sunk in battle; 19 went ashore in Scotland and England; and of 35 there was no history. As to the wrecks it seems to be preferable to take the English account. There were 4 wrecked in Scotland, and 1 of the 2 hospital ships after making the round of England and Ireland was lost on the south coast of Devon in November. Besides the 15 or 16 ships lost in Connaught, to which Bingham attests, he says there were others in Ireland, perhaps 5 or 6 more, so that the total number of wrecks may have been 25 or 26 instead of 19, as Duro says, with corresponding reduction in the number which he says foundered at sea.

As for the losses in men, the crews of the ships which did not get home numbered about 13,400 or half the total force. The losses of the other half in killed and dead of famine and exposure can only be guessed at. It was as high as 40 per cent on the Real, and two or three were said to die every day on the other ships, after rounding Scotland. If we rate the deaths from sickness and battle at only 25 per cent on board those ships that got home, only about 11,000 arrived in Spain. Under date of September 27, Don Alonzo reported 7,184 soldiers and 2,948 sailors were on board the ships that had already reached port (Duro, vol. 2, p. 302). To these we must add those who got home from Scotland or were ransomed after being captives in England and Ireland. Three hundred Turkish slaves who escaped from the galleass were returned to the Sultan by the King of France. Parma offered a small ransom and, as a result, the Lord Deputy in Ireland issued a proclamation which brought in a number of Spaniards who had been kept in hiding by the native Irish. All these numbered about 1,300.

Result of the Campaign of 1588

The defeat of the Armada marked the end of the great days of Spain. For the greater part of a century she had imposed herself on the world to an extent unwarranted by her population and resources. She had relied on the bullion from the American mines and, latterly, on the spices from the East. Under the Emperor Charles V she united the greater part of Italy and the wealth of Burgundy with the Empire, but after his death and the outbreak of revolt in the Netherlands, Spain's strength was fictitious. This was hidden at the time and was only slowly understood either by England or Spain, or, indeed, by any part of Europe. When the Armada returned to Spain, the half-ruined towns offered money and the monasteries found treasure to pursue the "enterprise" and obtain revenge on heretic England. Philip alone understood that, for the moment at least, his opportunity had passed. He told his people to be patient and that he would act when the time came. He did not entirely give up hope, nor seek peace, and for years longer the war dragged on to no purpose. Yet it is worth while to glance briefly at its course before closing this chapter, in order to note the strategic errors in its management.

The War After the Destruction of the Armada

The destruction of the Armada restored the initiative to England and for once the Queen was anxious to do something; yet the years of war yet to come proved an anti-climax after the great victory, just as the war after Lepanto was an anti-climax. The Queen wished to send out the fleet immediately. That was impossible, for the ships needed overhaul and the crews were reduced by sickness. She at last realized nothing could be done until spring. In her plans, the Queen was governed by the question of cost to her exchequer rather than by military advantage. Although she had £500,000 to draw upon, she did not wish to spend it. So early in 1589 a public company was organized with the Queen as principal stockholder to undertake a great expedition. Drake was to command the fleet and Sir John Norreys, who was the most distinguished British soldier of the day, was to have the army. The expedition included a number of Dutch ships which Drake met at sea and persuaded to join him at Plymouth where the expedition was mobilizing. The people of the countryside flocked to join and the generals soon had a force alleged to have numbered over 20,000 men, although Hakluyt says there were no more than 11,000 soldiers and 2,500 sailors, with over 125 ships.

Drake's sound strategic plan was to attack Spain in her weakest point by capturing her treasure ships on whose riches Philip's military strength was based. Doubtless his predatory instincts led him in this direction, but it was, none the less, the right road to national victory. But the commission under which the two generals acted made this the secondary objective. Their instructions were to make an attack on the Spanish shipping in port from Lisbon to the French frontier. If, in these efforts, they found the conditions in Portugal were favorable and the Spanish troops not too numerous, they might attempt to put the Portuguese pretender, Don Antonio, on his throne. But if this was not done, they might then go to the Azores to attack the treasure ships.

The generals were thus committed to an unwise course. The remains of the Great Armada were already negligible and the attempt to encourage a revolution in Portugal would bring raw English troops against the re-nowned Spanish veterans. The strength of England was on the sea, as had been shown only the year before, and important operations on shore were contra-indicated. The use of the army to seize a fleet base in the Azores would be, however, eminently proper.

By the Queen's usual parsimony the expedition was in desperate lack of food before starting, and Drake and Norreys told the government that if they could not get a month's supplies, they would be obliged to turn 20,000 men on the countryside, unpaid and unfed. The prospect brought some relief from Elizabeth and, on April 18, the fleet was able to sail with hope of receiving additional stores at some future rendezvous.

As the wind failed it to go to Santander, the fleet reached Corunna on the 24th and landed troops who occupied the lower part of the town. The soldiers got drunk and laid the seeds of later disease, but provisions were obtained and foraging parties secured cattle, so that the ships were supplied and sailed to attack Lisbon, having put the enemy on his guard.

The army was landed at Peniche, 40 miles north of Lisbon, and marched across country, while Drake took the fleet to Cascaes outside the mouth of the Tagus. Here many neutral ships laden with supplies were captured. When the army got to Lisbon the men were sick and no popular movement in favor of the Pretender took place. With little but his own resolution to support him the Governor was able to keep the English out. Drake did not feel able to pass the forts on the sea front and come to the army's aid, and in a few days the latter retired to Cascaes and embarked. It was now the intention to undertake what should have been the only objective, the movement to the Azores, but bad weather came up, the fleet was scattered, and in the end it returned to Plymouth. Only about 6,000 men seem to have got home. The survivors received only their pay and the expedition was held a loss, although it had secured £30,000 in prize money. The generals were called on to answer charges of disobeying instructions, which they seem to have answered successfully, but the Queen had lost money in an aggressive measure such as she had never before undertaken, and she reverted to less enterprising projects. Yet at the time, and after thorough discussion, the historian Camden wrote England was so far a gainer by this expedition as from that time to apprehend no incursions from Spain. The campaign failed because it was wrongly directed against the mainland of the peninsula instead of against the islands and the flotas.

The political situation in all Europe was changed this year of 1589 by the death of King Henry III of France and the succession of Henry of Navarre. King Philip now extended the warlike enterprises to which he was already unequal by promoting civil war in France with the object of unseating the Protestant Henry IV and adding France to the Spanish dominions. He sent an army into Northern France under the Duke of Parma to aid the French Catholic League and with the same object seized a naval base in Brittany, at Blavet (now L'Orient). Now was the chance for Queen Elizabeth to press King Philip, but she saw her opportunity in quite another way. She thought it was the time to use a small force of ships to hamper Parma's efforts to aid the Catholic League, while working against the Spanish communications with the Indies. But neither King Philip nor Queen Elizabeth spent enough money to obtain success. The King did not have it and the Queen would not part with what she had. For several years the English fleet undertook only minor operations; the flotas crossed the ocean in safety and Philip did not become entirely bankrupt. He took advantage of the moneys the flotas brought him to build 100 ships of 48,000 tons with 981 guns to replace the losses of 1588.

It was not until 1594 that reports of the growth of the Spanish fleet caused Queen Elizabeth any serious alarm. Really, King Philip was thinking more of defending the coasts of Spain and the traffic with the Indies than he was of invading England, but the Queen failed to realize that Spain was decadent and England growing. So, fearing Spain once more, the Queen recalled Drake to service and, in August, 1595, he and his cousin, John Hawkins, sailed on their last cruise to attack in America the sources of the Spanish revenues. But, as before, the Queen wanted them to undertake secondary affairs. She wished the expedition to see that Ireland was safe from invasion, and then to cruise for a month to intercept the flotas before crossing to America. The two admirals quarreled and missed a rich flota of 30 vessels, which got to Seville a few hours before the English arrived off the port. Then they went to Puerto Rico where it was known there was treasure, but they stopped at the Canaries where an unsuccessful raid betrayed their purpose and news was sent to America of their coming. Hawkins died as they sighted Puerto Rico. The attack there failed and later Drake died off the Isthmus of Panama. By great exertions Philip got a squadron out to the Caribbean which met the English, but the action which followed was a drawn one and the English squadron returned home in May, 1596, much reduced in numbers and as a failure, while about the same date the flota arrived at Seville with 20,000,000 ducats ($45,480,000).

The dread of an invasion continued to disturb the Queen, for in April, 1596, the Spaniards captured Calais and held it with 5,000 men. To forestall action against England, she fitted out a great expedition under Lord Howard of Effingham, Lord High Admiral, and the Earl of Essex, which had orders to "burn the King's ships and magazines of victuals so that he cannot go to Ireland."

The expedition sailed in June, 1596, with 11 Queen's ships, 12 London merchantmen, and 18 Dutch men-of-war with 70 transports and 7,000 soldiers. The secret had been well kept and the English appearance at Cadiz was a surprise. The fortifications were out of repair, the harbor was full of ships whose principal commanders were absent. The English entered with little difficulty and most of the Spanish vessels were destroyed, either by the English or by their owners to prevent their capture. The troops were then landed and the city occupied after offering very slight resistance. After 15 days' occupation, Cadiz was sacked and burned and the English fleet put to sea. The amount of booty was placed by the Spaniards at 20 to 22 million ducats ($45 to 50 million).* The Spanish

---

* This sum seems incredibly large.

loss was absolute, but the English gain was much less, for the loot was never properly appraised. The generals quarreled and, although the expedition was a success, the English people did not realize it; nor did it please the Queen, for it brought her little money. Neither did it serve to check the Spanish expedition to invade Ireland, because that was preparing in the northern ports.

This first great effort of Spain since 1588 sailed from Corunna on October 23, 1596, with 98 ships and 16,000 men. The vessels were unseaworthy and ill-supplied and were immediately scattered by a gale, in which many were lost with their crews, and they returned to port without seeing Ireland. In 1597 another expedition was a similar failure. In 1598 King Philip II died and his successor, Philip III, might have made peace, had not Ireland revolted and he felt encouraged to make another effort. So in 1599 another fleet was collected in Lisbon numbering over 100 ships.

England was much alarmed, but, as usual, the Spanish vessels were unseaworthy, the food was bad, and plague and famine prevailed throughout Spain. The fleet made no attempt to reach Ireland, but merely went to the Azores to escort the treasure ships and lost one-quarter of its strength in its task. At last, late in 1601, the Spaniards landed a force of 3,000 soldiers at Kinsale in Ireland, but early in 1602 both the Spaniards and the Irish rebels were totally defeated in battle and Spain could do no more. At the end of 1602 Olivares, the new King's minister, proposed peace. A few weeks later King James VI of Scotland succeeded Queen Elizabeth on the throne of England and peace was not difficult to arrange, for James had always wished to be on good terms with Spain. In August, 1604, peace was signed, the King yielding much that Elizabeth had prized. English aid to the Dutch was to cease, no English ships were to trade with the Indies, and Englishmen who offended the Inquisition on Spanish soil were liable to seizure. Neither English seamen who had profited by the war against shipping nor Spanish churchmen were pleased by the treaty.

SUMMARY OF TACTICS OF 1588

The tactical development of this war was the substitution of great-gun fire for hand-to-hand fighting of boarders as the chief effort. Eventually this entailed the substitution of the column for the frontal line of galleys, but nothing of this change appears in any of the combats in the Channel in 1588. So far as can be seen, the English leaders realized the frontal line was not suitable for their ships, but they had nothing to replace it, and so the English observed no formation at all. The bravest captains followed the principal leaders into action and, as Sir William Wynter suggests, the less enterprising ones lagged on the edge of battle. The method of fighting of the English ships seems to have been to run down on the Spaniards, firing the bow guns when at convenient range, then coming by the wind to discharge the broadside guns and, later, wearing to discharge the other broadside when the movement of the enemy rendered that advisable. Although Wynter says he fired faster, I do not believe the rate of fire was over two broadsides an hour on the average, although the interval between any two may sometimes have been only a few minutes.

The Spaniards had more respect for conventional formation than the English, but practically neither did they maintain any. They had not much considered the development of gunfire as the chief thing, for it was their expectation to maintain the usual line and let the English attack in the customary way. So when the speedy and weatherly English ships ignored the general line to attack only the weathermost Spaniards, the medieval idea of gaining personal distinction in battle caused the principal Spanish leaders to break their formation and seek to cover the Duke or draw the enemy to themselves and show their own gallantry. The result was a series of group fights, in which the English came off with advantage because their ships were faster and more handy, and the individual ships' batteries were heavier and better handled. So they baffled every attempt of the enemy to board.

Nevertheless, the English gunfire did not accomplish a great deal. One ship only, the *Sta. Ana,* was seriously injured by hostile gunfire before reaching Calais. After leaving Calais, gunfire obliged *S. Felipe* and *S. Mateo* to leave the fleet and apparently two others were sunk at that time. The defeat of the Spaniards was primarily owing to their wretched equipment and to the fact they were not fast enough to catch the English ships and make them fight Spanish fashion. Consequently the soldiers lost heart when foiled by the superior speed of their enemy. What the Spaniards called "English cowardice" ruined Spanish morale. Only the most distinguished leaders brought their vessels into action while the rest sheltered behind them. The entire neglect of tactical formation on both sides caused the fighting to be done only by the principal leaders and a few of their best followers, while the others lagged in rear. It was not until two generations or more that naval men learned how to oblige all ships to take their share in a broadside gun fight by adhering to a column formation suitable for developing the whole power of the fleet, and in which no one could fail to be at his post without discredit.

As for the strategy of the campaign of 1588, Parma, like Napoleon two centuries later, could not cross till his fleet had cleared the sea and this was a task beyond its powers. Had Parma got across in face of the Dutch fleet and Seymour's squadron, the English army would have been found very inferior.

The strategy of the whole war was poor on both sides. They were not spending enough money to accomplish anything great. Queen Elizabeth should have struck at the flotas with a sufficient force every year, and the Spaniards fitted out such worthless fleets that they accomplished nothing, yet war continued because neither pressed the other beyond endurance, and English business on the seas was thriving.

PRINCIPAL AUTHORITIES CONSULTED FOR THIS CHAPTER

CORBETT, SIR JULIAN S., *Drake and the Tudor Navy*.

CORBETT, SIR JULIAN S., Editor, *War of 1585-87* (Navy Records Society).

DURO, CESAREO FERNANDEZ, *La Armada Española*.

DURO, CESAREO FERNANDEZ, *La Armada Invencible*.

LAUGHTON, J. K., Editor, *State Papers relating to the defeat of the Spanish Armada* (Navy Records Society).

LAUGHTON, J. K., *Cambridge Modern History*, vol. 3, chap. 9.

OMAN, CHARLES, *History of the Art of War in the Middle Ages*.

OPPENHEIM, M., *Administration of the Royal Navy*, 1509-1660.

PIGAFETTA, FILIPPO, *Discorso sopra l'Ordinanza dell' Armata Catolica*.

UBALDINO, PETRUCCIO, *Commentario dell' Impresa fatta contra il Regno d'Inghilterra*.

WILTON, WILLIAM F., *Die Katastrophe der Spanischen Armada*.

APPENDIX TO CHAPTER X

At Lepanto the issue turned chiefly on archery against hackbuts (or arquebuses), although personal weapons (short arms), swords, pikes, etc., also played a considerable part. Yet only 17 years later, in the Anglo-Spanish war, heavy artillery was the only important weapon. There was no boarding nor any hand-to-hand fighting. By the end of Queen Elizabeth's reign the long-bow was no longer the English national weapon, and thereafter firearms were dominant in naval warfare. This great change in weapons in these few years makes it opportune here to trace briefly the development of firearms.

GREAT GUNS

Great guns became practical weapons, chiefly for siege work, much sooner than portable small arms. The first gun of which we have any record appears in a drawing of about 1325 (reproduced in *Encyclopedia Britannica,* "Ordnance," edition of 1929). The weapon has the shape of a soda-water bottle and is about 3½ feet long. A man is shown applying a match by hand to the rear of the bore, from the muzzle of which is issuing an iron-feathered bolt (or quarrel) about a yard long. The instrument is mounted on an ordinary table. Records of a few years later show that the powder charge for these primitive guns was an ounce or less. Considering the impure materials and their imperfect mixture, it is doubtful if they gave an initial velocity of as much as 400 foot-seconds to the quarrel. The blow of the projectile was probably less than that of the larger sizes of mechanical artillery; yet the higher velocity gave the firearm a greater range, in which was its advantage.

Guns soon began to use iron or lead balls instead of arrow-like bolts. As guns grew in size they were made of iron or of cast bronze.

GUN MOUNTINGS

As guns were at first used chiefly for siege work, they had no carriages, being dragged on sledges to the point of service, where they were placed on mounds of earth and wedged and levered until properly pointed.

FIG. 48.—BOMBARD ON SHIP'S DECK MOUNT

Small mortars or bombards were early used in the Navy. A bombard of 6¼-inch caliber would take a stone ball of 10 pounds weight. The one shown is in the Metropolitan Museum and is on a non-recoil mount suitable for ship-board use on the upper deck. The bore is a flaring one and only 7 inches deep. Allowing for poor quality of powder and excessive windage, it is not probable that this bombard developed an initial velocity of as much as 400 foot-seconds. Courtesy of Metropolitan Museum of Art.

As guns grew larger, stone shot began to replace iron balls, as the latter were very expensive.

Before the end of the fourteenth century field guns mounted on carts came into use. Naturally they were small to travel over the wretched roads. The early type of field gun was soon adopted for use on board ship, being mounted on the deck in a non-recoil mount (Fig. 48.) Then larger guns were mounted on the upper deck, under the forecastle to fire directly ahead. They were securely fastened to heavy timbers which recoiled with them, between 2 guide pieces bolted to the deck. The use of the helm was necessary to point these guns, which fired point blank, the earliest having no means of elevation (see Fig. 50). A later type had trunnions. As long as the heavy guns were mounted in this way the battle tactics of ships and fleets retained much resemblance to that of armies, for the opponents had to head at each other to get into action.

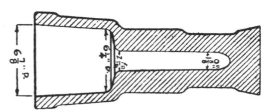

FIG. 49.—DRAWING OF A BOMBARD
IN THE METROPOLITAN MUSEUM, NEW YORK
Courtesy of the Museum

After guns began to be placed on board sailing ships, it was soon found practicable to mount them in broadside on the upper deck by cutting ports through the light bulwarks which entailed no sacrifice of structural strength of the ship. Soon after the beginning of the sixteenth century shipbuilders first cut ports through the sides below the upper deck. Thereafter the number of decks bearing guns slowly increased until at the end of the sailing ship period there were 3 covered gun decks on a few ships of the largest size. The U.S.S. *Pennsylvania* was one of these with 120 guns. For stability, the heaviest guns were always on the lowest deck. With guns between decks, the importance of sailing ships grew and they proved dominant in the Anglo-Spanish war. The mounts for broadside guns at first had 2 wheels in front and a trail at the rear, as shown in the Italian drawing reproduced in Fig. 50. Later a 4-wheel carriage lasted with little change till the middle of the nineteenth century when the weight and power of muzzle-loading guns notably increased. An early type of 4-wheel

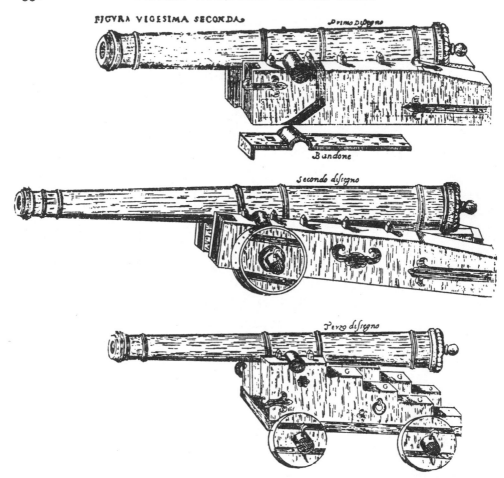

FIG. 50.—UPPER GUN—CANNON TYPE. MIDDLE AND LOWER GUNS—CULVERIN TYPE.
From *L'Artiglieria* of Pietro Sardi, printed in 1689. Showing 3 types of mounts. (1) Corsia type, pointed by the helm and with little or no elevation. (2) Carriage with 2 wheels and capable of pointing without use of helm. (3) Carriage with 4 wheels capable of pointing and elevation. This type lasted from sixteenth to eighteenth century.

mount is shown in Fig. 50 with steps at *G* which supported quions for holding the gun at various elevations.

TYPES OF GUNS

At the time of the Armada guns were divided into three classes according to length and weight in proportion to their caliber. The culverin type,

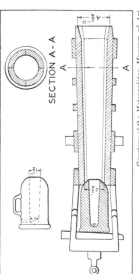

Courtesy of the Metropolitan Museum of Art

SECTION A - A

FIG. 51.—BREECH-LOADER ON SWIVEL RAIL MOUNT WITH SECTIONAL DRAWING

A type of breech-loading gun much used on ship board in the sixteenth century. It is a built-up gun of 4 longitudinal bars bent into quadrants to form the body of the gun and these are held together by shrunk-on hoops. The powder chamber is detachable, as shown in the diagram. Usually 2 or more chambers were provided for each gun. The flare of the bore permits a variation of some degrees in the course of the projectile while still within the bore. The gun weighs 140 pounds and fires a ¾-pound stone ball. The chamber holds a scant 4 ounces of powder. Owing to the great windage, it is scarcely probable that the initial velocity was as high as 800 foot-seconds. By Courtesy of Metropolitan Museum of Art, New York.

giving high velocity to the projectile, was over 30 calibers long with walls thicker than the diameter of the bore, and weighed 250 to 280 times its projectile. The powder charge was ¾ the weight of the iron shot. The initial velocity of the shot must have approached 1,900 foot-seconds. The point-blank range was about 400 paces (666 yards) and the extreme range about 2,500 paces (4,166 yards). The principal sizes of this type of gun were the culverin proper, of 17 to 18 pounds weight of shot; the demi-culverin of 9 pounds; and the saker of 5 to 6 pounds.

Cannon type.—The cannon was a shorter gun, nearly as stout in its walls, weighing 130 to 160 times its iron shot. There were a few 60-pdr. guns of cannon type, but the largest size in general use on shipboard was the 30-pdr., demi-cannon of 6.3-inch bore and 18 to 20 calibers long, firing a 6-inch shot. The initial velocity of cannon shot was probably nearly 1,700 foot-seconds and the point-blank range of the 30-pdr. 340 paces (566 yards) and extreme range 1,700 paces (2,833 yards).

Periers.—As their name indicates, periers threw stone projectiles of about ⅓ weight of the same size of iron shot and used small charges. They were light and short, weighing only 60 to 80 times as much as their stone shot, and only 8 or 9 calibers long. Their shot had low velocity, probably scarcely reaching 1,100 foot-seconds, and with proportionately short ranges.

NOTE: The common naval term "gun-shot-range" meant a distance of about 400 yards, beyond which precision of aim was wanting and the striking power reduced.

BREECH-LOADERS

Breech-loaders were early introduced. The powder was placed in a separate container, known as the "chamber" (see Fig. 51). There were two or three chambers for each gun, which were used in succession for quick firing. After each discharge the chamber was washed out and sent below for refilling. To the rear of each gun barrel was welded a holder for the chamber projecting to the rear, and shaped something like a stirrup. A bar under the stirrup prevented the chamber from falling through (see Fig. 51). In loading, a wad was first placed in the bore; the shot followed; and then the chamber, already filled, was placed in the stirrup, with its tapering front end thrust into the breech. Lastly, the butt of the chamber was wedged fast and the piece was ready to fire. There

were many accidents, for the chamber was not securely locked. All types
of guns were usually fired by a slow-match.*

The vent was first filled with quick-burning power (priming) and some of
it was left in the little pan shaped around the vent. When ready to fire
the gunner applied his slow-match.

GUNPOWDER

Gunpowder is made of saltpeter (nitrate of potash), charcoal, and
sulphur in varying proportions. In the sixteenth century a not unusual
blend was saltpeter one-half, charcoal one-third, and sulphur one-sixth.
Later the proportion of the first was greater. Originally the mixture was
made when the ingredients were dry and usually very impure. Sometimes
they were not mixed until just before use. Consequently, the variation in
effectiveness was great. Besides, the shape and weight of the projectiles
of nominally the same size varied; the allowance for windage was not
regular and many of the early guns flared towards their muzzles so that
there was excessive leakage of gas as the shot moved forward. The powder
was much affected by poor storage and consequent dampness. So inac-
curacy in aim was great, and the force of discharge was variable.

Although the work obtainable from a given weight of gunpowder may
now be closely estimated, we know little of the effectiveness of powder
before the middle of the eighteenth century and can only say that it may
perhaps have been one-quarter to one-half that of good powder of a century ago, with a further reduction for excessive windage and the flare of
the bore.** In the fifteenth century powder was improved by mixing it in a
moist condition and this conduced to safety in manufacture. The dry-mixed
powder was known as "serpentine" and was about 6/7 as strong as the
wet-mixed, called "corned" powder from the shape of its grains.

Saltpeter was very expensive at first and in the fourteenth century cost
18 pence a pound, or as much as three days' wages for a good mechanic.

---

* The slow-match was a loosely twisted cord, soaked in a solution of saltpeter and
quick lime, with some ashes. The cord was then dried and after ignition it smouldered slowly
like a cigar and was available for kindling. The slow-match cord was conveniently carried
by a wooden holder known as a "linstock." When the writer first entered the Navy, there were
some gunners who still preferred to fire their salutes using a match, instead of the quill per-
cussion-primer.

** In the eighteenth century in a 30-pdr. cannon 18 calibers long, 10 pounds of
corned powder would give about 39 foot-tons per pound.

It was a product of slow spontaneous growth in manure piles, on the walls and in the earth floors of cellars and caves. Governments took rigorous measures to obtain it. At the beginning of the first Anglo-Dutch war the British Commonwealth licensed certain persons to send their deputies into private houses to tear up floors over cellars (subject to replacement at government expense) to gather the saltpeter which might be found there. The collected earth and scrapings were washed to extract the nitrate and the liquor was then concentrated by boiling as in salt-making.

SMALL ARMS

Practical small arms developed slower than great guns. Already in the fourteenth century small gun barrels began to be attached to pike handles for use by infantry. As Oman says in his *History of the Art of War*, these little guns were only toy cannon, lit by slow-match in the same way as artillery. Towards the end of the fifteenth century a small arm was adopted, still without firing mechanism of any kind, which was so heavy that it had a crew of two men, one to hold it and point while the other applied the match. But this did not prove serviceable.

The hackbut.—Early in the sixteenth century the hackbut, or arquebus, came into general use. It was the first practical portable gun. By reduction in the weight of the piece and the addition of a firing mechanism to carry and apply the match, it became possible for one man to transport and use his weapon. The iron barrel of the hackbut was mounted on a wooden stock for convenience in handling. The powder was poured into the muzzle by hand; a wad followed and then the ball was rammed into place. At the rear of the bore there was a horizontal vent hole at right angles to the line of sight, under which was a small pan, with a lid, which held the priming powder to ignite the main charge. A burning slow-match was fastened to the head of a hammer or cock pivoted to the stock, and able to reach the pan. The hammer, with its match, was raised to firing position against the tension of a spring and remained in readiness subject to release by a trigger. To discharge his piece the hackbuteer first uncovered the pan to expose the priming, then adjusted the match and blew on it to freshen the spark. Not until then did he point his gun and pull the trigger, releasing the hammer which pressed the match into the priming and so discharged the weapon.

It was an unsatisfactory method of firing for the match was often put out by rain and dampness spoiled the priming. The time needed for reloading was so great that it is apparent why at short ranges archery was so long preferable to the gun.*

Yet to this day the match-lock is not entirely out of use in Central Asia.

Rifled small arms using spherical bullets came into use about the same time as match-locks and, being superior in accuracy and hitting power, they were in continuous, although restricted, use until breech-loaders displaced muzzle-loaders about the middle of the nineteenth century. So much time and labor were needed to force home the tight fitting bullets that smooth-bores were preferable for general service by infantry.

The wheel-lock.—Before the middle of the sixteenth century the wheel-lock was supplanting the match-lock. The new device did away with the match and generated fire anew for each discharge. In contact with the pan containing the priming powder was a serrated steel wheel which was rotated by a strong clock-spring. The latter was wound up before firing and held in tension by a trigger. Instead of a match the hammer of the gun carried a piece of hard iron pyrites (later a flint-stone) and when ready to fire the hammer was eased down on the wheel, against which it was pressed by a spring of its own. When the trigger was pulled the wheel revolved and struck sparks from the flint. These fell into the priming and discharged the gun.

The flint-lock.—Going a little beyond the period covered by this book, it may be said that about 1630 the wheel-lock gave way to the flint-lock, which remained the service weapon of armies for over two centuries. In this mechanism the hammer and its flint were unchanged. To the lid, or cover, of the priming-pan was added a serrated steel wing which took the place of the wheel in the wheel-lock. This wing on the lid was set in such a position and at such an angle with regard to the path of the descending flint that when the latter struck the wing it was thrown back and uncovered the pan at the same time that a shower of sparks fell into the pan. Arrangements were made to hasten loading. The vent hole was pierced at such an angle that when loading the main charge a part of it worked through into the priming pan and thus obviated priming as a separate operation.

---

* In his *Memoirs,* Baron Marbot states that so late as at Leipzig in 1813, 20,000 mounted archers formed part of the Russian army and he was himself wounded by an arrow.

The powder was measured off in paper cartridges, pre-attached to each bullet. When ready to load the soldier merely tore the cartridge and poured the proper amount of powder into the muzzle. Pointing was very inexact.

By the middle of the eighteenth century the small arm had acquired an extreme range of not over half a mile, but in practice it was little used at over 200 yards and not markedly effective at more than 100 yards. In the sixteenth century ranges were not so great. In navies the term "musket-range" meant under about 180 yards. The bore was about ¾ inch and the weight of a lead bullet 1.4 ounces. The size was not invariable, some guns were smaller. As for rapidity of fire from flint-locks, by continual drill Frederick the Great made his army capable of firing 5 shots per man per minute, far faster than any other service. On shipboard, however, such fast firing was never attained.

At Lepanto the principal weapon of the Christians was the arquebus to which the victory was chiefly due. In the Armada campaign the Spaniards hoped again to make it the instrument of victory, for they had many more soldiers. But the faster English ships would not permit the Spaniards to close within small-arm range. This campaign taught navies that the great gun was thereafter to be the principal weapon of ships, while small arms became no more than an important auxiliary weapon.

INDEX

Aarhus, Battle of, 80

Abantus, General of Licinius, His naval battle, 6

Administration, Naval, 113

Adrianople, Battle of, 5

Alexander the Great, 31

Alexandria, Imperial dockyard at, 33; Dockyard developed by Saraceus, 35

Alexius, Son of Byzantine Emperor Isaac, asks Crusaders to Constantinople, 119; Killed, 125

Alexius, Byzantine Emperor, 119; Threatens French camp, 123; Flees from city, 124

Alfred, King of England, develops a navy, 72

Alghero, Tactics of sailing ships at battle off, 141

Ali Pasha, Second in command Turkish fleet, 151; Made Turkish C-in-C, 166; Has 250 ships, 166; Movements of fleet, 171; Avoids attack on Spanish possession, 171; Scouts to find enemy, 172; Harries Corfu, 172; Sultan orders destruction of Christian fleet, 172; Christian opinion of his fleet, 176; Misinformation as to hostile fleet, 186; Strength of his fleet, 186; His early life, 186; Council before battle, 187; Sultan's orders, 189; Decision to seek enemy, 190; Fires opening shot, 193; Preparations for battle, 194; Address to his crew, 194; Commands center squadron, 195; His sons in battle, 195; Passes between galleasses, 195; Attacks Don John, 201; Personal share in battle, 202; His death, 203

Alliance, The Christian, 1571; Formation of, 167; Its terms, 168

Alphonso, King of Aragon, succeeds Peter as King, 139

Alva, Duke of, Governor of Netherlands, 243; Suppresses rebellion in Belgium, 243

Amalfi, Commerce with East, 47; Takes part in First Crusade, 54

Amru conquers Egypt, 33

Ancona, Siege and blockade of, 18

Andrada, Gil d', Returns from scouting expedition, 179, 183; Takes Spanish squadron to Corfu, 218; At battle off Cerigo, 221; Defies Don John, 222

Anglo-French War, 1213-17, 89; Invasion of England, 91

Anjou, Duke of, His death alters European policies, 246

Antonina, wife of Belisarius, 10; Provides drinking water, 11; Brings up infantry, 13; At siege of Portus, 17; Goes to Constantinople, 18

Antonio, Don, Claimant to throne of Portugal, 245; English effort in his favor, 330

Aragon, Navy of, 133; King of France attacks Aragon, 135

Aramburu, Marcos de, on board Almiranta of Castile, Position of ship August 30, 1588, 322; Sights Ireland, 322

Aranda, Spanish Auditor General, Will not hang Cuellar, 321; Drowns, 323

Arceo, Secretary to Medina; reports Parma unready, 307

Archelaus, General under Belisarius, Offers plan to attack Carthage, 12; Cannot control seamen, 13

Ark Royal, Lord Howard's flagship, 294

Armament, English, 289; Classes of guns, 290

Army, English, untrained, 280; Dispositions of, 319

Arquebus becomes serviceable in 16th century, 143; Christians armed with, 187

Artillery, Mechanical, in galleys, 112

Assentista, Definition of, 154

Astrid, mother of Olaf Tryggevesson, 77

Athenian fleet, Organization of, 59

Aubigny, Philippe d', at Battle of Dover, 93

Avila, Spanish Captain of *Sta. Barbara*, hanged summarily, 321

Babington conspiracy, 252

Barbarigo, Agustino, Venetian Proveditore, Commands allied left wing, 177; Reconciles Don John and Veniero, 183; Repre-

345

sents Veniero in Council, 183; Management of left wing, 199; Death of, 201

Barbaro, Venetian Ambassador to Turkey, held as prisoner, 151

Barbavera, Commanding galleys at Sluys, 98

Barcelona, Naval dockyard at, 133

Basiliscus, Roman Emperor, opposes Gaiserio and is defeated, 8

Bayeux Tapestry, 88

Bazan, Don Alvaro de, Marquis of Santa Cruz, Commands reserve at Lepanto, 177; Soothes quarrel of Don John and Veniero, 183; Not at hand for battle, 192; Reserve squadron in battle, 198; Sends men to Don John, 202; Saves Capitana of Malta, 207; Makes sole prize in 1572, 226; Defeats French adventurers in the Azores, 245; Urges conquest of England, 246; Submits plan for same, 246; Details of same, 250; King directs him to form fleet at Lisbon, 251; Lacks men to pursue Drake, 256; King wishes him to go to England, 260; Death, 262

Behuchet, French Admiral at Sluys, 99; Wounds King Edward, 101

Belisarius, Roman General, Commander in chief Vandalic War, 10; His army and fleet, 10; Seeks information at Syracuse, 12; Takes Carthage, 13; Holds triumph, 14; Commands in Gothic War, 15; Not well supported by Emperor, 16; Engagement at Portus, 16; Reoccupies Rome, 18; Recalled to Constantinople, 18

Bertendona, Martin de, Commands Levantisca Squadron, 268; Refuses to attack any but *Ark Royal*, 300

Bessas, Belisarius' General at Rome, 16; Escapes from Rome, 17

Bingham, Sir Richard, Governor of Connaught, Tells of execution of 700 Spaniards, 323; Reports ships lost in Ireland, 323

Blachernae, Imperial Palace at Constantinople, 122, 128

Black Book, British, navy regulations, 105

Blanche of Castile, sends aid to Prince Louis, 93

Bobadilla, Francisco de, Camp-master general, 268; Acts for Medina, 321

Bohemund, Prince of Antioch, Commands fleet of Robert Guiscard, 48; Commands

army in Illyria, 50; Becomes Prince of Antioch, 55; Gives trade privileges to Genoa, 55; Attacks the Empire, 57

Bonaparte, Napoleon, His flotilla in 1803, 27

Boniface, Count, Governor of Africa, 7

Borough, Sir William, Vice Admiral to Drake, 257; Disagrees with Drake, 258

Bosphorus, Naval battle in, 6

Bow, Turkish, At Lepanto, 187

Bragadino, Governor of Famagosta, is killed after surrender, 171

Brill, Dutch town, Seizure of, 244

Burghley, William Cecil Lord, Secretary to Queen, Heads peace party, 245; Correspondence with Borough, 258; Letter from Drake, 258; Letter from Howard, 318

Busta Gallorum, Battle at, 21; Tactics there and at Sena Gallica compared, 22

Byzantine Empire, Commerce of, in 7th century, 30; War with Saracens, 33; Greatly develops Navy, 35; Its defense of Western Europe, 40; Trade and commerce, 40; Division of, by Crusaders, 127; Reestablishment of, 128

Byzantium, 5; Name changed to Constantinople, 6

Caetani, Honorato, Commands Papal infantry, 169; Reports results of fleet inspection, 182; Experience in the battle, 209; Saves Papal ship, 210

Calais, British Navy at siege of, 96

Callinicus, inventor of Greek Fire, 36; As to his use of saltpeter, 44

Calonymus, Admiral under Belisarius, 10; Pillages Carthage, dies insane, 14

Canale, Antonio da, member of Venetian Counsel, 160

Canterbury, Archbishop of, Chancellor of England, protests against campaign of Sluys, 97

Canute, King of Denmark and England, 76; His great ship, 73, 76; His fleet in 1026, 76

Carabink, Bey of Caramania, Turkish Admiral, 187; Opposes battle, 188

Caracoggia, Turkish corsair, Visits Christian fleet, 184; Acquires false news, 186

Caramusciale type of ship, description, 151

Caravans of shipping, Annual, 109

Cardona, Don Juan de, Commands advance

guard, 177; Absence when enemy is seen, 185; Self and ship badly injured, 207

Carleill, Christopher, commands infantry under Drake, 248

Carlos, de la Cerda, commands Spanish squadron at Winchelsea, 103

Carrara, Lord of Padua, 148

Cartagena (South America) captured by Drake, 248

Carthage, Taken by Vandals, 7; Taken by Belisarius, 14; Taken by Mohammedans, 37

Castile, Kingdom of, War against England, 103

Celsi, Giacomo, member of Venetian Counsel, 160

Cervantes de Saavedra, Miguel, 147; Account of death of Mamut, 226

Chalcedon, Crusaders land at, 120

Chandos, Sir John, at battle of Winchelsea, 103

Charles, Count of Anjou, becomes King of Two Sicilies, 133

Charles II, King of Naples, peace with Aragon, 139

Charles V. Emperor of Germany, Expeditions to Africa, 148; Treachery towards Venice, 149; Policy towards France, 240; Income from Netherlands, 243

Chaves, Alonzo de, Treatise on naval tactics, 143

Chioggia, War of, 148

Cinque Ports furnished ships to Kings, 89

Clearing ship for action, 144; At Lepanto, 191

Cogs (cocche), type of ship, 113; Against galleys, 141

Colonna, Marc Antonio, Duke of Tagliacozzo and Paliano, Papal C-in-C, 154; His squadron, 155; Joins allies at Candia, 159; Letter from King Philip, 160; Quarrels with Doria, 164; Loses his squadron, 165; Lieutenant-General of the League, 168; Station in center of fleet, 177; Pope orders him to fight, 181; Preserves peace between Veniero and Don John, 183; Receives report on the enemy, 191; Runs along the battle line, 192; Overcomes his opponent, 202; Again makes peace between Veniero and Don John, 213; Sails for Messina, 213; Commands Papal fleet in 1572, 216; Sails for Corfu, 218; Takes

allied force to Cerigo, 219; Maneuvers off Cerigo, 220; Refuses to fight without nefs, 221; Action off Cape Matapan, 221; Change in plan of battle, 221; Fears to punish captains, 221; Convinced nefs and galleys cannot work together, 222; Joins Don John, 222; Proposes land attack on Modon, 225; Reconciles Don John and Foscarini, 227; Comments on his tactics, 228

Commerce, Maritime, in Mediterranean in 13th century, 109

Commerce of Venice, 115

Comnena, Anna, historian, On Greek Fire, 42; On her father's wars, 46

Comnenus, Alexius, Byzantine Emperor, Hostilities with Robert Guiscard, 47; Fights Pisan fleet, 56; Successful against Bohemund, 57

Constans II, Byzantine Emperor, defeated at sea, 35

Constantine the Great, Civil war of, 4

Constantine Porphyrogenitus, Byzantine Emperor, His allowance table for ships, 61

Constantine, Byzantine Emperor in 672, First siege of Constantinople, 36

Constantinople, formerly Byzantium, 6; Commerce of, 30; Revenues, 31; First siege, 36; Second siege, 37; Its walls, 39; Trade and commerce 8th century, 40; Treaty with Venice, 47; First Crusade, 53; Fourth Crusade, 117; Crusaders decide to attack, 121; Landing at, 121; First attack upon, 122; First fire, 123; Second fire, 124; Greeks attack Venetian fleet, 124; Second attack upon, 126; Third attack upon, 126; Third fire, 127; City sacked, 127; Wealth of city, 127

Contarini, John Baptist, sinks a Turkish Ship, 202

Contarini, Marino, aids Barbarigo at Lepanto and is killed, 199

Corfu, Naval battle off, 51; Fourth Crusade at, 120; Advanced base of fleet, 179

Cornia, Ascanio della, General of allied infantry, His address at Messina, 173; His second address, 175

Cosimo, Grand Duke of Tuscany, provides two galleasses, 217

Council, General—of Allies, Military decisions by Council, 160; Meets at Suda Bay, 161; Meets at Castel Rosso, 163; Meets at

Scarpanto, 164; Meets at Messina, 173; Meets on voyage to Corfu, 180; Meets at Corfu, 181; Meets at Sta. Maura, 213; Meets at Corfu 1572, 223; Meets at Zante, 223; Meets at Modon, 223; Reconnoiters hostile fleet, 225; Refuses to land soldiers, 225

Council, Queen's Privy, Plan of campaign, 281; Leaves all to Lord High Admiral, 283

Council, Spanish fleet, Called at Corunna, 273; Off Plymouth, 291; Off Isle of Wight, 303; In North Sea, 315

Council, Venetian, 160

Crete taken by Venice, 127

Crews in Hundred Years' War, 95

Crew space, 75

Crispus, Constantine's son, commands the fleet, 6

Croft, Comptroller to Queen, in Spanish pay, 281

Crossbow, Description, 107; Ballistics of, 108; Use forbidden by Pope, 108

Crosse, Captain Robert, of the Hope, Spanish ship sinks alongside, 316

Crusade, First, numbers in, 53; Emperor opposed to crusaders, 55

Crusade, Third, 117

Crusade, Fourth, 117; Venice provides shipping, 117; Strength of forces, 118; Siege of Zara, 118; Change of objective, 119; Capture of Constantinople, 121-27; Comments on campaign, 127

Cuellar, Francisco, Captain of San Pedro, Sentenced to death, 321; Reprieved, 321; Ship wrecked, 322; Reaches Antwerp, 323

Cyprus seized by Mohammedans, 35

Cyprus, War of, 143; Political situation, 147; Opening of war, 150; Turkish mobilization, 151; Siege of Nicosia, 152; Siege of Famagosta, 163; Campaign of 1571, 168; Campaign of 1572, 215; Peace, 227; Comments on, 227-28

Cyzicus, base for Mohammedan fleet, 36

Dalmatia, Insurrection in, 118

Damme, Battle off, 91

Dandolo, Enrico, Doge of Venice, Heads Fourth Crusade, 117; Induces crusaders to attack Constantinople, 120; Leads First Venetian attack, 123

Davalos, Alonzo, brave Spanish soldier, 211

Davalos, Don Cesar, Commands nefs, 178; Battle instructions, 178

Delbrueck, Hans, Size of armies 4th century, 5; Estimate of Norman strength at Hastings, 88

Diocletian, Roman Emperor, 4

Disdain, Pinnace, defies Spanish fleet, 293

Doria, commanding Genoese fleet in 1380, 148

Doria, Andrea, Commander in chief, allied fleet in 1538, 149

Doria, Gian Andrea, Prince of Melfi, Displeasing to Venice, 153; Commands Spanish-Sicilian squadron, 153; Its strength, 154; Visits Africa, 159; Joins allies at Candia, 159; Orders from King Philip, 160; At the General Council, 161; Thinks little of Venetian fleet, 162; Quarrels with Colonna, 164; Commands right wing at Lepanto, 177; Not allowed on Venetian ships, 182; Sights Turkish fleet, 190; Forms battle line at Lepanto, 191; Maneuvers before battle, 197; Rumors of treachery, 204; Takes down his lantern, 204; Maneuvers in battle, 205; Part of his ships forsake him, 206; Enters battle, 207; Ship slightly injured, 212; Commands Sicilian Squadron in 1572, 218

Doria, Oberto, Battle of Meloria, 130

Dover, Siege of, 92; Siege raised, 93; Naval battle of, 93; Comment on battle, 94

Dromon, type of ship, 10; Of Belisarius, 28; In 8th and 9th centuries, 61; Tactics, 62; Construction, 63; Crew, 63; About 900 A.D., 64; About 950 A.D., 65; In 1189 A.D., 65

Drake, Sir Francis, Engaged in illicit trade, 242; Cruise around world, 245; May attack West Indian ports, 247; Loots in Spain, 248; Success in West Indies, 248; Commands fleet, 253; Enters Cadiz, 254; Breaks up Spanish expedition, 256; Captures position near Cape St. Vincent, 256; Quarrels with Vice Admiral, 257; Tales of his magic power, 259; Prepares for cruise to Spain, 281; Opposed to plan of Council, 282; Is made Howard's Vice Admiral, 284; Hears news of Spanish fleet, 287; Guides English fleet, 297; Takes Nuestra Señora, 297; Commands one squadron, 303; Drake leads in battle off Gravelines, 312; Commands fleet in 1589, 329; His plan not followed, 330; Failure of expedition, 331; Expedition to West Indies, 332; Death near Panama, 332

Duodo, Antonio, Commands Venetian galleasses, 177; His fire brings down Ali's lantern, 201; Commended by Don John, 210

Dupplin Moor, battle in Scotland, 100

Durazzo (Dyrrachium), Siege of, 48; Naval battle at, 49; Surrenders, 50; Attacked by Bohemund, 57

Edward III, King of England, Invades Scotland, 96; Sends protective army to Flanders, 97; At battle of Sluys, 97-101; Siege of Calais, 102; At battle of Winchelsea, 103

Edward, Prince of Wales, at Winchelsea, 103

Egypt, conquered by Arabs, 33; Its Navy, 35

Einar Tambarskelver, his fleet, 76

Eleemon, Count, Byzantine seaman, fights battle with Pisans, 56

Elizabeth, Queen of England, Renounces Spanish policies, 241; Seizes Spanish money, 243; Favors Netherlands freebooters, 244; Is tendered sovereignty of Netherlands, 245; Share holder in Drake's expedition, 245; Authorizes Drake's expedition, 247; Sends army to Low Countries, 249; Her objective there, 249; Neglects to prepare for war, 251; Negotiations with Parma, 251; Sends restraining order to Drake, 254; Disavows Drake's action in Portugal, 259; Fails to pay her army, 260; Reluctant to make war, 281; Reduces crews, 281; Treats with Parma, 281; Forbids fleet to go to Spain, 285; Controls fleet by limiting supplies, 287; Proclaims Thanksgiving, 320; Organizes stock company, 329; Loses money on it, 331; Will not spend enough money, 331; Sends Drake and Hawkins to W.I., 332; Expedition to Cadiz, 332; Death in 1603, 333

England, Commerce with Spanish colonies, 242; Her seamen seek redress, 242; Sympathizes with Netherlands, 243; Sends men and money to Netherlands, 246; Military situation in, 319; Invasion of, in 1215, 92

Enriquez, Don Diego, Manner of death, 323

Epirus taken by Venice, 127

Eric, Earl, commanded at battle of Svold, 76, 79

Erling, Skakke, at battle of Gotha River, 86

Essex, Earl of, Expedition to Cadiz, 332

Euboea (Negropont) taken by Venice, 127

Eustace, The Monk, Takes French army to England, 92; Takes fleet to England, 93; Battle of Dover and death, 94

Eystein, King, His fleet, 76

Eystein, Son of King Harald, 84

Famagosta, Siege of, 163; Is supplied by Quirini, 166; Continuation of siege, 170; Surrender of, 170; Christian fleet hears of surrender, 184

Farnese, Alexander, Prince of Parma, his deeds at Lepanto, 210

Fenner, Captain Thomas, Adviser to Lord Howard, 281; Letter to Walsingham, 317

Finn Arneson, At battle of Nisaa, 83

Fire ships, English attack with, 309; Dutch fire ships at Antwerp, 310

Flanders, Count of, Will not attack England, 91; Asks help from England, 91; In Hundred Years' War, 96

Fleet, Allied, Question of command, 159; Strength in 1570, 162; Advances on Cyprus and withdraws, 163; Mobilizes at Messina 1571, 172; Its strength, 174; Condition of ships, 175; Organization, 177; Instructions for battle, 178; Leaves Messina, 179; Arrives at Corfu, 180; Inspection of fleet, 182; Comparison with Turkish fleet, 187; Battle of Lepanto, 190-212; Losses at Lepanto, 212; Returns to Corfu, 212; Neglect of crews, 215; Preparations for campaign of 1572, 216; Begins assembly, 217; France delays movement, 217; Mutual distrust, 217; Change in French government releases allied fleet, 218; First campaign of 1572, 218; Encounter off Cerigo, 219; Encounter off Matapan, 221; Returns to Corfu, 222; Second campaign, 1572, 223; Reconnoiters enemy at Modon, 225; At Navarino, 225; Partial engagement, 226; Returns to Zante, 226; Fleet breaks up at Corfu, 227; Neglect of crews, 227

Fleet, English, Mobilized in 1587, 280; Queen's ships at Chatham, 280; Demonstrates off Flushing, 281; Kept short of supplies, 283; Heads for Corunna, 286; Revictuals before battle, 287; Sickness, 287; Gets out of Plymouth, 288; Numbers and strength, 288; Tonnage, 289; Target practice, 290; Formation July 31, 293; J. S. Corbett's opinion as to formation, 293; Action July 31, 294; Action August 2, 299; Receives ammunition and men, 303; Reorganization, 303; Merchantmen of little service, 303; Action of August 4, 304; Out of ammunition, 306; Anchors off Calais, 307; Sends fire ships, 309; Battle off Gravelines, 310; Method of attack, 312; Expenditure of ammunition, 313; The chase, 315; Losses in battle, 318; Pestilence, 318; Total losses, 319; Expedition to Lisbon, 329; Expedition to Cadiz, 332

Fleet, Spanish, Assembly at Lisbon, 255; Condition in March 1588, 263; To impress foreign seamen, 264; Pay lacking, 264; General orders, 264-66; Rations, 267; Chief officers of, 268; Numbers and strength, 269; Types of ships, 269; Armaments, 270; Leaves Lisbon, 272; Enters Corunna, 272; In bad condition, 273; Formation as described in Pigafetta, 275; Voyage to England, 278; British fleet sighted, 279; Comparison with English fleet, 289; Action of July 31, 293; Formation, 292; Loses morale, 298; New organization, 298; Action of August 2, 299; Action on August 3, 303; Action on August 4, 304; Anchors off Calais, 306; Flees before fire ships, 309; Action off Gravelines, 312; Losses not severe, 314; The chase, 315; Short rations, 316; Voyage home, 320; Battle casualties, 321; Scottish pilots, 321; Ships separate, 322; Distribution of crews, 327; Neglect of crews, 327; Summary of losses, 328; Expedition to Ireland, 333; Second Expedition to Ireland, 333

Fleet, Turkish, Strength of, 186; Council before battle, 187; Opinions of enemy, 188; At Lepanto, 193; Preparation for battle, 194; Organization, 195; Losses in battle, 212; Renewal of fleet, 216; Harries Venetian islands, 217; At Malvasia in poor shape, 219; Maneuvers off Cerigo, 220; Partial engagement off Matapan, 221; Is secure at Modon, 223; Confronts allies, 225; Partial engagement, 226

Fleming, Captain, commands *Golden Hind* and sights Spanish fleet, 287

Flemings at Battle of Sluys, 101

Foscarini, Jacopo, Venetian General-at-Sea, 1572, 217; Urges search for enemy, 219; Quarrels with Don John, 227; Small success at Cattaro, 227

Frederick II of Germany, King of Two Sicilies, 133

Frederick, Regent of Sicily, 139; King of Sicily, 139; Defeated at Cape Orlando, 140; Established rule in Sicily, 141

Frobiser, Captain Martin, Adviser to Lord Howard, 281; Commended by Lord Howard, 285; Abuses Drake, 312

Gaiseric, King of Vandals, At Carthage, 7; Plunders Rome, 7; Raids Peloponnese, 7; Destroys Roman fleet, 8

Galata, suburb of Constantinople, 121; Crusaders winter there, 124

Galleass, French, Description of, 237

Galleasses, Four in Armada, 269; Armament, 271; Damaged August 4, 304; Flagship captured, 311

Galleasses, Tuscan, 217

Galleasses, Venetian, Extemporization, 156; Numbers in service, 1570, 156; Numbers at Lepanto, 174; Don John's opinion, 178; Very sluggish, 178; At Lepanto, 198, 201, 205; Description, 235

Galleys, Price for services, 154; Cruising speed of, 169; In 16th century (description), 230; Armament, 232; Replacement by sailing ships, 233; French, in 17th century, 234; Life on board, 234; Fail at Cadiz, 255; Four galleys in armada, 269; Their armament, 271; Leave the fleet, 278; A Spanish opinion of, 321

Galleys, Italian, in 12th and 13th centuries, 110

Galliot, small galley, Description of, 151

Gelimer, Vandal King, 9; Revolt against, 12; Attacks Belisarius, 13; Final defeat, 14

Genoa takes part in First Crusade, 54; Sends squadron to Antioch, 55; Secures trade privileges, 55; Draws seamen from Riviera, 110; Develops commerce at expense of Venice and Pisa, 128; War with Pisa, 128; Naval battle in 1283, 129; Battle of Meloria, 130; Declines to destroy Pisa,

133; Supplies three galleys for Lepanto, 174

Geoffrey, de Vinsauf, describes Dromon in 1189, 65

Gerona, Siege of, 135; Surrender of, 138

Gherardesca, Ugolino della, Pisan admiral, 130; Defeated at Meloria, 132; Death, 132; Saves Pisa from ruin, 133

Gil, Juan, Sent in zabra to scout, 292; Takes message to Parma, 298; Reaches Parma, 307

Giustiniano, Fra, Prior to Messina, Commands Maltese ships, 176; Dispute as to precedence, 176; Nearly loses his capitana, 180; Refuses to occupy assigned position, 184; Ship is captured, 207

Godfrey of Bouillon, King of Jerusalem, asks aid of Venetian fleet, 55

Gokstad ship, 72

Golden Horn, harbor of Constantinople, Secured by Crusaders, 122; Second attack on, 125

Gomenizza, Turks make prisoners at, 182; Quarrel at, 183; Fleet inspected at, 182

Gotha River, Battle of, 84

Gothic War, 14

Goths, Maritime incursion in 3d century, 4

Graecus, Marcus, writer on Greek fire, 41

Great Armada, Campaign of, 240; Used tactics of 1572, 246; Political situation before war, 240

Great Christopher, ship at battle of Sluys, 98-100

Great Serpent, ship of King Olaf, 73

Greek Navy, Organization of, 59

Greek fire, 41

Gregorius at battle of Gotha River, 86

Gregory XIII, Pope, Follows policy of Pius V, 216; Angry at Venetian peace, 228

Guzman, Don Alonzo de (see Medina-Sidonia, Duke of)

Guiscard, Robert, Conquers South Italy, 46; Hostilities with Venice, 47; Hostilities with Empire, 48

Guise, Duke of, May unite with Spaniards, 286; Will not help Spaniards, 304

Gyda, wife of Olaf Tryggevesson, 78

Hakon, petty king in Norway, 78

Hakon, Ivarsson, at battle of Nisaa, 83

Hakon, Sigurdsson, Fight at Gotha River, 84

Halidon Hill, battle in Scotland, 100

Harald Haarfager, 77

Harald Hardrada, of Norway, Raid in Denmark, 71; Raids in England, 76; Battle of Nisaa, 80; His great ship, 81

Harald (or Harold), King of England, 77; Opposes fleet to Norman William, 88

Hassan, son of Barbarossa, Turkish admiral, urges battle, 187

Hawkins, Sir John, Engaged in illicit trade, 243; Adviser to Lord Howard, 281; Commands division in fleet, 303; Off Isle of Wight, 304; Off Gravelines, 312; Expedition to West Indies, 332; Death off Puerto Rico, 332

Henry III, King of England, 92

Henry IV of France, Accession to throne affects all Europe, 331

Heraclius, Roman Admiral, commands fleet against Gaiseric, 8

Howard, Charles, Baron Howard of Effingham, Lord High Admiral, British Commander in Chief, 280; Moves fleet to Plymouth, 283; Intends to go to Spain, 284; Driven back, 284; Learns Spaniards have sailed, 285; Objects to order to remain in port, 285; Hears of Spanish ships off Scilly, 286; Sails for Corunna, 286; His mistaken strategy, 286; Sends "defiance," 293; Action on July 31, 293; Asks for ammunition, 295; Action on August 2, 301; Commands one squadron, 303; Action on August 4, 304; Attacks with fire ships, 309; Engages singly with galleass, 310; Joins fleet, 312; Does not realize Spanish defeat, 316; Returns to North Foreland, 317; Reports to Walsingham, 317; Reports pestilence, 318; Expedition to Cadiz, 332

Howard, Lord Thomas, commands *Golden Lion*, 304

Hormigas, Las, Battle of, 136; Comment on, 139

Huntington, Earl of, captures French ship at Sluys, 101

Hundred Years' War, 95; Origin of, 96

Hunsdon, Lord, commands Queen's body guard, 319

Hubert de Burgh, King's justiciary, his fleet attacks Eustace the Monk, 93

Inge, King of Norway, Kills his brother, 84; Fight at Gotha River, 84; Death, 86

Ionian Islands taken by Venice, 127

Isaac, deposed Byzantine Emperor, 119; Restored to throne, 124; Makes treaty with crusaders, 124; Imprisoned, 125
Isaac, Belisarius' General, at Portus, 17
Italian naval wars, 109

James I, King of England, makes peace with Spain, 333
James, regent of Sicily, 135; Becomes King of Aragon, 139; Makes peace with Naples, 139; Fights his brother at Cape Orlando, 140
John of Austria, Made General of the League, 168; High Admiral of Spain, 170; Arrives at Messina, 170; His battle station, 177; Accused of not wishing battle, 180; Resents execution of Muzio, 183; Murmurs against, 184; His Spanish counsellors oppose battle, 190; His own ardor, 190; He receives a report as to enemy, 191; Address to crews, 192; Address to Veniero, 192; His share in the battle, 201; Receives captains after battle, 210; Thanks Duodo for service of the galleasses, 210; Banquet, 212; His attention to duty, 212; New quarrel with Veniero, 213; Welcome at Messina, 214; Commander in Chief, 1572, 216; Obliged to stay at Messina, 217; Goes to Corfu, 218; Leaves squadron at Messina, 218; Childish rage at Corfu, 222; Takes fleet forward, 223; Restrained by Spanish council, 223; Chases Turkish division, 226; His fleet retires, 226; Quarrels with Foscarini, 227; Returns to Messina, 227
John, Imperial General, 19; Joins his fleet to Valerian's, 19; Battle at Sena Gallica, 19
John, King of England, His fleet, 89; War with France, 90; His death, 92
John of Gaunt, At battle of Winchelsea, 103
John of Joinville, writer, tells of Greek fire, 42
Josephus, historian, strength of Pontic navy, 60
Justinian, Roman Emperor, 9; War with Vandals, 10; Gothic War, 14; Sends new army to Italy, 16; Develops silk industry, 31
Justinus of Orange, Commands Dutch fleet, 279; The importance of his fleet, 307; Goes to Dover, 320

Khaireddin Barbarossa, 149
Klysma, Imperial dock yard at, 33
Kolbiorn, Marshal to Olaf Tryggevesson, 79

Laiazzo, battle between Venetians and Genoese, 141
Lancaster, Earl of, at Winchelsea rescues Prince of Wales, 104
Landulph, Byzantine Admiral, fights the Pisans, 56
La Riche, ship at Sluys, 99
Lauria, Ruggiero di, Commands Catalan fleet in Sicily, 135; Brings fleet to Aragon, 136; Battle of Las Hormigas, 137; Battle of Cape Orlando, 140
Leicester, Robert Dudley, Earl of, English Commander in Chief in Netherlands, 249; Queen disputes with him, 251; Slight opinion of Spanish navy, 252; Commander in Chief English army, 319; Dines with Queen in camp, 319
Leo I, Emperor, opposes Gaiseric, 7
Leo, the Isaurian, Byzantine Emperor, saves Constantinople, 37
Leo VI (the Wise), Emperor, His tactics, 19; Remarks on Greek fire, 41; His institutions, tactics for dromons, 61; Construction of dromons, 63
Lepanto, Campaign of, 143; Records regarding, 146; Political situation regarding, 147; Strength of Christian fleet, 174; Strength of Turkish fleet, 186; Description of battle, 190; Turkish losses, 212; Christian losses, 212; Comments on battle, 215
L'Espagnols sur mer, See Winchelsea, Battle of
Leyni, de, commanding Savoyard ships disputes with Prior of Messina, 176, 184
Leyva, Don Alonzo de, Captain General of the Armada, 268; Wishes to enter Plymouth, 292; Commands fleet vanguard, 292; leaves station to fight Howard, 294; Thinks fleet should stay with Parma, 315; Loses ship on Irish coast, 322; Transfers to galleass, is lost, 322
Licinius, Roman Emperor, Civil war of, 4
Lincoln, French army defeated at, 92
Lisbon, Expedition against, 329; A wrong objective, 330; Lands at Corunna, 330; Lands at Peniche, 330; Reëmbarks, 330; Returns to England, 331
Lodeve, French admiral, 135
London occupied by French army, 92
Long-bow, Accuracy of, 106; Range, 106; Ballistics, 107, Comparison with musket, 108

Louis, Prince of France, Offered throne of England, 92; Invades England, 92; Besieges Dover, 92; Evacuates England, 94

Louis IX, King of France, 133

Luzon, Don Alonzo de, camp-master Neopolitan regiment, testimony as to his wreck, 324

Lyn, a type of round ship, 135

Magnus, King of Norway, at battle of Aarhus, 80

Mahomet, Unifies Arabia, 31

Majorian, Roman Emperor, opposes Gaiseric and is beheaded, 7

Malta, Knights of, action of Maltese squadron pretext for war of Cyprus, 150

Mamut, Turkish captain, son of Dragut, killed by Christian crew, 226

Manny, Sir Walter, at battle of Sluys, 100

Manrique, Jorge, Inspector General, advises delay, 273

Manzikert, Battle at, 53

Marcellinus, Commands forces against Gaiseric, 7; Killed, 8

Margaret and John, English ship, At capture of galleass, 310; Her crew pillage French officers, 311

Margariti, fortified position attacked, 157; Sortie from, 181

Maritime conditions, 11th and 12th centuries, 88

Mary, Queen of England, desirous of following Spanish policy, 241

Mary, Queen of Scots, Conspiracies regarding her, 245; Execution, 252

Medieval Wars of French and English, 88

Medici, Cosimo di, Grand Duke of Tuscany, Furnishes galleys to Pope, 169, 216; Hires out two galleasses, 217

Medina-Sidonia, Duke of, Chosen to command fleet, 262; Unwilling to serve, 262; Correspondence with king, 263; Instructions from king, 264; Orders to fleet, 266; Recommends peace, 273; Reports on state of fleet, 274; Describes fleet formation, 277; Letter on sighting England, 278; Commands center, 292; Measures to enforce good conduct, 298; Alters organization of fleet, 298; Orders galleasses to attack, 300; Reproaches their commander, 300; Engages enemy, 301; Expects victory on August 4, 304; Message to Parma, 306; Hears Parma unready to sail, 307; Asks Parma

for ships, 309; Gets under way, 309; Personal bravery, 310; Tries to reform fleet, 311; Disobeys order from Parma, 316; Letter to king, 322; Arrives off Santander, 325; Reports arrival to king, 326; Authorized to go home, 327

Mehemet, Bey of Negropont, Collects troops and supplies, 185; Against battle, 188

Mehemet Sirocco, Bey of Alexandria, Turkish admiral, 186; Opposed to battle, 188; Commands right wing, 195; Escapes to shore, 200; Capture and death, 201; His squadron destroyed, 201

Mehemet Sokolli, Turkish Grand Vizier, Opposes war, 150; Wants peace in 1571, 167; Rebuilds Turkish fleet, 216

Mejia, Don Augustin de, commands *San Luis*, August 2, 301

Meloria, Battle of, 130; Comment on, 133

Merchant galley, Description of, 112

Mercury promontory (Cape Bon), Naval battle near, 8

Messina, Fleet base in 1571, 168; Welcome to fleet, 214; Fleet base in 1572, 217

Michiel, Giovanni, commands Venetian fleet, 56; Treaty with King of Jerusalem, 56

Misenum, Roman fleet base, 3

Miranda, Don Luis de, member of Medina's staff, Tells of nimbleness of English ships, 304; Reports casualties, 321; His opinion of galleys, 321

Moaviah, Governor of Syria, Starts a navy, 35; Seizes Cyprus, 35; Tries to be made Caliph, 35; Besieges Constantinople, 36

Mobilization, Turks in 1570, 151; Spaniards in 1570, 153; Papal in 1570, 154; Venetian in 1570, 155; Venetian in 1571, 168; Papal in 1571, 169; Spanish in 1571, 170; Turkish in 1572, 216; General allied in 1572, 217

Modon taken by Venice, 127

Mohammedanism, Rise of, 31

Moist fire, 38; Nature of, 43

Moncada, Don Hugo de, commander of galleasses, Disobeys order to attack, 300; Reprimanded, 300; Death, 311

Morley, Robert de, Protests to king, 97; At battle of Sluys, 100

Morosini, Pisan Admiral, 130

Moslemah, Leads army against Constantinople, 37; Retires from Constantinople, 39

Mourzouphles, Byzantine Emperor, Seizes throne, 125; Driven from city, 127

Muda, squadron of merchant ships, 115

Muñoz, Martin, Spanish sergeant, gallant warrior, 211

Mustapha, Pasha, Commander in Chief, 1570, 151; His forces, 151; Besieges Nicosia, 152; Assaults Nicosia, 162; Besieges Famagosta, 163; Refuses to fight allied fleet, 164; Sends fleet home, 165; Pushes siege of Famagosta, 166, 170; Violates terms of surrender, 171; Returns to Constantinople, 171

Muzio, Execution of, 182; His death known to Turks, 190

Nani, Federigo, flag captain to Barbarigo, repulses boarders, 200

Narses, Justinian's general, 18; Assumes command in Italy, 20; Battle of Busta Gallorum, 21

Naval officers, Rank and duty, 114.

Naval situation in Mediterranean in 13th century, 128

Naval tactics, Vikings', 79; Italian, 115; Status of, 16th century, 143; Treatise on, by Chaves, 143; Method of handling ship, 144; Method of handling fleet, 145; Battle, 146; Method in 1588, 312; English observed no formation, 334; Spanish did not preserve formation, 334

Navarino, Allied fleet at, 225; Attack on, 225

Nave (See Nef)

Navy, Byzantine, Expedition to Carthage, 10; Battle of Sena Gallica, 19; Tactics, 22; Defeated in 655, 35; Regenerated in 697, 36

Navy, Mohammedan, 36

Nefs, (nave) type of ship, Description of, 113; In 1570, 162; In 1571, 178-179; Their cargo, 180; In 1571 Christians will not fight without them, 221; At Zante, 223; At Navarino, 225; Description, 237

Netherlands, Revolt in, 243; Rebel flotilla, 244; Northern provinces prosper, 244

Nicosia, Siege of, 152; Allied fleet resolves to relieve, 161; Assault of city, 162; Spoils to Constantinople, 163

Nisaa, Battle of, 80

Norreys, Sir John, commands army bound to Spain, 329

Northampton, Earl of, at battle of Sluys, 100

Norway, Organization, 71

Nuestra Señora del Rosario, flagship of Recalde, Fouls another ship, 296; Taken by Drake, 297; Powder sent to English fleet, 297

Olaf, ruler of Vendland, 78

Olaf Tryggevesson, King of Norway, 73; Builds Great Serpent, 73; Battle of Svold, 76; Sketch of life, 77; Drowned at Svold, 79

Olaf II, the Saint, King of Norway, His fleet in 1026, 76; His army in 1030, 77

Olivares, Spanish Minister, proposes peace with England, 333

Oquendo, Miguel de, commands squadron of Guipuscoa, 268; Aids Medina, 301; Dies of grief, 325

Orlando, battle of Cape, 139; Victors derive no advantage, 141

Palaeologus, George, commands at Durazzo, 48

Pallavicino, Sforza, Commands troops in Venetian fleet, 155; Expedition to Margariti, 157; Member of council, 160

Palmer, Sir Henry, commands squadron, 280

Pamphilo (See Sagitta)

Panormus (Palermo), Belisarius conquers, 15

Papacy, The, and the Turks, 149

Papal fleet in 1570, 155; Method of recruitment, 155; At Otranto, 158; Losses in 1570, 165; Losses in 1571, 212; Returns to Messina, 214; In 1572, 217

Paris, Vikings besiege, 69

Parma, Alexander Farnese, Duke of, Governor of Netherlands, 246; Negotiations with Elizabeth, 252; Forces he needed for invasion, 252; Prepares for invasion, 260; Italian reënforcements, 261; Disease in army, 261; Negotiations with England, 261; Sends message to Medina, 272; Negotiations with England continued, 280; Army ready to embark, 307; Disembarks army, 320; Leads army into France, 331

Pay and rations, Italy, 114

Pembroke, Richard, Earl of, gathers fleet at Rye, 92

Peloponnese taken by Venice, 127

Peñafiel, Marquis of, Commands *San Marcos,* 301; Off Gravelines, 311

Perichytes, Peloponnesian seaman, fights Pisan fleet, 56

Perinthus, Belisarius stops at, 11

Persia, conflict with Rome, 9; End of war, 9; Conquered by Saracens, 33

Personnel, Maritime, Ship's officers titles, 113

Pertau, Pasha, Commanding troops, 187; Opposed to battle, 189; Flees from his ship, 202

Peter, King of Aragon, Assumes Crown of Two Sicilies, 133; Death, 139

Peter, King of Castile, makes peace with England, 105

Philip, King of France, Attacks Aragon, 135; Besieges Gerona, 135; Naval base in Bay of Rosas, 135; Strategic situation of army, 136; Takes Gerona, "Las Hormigas" obliges him to leave Spain, 138; Comments on campaign, 139

Philip IV, King of France, Aids Scotland against Edward III, 96; Declares war on England, 96

Philip II, King of Spain, Accepts Pope's request to aid Venice, 153; Mobilizes his Sicilian squadron, 153; Doubts Venetian sincerity, 158; Sends squadron to Africa, 159; Objective in the war, 167; Accused of double dealing, 180; Refuses to move fleet, 217; Permits Don John to advance, 218; Indifferent at Venetian peace, 228; Marries Mary, Queen of England, 241; Desires unity of church, 241; Policy in Netherlands, 243; Becomes unfriendly to England, 245; Thinks of invading England, 246; Seizes English ships, 247; Resolves on war, 249; Seizes English ships, 249; His finances, 241, 261; Correspondence with Medina-Sidonia, 262; Instructions to General-at-Sea, 263, 264; Forecast as to English tactics, 266; Conditions acceptable for peace, 266; Urges Medina to hurry, 273; Plan if English fleet is divided, 282; Receives favorable news, 324; Kind letter to Medina, 327; Directs bishops to cease prayers for success, 327; Sends army into France, 331; Builds new fleet, 331; Captures Calais, 332; Expedition to Ireland, 333; Death, 333

Philip III, King of Spain, Supports revolt in Ireland, 333; Expedition to Ireland, 333; Makes peace, 333

Philip, Duke of Swabia, 119

Philip Augustus, King of France, Makes War on Richard of England, 89; Prepares to invade England, 91

Philippa, Queen of England, Hostage for Edward III, 100; After battle of Winchelsea, 105

Piali, Pasha, Commands Turkish fleet, 151; Scouts for news, 158; Sends soldiers to Nicosia, 162; Refuses to attack Venetian fleet, 165; Relieved of command, 166

Pigafetta, Filippo, publishes fleet formation, 275

Pimentel, Don Diego, Commands *San Mateo* in battle July 31, 294; Will not abandon ship, 314; Captured by Dutch, 314

Piracy, 3

Pisa, Takes part in First Crusade, 54; Archbishop commands fleet, 55; Fights Venice, 55; Fights Emperor off Rhodes, 56; War with Genoa, 128; Political situation in 1282, 128; Battle in 1283, 129; Battle of off Meloria, 130

Pius V, Pope, Agrees to aid Venice, 152; Forms triple alliance, 168; Has vision of the battle, 193; Institutes perpetual festival, 214; Death checks allied ardor, 216

Pliny (the Elder), Admiral at Misenum, 3

Pompeii, Wall paintings of ships, 24

Pope claims Two Sicilies in 1262, 133

Porcia, Count of, aids Barbarigo, 200

Porto Quaglia, Venetian raid on, 157

Portus, port of Rome, base for Belisarius, 16

Priests, Christian, At Lepanto, 193; One's bravery at Lepanto, 211

Priuli, Vicenzo Maria, Venetian ship captain, Desperate single ship action, 165

Procopius, historian, secretary, 10; Scouts for Belisarius, 11

Propaganda at Lepanto, 193

Quick lime used at Battle of Dover, 94

Quieret, French Admiral at Sluys, 99

Quirini, Marco, Commands Venetian squadron, 155; Raids Porto Quaglia, 157; Scouts for news, 158, 161, 163; Watches Famagosta, 166; Commands 60 ships in Candia, 171; Arrives at Messina, 174; Battle station, 177; Skillful maneuver in battle, 199

Ravenna, naval base, 3

Recalde, Juan Martinez de, Admiral of Spanish fleet, Commands squadron of Viscaya, 268; Commands rear guard, 292; Engages several ships in *Sta. Ana*, 295; Attacked on August 2, 301; Reaches Ireland, 322; Arrives home, dies of grief, 325

Reprisal, British make reprisals against Spain, 242; Spanish counter reprisals, 243

Requesens, Don Luis de, Commendador Real of Castile, Inspects Venetian ships, 182; Encourages Don John, 192

Revenge, Drake's flagship, 297

Richard I, King of England, His fleet, 89; His galley, 110

Richard, son of King John, at Battle of Dover, 93

Robert of Courtenay commands French Reenforcements, 93

Roebuck, English ship, takes prize into Torbay, 297

Roger of Hauteville conquers Sicily, 46

Roman Empire, Its maritime peace, 3; In 3d-4th centuries, 4

Roman fire (See Greek fire)

Roman Navy, Organization during Republic, 60; Organization during Empire, 60; Signals, 62; Formations, 62; Tactics, 62

Rome, Siege of, 536 A.D., 15; Siege of 546 A.D., 16; Taken by Goths, 17; Reoccupied by Belisarius, 18; Taken by Goths, 18

Romegasso, Counselor to Colonna, 202; Advises Don John to cease pursuit, 209

Rosas Bay, Battle of, 135

Sagitta, despatch boat, 112

St. James, French ship at Sluys, 101

Salisbury, Earl of, Naval battle at Damme, 91

Salle du Roi, ship at Winchelsea, 104

Saltpeter, 44

Salvo firing, Casualties of, 182

San Domingo (West Indies), captured by Drake, 248

San Felipe, flagship, Battle of Gravelines, 314; Captured by Dutch, 314; Sinks with prize crew, 314

San Felipe, East Indian ship, captured, 259

San Juan de Sicilia sinks in battle off Gravelines, 314

San Lorenzo, flagship of galleasses, captured at Calais, 310

San Martin, flagship Capitana Real, 268; Battle of July 31, 294; Battle of August 2, 300; Battle of August 4, 304; Gets under way August 8, 309; Battle off Gravelines, 312; Injuries and losses, 314; Arrives at Santander, 325; Medina's report on losses, 327

San Salvador, Almiranta of Guipuscoa, Explosion on board, 297; Abandoned and captured, 297

Santa Ana, Recalde's flagship, 295; Repairing damage, 298; Attacked by English, 301; Expenditure of ammunition, 304; Wrecked, 306

Santa Cruz, Marquis of, (See Bazan, Don Alvaro de)

Saracens, Naval wars of, 30; Who they were, 31; Adopt Mohammedanism, 31; In Western Mediterranean, 46

Savoy, Duke of, provides three galleys for Lepanto, 174

Scandinavia, Migrations of people of, 69; Population, 70; Organization of, 71

Scutari, town opposite Constantinople, Crusaders at, 120

Seamen, Pay of, 114

Seapower, Comparison of Italian, with Athenian, 110

Selim, Turkish Sultan, Wishes possession of Cyprus, 150; Undismayed by Lepanto, 215

Sena Gallica, Battle at, 19; Comparison with Busta Gallorum, 22; Type of ships at, 29

Sereno, soldier on board *Grifona* and historian of campaign, tells of his ship, 209

Seymour, Lord Henry, Blockades Flanders, 283; Notified of Spanish approach, 296; Thinks merchantmen did little in battle, 303; Joins main fleet at Calais, 307; Plan of battle August 8, 310; Returns to blockade duty, 316

Ships in Hundred Years' War, Size of, 95; British vessels in 1346, 96

Ships, In 2d century A.D., 24; Of Belisarius, 27

Sicilian vespers, 133

Sicilian wars, 133

Sicily, Recovered by Romans, 15; Conquered by Totila, 18

Sigurd, son of King Harald, 84

Sigurd of Royr, Exhortation before battle of Gotha River, 85

Silvio, Doge of Venice, leads fleet against Robert Guiscard, 48

Sluys, Battle of, 96; British strength, 98; French strength, 98; British tactics, 100; Losses in battle, 101; Comments on battle, 101

Smoke screen, Turkish maneuver behind, 221

Soldiers in Italian navies, 115

Solyman, Turkish Sultan, 149

Sopoto, Venetian raid on, 157

Soranzo, Benedetto, destroys ship with own hand, 207

Sosthenion, harbor on Bosphorus, 38

Svend, Earl, At battle of Aarhus, 80; Now king at battle of Nisaa, 80

Svold, Battle of, 76, 79

Spain, Opposes Turkish piracy, 148; Has policy opposed to Venice, 148; Economic situation, 241; Colonies closed to foreign goods, 242; Defeat of Armada marks end of her greatness, 328; Peace with England, 333

Spur, the medieval ram, 143

Stein Herdisarson, a singer, at battle of Nisaa, 83

Strategy in 1588, Parma could not cross without fleet, 335; England should have struck at flotas, 335; Neither side spent enough money, 335

Suleiman, Caliph, Besieges Constantinople, 37; Death, 38

Suleiman, Moslem general, 37; Death, 38

Syria, conquered by Arabs, 33

Tancred of Hauteville, His sons conquer South Italy, 46

Tarida, type of galley, 112

Themes, Maritime, 60

Theodora, wife of Justinian, 18

Theodoric, Gothic King, Died in 526, 14; Built dromons, 29

Thessalonica, naval base, 5

Thiodolf, Norwegian singer, 81

Thomas, flagship of Edward III, Crew, 95; At battle of Sluys, 97; At battle of Winchelsea, 104

Thyra, wife of Olaf Tryggevesson, 79

Toledo, Don Francisco de, camp-master, Commanding San Felipe, Battle off Gravelines, 313; Stays by his ship, 314; Escapes to a boat from shore, 314

Tomson, Richard, Lieutenant, Reports as to captured galleass, 310; Answers Governor of Calais, 311

Torre, Father Geronimo de la, describes voyage home, 325

Totila, Gothic King, Regains South Italy, 16; Besieges Rome, 16; Cannot make peace, 17; Takes Rome, 17; Occupies Sicily, 18; Creates strong navy, 18; Occupies Sardinia and Corsica, 20

Trade of Empire, 109

Trajan's, Column, 3, 24

Triumph, Frobiser's flagship, Battle of August 2, 300; Battle of August 4, 305

Tromba, weapon used at Lepanto, 187

Tryggeve, King of Norway, 77

Turks, Ottoman, Rise of, 148

Turks, Seljuk, Conquer maritime provinces of Empire, 47; Secure Asia Minor, 53

Tzazon, brother of Gelimer, recalled from Sardinia, 14

Ulf, Marshal, at battle of Nisaa, 83

Uluch Ali, Dey of Algiers, Takes squadron to Piali, 159; His character, 159; Joins Ali Pasha, 171; His movement to Modon, 185; Urges battle, 188; Commands left wing, 195; Tries to outflank Doria, 197; Maneuvers in the battle, 206; Attacks Christian stragglers 206; Captures Capitana of Malta, 207; Escapes from battle, 209; Commands new fleet, 216; Harries Venetian Islands, 217; Will not fight nefs, 220; Maneuvers, 220, 221; Takes position at Modon, 223; Cannot attack at Navarino, 225; Disobeys Sultan's order, 226; Great credit due him, 227

Usciere, type of ships (See Vissier)

Vacchette, small craft, Description of, 112

Valdes, Diego Flores de, Commands Castilian galleons, 268; Advises Duke to forsake Nuestra Señora del Rosario, 296

Valdes, Pedro de, Commands Andalusian Squadron, 268; Alone urges forward movement, 274; Stands by crippled Santa Ana, 295; Abandoned by fleet, 296; Surrenders to Drake, 297

Valerian, Imperial General in Italy, 19; Joins his fleet to that of John, 19; Naval battle at Sena Gallica, 19

Vandals, Piratical power, 6; Capital at Carthage, 7; Plunder Rome, 7; Overthrow of, by Romans, 9

Vanegas, commanding company on *San Martin*, Tells of "broken spirit," 298; Losses on August 2, 301

Venetian commercial squadrons, Nature of cargoes of, 115

Venice, Becomes a sea power, 47; Hostilities with Robert Guiscard, 47; Treaty with Emperor, 47; Firm as maritime power, 48; At siege of Durazzo, 49; Fleet defeated at Corfu, 51; As maritime power, 52; Takes part in First Crusade, 54; Fights Pisa at sea, 55; Aids Godfrey of Jerusalem, 56; Commerce supported her navy, 110; Seamen from Dalmatia, 110; Provides shipping for 4th Crusade, 117; Does not wish to attack Egypt, 119; Byzantines attack Venetian fleet, 124; Spoils from Byzantine Empire, 127; Loses maritime advantage at Constantinople, 128; Political situation in 1570, 147; Fire in arsenal, 150; Refuses to surrender Cyprus, 151; Asks for help, 152; Mobilization, 155; Strength of navy in 1570, 156; Navy crippled by pest, 157; Negotiations with Sultan, 167; Objective in the war, 167; Alarmed by Ali Pasha, 172; Peace with Sultan, 227

Veniero, Sebastiano, Venetian Proveditor, 157; Raids Sopoto, 157; Becomes General at Sea, 165; Distribution of ships, 169; Takes Spanish soldiers on board, 175; Station in center of fleet, 177; Resents inspection by Doria, 182; Quarrel with Don John, 183; Personal share in battle, 202; Visits Don John after battle, 210; New quarrel with Don John, 213; Report to Venice, 214; Removed from command, 217; Doge of Venice, 217

Viking fleets, Size of, 76

Vikings, Their people, 69; Siege of Paris, 69; Population, 70; Organization, 71;

Early raids, 72; Their arms, 79; Naval tactics, 79, 86

Viking ships, Average size of, 76

Villehardouin, Geoffroi de, Historian of 4th Crusade, 118

Vissier (Usciere), type of ship, Description of, 113

Waldemar, King of Novgorod, 78

Walsingham, Sir Francis, Secretary of State, 245; Favors war with Spain, 245; Letter from Howard, 285; Letter from Wynter, 313; Letter from Howard, 317; Writes to Howard about reducing crews, 319

William the Conqueror, His fleet, 88; Invasion of England, 88; Strength of army, 88

William, Prince of Orange, Leads insurrection in Netherlands, 243; Murder of, 246

Winchelsea, Battle of, 103; Comments on, 105

Witigis, Gothic King, 15

Women, Loose, not allowed in Armada, 263; Charter their own ships, 263; Wives clamor for husbands' discharge, 275

Wynter, Sir William, Commands *Vanguard*, 291; Expenditure of ammunition, 291; Merchantmen make a show only, 303; Describes action off Gravelines, 313

Zaccaria, Benedetto, Genoese Admiral, 130; At Meloria, 131

Zacynthus, Belisarius stops at, 11

Zanne, Girolamo, Venetian General at Sea, 155; Attacks Margariti, 157; Sails for Candia, 158; His council, 160; Submits to Doria's demand, 161; Renounces effort to aid Cyprus, 164; Dies in prison, 165

Zara, Siege of, 118

Zeno, Roman Emperor, Treaty with Vandalic Kingdom in Africa, 9